CANADIAN PUBLIC POLICY AND ADMINISTRATION:

THEORY AND ENVIRONMENT

V. SEYMOUR WILSON
Carleton University

McGraw-Hill Ryerson Limited

Toronto   Montreal
New York   St. Louis
San Francisco   Auckland
Bogotá   Guatemala
Hamburg   Johannesburg
Lisbon   London   Madrid
Mexico   New Delhi
Panama   Paris
San Juan   São Paulo
Singapore   Tokyo

CANADIAN
PUBLIC POLICY
AND
ADMINISTRATION:
THEORY AND
ENVIRONMENT

ISBN 0-07-092428-7

1 2 3 4 5 6 7 8 9 0 D 9 8 7 6 5 4 3 2 1

Printed and bound in Canada

Care has been taken to trace ownership of copyright material
contained in this text. The publishers will gladly take any information
that will enable them to rectify any reference or credit in
subsequent editions.

Canadian Cataloguing in Publication Data

Wilson, Vincent Seymour.
  Canadian public policy and administration

Includes index.

ISBN 0-07-092428-7

1. Public administration—Canada. 2. Policy
sciences. 3. Canada—Politics and government.
4. Bureaucracy. I. Title.

JL108.W54   354.7107   C80-094760-6

CONTENTS

PREFACE

This book represents an attempt to synthesize and integrate relevant knowledge in the field of public policy and administration. This field could logically be divided into four areas: theoretical considerations, environmental concerns, bureaucratic processes and bureaucratic performance. This book deals with the first two areas. A forthcoming publication will be concerned mainly with process and performance, although the strong linkages to theory and environment will be continuously emphasized.

Even within this narrow focus, it is impossible to be comprehensive on all aspects of theory and environment. For example, I have had to resort to broad-brush treatments of Canadian and British administrative history, decision theory, theories of organizations and public policy studies. In a way much depth is sacrificed for breadth, but I justify this treatment of the subject matter by arguing that the reader is given an opportunity to see the forest for the trees. A more in-depth assessment of the different tree species, the seedlings, and the flora and fauna can be undertaken after the forest is recognized and identified. To this end, I have supplied short bibliographies at the end of each chapter for further study.

Although I have given a synthesis of already well-known but disparate facts about public policy and administration, I have attempted to put some clear interpretations on this subject matter. For example, in Section I, I am particularly excited about the new perspectives of Max Weber's work appearing in the late 1970s. Neo-Weberian studies are now challenging many of the assumptions and misunderstandings that were prevalent about Weber's work only a decade ago: his use of the "ideal type"; his concept of rationality; his "determinism" purportedly implicit in the Weberian view of Western societal evolution. Some of this recent analysis is touched upon here. For example, I have attempted a reinterpretation of the administrative state given Weber's prognosis on this matter (Chapter Three), and this has led me to further insights on the policy/administration dichotomy (Chapter Four). I have also argued that a clearer connection between decision theory and policy studies should be made.

Similarly, in Section II, I have tried to furnish some perspectives into ministerial responsibility, the concept of central agencies, and the origins of the ministerial department. These insights already existed in the literature. All I can claim is that I have provided a service in bringing this material together for the consideration of public policy and administration students.

The photographs of the persons appearing in this work were solicited and very readily given by all of them. Some of these prominent people even read parts of this manuscript and freely gave of their advice and constructive criticisms. I extend my sincere thanks to all of them. My colleagues Bruce Doern, Sharon Sutherland, Michael Prince and Ken Kernaghan all read parts of this manuscript and gave their insightful views and criticisms. In particular, a special thanks is extended to my friend and colleague Michael Prince. Many a day I have "cornered" Mike in his small office where he has a convenient blackboard, and badgered him with my half-baked syntheses and false starts. He has always been a patient listener, and much of his advice, criticisms and insights have been gratefully heeded. None of the above are, however, responsible for the errors of commission or omission found in this work.

The Canada Council provided financial support for this project by awarding me a leave fellowship during 1977-78. Part of that leave was spent on this project. In addition, Carleton University supplied small grants of money on two occasions to help defray sundry incidental expenses. I wish also to thank the secretarial staff of the School of Public Administration at Carleton University, in particular Judy Smith and Linda Mellon, for some typing help in the early stages of this work. Further secretarial help was cheerfully given by Caroline Caiger of the Dean's Office. My heartfelt thanks also is extended to my research assistant, David MacMartin. Dave read virtually the whole manuscript, responded to it by giving me detailed criticisms about what he read, and cheerfully completed the arduous task of double-checking my footnotes and quotations. My grateful thanks go out to a young and fine mind. Finally, I wish to thank members of my family for their patience and understanding while I completed this work.

V. Seymour Wilson

May 1980
School of Public Administration
Carleton University

Unless otherwise specifically mentioned, all italicization of quotations throughout this book is made by the author for emphasis.

To the
memory
of my
loved ones

This book
is dedicated
In deep
gratitude
and
affection.

Lena J. Superville
(1894-1978)

Randolph A. Pierre
(1898-1979)

An Introduction to Some Polemics and Key Theoretical Concepts

Theory will not
perish from the
earth so long as
rational curiosity
exists—a desire
for justification
and explanation
in terms of
motives and
reasons.

Sir Isaiah Berlin

CHAPTER ONE

PUBLIC POLICY AND ADMINISTRATION: WHAT'S IN A NAME?

The modern method of social control involves the application of rationality to all social relations. In production we call it technology. In exchange it is called commerce or markets. In social structure we have here called it differentiation. *Rationality applied to social control is administration. Administration may indeed be the sine qua non of modernity.*

Theodore Lowi

"When I use a word," Humpty Dumpty said in rather a scornful tone, "it means just what I choose it to mean—neither more nor less."

Lewis Carroll,
Through the Looking Glass

Humpty Dumpty, one of the characters of our childhood fantasies, certainly had a most convenient way of dealing with troublesome words, phrases and situations. By defining them in accordance with his own whims and fancies he of course felt that he authoritatively settled matters once and for all. His acquaintance, Alice, was rather puzzled by all this, but Humpty Dumpty made sure that he was clearly understood the second time around:

"The question is," said Alice, "whether you can make words mean so many different things." "The question is," said Humpty Dumpty, "which is to be master—that's all."

In the real world in which we live things are, however, not that simple. And so it is with the subject matter of this book, public policy and administration. How can the field be defined for the student?

Most students know that the subject matter has something to do with governmental bureaucracy, but exactly what is not entirely clear. We can, therefore, be like Humpty Dumpty and be rather pragmatic, calling it like it is, as we see the situation. And what the average Canadian "sees" about anything to do with government is rather formidable. In the first instance one recognizes that government is involved in the making of decisions and in the process of providing *services* for all Canadians. As examples, for the poor and the unemployed it is the welfare agency and unemployment benefits; for senior citizens, it is the monthly social insurance cheques; and for the sick and infirm, it is the hospital and the health insurance commission.

Secondly, one is also aware of governmental action in the enforcement or implementation of *regulations* for the benefit of all society:[1] the setting of standards for food and drugs, the implementation of wages and prices control under anti-inflation programs, the enforcement of fair housing, rental and employment regulations and so on. The average Canadian quickly realizes that government is heavily involved in the processes of social change and that large organizations are the indispensable instruments used for the implementation of social policies to effect those changes.

Moreover, on a little reflection, our average Canadian quickly realizes that most people act out their lives in the context of an organization. From birth, during school years and on through a working career, almost everyone is in constant touch with the realities of organizational structure. It shapes and defines our very existence. To some, or perhaps to most people, this reality of life, this inescapable juggernaut, is imposing, frustrating and alienating. Be that as it may, organization cannot be escaped in the Canada of the twentieth century. Organization, especially governmental organization, is too big to go away and too crucial to ignore. In attempting to deal with reality we must analyse what this phenomenon is all about and try to understand why it seems such an inescapable fact of our existence.

The perception thus described above is one which the average Canadian has and tacitly accepts about everyday existence. But governmental organization is much more complicated than it first appears and it is our task in this chapter to briefly explore some of the clues we have already been given in the everyday perceptions of our average Canadian. For example, we take as granted that public policy means *"making decisions"* for society; that this involves some *means of implementation;* and that implementation involves us in *the controlling of the environment* so as to achieve our goals. Furthermore, we try to do all this within *organizations,* a nice synonym for *bureaucracy*—that inefficient overpowering *bane* of our existence which *manages* just about everything in our lives.

Our conception of what the making of public policy and its administration is all about takes in a multitude of words and phrases which seem all interconnected but rarely defined in any precise way.[1] Key words used are "decision," "decisions over time," "means of implementation," "control of the environment" (or social control), "organization," "bureaucracy," "inefficiency" and "management". If we look at these words a little more closely we discover that they are a mixture of abstract images or airy concepts (social control, bureaucracy meaning red tape, power over our lives and inefficiency) and commonly used words with everyday meanings (decision, management, inefficient).

What is being suggested is that an understanding of what public policy and administration is all about involves an imprecise consideration of a series of key words and phrases, not an encouraging sign for a reader seeking definitional purity. The aim of this chapter is to explore, in a preliminary way, the subtleties of meaning involved in these words and phrases.[2] Why explore the topic in this fashion? First, while it is true that no single one-sentence definition is given it is hoped that this exploration of meanings would help to mitigate many semantical pitfalls so common in the usage of these words.[3] Second, the exploration of the phenomenon of governmental organization in this way opens up a whole gamut of issues concerning the relations of individuals to abstract organizational features (power, control, the relationships of environment to organization and so on). What, therefore, is in a name? Quite a lot really. It is hoped that our preliminary definitions will form the basis for further analysis, but in the end all this information can be boiled down to one basic fact: "we cannot expect this name to tell us anything more than the fact of relationship, of historical and logical connection between these problems. But that single piece of information is important enough for academics [students] and citizens alike."[4]

The Matter of Definition: Part I

Public Policy and Rationality

What is our preliminary conception of the word "public"? For short we can say it means *governmental* or *state related*. But such qualifying words or adjectives, although as precise as we can get, do not eliminate the many subtleties and complications which surface in the real world when this definition is applied. For the concept of public or governmental has become somewhat obscured by the close interaction or interpenetration of the public and private sectors everywhere in Western liberal democracies. This is best illustrated by exploring the distinctions between "public" and "private" organizations. Many "private" institutions in Canada operate on a heavy subsidy of public tax dollars (for example, Pan Arctic Oils of Canada Ltd.)[5]; are regulated and otherwise dictated to in rather extensive ways, from prices charged for service to modes and places of operation (for example, private rail, air transportation and certain communication services); make decisions that affect the "public interest" to a large degree; and perform functions identical to those found in government.

Some "public" institutions operate on a "cost-recovery" or "self-support" basis; some utilize business-type financial and operating methods to a large degree (for example, Department of Supply and Services); carry out their functions primarily through private institutions (e.g. Defence Research Board); make decisions that affect the "immediate public interest" to a relatively small degree (e.g. esoteric research activities of many sections of government departments, for example, Agriculture); and perform functions identical to those found in the private sector (e.g. Eldorado Aviation Ltd.). In other words sectoral distinctions tend to shade imperceptibly into one another making "public" and "private" differentiation far from clear cut. While this aspect of governmental organization is not explored in any detail in this book, suffice to state here that it is a major issue in the study of public policy and administration, which cannot be entirely ignored. For our preliminary purposes, however, it is sufficient to point out that the major distinguishing features differentiating *public* from *private* organizations are found in basic differences in the *political bases of organizations* and in their mechanisms of *economic resource procurement.*[6]

When the question of allocation of all resources within an organization can be superseded at any point in time by considerations having to do with the authoritative allocation of values in society that organization can be regarded as "public."[7] In a "private" organization the tendency would be for considerations dealing with the maximization of profit to predominate. Figure I illustrates the fact that the regulation of economic activity by governmental control is not the baseline difference between public and private organizations. Rather, the baseline (represented by the black horizontal line) is *political.* Public policy and administration has that unique and overriding consideration about it, namely its political characteristics. Politics is centre stage here, and throughout this book we will consistently stress this dimension as a foremost and overriding one.

This takes us to the key term "public policy" and what is meant by it. A good definition advanced by W. I. Jenkins is:

FIGURE I

A CONTINUUM SHOWING SOME OF THE AVAILABLE CHOICES OF ORGANIZATIONAL FORMS BETWEEN GOVERNMENT OWNERSHIP AND PRIVATE ENTERPRISE

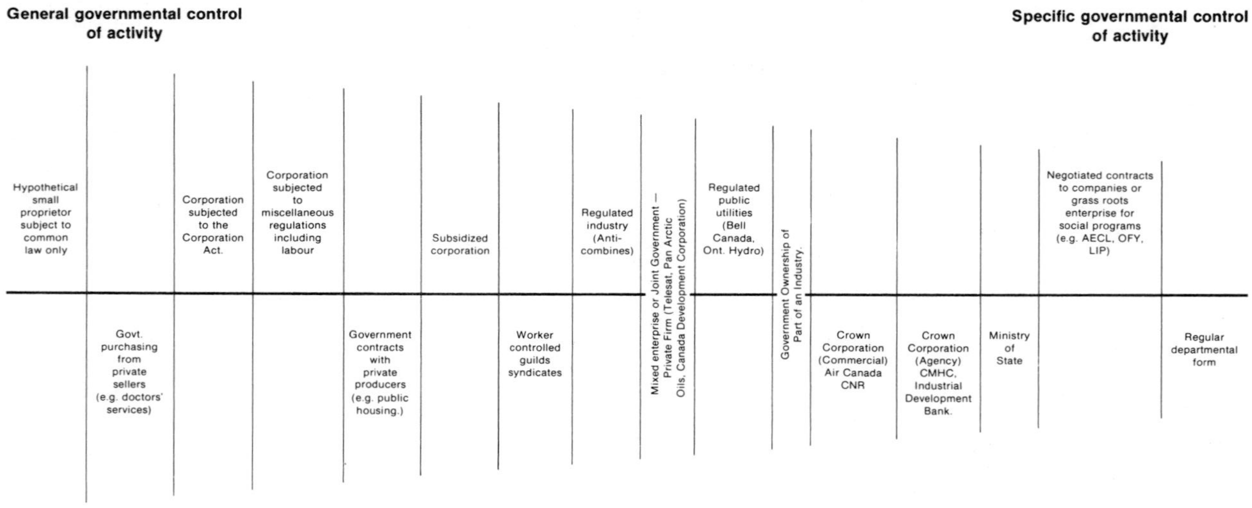

General governmental control of activity

Specific governmental control of activity

- Hypothetical small proprietor subject to common law only
- Corporation subjected to the Corporation Act.
- Corporation subjected to miscellaneous regulations including labour
- Regulated industry (Anti-combines)
- Regulated public utilities (Bell Canada, Ont. Hydro)
- Negotiated contracts to companies or grass roots enterprise for social programs (e.g. AECL, OFY, LIP)
- Regular departmental form

Government Ownership of Part of an Industry.

Mixed enterprise or Joint Government — Private Firm (Telesat, Pan Arctic Oils, Canada Development Corporation)

- Govt. purchasing from private sellers (e.g. doctors' services)
- Government contracts with private producers (e.g. public housing.)
- Subsidized corporation
- Worker controlled guilds syndicates
- Crown Corporation (Commercial) Air Canada CNR
- Crown Corporation (Agency) CMHC, Industrial Development Bank.
- Ministry of State

Above the line: organizational forms described as "private enterprise," "free enterprise," "reprivatization," "hiving off," "private industry."

Below the line: organizational forms popularly described with words such as "nationalized," "socialized," "government ownership" and "public enterprise"

On the line: organizational forms thought to be neither clearly public nor private.

A set of interrelated decisions taken by a political actor or group of actors concerning the selection of goals and the means of achieving them within a specified situation where these decisions should, in principle, be within the power of these actors to achieve.[8]

This definition highlights several important considerations about public policy. First, the definition indicates that decision-making is crucial to public policy making but normally the decision *per se* is only one aspect of public policy making. In other words, one swallow does not make a summer (one decision is normally not the policy). In the vast number of instances, *a series of decisions extending over time* is the crucial distinction between policy making and decision-making. We will explore the theoretical distinctions involved in this difference in Chapter Five. Secondly, the definition strongly implies the need to attain a thorough knowledge not only of the technical and social considerations, but also of the *institutional setting* (or loosely put, the environment) within which a given policy or policies are to occur. This emphasis forms the core of Section II of this book. Thirdly, the definition leaves open the notion that *inaction is in itself a decision* by the political actor or actors and this must be taken into consideration in our notions as to what policy making is all about. Finally, the latter part of the definition makes a conceptual distinction between *policy process* which is the strategies, techniques and methods of policy making and *policy content* which is the substance of policy. Later in this chapter we will again consider policy content versus policy process from a different angle when we look at the conceptual distinction involved in *administration* as opposed to *management*.

Construing public policy in terms of the deliberate "selection of goals and the means of achieving them "conjures up another word commonly used in describing aspects of the public decision-making process, namely rationality. The epigram by Theodore Lowi for this chapter states categorically that "the modern method of social control involves the application of rationality to all social relations." Obviously, the concept has very important implications for public policy and administration. Rationality, however, means a host of different things when used in different contexts. As Chapter Two would argue, even experienced scholars of bureaucracy get confused over the different meanings.

The most conventional meaning of the word is the equating of "rationality" with "efficiency." Efficiency and rationality are almost synonymous words in the layman's lexicon. Furthermore, the meaning takes an almost mechanical attitude toward human behavior and motivation as conditioned by considerations of self-interest or financial motives. (In neo-classical economics it is irrational for a business executive not to have profit maximization as his chief or overriding interest). A familiar example of this concept of rationality is the search for greater efficiency or for "the one best way" of expediting a job, a theme which the student will encounter in considering the organizational theories of scientific management in Chapter Four.

This notion of rationality is also closely associated with reason, formal logic and the methods of mathematical, scientific and economic inquiry. According to this concept, the decision-maker looks at the ends and then considers the most efficient means necessary to achieve these ends. This accounts for the fact that this type of rationality is frequently referred to as the means-ends approach to administrative behavior.[9] One is reminded here of the essay, "A Dissertation Upon Roast Pig" by the English literary critic, Charles Lamb. The story, it will be remembered, is that roast pork was first enjoyed when a house in which pigs were confined was accidentally burned down. While searching in the ruins, the owners touched the pigs that had been roasted in the fire and scorched their fingers. Impulsively bringing their fingers to their mouths to cool them, they experienced a new taste. Enjoying the taste, they henceforth set themselves to building houses, enclosing pigs in them, and then burning the houses down. Does the end justify the means? Or to put it in another way, given the end, would it not have been wiser to consider the cost and consequences of alternative available means? Reasoned in this way, rationality construed also in *terms of procedure* takes on a different meaning, a point to which we will return in a moment.

A second meaning of the concept of rational refers to the attempt to objectively understand human behavior—to describe, measure and predict it. We are here referring to the attempt to do so accurately by means other than precise, calculating logical methods. The English political philosopher Michael Oakeshott refers to this rationality as "practical knowledge" which exists "only in use, is not reflective, and (unlike technique) cannot be formulated into rules" (precise logical rules). The cook who makes a superb meal without ever having considered a recipe, or the genius of a painter who "just paints" is very rational according to Oakeshott.[10] Likewise, the skillful administrator has the ability to sense how people are going to react to various administrative actions and decisions made, and attempts to shape those actions and decisions to minimize adverse reception on the part of those affected. To the extent that the professionally trained administrator is unable to do this with legislation or a job delegated, the administrator is, in Kenneth Burke's echolalic phrase, "unfitted by being fit in an unfit fitness,"[11] namely, that past "rational" training may have become an incapacity. In many respects this type of decision-making is the very heart of administrative behavior. This flexibility, this ability to accurately judge the consequences of one's administrative decisions, we call administrative "experience." It can only be obtained on the job where the administrator takes into account the probable human reactions to decisions and actions taken. In doing so one is engaging in prediction, although one would not call it that.

The third meaning of rationality is derived from a combination of normative values and technical considerations. This meaning of bureaucratic rationality is pervasive throughout this book, and it is in this sense of the term that Max Weber used it extensively in his study and analysis of bureaucracy. Weber's conception of rationality involved two central characteristics: *the intention* in the design of an administrative rule, and the *procedure* involved in the rule's application.[12] What is meant by this? A rational act is one designed to accomplish certain specific goals, no matter what the goals may be. Simply put, the Nazi bureaucratic act of working out technical rules to aid in the "expediting and processing" (read genocide) of millions of Jews and other "undesirables" was rational. Or for a more recent analogy closer to home, the cold calculating rules devised to record and report "body counts" and "kill ratios" in the bureaucratic war called Vietnam were perfectly rational. Weber's meaning encompasses another aspect as well: the term *rational* was not only appropriate to rules because of the intention behind them but also it could be used to designate the procedure of applying rules to particular cases. In today's world it has become increasingly necessary to employ qualified people with appropriate skills to apply technical rules and procedures to achieve certain goals. Martin Albrow is enlightening on this point:

Two separate statements Weber made about the specific nature of the rationality of bureaucracy support such an interpretation: "Bureaucratic administration signifies authority on the basis of knowledge. This is its specifically rational character"; and, "Bureaucratic authority is specifically rational in the sense of being bound to discursively analysable rules." Only *if one realized that Weber regarded the implementation of rules in the modern organization as a matter for the expert can one grasp the compatibility of these apparently divergent judgements. This procedure of expert application of rules was central to what Weber called the formal rationality of bureaucracy.*[13]

This concept of rationality is different from rationality in the sense of efficiency. As Albrow shows, Max Weber's formal rationality certainly encompassed techniques (such as accounting and filing to achieve certain administrative standards). But, more importantly, this rationality meant legal expertise, the interpretation of law and codes by experts versed in those interpretations. Thus administrative action was guided both by *technique* and by *norms*. In short, we have from Max Weber a statement of the formal procedures which are prevalent in modern administration, a theme to which we will return in the next chapter.

A Matter of Definition: Part II

Organization, Administration, Management and Bureaucracy

How do we view these terms and distinguish between them? Again, the fact that precise definitions cannot be given for these terms demonstrates something of the meaning of these complex concepts. One conception of organization is rather straightforward and generally acceptable to most people. Formal (or complex) organizations, in the words of a recent text, have "been established for the explicit purpose of achieving certain goals" possessing both rules (designed to shape and anticipate behavior in the direction of these goals) and "a formal status structure with clearly marked lines of communication and authority."[14] In other words, organizations are instruments concerned with means and ends, with goals and with technological efforts to achieve such goals. As instruments, their chief *raison d'être* is to help fashion, serve and otherwise control human behavior in the achievement of goals specified for the organization (be it by the state or some private purpose).

But what about administration? Can it not be conceived as the same thing as organization? A clue to a subtle difference between the two is provided in our opening epigram by Lowi when he asserts that rationality applied to social relations is administration. Practitioners of administration do two things simultaneously: first they are concerned with the proper exercise of applied logic and other instrumental means of organization, but simultaneously they must initiate values and practice ethics. *Above all, administration must be concerned with cultural and value considerations—the available roles, skills, beliefs, values and other environmental concerns which help to shape social relations.*[15] As one writer recently put it: "Administration is philosophy in action . . . By philosophy I mean in barest essence the process of correct thinking and the process of valuing: rationality, or logic and values. These constitute the dual aspects of activity whereby administration becomes philosophical."[16]

When we study public administration we are therefore (or should be) heavily preoccupied with values and ethical considerations and how these are authoritatively allocated through public organizations. Hence our main preoccupation with environmental concerns in Section II of this book.

But as Christopher Hodgkinson points out, philosophy in action is like the image of Janus, for there are two aspects to it: "the process of valuing" and "the process of correct thinking." Administration is more concerned with valuing, that is, with *ends*, while the concept of management is more preoccupied with rational (*intentional* and *procedural*) action, that is, with *means*:

> . . . we can consider administration to be the art of influencing men to accomplish organizational goals while management is the ancillary and subordinate science of specifying and implementing means to accomplish the same ends. Administration is ends-oriented, management is means-oriented. The pure administrator is a philosopher, the pure manager a technologist. *But there is no approximation to purity at either end of the spectrum in the fact and practice of administration or management. The distinction is obscured and sometimes deliberately so.*[17]

We believe this distinction to be fundamentally important. For conceptual and practical reasons we have utilized it in this book, for administration is here construed in terms of ethical concerns and other environmental influences. A later volume on Canadian public policy and administration will be more preoccupied with what is commonly referred to as the *processes* and *performance* considerations of the bureaucracy, namely managerial concerns. However, we contend, with all the emphasis we can here muster, that in practice managerial (or means-oriented) concerns *cannot and should not* be divorced from administrative (or ends-oriented) concerns. That is why we have titled this book *Canadian Public Policy and Administration*. It is fashionable to make a distinction between policy and administration particularly by those who have never given the concept of administration a second thought. We contend that policy *is* administration and that administration and management are inextricably linked.

We finally come to the concept of bureaucracy. Where did the word come from? Initially the word "bureau" was coined in France during the eighteenth century to refer to the cloth covering the desks of French government officials. Later the term "bureau" was linked with the Greek suffix (KpaTOS) (or kratos) meaning strength, power, dominion, rule or mastery.[18] But exactly how it is to be understood in usage is not entirely clear from this history of its roots. A few examples would suffice to illustrate how Humpty Dumpty could have a great time with this one. The roots of the word would suggest that the best definition would seem to be a state of affairs where power is exercised by officials who are supposed to carry out the commands of another group with sovereign power but in fact usurp that power to themselves. Or it could mean merely rule through, rather than by, officials. Or it could mean that the impersonal nature of the system has taken over, that rationality (a mixture of *intentional* and *procedural* considerations) has predominated by giving birth to an automatic and relentless system. With all these various meanings it is obvious that usage could lead to various conceptual difficulties. It is therefore necessary to explore in greater detail these various meanings, for they are all found, in one form or another, in both the popular and intellectual literature on the subject.

The first general conception of bureaucracy is one already familiar to us from our discussion of rationality, namely efficient organization. We need not dwell on this theme here, but an example of this conception in the literature is the notion that bureaucracy should be defined as "organization that maximizes efficiency in administration"[19] or as "the organizational structure where there is heavy emphasis on administrative efficiency."[20] This theme of bureaucracy as rational or efficient organization remains of central importance in the present-day growth of the "sciences" of decision-making, of organizational tools such as operations research, and certainly in the language of the budgetary processes of bureaucracies.

A second conception of bureaucracy is a very popular one with the lay person and with politicians everywhere. This conception associates *bureaucracy with inefficiency and "red tape."* The origin of this idea is again of interest. Bureaucracy's central function is to maintain continuity, stability and predictability in the ongoing day-to-day activities of government. Therefore it follows that all transactions and dealings must be recorded in writing and preserved to ensure the stability of the ongoing process. But it is exactly these transactions which create symbols. The term "red tape," for example, is derived from the red ribbons used to bind up those rows upon rows of daily transactions and files at the United States State Department as these excess papers overflowed the filing cabinets during the American Civil War.

And the term continues to plague bureaucracy to the present day. Lay proponents of the notion of bureaucracy as red tape argue that the only effective remedy for this pathology lies in constantly sensitizing bureaucrats to their own bureaucratic nightmares.[21] Academic writers as well have also emphasized the problems of inflexibility and red tape in organizations and have defined bureaucracy in these terms. Professor Marshall Dimock has referred to bureaucracy as "the composite institutional manifestations which tend towards inflexibility and depersonalization,"[22] and another writer reserved the term for "the many imperfections in the structure and functioning of big organizations."[23] In a classical article written almost four decades ago, sociologist Robert K. Merton argued that bureaucratic emphasis on precision, reliability and predictability may well have self-defeating consequences, for rules designed as means to ends can easily become ends in themselves. This bureaucracy can readily lead to administrative delays and public complaints of red tape and secrecy.[24] In the study of public administration this theme has constantly appeared under the title of administrative responsibility and control and also in the literature on participatory administration. We will have occasion to return to this perception of bureaucracy in later chapters of this book.

A third conception of bureaucracy has also received attention from conservative thinkers on the one hand, and Marxists, Neo-Marxists and members of the New Left movement on the other: *the notion of bureaucracy as rule or government by officials.* Some conservative critics have viewed bureaucracy as an insidious system of societal control, slowly but inexorably threatening the values and liberties of Western democracy.[25] Marxists were, however, among the first students of twentieth century bureaucracy to infer this association of bureaucracy with power over the proletariat, but there has always been some ambivalence with this meaning. At first the explanation was a simple one. The logic of Marxist theory, and more specifically dialectical materialism, led to the conception of the state apparatus functioning as a mere tool for the continued hegemony of the dominant class, that is the economic class interests of society. This instrumental perception of bureaucracy led many Marxist writers at first to conceive bureaucracy as parasitic, serving the interests of the dominant economic interests but deriving its sustenance from the surplus labour of the proletariat.[26]

Social democrats and some Marxist followers however, were to question this passive conception of bureaucracy and bureaucratic power. In the early 1930s England's influential socialist intellectual, Harold Laski, defined bureaucracy as "the term usually applied to a system of government, the control of which is so completely in the hands of officials that their power jeopardises the liberties of ordinary citizens."[27] The most concerted attack on Marx's theory of the state apparatus came in the work of Milovan Djilas, author of the book, *The New Class*. Djilas argued that communist states are run by the party which is a bureaucracy. The bureaucracy is a class since it uses and disposes of state property. But this mechanism of party rule is not firmly embedded in the socio-economic order, so force and ideological dogmatism are used by the mechanism to secure its power.[28] He spent seven years in jail for exploring this line of logic and for openly proclaiming it to be the truth.

In the recent literature Neo-Marxists have concentrated more on expounding reformulations on bureaucracy. The notion of bureaucracy as a tool of the dominant economic interests is still present, but Marxist followers have now addressed themselves to such questions as: why the bureaucratic form of organization? Why do state bureaucrats think and act much like corporate managers? And why especially do state enterprises fail to act differently from corporations?[29] Aspects of these themes will be briefly dealt with in Chapter Three.

Whereas Marxist and socialist literature have been ambivalent to the phenomenon of bureaucracy, over the last decade the diffuse and short-lived movement known as the New Left has treated the whole concept as "a plague on both your houses." The stringent protests and demands of the Paris student revolt of May 1968 bear out this assertion. Socialism is defined as "a rejection of all bureaucracy, of all centralized direction, by granting power to the producers at their point of production."[30] Thus, bureaucracy in the form of all hierarchy, specialization, authority or any form of alienation in society is anathema. This philosophy is best summed up by a popular bit of graffiti expressed on the walls of Paris during the 1968 revolt: "When the last bureaucrat and the last technocrat are hung by their [tripes], will we still have problems?" Thus we have come full circle: from a discussion of the inevitability of bureaucracy in modern society, to a lashing out at its "pathological" symptoms, to a Marxist and socialist ambivalence, and finally to a New Left ideology which has made organizational structure, rather than the class system, its main target of attack.[31]

As the reader by now would have realized, no definition of public bureaucracy can be simple and straightforward. While it is true that the idea of bureaucracy and its derivatives arose out of a concern for the adequate understanding of the official in modern government, that concern has changed with changing times. Thus, in the foregoing analysis the definition of the topic under study was construed in terms of its relationships to the values of democracy, and as these values changed so have the conceptions of the phenomenon. There are other attempts, however, to understand bureaucracy with somewhat different emphases. The most important of these holds that the bureaucratic phenomenon can only be truly understood if its cause-and-effect sequences occurring in the world of nature are established.

For example, despite all the rantings and ravings about its inefficiency, mediocrity and red tape, why does bureaucracy, or forms of organization close to it, exist in every culture known to man? In order to obtain a meaningful answer to this question this viewpoint further maintains that systems of ethical evaluation have to be at least bracketed, (but certainly not ignored), to permit the examination of social relations apart from values. This is the so-called "scientific method" of the social sciences, and it forms the basis of the views on bureaucracy amplified in both Chapters Two and Three of this book.

These perceptions represent the first two most important attempts to subject bureaucracy to vigorous, systematic analysis and to facilitate an understanding, not only of bureaucracy's relation to its environment but its internal processes as well. Thus, these perceptions have occupied a central place in the corpus of knowledge about bureaucracy during the last eight decades, and represent the starting point of the so-called "scientific" theories discussed in Chapter 4.

Conclusions

In this chapter an explanation of the meaning and development of public policy and administration is attempted through a brief semantic exposition of the different ways in which, and the different purposes for which, the name has been used and the changes which the concepts associated with the name have undergone in the course of time. This exposition reinforces the now accepted belief that the scope of the study of public policy and administration has been so extensively broadened in recent decades that a brief definition of the subject would therefore be impracticable. It is our purpose to continue this semantic exposition in greater depth in each chapter, indicating to the student the relationship between ideas and practice, between theory and application. We also emphasize here that both the *study* and *practice* of public management are conceived as public policy and administration. We concur with Nicholas Henry's contention that " . . . public (policy and) administration is a broad-ranging and amorphous combination of *theory* and *practice* designed to promote a superior understanding of government and its relationship with the society it governs . . ."[32]

This relationship with society can only be meaningfully understood by coming to grips with how society defines the contextual nature of the phenomenon and studying the individual's role in that context. As Mason Haire argues:

Whenever we try to plan what an organization should be like, it is necessarily based on an implicit concept of man. If we look . . . at the outline of a "classical" organization theory and some more modern alternatives, we begin to see the change in the concept of man.[33]

As a parting shot in our opening chapter we return to the idea put forward earlier that public policy *is* public administration. One might suppose that public policy and public administration are simply different titles for the same thing, but in fact not everyone would agree with this, for these terms denote fields of study which, in my view, are illogically distinct.

The gap which must be filled in public policy studies is the neglect of the administrative element.[34] In our increasingly bureaucratic society a proliferation of studies and books have appeared, and will continue to appear, on the subject of the "philosophy and politics" of public policy and of the new "managerial" styles of rational decision and planning. Both sets of writings totally disregard the administrative element: *administration in the seemingly prosaic sense of values merging with programs, of control, surveillance, institutional considerations and policy implementation* have all somehow received very little, if any, attention from the so-called policy analysts. This, in our view makes no sense whatsoever, for failing to study the administrative element only in fact assumes away the real problems of administration. Our hope is that in succeeding chapters we have, in some small measure, helped to rectify that regrettable neglect.

The Democratic Political Process: Lifeline to an Open Society

The thing that is most fatal to the political process is conclusions: when once the train of thought has reached a terminus, everybody might just as well get off it.

Kenneth Boulding,
The Organizational Revolution

Footnotes

1. To the initiated in public policy and administration, precision is a real problem, because there is very little common agreement of the use of terms in the literature. One recent study identified fifteen different English uses of "administration." See Andrew Dunsire, *Administration: The Word and the Science* (London: Martin Robertson, 1973) 228-229.

2. We concur with Professor Dwight Waldo's description of the problem in the study of public administration. "The immediate effect of all one-sentence or one-paragraph definitions of public administration is mental paralysis rather than enlightenment and stimulation. This is because a serious definition of the term . . . inevit-

ably contains several abstract words or phrases. In short compass these abstract words and phrases can be explained only by other abstract words and phrases, and in the process the reality and importance of "it" become fogged and lost." D. Waldo, *The Study of Public Administration* (New York: Doubleday, 1955) p. 2.

3. It is nevertheless true that simple definitions do help us to begin our analysis and to arrive at some common perceptions. Again to quote Waldo approvingly: "This disposition to get on is no doubt healthy, and diminishes a picayune and wasteful squabbling over words alone. But it must not be forgotten that definitions are important to fruitful study and effective action." *Ibid.*, p. 3.

4. Martin Albrow, *Bureaucracy,* (London and Basingstoke: Macmillan and Co. Ltd., 1970), p. 125.

5. More correctly, this example is a public-private consortium with government providing most of the funds but having a disproportionate say in the decisions of the consortium. If the private sector representatives had their way, this input of government would be even less than it is now.

6. R.A. Dahl and C.E. Lindblom, *Politics, Economics and Welfare,* (New York: Harper and Row, 1963).

7. David Easton, *The Political System,* (New York: Alfred A. Knopf, 1965) pp. 129-141.

8. W.I. Jenkins, *Policy Analysis: A Political and Organisational Perspective,* (London: Martin Robertson & Co. Ltd., 1978) p. 15.

9. See A.W. Johnson, "Efficiency in Government and Business", *Canadian Public Administration,* Vol. 6, No. 3 (September 1963), pp. 245-260.

10. Michael Oakeshott, *Rationalism in Politics* (London: Methuen and Co., Ltd. 1962), p. 8. When Oakeshott uses the term "practical knowledge" he is referring to knowledge which is good for man. The end of "practical" knowledge is moral action. It facilitates the working out of broad criteria of moral choice and also guides the particular choices of the moral agent. The scientist-philosopher, Michael Polanyi, has also made this crucial distinction in his discussion of "tacit knowledge." See *The Tacit Dimension* (New York: Doubleday & Co., 1966).

11. Kenneth Burke, *Permanence and Change* (New York: New Republic, 1935), pp. 50.

12. Martin Albrow, *op. cit.,* p. 61-66.

13. Martin Albrow, *Ibid.,* p. 63.

14. Peter M. Blau and Richard W. Scott, *Formal Organizations: A Comparative Approach* (London: Routledge and Kegan Paul, 1963) pp. 1 and 14.

15. Robert D. Miewald, *Public Administration: A Critical Perspective* (New York: McGraw-Hill Book Company, 1978) especially Chapters One and Two (pp. 3-48).

16. Christopher Hodgkinson, *Towards a Philosophy of Administration*, (London: Basil Blackwell, 1978) p. 3.

17. *Ibid.*, p. 5.

18. Reinhard Bendix, "Bureaucracy," *International Encyclopedia of the Social Sciences*, (New York: Macmillan and Free Press, 1968), II, 206-219; Fritz Morstein Marx, *The Administrative State*, (Chicago: University of Chicago Press, 1957), pp. 16-21.

19. Peter M. Blau, *Bureaucracy in Modern Society* (New York: Random House, 1956), p. 60.

20. David E. Apter and R.A. Lystad, "Bureaucracy, Party and Constitutional Democracy: An Examination of Political Role Systems in Ghana," in G.M. Carter and W.O. Brown, *Transition in Africa: Studies in Political Adaptation* (Boston: University Press, 1958), p. 20.

21. In November 1977, the then Opposition Leader in our Federal Parliament, Mr. Joe Clark repeated a popular planned "shakeup" of the federal bureaucracy when the Progressive Conservatives came to power in Ottawa: "It would help the deputy minister of immigration to spend two weeks each year at Malton Airport, applying to prospective immigrants the rules and regulations the department establishes. It would do the chief statistician of Canada an immense amount of good to spend two weeks each year filling out forms." See "Tories plan shake-up of bureaucrats," *The Edmonton Journal*, Tuesday, November 29, 1977, Section BI.

22. Marshall E. Dimock, "Bureaucracy Self-Examined," *Public Administration Review*, Vol. 4, 1944, p. 198.

23. E. Strauss, *The Ruling Servants*, (London: Allen and Unwin, 1967), pp. 40-41.

24. Robert K. Merton, "Bureaucratic Structure and Personality" in *Social Forces* XVIII, (1940), pp. 560-568. Also found in Robert K. Merton *et al.*, (eds.) *Reader in Bureaucracy* (Glencoe, Ill.: The Free Press, 1952), pp. 361-71. For an excellent review and critique of the Merton theme see Harry Cohen, "Bureaucratic flexibility: some comments on Robert Merton's 'Bureaucratic Structure and Personality,' " *British Journal of Sociology*, Vol. 21, 1970, pp. 390-399.

25. See Jose Ortega y Gasset, *The Revolt of the Masses* (New York: W. Norton and Co., Inc., 1957), especially Chapter 12, "The Barbarism of Specialization" and Chapter 13, "The Greatest Danger, the State"; Herman Finer, "Critics of Bureaucracy," *Political Science Quarterly*, Vol. 60, 1945.

26. "The Eighteenth Brumaire of Louis Bonapart," (1852) in L.S. Feuer (ed.), *Marx and Engels: Basic Writings on Politics and Philosophy* (New York: Doubleday, 1959), p. 343. Marx himself fostered this conception. See his remarks about Louis XIV's "courtier group."

27. Harold Laski, "Bureaucracy," *Encyclopedia of the Social Sciences*, Vol. 3, (New York: Macmillan, 1930), p. 70.

28. Milovan Djilas, *The New Class* (London: Thames and Hudson, 1957).

29. See the various pieces in Leo Panitch, *The Canadian State: Political Economy and Political Power.* (Toronto: University of Toronto Press, 1977. An excellent discussion comparing the similarities and differences between Weber's and Lenin's thoughts on bureaucracy is found in Erik Olin Wright, *Class, Crisis and the State* (London: New Left Books, 1978) pp. 181-225.

30. J. Sauvageot, A. Geismar, D. Cohn-Bendit and J.-P. Duteuil, *The Student Revolt* (London: Panther Books, 1968), p. 60.

31. P. Jacobs and S. Landau, *The New Radicals* (London: Penguin Books, Hardmondsworth, Middlesex, 1968), especially the sixth section "The F.S.M.—Revolt against Liberal Democracy."

32. Nicholas Henry, *Public Administration and Public Affairs* (Englewood Cliffs, J.N.: Prentice Hall, Inc., 1975), p. 4.

33. Quoted in George B. Strother (ed.), *Social Science Approaches to Business Behavior* (Homewood, Illinois: The Dorsey Press, Inc., 1962), pp. 170-171.

34. A good example of this disregard, of public administration conceptualized as a "hole" in which public policy should not be allowed to get "stuck," see Richard Simeon, "Studying Public Policy," *Canadian Journal of Political Science*, IX, No. 4 (December, 1976), pp. 548-580.

Recommended Readings

Few books are recommended for further reading. Our main criticism of textbooks is that most of them simplify the introductory chapter to the extent of making the material a collection of truisms. We however recommend the following books and articles for further study.

Books and Articles

Martin Albrow, *Bureaucracy*.
This book is highly recommended. The book gives some examination of the history of the concept of bureaucracy and its evolution in meaning over the centuries. We found it particularly insightful in spelling out the various contemporary ways the concept of bureaucracy is referred to. Hard going in spots, but highly recommended nevertheless.

Nicholas Henry, *Public Administration and Public Affairs*.
For those wanting material on the intellectual development of public administration this book is recommended. Attempts to cover too much in its chapters on "focus" (which it defines as the specialized "what" of the field, the core of knowledge which has come to be known as administrative studies). Henry however covers the material for the American environment. For a Canadian perspective on developments, see the following:

James Iain Gow (ed.), *Administration publique quebecoise* (Montreal: Librairie Beauchemin Limitee, 1979).

W.D.K. Kernaghan, "Identity, Pedagogy and Public Administration: the Canadian Experience," *Public Administration* (Australia), Vol. 32, No. 1 (March 1973).

W.D.K. Kernaghan, "An Overview of Public Administration in Canada Today," *Canadian Public Administration*, Vol. II, No. 3 (Fall 1968).

Roland Parenteau, "Une nouvelle approche dans la formation des administrateurs publics: l'Ecole nationale d'administration publique," *Canadian Public Administration*, Vol. 15, No. 3 (Fall 1972)

A. Paul Pross and V. Seymour Wilson, "Graduate Education in Canadian Public Administration: Antecedents, Present Trends, and Portents," *Canadian Public Administration*, 19, no. 4 (Winter 1976) pp. 515-41.

Ralph P. Hummel, *The Bureaucratic Experience*.
This is an excellent book which attempts to bring together elements of sociological, political and psychological writings on bureaucracy in an attempt to explain bureaucracy to the average lay person. It succeeds, although it may be hard going for some in spots (the psychology of bureaucracy, for instance).

Robert D. Miewald, *Public Administration: A Critical Perspective*.
Part I of this book dealing with "Administration and Society" is highly recommended as good general reading. To give a flavor of the book's content I simply quote a section of the preface:

> Public administration is the heart of modern politics, largely because the nature of reality is not an abstract question for the bureaucracy; the formal rules describe what is and what is not. . . . We are done for if administration is regarded as a science which must be presented in a solemn and reverent fashion. The subject is fascinating because it is so large a part of our existence, and therefore every aspect of it ought to be subject to the liveliest discussion. (p. x).

Dwight Waldo, *The Study of Public Administration*.
This book is somewhat outdated, but it still remains a central classic in the field. We are not particularly happy with its narrow definition of rationality (efficiency) but it nevertheless comes to firm grips with other central concepts in the study of public policy and administration.

CHAPTER TWO

BUREAUCRACY AS RATIONAL ADMINISTRATION: MAX WEBER AND THE IDEAL TYPE

Positions of leadership are not much coveted by the Ik. They are backed by little power, and in so far as they confer any benefits (i.e. ngag, or food) upon the office-holder, that only serves to make him all the more edible.

Colin Turnbull,
The Mountain People

Introduction

In the previous chapter we dealt with, among other things, three commonly held notions about bureaucracy (as an inefficient phenomenon, as "rational" or "efficient" organization and as naked power broker). We come now to a fourth notion, *bureaucracy as administration by officials*. This latter concept is aimed at expressly relating bureaucracy to the *legitimate* environment of the society in which it is located, (the word "officials," for example, is used to connote legitimate power authorities). This notion emphasizes the fact that bureaucracy exists because there is a legitimate function for it to perform in the society in which it is found. Thus, an attempt is made to adequately link up the concepts of *power, authority* and *legitimacy* with that of *administration*. For example, it will be shown how the concept of "rational-legal bureaucracy" has a particular meaning, and how it is linked to and identified as a distinct phenomenon of Western liberal democratic culture. It was Max Weber, whose main interest was in the impact of bureaucratic organizations on the political structure of society as a whole, who further advanced the study of organizations by specifically dealing with these interrelationships. Weber was not concerned with the question of whether the bureaucracy would of necessity decline. Rather he argued that the sweep of history showed that its permanence and technical indispensability must be assumed, and he therefore concentrated his analysis more on the impact of bureaucracy on the social structure and, more particularly, on individual personality.

Accordingly, in this chapter we will first give a brief glimpse of Max Weber's conceptual scheme of characterizing organizations in terms of the authority relations both within them and also within the societies which these organizations serve. Secondly, we will elaborate on the rational-legal bureaucratic system. Thirdly, our analysis will explore some aspects of Weber's political sociology by discussing his use of "ideal types" and what he meant to accomplish by utilizing this explanatory tool of the social sciences.[1]

We wish to emphasize that amongst all the different interpretations of bureaucracy, the theoretical moorings Weber tries to establish should be grasped and adequately understood by everyone engaged in the study of bureaucracy. Max Weber was deeply committed to democracy but he also believed very fervently that the study of the potentialities and dangers of bureaucracy will make progress only if the underlying philosophical assumptions about the phenomenon are made explicit. Thus in terms of the influence it has exerted and the debate it has stimulated, Weber's writings on bureaucracy remain central in any theoretical discussion of public policy, administration and society.

Max Weber's Political Sociology

Max Weber (1864-1920) was born in Germany. His early education was in law, and after his doctoral studies he became a member of the faculty of Berlin University. Generally regarded as the founder of modern sociology, Weber had a primary interest in the historical development of civilizations through sociological studies of economics, religion, politics, the law and the arts.

Weber's range of interests and erudition was incredible. In his study of civilizations and their development, he discursively and thoroughly examined the major world religions, such as Christianity, Buddhism and Judaism, as well as tracing the pattern of economic development from prefeudal times. Throughout these discussions Weber repeatedly emphasized his strong belief that attempts to unify and systematize knowledge inevitably lead to narrow formalism, and that the best way to proceed is to work directly with the raw materials, seeking to impose no pattern on them other than that method logically necessary to accent their uniqueness. The result of this focus of

MAX WEBER (1864-1920).
Courtesy of the University of Heidelberg Archives.

interest and scholarly style was to produce his classical study of the impact of Protestant beliefs on the development of capitalism in North America and Western Europe.[2]

Weber's most important contribution to the study of organizations was his categorization of authority structures in terms of the authority relations within them.[3] To do this Weber spent considerable time in his writings exploring the concept of *social relation*. As Don Martindale explains: "This is the fundamental concept for making the transition from individual acts to patterns of behavior. It is the critical concept by which one moves eventually from social action either to the social person or to social groups, institutions, and communities."[4] Weber devoted much energy in developing the idea of a *Verband*. To quote Martindale once more:

A social relationship which is either closed or limits the admission of outsiders by rules, is a "corporate group" (Verband) so far as its order is enforced by the action of specific individuals whose regular function this is, i.e., a chief or head (Leiter) and usually also an administrative staff. Corporate groups may be self-governing or subject to the law of other groups. The types of order in corporate groups may be established by voluntary agreement or by imposition and acquiescence. The systems of order governing action in corporate groups may be administrative or regulative. The types of organization of corporate groups including the voluntary association and compulsory association, are organizations of *power* and *imperative* control.[5]

The "ordering of social relationships" as the specialized tasks of certain individuals within society formed the basis of Weber's understanding of bureaucracy. There are three aspects to this ordering: a leadership function (Leiter), an administrative staff which both gave and received orders (Verwaltungsstab), and the rest which received orders and routinely carried these orders out in the service of the bureaucracy. By definition, bureaucracies were *hierarchical tri-partite structures*. And yet this tripartite ordering is much more than just orders being given and carried out. To quote a former experienced student of Canadian bureaucracy: "Hierarchy is not essentially a matter of someone telling someone else what to do. It is an arrangement, or a system of roles which link up with one another in such a way that values are subordinated to one another. Thus the outcome of the work of the hierarchy is predictable. . . ."[6] In an administrative order, commands and rules were linked in such a manner that the rules regulated the scope and the possession of authority. Thus, administrative orders must be vested with *authority* and must be seen as *legitimate* in order to be carried out. Figure I attempts to present this conceptualization in graphic form. This relationship between the state and its administrative apparatus in a legal-rational system of authority embodies some crucial distinguishing characteristics to which we will return in the second half of this book.

To make his meaning clear Weber first differentiates between "power" and "domination." The concept of power (Macht) is a broad term used in dealing with all forms of social interaction where an individual might try to impose his will on others. However, as Weber himself puts it, "Power (Macht) is the probability (Chance) that one actor within a social relationship will be in a position to carry out his own will despite resistance whatever the basis of this probability may be." Domination or "imperative co-ordination" (Herrschaft) is defined as "the probability that certain specific commands (or all commands) from a given source will be obeyed by a given group of persons".[7] Thus domination or authority is a more precise concept. A person has this relationship with others only if he is operating with a corporate group and has an administrative staff to see that his orders are actually acted upon. Also, domination per se is more precise because the person obeying the orders must conceive them to be legitimate. Domination given without legitimacy leads to hypocrisy or it may be given as a result of weakness and helplessness.[8]

This concept of legitimacy is crucial to Weber's classification of organizations: "The foundation of all authority, and hence of all compliance with orders, is a belief in prestige, which operates to the advantage of the ruler or rulers."[9] He identified three principles of legitimate authority or domination as follows:

(i) *Rational-legal domination*. People believe that someone giving an

FIGURE I

THE RELATIONSHIP BETWEEN THE STATE AND ITS ADMINISTRATIVE APPARATUS
IN A LEGAL RATIONAL SYSTEM OF AUTHORITY

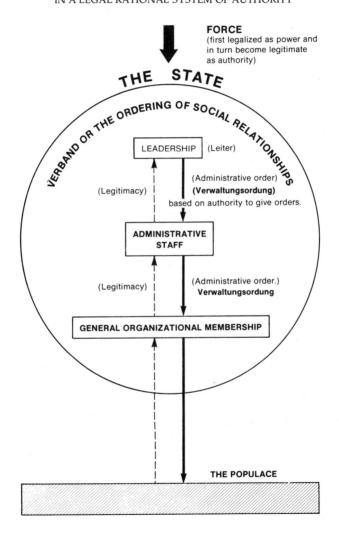

order is acting in accordance with one's duties as enumerated in a code of legal rules and regulations. Furthermore, the rationality base of the organization is exhibited by its ability to orchestrate the consequences of actions carried on within its boundaries. Rationality ensures predictability: experts with specific areas of responsibility, knowledge and the use of files guarantee a knowledge of the past behavior of the organization, and an ability to apply laws and procedures in a depersonalized and equitable manner.

(ii) *Traditional Domination.* Legitimation of power in this type is derived from the belief that the ruler commands by virtue of his inherited status. Custom is the predominant value system in such a circumstance. The extent of the leader's authority is proscribed by custom—he may be personal or arbitrary but he cannot go beyond the bounds of what is customary. The actual organizational form under a traditional authority system usually emerges in either one of two forms:

(a) the *patrimonial* form of traditional organization where officials are personal retainers dependent on the good graces of the leader for remuneration for their services.

(b) The *feudal* form of traditional organization which has more autonomy in its relationship with the ruler. Feudal officials are in reality allies of the ruler committed to his leadership by an oath of allegiance. Their sources of income are, however, dependent on a system of tithes, fiefs and beneficiaries which they independently collect.

(iii) *Charismatic Domination.* Weber uses the Greek term charisma, which literally means "gift of grace," to identify any quality of the individual leader's personality which sets him apart from ordinary mortals, and ensures that his specifically exceptional powers or qualities of leadership are extolled. This ensures that disciples accept the leader's domination because of the blind faith they must have in the person. The administrative apparatus for such a form of domination is actually unstable, and sooner or later, Weber argues, the organization loses its charismatic form becoming one of two types. If the succession to the organizational leadership is dictated by rules then a bureaucratic organization develops; but if hereditary considerations dictate the nature of the succession then the traditional form of organization emerges.

For the student, two aspects of this theory of legitimate domination must be kept in mind:

I. Max Weber was careful to point out that all these ideal-types *do not exist in pure form.* At most one could discover approximations with certain traits dominant and others simply non-existent. This follows, of course, from the logical nature of the ideal type—a theme to which we will return in a few pages. Suffice to state here that in the real world there can be found a blending of all three types in one organizational set-up. In other words, all forms of domination encountered in empirical reality are mixtures of the three types of domination, although in greatly varying combinations. The Canadian system of government is headed by a sovereign who possesses both qualities of charisma and tradition. And yet, as we would maintain throughout this text, the legal-rational bureaucratic form of organization provides us with some of the best insights of the organizational framework which executes the laws of this sovereign. Indeed, Weber has argued that the continued existence of charisma was essential for the maintenance of a legal-rational democratic order. [10]

II. The theory of the "three pure types of legitimate domination" was not intended to be a scheme which exemplified a linear perspective of world history leading from charismatic forms of government to forms of government which were more rational-legal or bureaucratic in nature. Neither had it anything to do with the various versions of a circular theory of world history. Weber deliberately put the type of rational-legal domination first, if only to forestall any misapprehensions about his "ideal types." Nevertheless, some of the confusion which remains in the minds of readers of his works were due to misunderstandings which Weber himself perhaps unintentionally created. [11] It is therefore fitting here to explain what Weber meant by rationality.

Weber's rationality has nothing to do with the rationalization of history which professedly directs human evolution along a path of universal progress and reason, equality and peace. Rational to Weber meant a process of scientific specialization and technical differentiation *peculiar to Western culture.* He does not view rationalization as some metaphysical force which inexorably leads world evolution in some determined direction with an ultimate Utopian goal. Rather it is a by-product of Western man who may or may not transmit it to the rest of humanity. Rationality in the Weberian sense may therefore be defined as the organization of an individual's daily activities through the division and coordination of legal authority. Why is rationality attributed to legal authority? We emphasize this concept of rationality throughout Section I of this book to ensure that Weber's use of the concept is understood. Bureaucracy is a form of legal authority and derives its rationality because of this fact. The legitimacy of legal authority is sustained by three crucial procedures:

(i) It is presumed that societal objectives and values can be formulated in a legal code.

(ii) The abstract rules of the code can be applied to specific cases, and administration involves the pursuit of interest within that framework.

(iii) The duties of persons in such a system are limited to specific tasks.[12]

Rationality encompassed two clear purposes implicit in the above enumeration: to help in the achievement of technical rules or to realize values (norms) and to designate the procedure of applying rules to particular cases. This is what Weber meant when he wrote, "Bureaucratic authority is specifically rational in the sense of being bound to discursively analysable rules."[13]

It is important to discuss this subject of rationalization because so much of the critical comments on Weber's "rational bureaucracy" could be dismissed as a misunderstanding or misinterpretation of his work.[14]

Let us examine for a moment why rationalization in the Weberian sense does not mean progress in the usual or enlightenment sense of the word. First, to Weber, rationalization affects *external social organization* rather than man's *private intellectual life*. Increased rationalization has not made man more peace-loving, moral or tolerant. The fact that the Mafia can now use computer techniques and jets to consolidate their crime empires in no way makes them more moral or better than secret criminal societies in medieval Europe. Indeed, the progress of science and technology has enabled man to stop believing in magic powers, in spirits and demons, but he has lost his sense of prophecy and above all his sense of the sacred. *He is now utilitarian in nature.*

Secondly, although rationality is partly based on "scientific techniques" it has nothing to do with individual enlightenment in the sense of a better understanding and appreciation of life. To paraphrase one of Weber's own examples on this, each morning we travel in buses or private cars, taking the shortest routes from A (our homes) to B (our places of work). We do not spend an inordinate amount of time getting there by foot, horseback or some other means less efficient. However, the majority of us haven't the foggiest idea how these machines work to get us to where we are going. Or, take another example. We all know the marvels of the modern supermarket: canned foods, dehydrated goods which can be stored for years without spoiling, and a vast array of synthetic edibles most of which the ordinary person hasn't the least idea what these items are made from. By contrast, "primitives" in the bush know infinitely more about the conditions under which they live, the tools they must use and the food they must be discriminatory about in order to survive. That is why, in order to stay alive and initially to understand the environment, modern people must go "primitive" in so-called "primitive" societies. Weber sums up this aspect rather concisely:

The increasing intellectualization and rationalization do not, therefore, indicate an increased and general knowledge of the conditions under which one lives. It means something else, namely, the knowledge or belief that if one but wished one could learn it at any time. Hence, it means that there are no mysterious incalculable forces that come into play, but rather that one can, in principle, master all things by calculation.[15]

And how was this to be accomplished? By procedure, as Albrow emphasizes:

Each of the propositions involved in his pure type of bureaucracy referred to a procedure where either legal norms or monetary calculation were involved, and where impersonality and expert knowledge were necessary. Any such procedure was for Weber intrinsically rational, irrespective of its relation to organizational objectives. In short, he was not offering a theory of efficiency, but a statement of the formal procedures which were prevalent in modern administration.[16]

Figure II presents in skeletal form the schema outlining the theory of legal domination which we have so far discussed. In greater detail, what sort of administrative staff flows from the nature of legitimate authority as outlined in this schematic presentation? Bureaucracy, according to Weber, is based on the following principles (for a schematic outline see Figure III).

(i) The existence of organizational forms clearly defined by law and regulations. This ensures the division and apportionment of powers of decision required for the performance of specific functions delegated by law. (#1 in Figure III).

(ii) General protection of officials in the exercise of their delegated functions.

(iii) Hierarchical organization of functions: structured in terms of levels of positions with provisions for appeal from the lower ranks.

(iv) Recruitment based on specialized training, qualifications. Officials appointed on a contractual basis after free selection.

(v) Regular remuneration in terms of a fixed salary, a pension after retirement, and salaries graded according to hierarchical ranking.

FIGURE II

THE THREE TYPES

Legal Domination

	According to instrumentally-rationally enacted rules	According to value-rational rules (for instance 'Natural Law')
Head of the system (type of 'master')	Official (civil servant)	Elected official(s) or collegiate body
Source of the authority of the head of the system (or 'master')	Delegation (sometimes according to the principle of seniority)	Delegation, or, more often, mandate given (either directly or indirectly) by the governed
Form of legitimacy of the system	Belief in the formal correctness of the enacted system of rules (a) because it has been agreed upon by the interested parties (b) because it was enacted or imposed by an authority considered to be legitimated to do so (it is all important that the rules are enacted in a formally correct manner)	Value-rational belief in the validity of the basic principles of the system of rules. The laws are considered merely explications of the fundamental principles
Type of administrative staff	Bureaucracy	Bureaucracy, or elected civil servants
Type of legal system	Instrumentally-rational formal law, enacted according to positivistic principles	Value-rational law, founded and derived from fundamental principles, yet otherwise strictly formal
Predominant type of social conduct	Instrumentally-rational social conduct	Value-rational social conduct

GITIMATE DOMINATION		
Traditional Domination		Charismatic Domination
Patriarchal rule	Estate-type rule	
Monarch or religious dignitary	Monarch or religious dignitary	Prophet, warlord, demagogue, leader
Tradition, or heredity, often supported by religious rituals	Tradition, or heredity, often supported by religious rituals	Emotional devotion of the 'retinue' to the charismatic leader (which is considered a duty that can be enforced by the leader)
Belief in the prescriptive order of things	Belief in the prescriptive order of things	Affectual or emotional belief in the extraordinary qualities of the charismatic leader, and in the values revealed by him
Personnel personally dependent on the head of the system ('Servants of the master')	Offices are appropriated either by tradition or by the representatives of an estate	Retinue of the leader all officials are personally devoted to the charismatic leader
Strictly traditional, yet material in its judication	Strictly traditional law, judicated in a formalist procedure	The ruler imposes or modifies the law at his discretion
Traditional social conduct	Traditional social conduct	Affectual, in particular cases: value-rational social conduct

Source: Wolfgang Mommsen The Age of Bureaucracy *pp. 76, 77.*

(vi) Promotion based on objective criteria rather than arbitrary decisions of higher-ups.

(vii) Complete separation of the office and the encumbent.

FIGURE III
ELABORATED SCHEMA ON THE RATIONAL-LEGAL TYPE OF DOMINATION

LEGITIMATE DOMINATION
Nature of Legitimate Domination

(1) Obedience is owed to the legally established impersonal order.

(2) Legal views may be established on any of a variety of bases (expediency, values).

(3) Abstract rules which are intentionally established are applied to specific cases.

(4) Person in authority occupies an "office."

(5) Person who obeys command obeys "only the law" not an individual.

(6) Offices arranged in hierarchical manner with appeal and grievance machinery.

(7) Because application of norms is a rational process, individuals in authority need specialized training.

(8) Officials separated from ownership of means of production; their private property strictly separated from public property.

(9) Office separated from living quarters.

(10) Official does not appropriate his "office."

(11) Written documents are heart of process; all final decisions in writing.

(12) Ultimate source of authority in a rational-legal system may well be in another order (i.e. charisma).

BUREAUCRACY
Nature of Administrative Staff

(1) Legal authority in its purest form utilizes bureaucratic administrative staff. Flowing from this are characteristics which relate to the structure and function of organization.

a) Business conducted on a continuous basis.

b) Organized in hierarchy of offices.

c) Hierarchy in structure means a systematic division of labour based on specialized training and expertise.

d) Each office has defined competence in the form of written rules and written records (files) of actions and decisions already taken.

(2) *Rewards and Consequences* for such conformance.

(a) Officials are paid in money; fixed, graded salary scale; pensions, as well as social status taken into account.

(b) Office is the primary occupation of the incumbent, i.e. separating the private affairs of the officer from the organization's affairs and property.

(3) *Rights of Officials*
The bureaucratic form of organization. To prevent the arbitrary use of power and to ensure a continual source of personnel, the following criteria are specified:
  (a) Each office is filled by free selection.
  (b) There is a career; advancement by seniority and for achievement.

(c) Official is subject to discipline in the conduct of his/her office
(d) Obedience (rank) is in the office holder and not in the individual. (Rank is in the job and not in the individual).
(e) Official subject to authority only in his/her official capacity.
(f) There is the right of appeal of decisions and to make statements on grievances.

Source: Adapted from Alfred Diamant "The Bureaucratic Model: Max Weber Rejected, Rediscovered, Reformed" in F. Heady and S.L. Stokes (eds.), Papers in Comparative Public Administration.

As Figure III shows, all these criteria can be classified under the following subheadings: those which relate to both the structure and function of bureaucracy; those dealing with rewards; and those which deal with protection from arbitrary authority.

Weber's Conception of the Ideal Type

Social science is a generalizing science. Although each observed historical event is unique, the social scientist must ignore these unique aspects of social events and subsume them under general categories or types in order to generalize about them. Let us elaborate.

Precision of expression is an axiomatic assumption of all scientific studies. That is why mathematics, with its precise logic and symbols undergird most, if not all, of the natural sciences. Concepts such as power, force, mass and energy become unambiguous when they are expressed in the empirical and logical language of mathematics. The social sciences are, however, not that fortunate, since a large part of what we study is not subject to rigorous empiricism. When dealing with such concepts as capitalism, socialism, protestantism and so forth, we have difficulty in being precise because the concept under study is fluid: it means different things to different people, and further, it changes over time. In his excellent discussion of the concept of capitalism, economist Joseph Schumpeter is careful in emphasizing this essential point about his model of capitalism:

The essential point to grasp is that in dealing with capitalism we are dealing with an evolutionary process. . . . Capitalism is by nature *a form or method of economic change* and not only never is, but never can be stationary.[17]

This evolutionary nature of their subject matter can present serious conceptual difficulties for social scientists. Each time a concept is used, the social scientist by necessity must define what is meant by the term. If this is not done, drawing conclusions about the nature of capitalism over time would become meaningless; for one could be attributing to capitalism in general a whole series of characteristics which are only valid for certain historical forms in the past.

Weber devised the "ideal type" to deal with this problem of conceptualization:

An ideal type is formed by the one-sided accentuation of one or more points of view and by the synthesis of a great many diffuse, discrete, more or less present and occasionally absent, concrete individual phenomena which are arranged according to those one-sidedly emphasized viewpoints into a unified analytical construct.[18]

No study, either the physical sciences or humanities or the social sciences, can ever hope to extract the "essence" of reality and to mirror this essence in one system or construct. Reality is infinite and therefore knowledge will always be hypothetical—new knowledge will always surpass the old, sooner or later. Weber applies this profound truth to his own work:

In science, each of us knows that what he has accomplished will be antiquated in ten, twenty, fifty years. . . . Every scientific fulfilment raises new "questions"; it asks to be "surpassed" and outdated. Whoever wishes to serve science has to resign himself to this fact.[19]

Weber's problem is therefore obvious but so complex: is it possible to formulate a precise definition of a unique piece of reality in the social sciences? Capitalism or socialism is definitely a particular manifestation of economic life. Can we develop a construct, which although it does not exist in reality, never has, and never will, would capture the unique enduring features of the phenomenon under study? Can we, in writing about capitalism in the seventeenth, eighteenth, or twentieth century, capture basic features of the phenomenon without having to resort to qualifications with every use of the word, having to eschew generalizations on the subject, and succeeding in gaining some insights into a phenomenon whose infinite reality, like all knowledge, will remain beyond the reach of total understanding?

Similarly, in our first chapter we have presented a variety of interpretations of bureaucracy. Each interpretation captures certain distinguishing features of the bureaucratic phenomenon. Can this variety be used in some way to further our understanding of bureaucracy?

To Weber the solution lay in the construction of an "ideal type." The concept should not be taken to mean "average type." Characteristic and distinctive elements are chosen and through a process of enlargement and amplification these characteristics are arranged in a unified analytical construct to form an ideal type.

Charles Dickens' Fagin in *Oliver Twist* is an ideal type of thief and miser rolled into one. The use of a herd of underfed, ragged urchins to pick the pockets of overfed and overdressed gentlemen of nineteenth century England was in many ways a unique phenomenon, but the enduring themes of roguery and avarice were present in that particular dereliction just as they are found today in twentieth century England. To construct his Fagin, Dickens did not choose every single imaginable trait of a thief and/or miser and average them out, but instead chose certain characteristic ones, which he exaggerated and amplified, and created Fagin. By so doing, Dickens gives us a whole series of insights into roguery and avarice, while at the same time we know that no one individual embodies the characteristics possessed by Fagin, that pathetic figure of the nineteenth century.

Likewise, as Schumpeter has shown, the ideal type of capitalism is an analytical construct uniting those characteristics which give it its originality as an economic doctrine, although these characteristics can be found only as diffuse phenomena in reality. Because of exaggeration, amplification and logical construct, many of these characteristics may be missing in any one concrete organization. For example, the ideal type could have as one of its logical characteristics the final goals or objectives of the phenomenon, although these objectives may not be attained (or never will) in reality. This is what Weber meant when he wrote of "one-sided accentuation" and the "synthesis of a great many diffuse, discrete, more or less present and occasionally absent concrete individual phenomena."

Let us make a few observations on the ideal type construct. First, there is nothing sacrosant about an ideal type. The proof of its utility is its heuristic value in establishing unambiguously the meaning of the subject under investigation. Every social scientist uses ideal types in teaching and everyday conceptualization in research. To deny this is to pass off, on occasion, one's value judgements as "scientific" conclusions. Such generic concepts as Marxism, Christianity, feudalism, the administrative state and industrial and post-industrial society are all ideal types.

Second, the ideal type is not "ideal" in an ethical sense. We use no judgment as to whether the type is the best of all possible worlds (i.e. what ought to be). The ideal type seeks perfection of a logical not a moral order. However, it is possible to construct an ideal type of what ought to be as well (for example, what Christianity or Marxism, or Capitalism regard as their ethical, final goals).

Third, it is clear from what has so far been written that one can construct a series of ideal types for heuristic purposes in research. The value of such ideal types are determined solely by their helpfulness and effectiveness in research. If an ideal type has outlived its usefulness, by lacking in insight or failing as a tool to help us generate useful judgements involving causal imputation, then it should be discarded for a new ideal-type construction. The proof of the pudding is in the eating. Because reality is infinite, the social scientist must continually clarify meaning: concepts which the sciences use are constantly outstripped since it is through such outstripping that knowledge advances. Max Weber has this to say on the topic:

Indeed, it is just because the content of historical concepts is necessarily subject to change that they must be formulated precisely and clearly on all occasions. In their application, their character as ideal analytical constructs should be carefully kept in mind, and the ideal type and historical reality should not be confused with each other. It should be understood that, since really definitive historical concepts are not in general to be thought of as an ultimate, and in view of the inevitable shift of the guiding value-ideas, the construction of sharp and unambiguous concepts relevant to the concrete individual viewpoint which directs our interest at any given time affords the possibility of clearly realizing the limits of their validity. [19]

Fourth, as a kind of yardstick we use the ideal type to determine what is unique about a course of events by comparing to what extent reality departs from the unified and unreal analytical construct. Let us take as an example industrial society. Economists such as Shonfield, Schumpeter, and Galbraith have enriched our knowledge of industrial society. We can construct an ideal type based on the distinctive features of the organization of this kind of society. We can then see if it gives intelligibility to our experience and provides us with some new understanding which previously escaped our attention. This may give us the knowledge as to whether late nineteenth up to mid-twentieth western society was strictly an industrial society or whether, on the contrary, elements of some other economic system were apparent in it. This is exactly what the whole debate about the post-industrial society today is all about. Ideal types in scholars' minds were created and utilized to produce insights into the nature of our society in the 1980s and beyond.

Fifth and lastly, although his ideal-typical construct of bureaucracy afforded Weber a precise and unambiguous means of expression, he was by no means unambiguous as regards the logical consequences of the ideal type. As Wolfgang Mommsen argues:

He (Weber) was haunted by the prospect of a steady growth of the bureaucratic structures which was likely to put all individual freedom more and more in jeopardy. He considered stagnation and ossification the real dangers of his age, rather than charismatic break-throughs. In his opinion, the fatal decline of dynamism and mobility in politics could be cured only by one antidote, namely "charismatic leadership." Charismatic leaders had to check the aspirations of the bureaucracy. They had to break up its deadly rule of routine by their unique capacity to set new goals and to open up new paths in societies hampered by political stagnation and bureaucratic routine. It was up to them to keep the "open society" open against the inhuman forces of bureaucratization.[21]

This in barest outline is Weber's ideal-type bureaucracy. On one level of analysis Weber attempted to give us a description of the phenomenon. Bureaucracy simply meant administration by appointed officials wedded to a wider framework of organizational analysis in which bureaus were seen as tripartite structures. Blau and Scott give a further elaboration on this meaning:

Colloquially, the term "bureaucracy" connotes [among other meanings] rule-encumbered inefficiency. In sociology, however, the term is used neutrally to refer to the administrative aspects of organizations. If bureaucratization is defined as the amount of effort devoted to maintaining the organization rather than to directly achieving its objectives, all formal organizations have at least a minimum of bureaucracy—even if this bureaucracy involves no more than a secretary-treasurer who collects dues. But wide variations have been found in the degree of bureaucratization in organizations, as indicated by the amount of effort devoted to administrative problems, the proportion of administrative personnel, the hierarchical character of the organization, or the strict enforcement of administrative procedures and rigid compliance with them.[22]

American students of bureaucracy writing in the European tradition also find Weber's analytical construct useful.[23] Thus in analysing bureaucratic administration such comparative observations of bureaucracy as the impersonality of rules, specialization of tasks, the strata isolation in bureaucratic structures and the system of records and personnel with specialized skills and roles are emphasized. All these descriptive aspects of bureaucracy appear to have universal application and the Canadian experience has been no exception. And on another level of analysis Weber was also concerned with normative problems associated with bureaucracy.

His conception of bureaucracy presents us with a curious set of dilemmas, the analysis of which will be one of the central themes of this text. As noted earlier, Weber's insights into bureaucracy emphasized that rationalization meant specialization. The importance of the skill element in modern administration is such that power in the state cannot be exercised without a professionally trained bureaucratic apparatus. But at the same time this specialization has led to increasing professionalization in bureaucracy, a trend which is likely to increase bureaucracy's predictability and reliability as instruments of policy.[24] *Thus the indispensability of specialized bureaucrats makes modern bureaucracy autonomous, but professionalization helps to make it more predictable and reliable, to serve as a subservient tool of the state.*

A second aspect of this curious dilemma is Weber's analysis of modern bureaucracy possessing a monopoly of legitimate coercive powers. Weber noted that control over this bureaucratic phenomenon cannot be achieved by attempting to destroy it, since under modern conditions bureaucracy was absolutely indispensable for running the state.[25] Only shifts in the control over modern bureaucracy can be obtained either through the liberal democratic method of representation or through revolutionary means (the replacement of one group by another to control the bureaucracy). Bureaucracy is like the Rock of Gibraltar: whichever group is in power is faced with the unchallengeable position of the bureaucratic phenomenon which gives the government its monopoly of power. But unlike Marx's analysis, Weber's treatment of bureaucracy emphasizes *administrative rationality* as the overriding emphasis of modern bureaucracy. This concern for administrative rationality has inevitably led to an overriding emphasis on technical competence: thus the mechanisms of wielding power strictly for its own purposes are beyond bureaucracy's concern or competence. *The politicians perform this function of legitimacy and power brokerage.*[26] *Thus bureaucracy is all-powerful and at the same time incapable of determining how its power should be used.*[27]

These are some of the most central dilemmas posed by bureaucracy in modern society, and it was Weber's insightful analysis which has pinpointed them as significant criteria for analysis and study. These dilemmas, however, place bureaucracy on a continuous tightrope act, an attempt to steer a middle course between the Scylla of becoming a "permanent politician"[28] and the Charybdis of being a political eunuch. These dilemmas of positions of bureaucratic leadership (Leiter) and staff administration (Verwaltungsstab) cannot be easily dismissed: like the Ik in this chapter's epigram, experienced bureaucrats are well aware of the extreme hazards of their positions, the enduring central dilemmas of bureaucracy.[29] These themes of *power* and *subservience* remain, in my view, the most central insights into the nature of bureaucracy. When we dealt with *administration* and *management* in Chapter One, we were in effect implicitly pinpointing these aspects of bureaucracy. Chapter Three on the administrative state is a further theoretical analysis of the same themes, while Chapter Four (the politics/administration dichotomy) is yet another analysis emphasizing the themes' socio-historical dimensions which have some direct relevance for the Canadian environment.

A prominent scholar of bureaucracy commenting on some Marxist "rhetoric" about organizations:
(The rhetoric)

The revolutionary group must clearly see that its goal is not the "seizure of power," but the dissolution of power—indeed that the entire problem of power, of control from below and control from above, can be solved only if there is no above or below. Above all things, the revolutionary group must divest itself of the forms of power—statutes, hierarchies, property, prescribed opinion fetishes, paraphernalia, official etiquette—in short, the subtlest as well as the most obvious of bureaucratic and bourgeois traits that reinforce authority and hierarchy, not only consciously but unconsciously. . . . Only . . . when the revolutionary movement is congruent with the decentralized community it seeks to achieve, can it avoid becoming another elitist obstacle to the social development and dissolve into the revolution like surgical thread into the healing wound.

(The comment):

Understanding the organization [both] *as an instrument and as a form of power* strikes me as being, in some ways, more "realistic" than much scholarly writing on administration and organization.

Alfred Diamant

Footnotes

1. This chapter owes an intellectual debt to the authors enumerated here. A large part of their contributions to the debate on Max Weber is both simplified and synthesized in this chapter. Alfred Diamant, "The Bureaucratic Model: Max Weber Re-

jected, Rediscovered, Reformed" in F. Heady and S. Stokes, *Papers in Comparative Public Administration* (Ann Arbor: Institute of Public Administration, 1962). Wolfgang Mommsen, *The Age of Bureaucracy: Perspectives on the Political Sociology of Max Weber* (Oxford: Basil Blackwell, 1974). Julien Freund, *The Sociology of Max Weber* (New York: Random House, 1968). Weber's most important writings on the subject appear in two different parts of an uncompleted draft of his work *Economy and Society*. The first part is presented in *Max Weber: The Theory of Social and Economic Organization*, trans. by A.M. Henderson and Talcott Parsons (New York: Free Press, Inc., 1966), and the second part appears in Max Weber, *From Max Weber, Essays in Sociology* trans. and ed. Hans Gerth and C. Wright Mills (New York: Oxford University Press, Inc., 1946).

2. Max Weber, *The Protestant Ethic and the Spirit of Capitalism,* trans. by Talcott Parsons (New York: Scribner, 1958).

3. For an excellent discussion of this theme see Don Martindale, *The Nature and Types of Sociological Theory* (Cambridge, Mass.: The Riverside Press, 1960), p. 389ff.

4. *Ibid.,* p. 389.

5. *Ibid.,* p. 391.

6. D.J. Gow, "Canadian Federal Administrative and Political Institutions: A Role Analysis" (unpublished Ph.D. dissertation, Queen's University, Kingston, 1967), p. 63.

7. A. Henderson and T. Parsons (eds.), *Max Weber: The Theory of Social and Economic Organization* (New York: Free Press, 1966), p. 324.

8. *Ibid.,* p. 326.

9. *Ibid.,* p. 382.

10. Alfred Diamant, "The Bureaucratic Model: Max Weber Rejected, Rediscovered, Reformed" in F. Heady and S.L. Stokes, *op. cit.,* p. 70.

11. In the earlier versions of his theory of legitimate domination Weber made some allusions to the fact that charismatic forms of domination are predominant in earlier periods of history whereas bureaucratic forms are a comparatively recent phenomenon of the modern world. Later, however, he systematically deleted his references to this teleological theory—the factor of historical evolution was systematically and deliberately deleted from his work.

12. Martin Albrow, *Bureaucracy* (London: Macmillan, 1970), p. 63.

13. The foregoing paragraph is a paraphrase of Albrow's excellent analysis of Weber's use of rationality in bureaucracy. Found on pp. 62-63.

14. Robert Miewald captures this important dimension in his excellent study:
    (Max Weber) was the first, and so far the most successful, in placing bureaucracy within a world historical context. There has been much carping about the Weberian

definition, just as there is about any great intellectual monument, but no one has come close to repealing it. Much of the confusion results from a failure to grasp what he was trying to do, namely to find out why Western civilization is moving in its particular direction. His bureaucracy is not descriptive. No such institution as he describes has ever existed. Bureaucracy was for him an analytical category for studying the real world and not reality itself. The abstraction which he called bureaucracy was based on the first premise of modern organizational behaviour: What is the most rational method of conducting large-scale, complex administration?

Robert D. Miewald, *Public Administration: A Critical Perspective*, p. 43.

15. H.H. Gerth and C. Wright Mills, *From Max Weber: Essays in Sociology* (New York: Oxford University Press, 1946), p. 139.

16. M. Albrow, *op. cit.*, p. 65.

17. Joseph Schumpeter, *Capitalism, Socialism and Democracy* (New York: Harper and Row, 1950), p. 82.

18. E.A. Shils and H.A. Finch, *Max Weber on the Methodology of the Social Sciences* (Glencoe, Illinois: The Free Press, 1949), p. 90.

19. From "Science as a Vocation" in H.H. Gerth and C. Wright Mills, *From Max Weber: Essays in Sociology*, p. 138.

20. E.A. Shils and H.A. Finch, *op. cit.*, p. 107.

21. Wolfgang J. Mommsen, *The Age of Bureaucracy: Perspectives on the Political Sociology of Max Weber* (Oxford: Basil Blackwell, 1974), pp. 93-94.

22. Peter M. Blau and W. Richard Scott, *Formal Organizations: A Comparative Approach* (San Francisco: Chandler Publishing Co., 1962), p. 8.

23. A good example of this genre is Reinhard Bendix, *Work and Authority in Industry* (New York: Harper and Row, 1956).

24. For an elaboration of this central dilemma see Herbert A. Simon, "The Changing Theory and Changing Practice of Public Administration" in Ithiel de Sola Pool (ed.), *Contemporary Political Science* (New York: McGraw Hill Inc., 1967), pp. 86-120.

25. For a treatment of this theme see Nicos P. Mouzelis, *Organisation and Bureaucracy* (Chicago: Aldine Publishing Co., 1968), Chapter I.

26. For a brilliant treatment of this theme, see Volker Ronge, "The Politicization of Administration in Advanced Capitalist Societies," *Political Studies*, Vol. XXII, No. 1, pp. 86-93.

27. For an early posing of these dilemmas for bureaucracy see Reinhard Bendix, "Bureaucracy and the Problem of Power," *Public Administration Review*, Vol. V, No. 3 (Summer 1945), pp. 194-209.

28. Referring to the permanence of senior bureaucrats, J. Donald Kingsley wrote "Their functional position is best described, perhaps as that of permanent politician," J. Donald Kingsley, *Representative Bureaucracy* (Yellow Springs: The Antioch Press, 1944), p. 269.

29. This distinction is not appreciated or even acknowledged by some experienced observers. As seasoned a politician as former M.P. and cabinet minister Paul Hellyer contends that the merging of political and bureaucratic roles takes place at the highest levels anyway, with no real meaningful differentiation. See his "How they killed public land banking: a political memoir," *City Magazine*, Vol. 3, No. 2 (December 1977), pp. 31-38.

Recommended Reading

In our experience the reader would do well to stay away from much of the theoretical interpretations of Max Weber's work on bureaucracy, particularly most of the North American interpretative pieces. Max Weber was "discovered" by North American social scientists immediately after World War II, partly because European scholars who fled the Nazi scourge began to introduce their North American peers to his work. Part of the reason however is that North American social science has been traditionally myopic, leading to a neglect of European scholarship before that time. Here are some of the more important interpretative sources of Weber for further exploration:

1. Martin Albrow, *Bureaucracy* (London: Macmillan and Co. Ltd., 1970).
This is an excellent little book and highly recommended. Indeed, we feel it might be highly useful for the student to read our whole theoretical section in conjunction with this book. The concept of bureaucracy is lucidly treated, and the student is given a full sense of the various meanings of the concept.

2. Julien Freund, *The Sociology of Max Weber* (New York: Random House, 1968).
This book by a leading European scholar of Max Weber's works is invaluable to anyone studying Weber's methodology. The concept of the ideal type is sympathetically explored in addition to other aspects of Weber's sociology not particularly germane to our study of bureaucracy.

3. Ralph P. Hummel, *The Bureaucratic Experience* (New York: St. Martin's Press, 1977).
For the student we believe this book is an excellent attempt to interpret Weber, Talcott Parsons and other writers on Weber's works and place these interpretations in everyday practical situations. Highly recommended for supplementary reading.

4. Alfred Diamant, "The Bureaucratic Model: Max Weber Rejected, Rediscovered, Reformed," in Ferrel Heady and Sybil L. Stokes, (eds.), *Papers in Comparative Public Administration* (Ann Arbor Michigan, 1962).
This is an advanced treatment of Weber's work on bureaucracy, but for students who have been reading Weber and interpretative works on his works it remains one of the more important review articles in the literature to date.

5. Nicos P. Mouzelis, *Organisation and Bureaucracy: An Analysis of Modern Theories*.
A good supplementary source for the whole of Section I of this text. The treatment of

Max Weber's work, particularly his use of the ideal type, leaves something to be desired, but Mouzelis' analysis of the Marxist position on the study of bureaucracy is good (at least up to the 1960s), and his Part II "The Managerial Tradition" certainly supplements Chapter Five of this text. Recommended as supplementary theoretical reading.

CHAPTER THREE

BUREAUCRACY AS THE GENIE OF ARAB MYTHOLOGY: ASPECTS OF THE ADMINISTRATIVE STATE*

Since bureaucracy has a "rational" character, with rules, means-ends calculus, and matter-of-factness predominating, its rise and expansion has everywhere had "revolutionary" results . . . as had the advance of rationalism in general.

Max Weber

Since 1789 the State, or if you like to have it so, La Patrie, has taken the place of the sovereign . . . thus Bureaucracy, the giant power wielded by pigmies, came into the world. Bureaucracy [has] . . . a natural kindness for mediocrity, a predilection for categorical statements and reports, a government as fussy and meddlesome, in short, as a small shopkeeper's wife.

Honoré de Balzac

Bureaucracy [is that] . . . continental nuisance . . . I can see no risk or possibility in England. Democracy is hot enough here.

Thomas Carlyle

I. Introduction

That French master of drama, epic realism and biting satire, Honoré de Balzac, and his somewhat dour Scottish contemporary, philoso-

---

* *The word genie is often used in English for jinni, the Arabic name for a kind of demon. In Arab mythology the jinni could be a schizo or split personality, a Dr. Jekyll or Mr. Hyde as it were: it was extremely intelligent, stayed out of the limelight, and when called upon it was capable of carrying out heavy labours at its master's bidding (as in* Aladdin's Lamp). *However, on occasions the jinni, acting independently, could be equally mischevious, creating havoc and destruction if not carefully controlled by its owner (as in many of the other stories in* The Arabian Nights). *As we will argue in this chapter, both* subservience *and* autonomy *are the two paradoxical images which bureaucracy as the administrative state projects.*

pher Thomas Carlyle, were miles apart in personality but they certainly had one thing in common: their view of bureaucracy as humbug, an administrative disease which plagued the early nineteenth century countries of Western Europe (red tape, mass democracy and pettifogging, power-hungry clerks). As we have indicated in Chapter One, that perception is still held by many to this present day. For example, as late as 1937 the renowned English political scientist, Herman Finer, was strongly echoing Carlyle's sentiments by asserting that "in the continental sense, England has no bureaucracy."[1]

Side by side with this view of bureaucracy as a dangerous and autonomous power usurper there has been another view briefly mentioned in the previous chapter which construes bureaucracy as a rationalized effective machine, an instrument to be fine-tuned and fashioned after the dictates of its "elected masters," the politicians. Implicit in this view is a strongly held belief that the administrator is ancilliary to the policy maker, a tool subservient to the policy maker's wishes. At first glance both views appear rather contradictory, as do the three epigrams of this chapter. Our task in this chapter is to outline the view that the phenomenon is much more complicated than what a Carlyle or a Balzac would have wished to concede. Max Weber, however, deeply understood the nature of bureaucracy when he asserted that bureaucracy, like the genie of Arab mythology, had the distinguishing characteristics of an autonomous power as well as a subservient efficient tool at the beck and call of its hierarchical political superiors. This basic insight constitutes the first and most important characteristic of the partial model known as the administrative state.

Before attempting a definition of the administrative state we should pose the question as to why we hold this paradoxical position towards one of our most fundamental societal institutions. Where did this genie image come from? Simply put, it stems from the fact that Western democratic theory has always been saddled by a fundamental ambiguity towards the power of the state.[2] On the one hand we idealize our historical process as one in which the community, constituted as the nation, gives expression to its basic values by institutionalizing its own distinctive state structures. For example, most of the chapters' topics comprising section II of this book pay particular attention to our historical past and attempt to show how this past has conditioned the nature of our bureaucratic institutions. One such fundamental value is that bureaucracy is essentially conceived as a machine at society's service, geared to expediting the policy initiatives dictated by the political executive. This is a conceptualization of the public service held by many of our political and intellectual elite.[3]

Here is former Prime Minister Joe Clark during his first week in office explaining his intention to transfer the Canadian embassy in Israel from Tel Aviv to Jerusalem:

We certainly intend to do that. Miss MacDonald [the new minister of external affairs] will be indicating to officials in External Affairs that we will be expecting from them recommendations fairly directly as to how it can be accomplished and what other policies will be followed, will be necessary to make that goal realizable. *I say that simply to indicate that the position she and other ministers will be taking in relation to matters that have been part of party policy in the election campaign will be to indicate that those questions are now beyond discussion as to their appropriateness and that what we will be seeking from the public service will be indications as to how we accomplish what we have undertaken to do.* [4]

On the other hand, since Max Weber we have become increasingly predisposed to the view that bureaucracy can have a powerful autonomy of its own fashioned by either of two considerations: first, that bureaucracy possesses considerable political powers due to its necessary and inevitable exercise of administrative discretion, and second, the always present fear that these powers, through human inertia or evil impulse, can serve to sabotage the political will of society. Thus we would readily agree with James Madison who first rhetorically asked, "But what is government itself but the greatest of all reflections on human nature?," then went on to assert:

If men were angels, no government would be necessary. If angels were to govern men, neither external nor internal controuls on government would be necessary. In framing a government which is to be administered by men over men, the great difficulty lies in this: You must first enable the government to controul the governed; and in the next place, oblige it to controul itself. A dependence on the people is no doubt the primary controul on the government; but experience has taught mankind the necessity of auxiliary precautions. [5]

These apparent ambiguities have deep roots in our historical past. Here is not the appropriate place to chronicle in specific detail this heritage, but perhaps a page or two of historical summary would give us an adequate backdrop to these somewhat paradoxical positions. [6]

In ancient times, the struggle for responsible government was a battle between estates of the realm, a universal church, feudal oligarchies of landed gentry, loose confederations of towns and cities on the one hand, and crowned heads on the other. The struggle was a very confused one, always in a state of flux or indeterminancy. Its gradual progress over the centuries was marked by alliances of one power with the other as class, personal whims or institutional interests might temporarily dictate. This anarchy ended with the eventual triumph of the Crown over all competitors for power in every nation in western Europe. The period of absolute monarchy then began, lasting for four centuries (between 1500 and 1900), but so did the saga of modern constitutional history which essentially began as the long struggle aimed at curtailing the now untrammelled powers of triumphant monarchs.

Absolute monarchy in western Europe came to an end by about the middle of the nineteenth century, at which time the machinery of representative democracy slowly but inexorably emerged. British political scientist Herman Finer gives us a lucid account of this liberal-democratic arrangement, basically fashioned in the nineteenth century:[7] a parliamentary body, increasingly chosen by the mechanics of universal suffrage, was the watchdog for the whole system. Foremost amongst its many functions Parliament provided a forum for deliberating on proposed legislation, giving its approval or rejection to this legislation placed before it by the political executive. Parliament also served the ancilliary purposes of being an open forum for voicing the grievances of the people and focusing at a central point the various opinions held by the growing electorate.

This parliamentary order was buttressed by an administrative arrangement which had also changed to suit the times. The retainer-officials who served the royal or princely households of the early Middle Ages were transformed by the 1900s into "public servants" now serving under the tutelage of the parliamentary officials elected directly by the people (the German word *Amt* meaning "office" goes back to a Celtic term meaning "servant").[8] In Great Britain this satisfying assymetrical arrangement (bureaucracy responsible to the political executive who in turn is responsible to Parliament which has ultimate responsibility to the people) reached its apogee in the 1870s. As we would demonstrate in Section II theory and practice meshed very well if only for a brief moment in time. The classical exposition of this theory is worthwhile noting:

In theory the business of the official is simply to serve his political master by sorting out the day's business, relating it and the government statutes and directives of higher political authority to what has been done in similar cases in the past, singling out the important from the unimportant, and then saying, in effect: "Here is the relevant data out of which you must decide. I have marshalled the arguments for and against and it seems that you should adopt course A rather than course B—but you may have other good reasons of your own to reject my advice and take another course." In part this theory of the role of the civil servant comes from Walter Bagehot's distinction between the intense perception of the specialist mind, and the wider vision of the non-specialist mind. Theoretically, the expert is "on tap" and the layman (the minister) is "on top."[9]

It is during this period that the powerful image of the *neutral anonymous* public official who administers "a service-rendering organization for the protection of rights and the enforcement of duties of a national citizenry" was formed. After all it was the public who paid his wages, so obedience through the control administered by the political executive could be expected.[10]

However, the background of historical development is not complete. The emergence in modern times of new problems of government which can only be solved by non-political techniques has altered essentially the conditions of the earlier struggle between the people and the executive power. The "new boy in town" was obviously the bureaucracy: modern administration consists largely of the manipulation of forces and factors for the most part beyond the ken of lay people, and clearly beyond the actual competence of representative bodies. In the metaphor of J. E. Hodgetts, it became patently obvious that "administration [was not] purely the slave of the politicians' policy lamp."[11] The growing "power" of the bureaucracy, we were told, was manifested in such factors as the prodigious growth of public service expert personnel, the proliferation of administrative boards and commissions, the steady expansion of the bureaucracy's rule-making power, and the increased attention paid to the bureaucracy by lobbies and other deputations. All these societal trends have raised new questions concerning the relation of bureaucracy to the distribution of power in the society at large. Thus another powerful image emerges, namely the autonomous power of the bureaucracy. This image is given further credence by the "Liberal in despair" musings of none other than Max Weber:

The question is always who controls the existing machinery. And such control is possible only in a very limited degree to persons who are not technical specialists. Generally speaking, the trained permanent official is more likely to get his way in the long run than his nominal superior, the Cabinet minister, who is not a specialist.[12]

Two powerful images thus merge. Bureaucracy is acknowledged to be indispensable for its service functions in Western societies. Apart from a few dissenters, most students of bureaucracy believe that

Western countries have no other tested solutions that can be adopted on a large scale. Without bureaucracy, the modern nation-state patterned after Western technological and industrial development is virtually impossible. However, the historical development of bureaucracy has become associated with the diminution of individual freedom, and a recognition that, as a structure of the nation-state, it has certain autonomous "powers," creating disturbing images in the minds of many. Thus from our historical experience this dichotomous image of "the administrative state" is born and pervades both our writings on bureaucracy and, on a broader scale, our conception of the role of bureaucracy in the relation between economy, state and society.

Based on these conflicting images our conception as to what is meant by the administrative state is therefore as follows. The administrative state as an ideal type is, first, one in which the state is the dominant institution in society, guiding and controlling all societal pressures. Second, the administrative (bureaucratic) sector in such a state is accorded a schizophrenic position in its relationships with other sectors of society. On the one hand, it is ideally construed as an instrument fashioned to implement or give expression to the public will as enunciated by the people's representatives, the politicians. On the other hand, this "instrument" projects an image of possessing strong autonomous powers, more important than the powers of political and participative organs in determining the behavior of the state and the course of public affairs.

If bureaucracy verges towards this ideal typical characterization, then some obvious questions follow: how did the original historical image of the bureaucratic phenomenon become transformed from one of subservience to one of autonomous power? How and from what sources is bureaucratic power derived? Does the increase of administrative power necessarily mean that the bureaucracy has a monopoly of power? The logic of the administrative state concept therefore leads us to seek answers to such questions in a discussion of the wider problem of the relation of bureaucracy to the distribution of power in society at large. Put in another way, a theory of bureaucracy really implies a larger philosophy of history to which the theory must inevitably lead back.[13] Thus we turn to the formulations in the academic literature which deal with the relationships between the state system and the economy. We have narrowed this discussion mostly to the Canadian literature on the subject to give a sharper focus to the ongoing theoretical debate and to illustrate, albeit briefly, Canadian thinking on these matters. What do these conceptions specifically say about bureaucratic power in Canada and its source?

II. Perspectives on the State System and the Economy: The Role of Bureaucracy

It is not coincidental that a large proportion of what social scientists now study about the relationship between economy, class, political stability and the classification of the polity were first explored by the Greek philosopher Aristotle. [14] Indeed, much of what is now done on the dynamics of systematic political change still has its basic roots in the Aristotelian typology of political systems. [15] In Greek thought the polity and society were one and the same and, to this day, this intellectual heritage has been extremely significant in Western political thought. In the eighteenth and nineteenth century political theorists such as Hobbes, Locke and Rousseau labored mightily in seeking to establish the sovereignty of the polity by arguing that the origins of social life were embedded in basic political contracts. Despite these philosophical onslaughts, Western political thought never broke from the Aristotelian tradition of assuming that the nature of the polity is greatly influenced by the non-political bases of social and economic life.

Thus all the perspectives on the state system we will discuss here make the explicit assumption that there are strong relationships between *economy, state* and *society*. To put this another way, most social scientists take it as axiomatic that the sociological and economic bases determine the nature of politics in all societies. The theories of Karl Marx are of course the most forceful in making these assumptions, but even the critics of Marxist theory have strengthened this tendency to view *politics as the dependent variable*, since they almost all assert that the relationship between economy and society to political behavior is more complicated than Marx has suggested. [16] As will be seen in Chapter Five when we present a classification of policy studies, there are more policy "theories" emphasizing policy as a dependent variable of economy and society than other "theories" assuming the opposite (that is, policy being the independent variable).

This relationship between economy, state and society has been analysed in a variety of ways. [17] For our brief discussion here aimed primarily at highlighting the role of bureaucracy in the various perspectives, we have classified the literature roughly into three categories: pluralist, instrumentalist and structuralist. [18] (See also Figure I.) Other more elaborate distinctions exist, especially within Marxist thought, but we deem this preliminary classification to be sufficient as a start. [19]

The pluralist perspective operates on two theoretical planes. First, it is an ideal emphasizing liberal democracy, individual liberties,

FIGURE I
A BROAD GROUPING OF SOME PERSPECTIVES ON STATE, ECONOMY AND SOCIETY

PLURALIST PERSPECTIVE	INSTRUMENTALIST PERSPECTIVE	STRUCTURALIST PERSPECTIVE
State is an aggregating mechanism in which outputs and plural structures are responses to demands and interests of competing groups.	State is viewed as a system of political domination.	State structures determined by (i) the contradictions inherent in capitalism or by (ii) the systemic constraints applied to ensure state's viability (corporatism).
(1) One strand of liberal-democratic thought, Weberian in its intellectual thrust, which emphasizes the concept of state dominance. *Societal circumstances have led to bureaucracy adopting an autonomous perspective of self-interest* (Cairns/Black, Hockin).	(1) Conventional Marxist position in which the state is an instrument of the ruling class. *As such, bureaucracy as a state structure is viewed simply as a pawn in the hands of the bourgeoisie.* This Marxist position is still extant but fast becoming a "non-viable theory" (Miliband, Panitch et al.).	(1) Institutionalization of interest and class conflicts assuring state control, co-optation of working class elites, and predictability of class conflict so as to ensure control of same. *Bureaucracy has a degree of autonomy but in the long run it acts on behest of the bourgeoisie* (Poulantzas, Panitch et al.).
(2) The elite-pluralist approach. Power of economic, political, bureaucratic and other institutions tend to be structurally differentiated. However, interaction required to ensure system maintenance. *In Canada this coordination verges on the "cozy" side, with the bureaucratic elite tending to be co-opted by other elite structures* (John Porter).		(2) Institutionalization of interest and class conflicts to enhance the political regulation of the economy. *Bureaucracy conceived both as an instrument and willing active participant in ongoing collaboration to make the system "work." An interdependent sector in the overall political system.* Paramountcy of collective interests and goals of system stressed (McLeod/Rea, Presthus).

equality, toleration and so on in the abstract sense, but it is also an explanation of what actually happens in modern Western democracies. Thorburn quite rightly points out the dangers inherent in confusing the two meanings:

> The former [that is the ideals] are aspirations achieved by no society; the latter the humdrum and sometimes sordid reality of every day. It is easy when using the term pluralism to refer to both, to attribute the virtues of the ideal to the less than idyllic reality. Here is where propaganda assists sloppy thinking to misperceive what actually happens, and produce complacency where there are serious shortcomings.[20]

One strand of liberal democratic thought has drawn heavily on Canadian economic and political history to explain the actual workings of the Canadian societal system. Briefly put, this school of thought, exemplified by the influential writings of Harold Innis, asserts that the origins and purposes of the federal government are to be understood in terms of an economic territory dependent upon the export of certain "staples," the commercially feasible production of which entailed heavy public expenditures on such capital facilities as railways and canals. The full development of this thesis is not of direct importance to us here. What is of significance is the concept that the state, represented both by its political and bureaucratic institutions, filled an important vacuum by being the substitute for private enterprise in this nation-building activity. As sociologist S. D. Clark puts it: "Geography, which favoured individual enterprise and limited political interference in the conduct of economic, social and religious affairs over a large part of the [North American] continent, favoured on this part of the continent *large-scale bureaucratic forms of organization and wide-spread intervention by the State.*"[21]

Taking this economic history as a point of departure, the writings of Black, Cairns and Hockin emphasize Canadian state dominance.[22] Black's views are tersely expressed.

> Among other purposes, the central government was expressly created in order to play a crucial role in compensating for the developmental and distributional failures of the private sector of the economy. The politician cannot usefully be viewed simply as the helpless tool of private capitalists for our elected chiefs from Macdonald onward have sought—and with frequent success—to harness private enterprise to public objectives.[23]

Both Cairns and Hockin have taken this analysis one step further. Hockin argues that the state in Canada, having been nurtured and given an active role in "national development" and the fostering of "local particularisms," *took on a life of its own:* "It created political units at confederation, it created, fostered and protected certain cultural and economic attributes, and it created and sustained certain demands and elites which are far more complex than are those of the bourgeoisie."[24] Cairns concurs on all this:

> The impact of society on government is a common theme in the study of democratic polities. Less common is an approach which stresses the impact of government on the political functioning of society. . . . I do not doubt that government rides such a tiger of social change that the sweet smile of victory is often on the face of the tiger. However, I am convinced that our approach to the study of Canadian politics pays inadequate attention to the weight of the rider, and his possession of reins to steer, whips to beat, and various inducements to make the tiger responsive to his demands.[25]

Bureaucracy has therefore become a necessity because private enterprise has been both unwilling and unable to take up the "slack of competition" in many areas of economic life in Canada. Bureaucracy has helped to fill this vacuum, and now because of its indispensability it has in time generated a life of its own. This perspective argues that administrative autonomy has grown, but no judgement seems to have been made as to the pervasiveness of this autonomy. Is bureaucracy in a position to remain uninfluenced by changes in the class structure, by the shifting weight of social conflict groups or by long-range changes in public opinion? To what degree does the bureaucratic elite actually *believe in the belief* of bureaucracy as a societal instrument? As yet, the answers to these questions remain inconclusive from the writings of Canadian academics.[26]

The elite-pluralist approach which has been developed by the late John Porter states that the power of economic, bureaucratic labour, military and other societal institutions tends to be structurally differentiated, because all these institutions and their elites perform different functions for a highly industrialized and urbanized society. Specialism is therefore inevitable, but there is, however, an important need for the various elite groups to interact with each other to ensure coordination and mutual agreement on various goals for society. If this coordination leads to an aggrandizement of power, or a collusion of elites, then the societal system is in need of reform. Porter ties together his normative social democratic concerns for the ideal of egalitarianism, technological advancement and greater social mobility with his realistic assessment of the actual workings of Canadian society. He shows very little sympathy for the arguments of ethnic pluralism, asserting that this concern has become a fetish in Canadian political life.[27]

Porter's analysis of bureaucracy illustrates the paradoxical position in which the bureaucracy is placed. He is not prepared to concede that the bureaucracy holds power although the elite here is equated with other elites in society. Only politicians have the "recognized right" to power: bureaucrats possess influence on that power. To the extent that influence is wielded then power is exercised in some measure. According to Porter, "a minister may . . . retain the ultimate decision-making power, but there is power also for the person who has access to him and who can sell him a plan."[28]Porter's ideal of a rationalized bureaucracy is one which is open and accessible to all, efficient and effective (rational, rivalled and open) and free of patronage.[29] Instead, he sees one which is too closely allied to the elite structures of other sectors of society. The ideal image of bureaucracy as subservient and efficient implementer is contrasted with his empirical image of an elite overly influential and tied to the political and economic elites of Canadian society. Canadian bureaucracy is therefore found wanting. In the tradition of a true social democrat he longs for "realistic and appropriate" reform: "If power and decision-making must always rest with elite groups, there can at least be open recruitment from all classes into the elites."[30]

Whereas elite-pluralism views a state institution like the bureaucracy as powerful through associational influence, the traditional Marxist view goes all the way by asserting that *all* state institutions, including the bureaucracy, are "instruments" of the ruling class or dominant elite. This approach takes its position from a specific interpretation of Marx's superstructural view of the state:

The bourgeoisie has at last, since the establishment of modern industry and of the world market, conquered for itself, in the modern representative state, exclusive political sway. The executive of the modern state is but a committee for managing the common affairs of the whole bourgeoisie. [Thus] the bourgeoisie has played a most revolutionary role in history.[31]

Thus despite all the formal trappings of the rule of law, parliamentary "sovereignty," "civil liberties" and such like, the fact of the matter is that the capitalist state remained a "dictatorship" of the capitalist class. Bureaucratic structures were simply an extension of this dictatorship, an instrument in the hands of the bourgeoisie. This position is illustrated in the works of two Western Marxists. American Paul Sweezy in his *Theory of Capitalist Development* argues that ". . . state power must be monopolized by the class or classes which are the chief beneficiaries. [The state is] an instrument in the hands of the ruling classes for enforcing and guaranteeing the stability of the class structure itself."[32] Marxist Ralph Miliband from the London School of Economics augments this view by inferring that the power of the capitalists is derived from the class composition of the people who hold the crucial bureaucratic, military, legislative and religious elite positions in society:

. . . it has remained a basic fact of life in advanced capitalist countries that the vast majority of men and women in these countries has been governed, represented, administered, judged and commanded in war by people drawn from other, economically and socially superior and relatively distant classes.[33]

This position, by making the state an instrument of the ruling class, allows no autonomy to state institutions. All state institutions are geared towards the fundamental needs of capitalist accumulation. This instrumentalist conception of the state certainly gave many Western Marxists some intellectual problems, for it was clearly evident that capitalist states had internal conflicts and were susceptible to confusing and conflicting behavior of which the simple instrumentalist theory could make very little sense.[34]

Even Ralph Miliband in *The State in Capitalist Society* seems to understand this inconsistency in Marxist-Leninist thought and in actual reality. Though his theoretical formulations pronounce the conventional Marxist-Leninist position of instrumentalism, he nevertheless concedes that bureaucratic personnel cannot be considered as either "mere servants" of the state or "power hungry apparatchiki."[35] The truth, it seems lies "somewhere in between" but exactly where still remains somewhat problematical:

. . . to view higher civil servants as the mere executants of policies in whose determination they have had little or no share is quite unrealistic. This is not to say that "bureaucrats" are necessarily "hungry for power," that they "run the country" and that ministers only provide a convenient façade for bureaucratic rule. That picture does not correspond to reality either. The true position lies somewhere in between these extremes: the general pattern must be taken to be one in which these men do play an important part in the process of governmental decision-making, and therefore constitute a considerable force in the configuration of political power in their societies.[36]

This statement nullifies the Marxist-Leninist instrumentalist perspective. But according to Marxist George Ross, a new Neo-Marxist perspective or a series of perspectives on the capitalist state had to be formulated to fill the vast vacuum left by the defunct Soviet theory of the capitalist state:

The hold of Soviet theories over much of the world socialist movement declined parallel with the disaggregation of world communism in the 1960s. In
the de-Stalinizing context which then emerged, most major oppositional
Communist parties (mainly in Europe but also in Japan) began to question
traditional Marxist-Leninist wisdom about the state. In almost all cases such
parties had long since adopted radical reformist, united-front strategies for
socialist change which *de facto* challenged much of Soviet dogma. De-Stalin-
ization, however, allowed such parties to come out of the theoretical closet on
the question of the capitalist state. But because the weight of tradition is still
heavy even in Eurocommunist parties, and because the problem of developing a workable new theoretical understanding is such a difficult one, official
Eurocommunist thought has thus far been quite tentative.[37]

In Marxist thought what we have had since the 1960s is a virtual
renaissance of theoretical thinking, particularly as regards the nature
of the capitalist state. No one particular theory has emerged as a
universally acceptable or as an all-encompassing Marxist theory of
the state. But the theoretical writings of Nicos Poulantzas and Louis
Althusser[38] which view the state structure as determined by the systemic constraints and contradictions of capitalism, have been widely
acclaimed by many Neo-Marxists, and so the structuralist perspective
which we present here is largely drawn from the work of Poulantzas.[39]

Implicit in Poulantzas' writings is the recognition that state structures are continuously being confronted with this schizoid problem of
identity referred to earlier in this chapter. The images of the capitalist
state structures as either being *autonomous* or *instrumental* do not fit reality: such structures, he contends, are neither derived from civil society (either of the economy or of the capitalist class) nor possess an autonomy completely divorced from the society. The capitalist state
exists to allow capitalist accumulation to occur. Thus the production
of a class structure that will allow capitalist accumulation becomes the
central problem for the capitalist mode of production.

In solving this problem the various sectors of society must each
contribute: the political, ideological and economic-technological sectors each has a contribution to make in separate ways, but ultimately
these contributions collectively allow accumulation. As Ross puts it,
"the capitalist state is, therefore, a critical constitutive element in the
production and reproduction of social relations of production, not
simply a product of these relations. The capitalist state is, then, relatively autonomous from the economy, with its own rules and purview which are quite as essential to accumulation as those of the
economy."[40]

FIGURE II
POULANTZAS' STRUCTURAL PERSPECTIVE IN DIAGRAMMATIC FORM

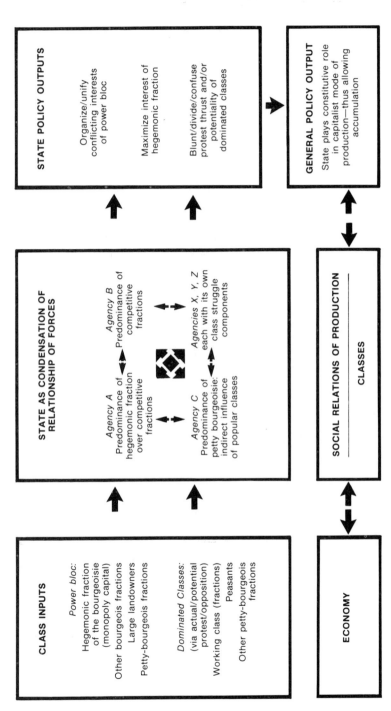

CLASS INPUTS

Power bloc:
Hegemonic fraction
of the bourgeoisie
(monopoly capital)
Other bourgeois fractions
Large landowners
Petty-bourgeois fractions

Dominated Classes:
(via actual/potential
protest/opposition)
Working class (fractions)
Peasants
Other petty-bourgeois
fractions

**STATE AS CONDENSATION OF
RELATIONSHIP OF FORCES**

Agency A
Predominance of
hegemonic fraction
over competitive
fractions

Agency B
Predominance of
competitive
fractions

Agencies X, Y, Z
each with its own
class struggle
components

Agency C
Predominance of
petty bourgeoisie:
indirect influence
of popular classes

STATE POLICY OUTPUTS

Organize/unify
conflicting interests
of power bloc

Maximize interest of
hegemonic fraction

Blunt/divide/confuse
protest thrust and/or
potentiality of
dominated classes

GENERAL POLICY OUTPUT

State plays constitutive role
in capitalist mode of
production—thus allowing
accumulation

SOCIAL RELATIONS OF PRODUCTION

CLASSES

ECONOMY

Source: George Ross, "Nicos Poulantzas, Eurocommunism, and the Debate on the theory of the Capitalist State" Socialist Review No. 44. Vol. 9. No. 2. March-April (1979) p. 149

This gives the state a very autonomous position in society, a point of view which almost borders on being non-Marxist. This position allows Poulantzas to include in his theoretical formulation new forms of property accumulation which have arisen in Western economies (monopoly rights derived from public contracts, rights of public employment, pension entitlements and so on which now supplement the older property rights).[41] Thus Poulantzas can claim that the state fosters on its own initiative specific divisions of intellectual and manual labor; it can stand as a symbol of *national* and *social* unity because it can promote social theories of individual liberty and freedom as well as ideologies legitimizing national-territorial aspirations and claims. Additionally, "it possesses the monopoly of legitimate violence which allows/forbids different behaviors, creating the rational-legal abstractions and norms without which predictable enlarged social reproduction would be impossible (here Poulantzas gives Max Weber his due, something that all too few Marxists, as yet, have been willing to do)."[42] The state as a societal structure is acceded a realm of independence in organizing and politically unifying the "power bloc" in society. Thus it must stand above all classes and class factions, and at various times it would appear even to be working against the segment of the ruling class (the "hegemonic fraction" of the bourgeoisie) which has a dominant position to play in the accumulation process in society.

Nevertheless, the effects of state power are circumscribed by the dominance of capitalism, so in the end the effects of this power can only correspond to the long-run interests of the "hegemonic fraction." In this way the state remains an instrument of monopoly capital. It acts to disorganize and divide dominated groups "confusing them by ideological offensives and/or concessions that will short-circuit their own attempts to organize into a coherent opposition."[43] The state thus presides over a dynamic struggle of classes in which the hegemonic fraction of the bourgeoisie has a disproportionate measure of influence and power. To complicate matters even further the state apparatus—regulatory agencies, departments, crown corporations, bureaus etc.—are themselves the loci and residues of class conflict. Thus the bureaucracy is in the midst of this general class conflict, some departments and/or sections of departments (such as Finance, or Trade and Commerce) being beachheads of "hegemonic fraction interests," while other agencies (such as the Department of Labour or perhaps sections of the Department of National Health and Welfare) represent working class interests or have a pronounced "petty bourgeoisie" bias.[44] The class struggle and the contradictions of capitalism, even within the bowels of bureaucracy, continue in full swing.

This theoretical formulation is posited by Poulantzas and his admirers as an ideal-typical situation. George Ross reminds us that "Actual class-conflict situations within a given social formation, the class-conflict densities of specific state agencies, existing relationships and hierarchies between such state agencies, and so on, all remain matters for further investigation."[45]

We must remind the reader that Poulantzas' theoretical formulations on the capitalist state remain only one theory among several Marxist theories. Poulantzas' views have, however, received wide acclaim not only in Marxist circles in Europe but in Canada as well. Bringing Marxist thought "out of the dark decades of Stalinism," is a process which has only just begun: theoretical formulations abound and disagreements over various interpretations and reinterpretations fill the Marxist publications.[46] However, as one Marxist has indicated, these disagreements should not be construed as fatal for "what matters is [the Marxists'] conceptual clarity in explaining the functioning of capitalist institutions generally."[47] The conceptual clarity referred to, common to all Marxist thought, is the view that state institutions, in the final analysis, function as agents of "repression (or coercion), legitimation (the ideological function) and accumulation."[48]

Among Marxist formulations we find Poulantzas' work interesting, for he has attempted to come to grips, in Marxist structural terms, with what we have dubbed here "the schizoid image" of bureaucratic institutions: a powerful arm in the formulation of policy while at the same time being a subservient implementer "engaged in meeting [and expediting] the systemic goals of society as a whole."[49]

We come now to our last theoretical formulation to be presented here on the relationship between economy, state and society, namely corporatism. The ideal-typical definition most often cited is given by Philippe Schmitter who defines corporatism as

. . . a system of interest representation in which the constituent units are organised into a limited number of singular, compulsory, non-competitive, hierarchically ordered, and functionally differentiated categories, recognised or licensed (if not created) by the state and granted a deliberate representational monopoly within their respective categories in exchange for observing certain controls on their selection of leaders and articulation of demands and supports.[50]

Schmitter concedes that there is a need to distinguish subtypes within this ideal-typical construct. Thus he discusses "state corporatism" and "societal corporatism" in his theoretical formulations. State corporatism, he argues, is characterized by the autonomy of interest associations from the state while societal corporatism more resembles fascism in that all interest associations are subordinated to the state and there is a repressive imposition of authoritarian control on all aspects of economy and society. As Mussolini used to express it: "Everything for the state; nothing against the state; nothing outside the state."[51]

This highly authoritarian and hierarchical model is, of course, not replicated in liberal democracies where there is a strong tendency to stress individual as opposed to collective interests and goals. Nevertheless, there are "tendencies" towards the ideal-typical model, and various scholars have noted these similarities and relationships. Robert Presthus in his *Elite Accommodation in Canadian Politics* describes corporatism as practised in Canada as "a conception of society in which government delegates many of its functions to private groups, which in turn provide guidance regarding the social and economic legislation required in the modern national state."[52] It is, he maintains, an *organic view* of society seeking to mitigate any semblance of class struggle, especially between labor and capital. Canadian corporatism seeks a solution to this class struggle by bringing in both big business and big labor into the governing councils of the state thereby co-opting them as partners or agents for the state.

As evidence of these tendencies Presthus sees groups, whose legitimacy is not open to further question, openly consulting, lobbying and making strong, matter-of-fact representations to the Canadian government. This they would be unlikely to do if, in the eyes of the decision makers, they were considered illegitimate. Presthus also detects an ongoing collaboration among the political executive, the public bureaucracy and the various functional groupings in Canadian society. *The bureaucratic elite is therefore conceived as a willing partner in this sharing of power among groups.* This elite acquiesce in much government delegation of its rule-making functions to select corporate groups. In other cases when delegated powers are not involved, a vast network of consultation is in effect to ensure agreement with the affected constituents.[53]

Hierarchical group structuring to effect this corporatist arrangement is helped considerably by Canadian political culture viewed as "deferential [in its] patterns of authority."[54] Essentially, K. J. Rea and J. T. McLeod concur with this characterization of the Canadian political and societal systems:

What we are asserting then, is that no liberal organic corporatism may be a pervasive fact of the Canadian political economy. Our political system's organization of power is not merely elitist, but corporatist. Elites interact and attempt to accommodate each other. The various elites often appear to clash, or pretend to clash, but usually maintain a realistic willingness to balance or harmonize their diverse interests and to preserve the interests of the community through collaboration with the state. When our elites perceive that they are threatened by external enemies, free trade, foreign competition, foreign investment, class divisions or inflation, the orthodox Canadian response is an organic corporatist response: to seek the cooperative interaction of various groups; to eschew market norms of liberal competition; to rally around the concept of a unique Canadian community.[55]

The effort aimed at combining the structures of sovereign parliamentary democracy with those of corporatism is called tripartism, a word which is frequently used in association with corporatism but very seldom defined. A definition given by Professor Bob Jessop is proffered here despite its rather cumbersome qualities:

Tripartism is a hybrid in which parliamentarianism and corporatism are combined into a contradictory unity owing to the formal participation in corporatist decision-making of representatives of the parliamentary executive ("government") and/or the delegation of corporatist policy implementation to the parliamentary bureaucracy and/or the formal participation of corporations in the decision-making of the parliamentary executive and/or the delegation of parliamentary policy administration to the corporations.[56]

Because of the political moves of the past Liberal administration in the late 1970s to inaugurate a system of wage and price controls in Canada, the issues of corporatism and tripartism have received considerable attention in both academic and popular journals. Some observers disputed the claim that Canada was or could move towards a tripartite arrangement: there were too many conflicting societal influences in Canada preventing such a coalition.[57] When applied to the nature of federal bureaucratic structures, some scholars saw no direct evidence to suggest that we are moving in a corporatist direction. Phidd and Doern conclude their analysis on the politics and management of Canadian economic policy by arguing that

. . . our analysis of the evolution of economic-management portfolios and departments would suggest a gradual pluralist unfolding of the recognition and institutionalization of values and groups who have pressed their claims on successive governments. [Furthermore] . . . our analysis also suggests the existence of a form of pluralism in which successive attempts at conceptualizing economic issues (e.g., regional policy, employment policy, incomes policy) not only compete in total for political attention in a highly competitive way, but also reflect *within* each category, the pluralism engendered by the public-private and intergovernmental divisions of the Canadian political economy.[58]

All of the perspectives we have of the interaction of economy, state and society are imprecise and still a long way from accurately specifying the role of state institutions in our liberal democratic society. It is advisable to keep D. V. Smiley's admonition in mind when he argues that "we should avoid arrogance and sectarianism on all sides of this dialogue and admit that the theoretical apparatuses we use and the information we have are both inadequate to the task [of explaining the connections between economy, state and society]."[59] Nevertheless, we must work with what we have, incomplete though these theories may be. All the theories mentioned earlier, with the exception of the Marxist intrumentalist perspective, take cognizance of the growth of bureaucratic power. But with the one exception of the Marxist structural theory of the state, none have specifically addressed themselves to the genie image of bureaucracy. Let us turn the question around to illustrate the point we are trying to make here. Why is it that despite its position of power bureaucracy has not challenged or usurped the role of the politician? Why is it that powerful bureaucrats are, in the final analysis, subservient to the dictates of our elected political executive? Marxist theory would logically answer that what we see being played out on such occasions is only a game amongst the bourgeoisie, aimed at obfuscating and mystifying the real issues of capitalist contradictions in the system. Is there no other explanation for this genie image?

III. A Concluding Note: The Problem Posed for Liberal Democracy

The truth of the matter is that theories dealing with the administrative state concept have really been attempting to come to grips with some central facts about the "administrative machine." Those concerned with normative problems in democracy recognize that the business of government has become more complex, that under these conditions, the administrator has become more important, and that granted a desire to maintain a democratic society, it is of the utmost importance to decide how the professional administrator fits in to this new conception of things. The realization of this evolution led, by 1945, to the coining of the term "the administrative state" to describe this change in bureaucracy.[60]

But the basis of the administrative state was laid much earlier than that. Long before the bureaucracy grew in importance in the late nineteenth century, the matter of who "owns" and "controls" the bureaucracy was discussed under the guise of accountability, which in turn was tied to the subservient implementer image. The theory became popularly known as the politics/administration dichotomy, namely that politicians were "on top" and bureaucrats "on tap." When the dichotomy was challenged in a most vigorous fashion and subsequently discarded as a public philosophy which no longer represented reality, the public bureaucracy was left without a clear conception of accountability.

But let us pause and take a step backward for a moment. At least in Canada and Britain it should have been remembered that this reality of change, of power accruing to the bureaucrat, was recognized and indeed sanctioned by liberal philosophy. That there is in politics a necessary place for experts was not only a principle of liberalism; on good historical grounds it might even be claimed as a discovery of liberalism. At the turn of this century one of the founders of the London School of Economics, Professor Graham Wallas, certainly recognized the issue's seminal importance in a philosophy for liberal-democratic administration, and Canada's R. MacGregor Dawson wrote his first book on the subject which he entitled *The Principle of Official Independence*.[61]

Nevertheless, it is true that when administrative pluralism was adopted as the working reality of Western liberal democratic bureaucracies, normative ideals became confused with the humdrum and sometimes sordid practicality of every day administration. Thus ideals which served the purpose of subjecting bureaucracy to a higher purpose were downgraded and in some cases discarded as useless (or close to being so) either in public discourse or in social science lexicon. As Theodore Lowi has argued such poetic terms as "the public interest," "the state" and "sovereignty," admittedly difficult to define in precise terms, were simply rejected by the "new philosophy of interest-group liberalism."[62] Thus in public administration we "discarded" the politics/administration dichotomy, and in political science such concepts as "sovereignty," "the state" and so on were challenged and rejected by the rising tide of behavioralism.[63]

The fact remained however that the image of bureaucracy as subservient implementer has a strong normative component, partly serving the purpose of ensuring the control of the bureaucracy. The image is a myth, not in the sense of an untruth, but in the sociological sense meaning, "the value-impregnated beliefs and notions that men hold, that they live by or live for. Every society is held together by a myth-system, a complex of dominating thought-forms that determines and sustains all its activities. All social relations, the very texture of human society, are myth-born and myth-sustained."[64]

Bureaucratic behavior is strongly conditioned by the myth of bureaucracy as instrument and Caliban. To paraphrase Hugh Thorburn from another context, at the bureaucratic elite level where power is held and the actual relationships are well known, the ideal of being society's servant is subscribed to in much the same way Voltaire praised religion—as a means of dissuading the servants from stealing the silver.[65] *The bureaucratic elite believes in the belief of subservience to society and to its political masters. To grasp this fact is of extreme significance.* The empirical studies of Robert D. Putnam, and the writings of C. H. Sisson emphasize this. As Putnam puts it in one of his articles:

> . . . a major premise of this study . . . is that bureaucrats' beliefs and values are a powerful determinant of the extent to which bureaucracy can be made compatible with democracy.[66]

It is therefore still possible to believe in the normative philosophy of the politics/administration dichotomy and yet to recognize that bureaucrats share significant power and influence in the political system. We will explore this seeming puzzle in greater detail in the next chapter.

The Paradoxical Reality of the Administrative State

> There is a paradox . . . in the long series of discussions over the theory of bureaucracy. During the last fifty years, many first-rate social scientists have thought of bureaucracy as one of the key questions of both modern sociology and modern political science. . . . On the one hand, most authors consider the bureaucratic organization to be the embodiment of rationality in the modern world, and, as such, to be intrinsically superior to all other possible forms of organization. On the other hand, many authors—often the same ones— consider it a sort of Leviathan, preparing the enslavement of the human race. Optimism and pessimism are mixed in various ways. Whatever their proportions, there is always a double belief in the superiority of bureaucratic rationality—in the domain of efficiency and in its threatening implications in the domain of human values.
>
> French sociologist Michel Crozier.

Footnotes

1. Herman Finer, *The British Civil Service* (London: George Allen and Unwin, 1937), p. 15.

2. I am including Marxist thought as well because for a long time Marxist ideology virtually ignored bureaucracy. Classical Marxism categorized bureaucracy as one aspect of the "state" which would eventually "wither away and die." *The instrumental character of bureaucracy was simply noted.* What was more important was the categorization of bureaucracy as an agent of class domination. Recent Neo-Marxist

thought, while not rejecting this image of implementer of class domination, has, however, begun to visualize the bureaucracy as an instrument with *some autonomy*. Marxist writings have recently been devoted to exploring this dichotomous theme.

3. Although it is accompanied by the usual caveats, see for example J.E. Hodgetts, *The Canadian Public Service: A Physiology of Government, 1867-1970* (Toronto: University of Toronto Press, 1973), p. 4.

4. Quoted in Geoffrey Stevens, "Watch Out," *Globe and Mail* (Toronto), Thursday, June 7, 1979, editorial page.

5. James Madison, "Paper Number 50," *The Federalist* (Franklin Center, Pennsylvania: The Franklin Library, 1977), p. 374.

6. For an excellent synopsis, see Reinhard Bendix, "Bureaucracy," *International Encyclopedia of the Social Sciences* (New York: Macmillan and Free Press, 1968), II, 206-219. The same text (and used here) can be found as Chapter Seven in Reinhard Bendix and Guenther Roth, *Scholarship and Partisanship: Essays on Max Weber* (Berkeley: University of California Press, 1971), pp. 129-155.

7. Herman Finer, *Representative Government and a Parliament of Industry*, (London: George Allen and Unwin, 1923). Ch. I. pp. 6-7.

8. Bendix, "Bureaucracy," p. 133.

9. J.R. Mallory, *The Structure of Canadian Government* (Toronto: Macmillan of Canada, 1971), pp. 111-112.

10. Ernest Barker, *The Development of Public Services in Western Europe: 1660-1930* (Oxford: Oxford University Press, 1944), p. 6.

11. Hodgetts, *The Canadian Public Service*, p. 4n.

12. Max Weber, *The Theory of Social and Economic Organization*, ed. Talcott Parsons (New York: The Free Press, 1947), p. 338.

13. Reinhard Bendix, "Bureaucracy and the Problem of Power," *(PAR) Public Administration Review* V:3 (Summer, 1945):194-209. Reprinted in Robert K. Merton et al., *Reader in Bureaucracy* (New York: The Free Press, 1952), pp. 114-135.

14. For a succinct discussion of aspects of this theme, see Gabriel A. Almond, "Political Systems and Political Change," *American Behavioral Scientist* VI:10 (June 1963):3-10.

15. For an example of this bridging of ancient theorists with twentieth century social science, see William T. Bluhm, "The Place of the 'Polity' in Aristotle's Theory of the Ideal State," *Journal of Politics* 24:4 (November 1962):743-753. Reproduced essentially as Chapter IV ("The Aristotelian Bridge: Aristotle, Lipset, Almond") in W.T. Bluhm, *Theories of the Political System: Classics of Political Thought and Modern Political Analysis* (Englewood Cliffs, N.J.: Prentice-Hall, Inc., 1965), pp. 105-153.

16. For aspects of this argument, see Lucian W. Pye, "Democracy, Modernization, and Nation Building" in J. Roland Pennock, ed., *Self-Government in Modernizing Nations* (Englewood Cliffs, N.J.: Prentice-Hall, Inc., 1964):6-25. Also, L. Pye, "The Formation of New States" in Ithiel de Sola Pool, ed., *Contemporary Political Science: Toward Empirical Theory* (New York: McGraw-Hill, 1967), pp. 182-203.

17. For one Canadian approach, see K.J. Rea and J.T. McLeod, *Business and Government in Canada: Selected Readings,* 2nd ed. (Toronto: Methuen, 1976), pp. 334-345.

18. This broad classification under which we subsume the Canadian "debate" is borrowed from G. Esping-Anderson, R. Friedland, and E.O. Wright, "Modes of Class Struggle and the Capitalist State" in *Kapitalstate: Working Papers on the Capitalist State* (Special double issue) 4-5 (Summer 1976). (San Francisco: Kapitalistate Group, 1976):186-220.

19. See, for example, the highly informative article by Bob Jessop, "Recent theories of the capitalist state," *Cambridge Journal of Economics* I:4 (December 1977):353-373.

20. Hugh G. Thorburn, "Canadian Pluralist Democracy in Crisis," *Canadian Journal of Political Science* XI:4 (December 1978):723-738 at 723-24.

21. S.D. Clark, "Canada and the American Value System," *The Developing Canadian Community,* 2nd ed. (Toronto: University of Toronto Press, 1968), p. 233.

22. Edwin R. Black and Alan C. Cairns, "A Different Perspective on Canadian Federalism," *CPA* IX:1 (March, 1966):27-44; Thomas A. Hockin, *Government in Canada* (Toronto: McGraw-Hill Ryerson Ltd., 1976).

23. Edwin R. Black, "The Fractured Mosaic: John Porter Revisited," *CPA* 17:4 (Winter 1974):640-653 at 645.

24. Hockin, *Government in Canada,* pp. 94-95.

25. Alan C. Cairns, Presidential Address to the Canadian Political Science Association, Fredericton, June 1977, p. 1 (mimeo). Essentially, although not entirely, reproduced as "The Governments and Societies of Canadian Federalism," *CJPS* X:4 (December 1977):695-725.

26. Hockin's answers in his text are somewhat inconclusive. After having strongly argued the autonomous nature of the Canadian bureaucracy he ends on the following note:
    "The state is driven to increased superordination in relation to everything around it. The public service, of necessity, plays a crucial role in mediating and extending this superordination, a task made somewhat easier in Canada by *the principle of a neutral public service.*"
    T.A. Hockin, *Government in Canada,* p. 170.

27. John Porter, *The Vertical Mosaic* (Toronto: University of Toronto Press, 1965), pp. 368-369.

28. Ibid., p. 432.

29. Ibid., pp. 418-420.

30. Ibid., p. 558.

31. Marx and Engels, *The Communist Manifesto*, ed. Samuel H. Beer, *Crofts Classics* (New York: Appleton-Century-Crofts, Inc., 1955), pp. 11-12. Reprinted from *The Communist Manifesto* edited by Samuel H. Beer with the permission of AHM Publishing Corporation, Arlington Heights, Illinois.

32. Paul Sweezy, *The Theory of Capitalist Development* (New York: Monthly Review Press, 1942), p. 243.

33. Ralph Miliband, *The State in Capitalist Society* (London: Weidenfeld and Nicolson, 1969), p. 67.

34. G. Esping-Andersen, R. Friedland, and E.O. Wright, "Modes of Class Struggle and the Capitalist State," pp. 186-220; George Ross, "Nicos Poulantzas, Eurocommunism, and the Debate on the Theory of the Capitalist State," *Socialist Review* Number 44 (Volume 9, No. 2) (March-April 1979):144.

35. Apparatchiki is the Russian word for "men of the bureaucratic apparatus."

36. Miliband, *The State in Capitalist Society*, p. 119.

37. Ross, "Nicos Poulantzas, Eurocommunism," p. 145.

38. Nicos Poulantzas, *Classes in Contemporary Capitalism* (London: New Left Books, 1975); Louis Althusser, "Ideology and Ideological State Apparatuses," *Lenin and Philosophy* (New York: Monthly Review Press, 1971).

39. I am indebted to the excellent review of Poulantzas' work by George Ross for the following summary.

40. Ross, "Nicos Poulantzas, Eurocommunism," p. 146.

41. In a review of Leo Panitch's *The Canadian State* Professor D.V. Smiley points to this problem in Marxist formulations, but it seems to me that a reading of Poulantzas' latest book would allow his theory to include these new forms of property accumulation within the purview of the "autonomous state." See D.V. Smiley's review of Leo Panitch, ed. *The Canadian State: Political Economy and Political Power*, in *Canadian Journal of Political Science* XI:3 (September 1978):656-659.

42. Ross, "Nicos Poulantzas, Eurocommunism," p. 146.

43. Ibid., p. 147.

44. Professor Rianne Mahon has subjected Poulantzas' theoretical formulations to empirical enquiry. See her "Canadian public policy: the unequal structure of representation" in Leo Panitch, ed. *The Canadian State*, pp. 133-198.

45. Ross, "Nicos Poulantzas, Eurocommunism," p. 147.

46. See, for example, Bob Jessop, "Recent theories of the capitalist state," *Cambridge Journal of Economics* I (1977)

47. Henry Milner, "The decline and fall of the Quebec Liberal regime: contradictions in the modern Quebec state" in Leo Panitch, ed. *The Canadian State,* pp. 101-132 at p. 105.

48. Ibid., p. 105.

49. B.F. Hoselitz, "Levels of Economic Performance and Bureaucratic Structure" in Joseph La Palombara, ed., *Bureaucracy and Political Development* (Princeton, New Jersey: Princeton University Press, 1963), pp. 171, 198.

50. P.C. Schmitter "Still the Century of Corporatism?" *Review of Politics* 36:2 (April 1974):85-131 at pp. 93-94; see also his "Modes of Interest Intermediation and Models of Societal Change in Western Europe," *Comparative Political Studies* 10:1 (April 1977):7-37.

51. Luciano Lanza, "Fascism and Techno-Bureaucracy," *Our Generation* 12:1

52. Robert Presthus, *Elite Accommodation in Canadian Politics* (Cambridge: At the University Press, 1973), p. 25. Chapter 2, containing his views on Canadian political culture and the Canadian system of elite accommodation, provides the gist of the summary here. (See pp. 20-63.)

53. Ibid., chapter 7.

54. Ibid., p. 20.

55. K.J. Rea and J.T. McLeod, eds., *Business and Government in Canada,* 2nd edition, (Toronto: Methuen, 1976), pp. 339-340; see also Carolyn J. Tuohy, "Pluralism and Corporatism in Ontario Medical Politics," pp. 395-413 in the same edited book.

56. Bob Jessop, "Corporatism, Fascism and Social Democracy," unpublished paper (mimeo), p. 15.

57. D.V. Smiley, "The Non-Economics of Anti-Inflation," *Canadian Forum* (March 1976). Reproduced in K.J. Rea and J.T. McLeod, eds., *Business and Government in Canada,* pp. 444-448.

58. Richard W. Phidd and G. Bruce Doern, *The Politics and Management of Canadian Economic Policy* (Toronto: Macmillan of Canada, 1978), p. 558.

59. D.V. Smiley, "Review of Leo Panitch (ed.) *The Canadian State: Political Economy and Political Power,*" *CJPS* XI:3 (September 1978):659.

60. The term was first popularized by Dwight Waldo. See D. Waldo, *The Administrative State: A Study of the Political Theory of American Public Administration* (New York: The Ronald Press Co., 1948).

61. R. MacGregor Dawson, *The Principle of Official Independence* (London: P.S. King and Son Ltd., 1922). See also Graham Wallas' "Introduction" to this book.

62. Theodore J. Lowi, *The End of Liberalism: Ideology, Policy, and the Crisis of Public Authority* (New York: W.W. Norton and Co., Inc., 1969), pp. 48-49. See also Chapter 3, "The New Public Philosophy: Interest-Group Liberalism," pp. 55-97.

63. See A.P. d'Entrèves, *The Notion of the State* (Oxford: Oxford University Press, 1967), pp. 33-34, 62-63, on the concept of the state and on the hostility of social scientists in liberal democracies to its employment. See also David Easton, *The Political System* (New York: Alfred A. Knopf, 1965), pp. 106-115.

64. R.M. MacIver, *The Web of Government* (New York: The Macmillan Co., 1947), p. 4.

65. Hugh G. Thorburn, "Canadian Pluralist Democracy in Crisis," *CJPS* XI:4 (December 1978):737-738.

66. Robert D. Putnam, "The Political Attitudes of Senior Civil Servants in Britain, Germany and Italy," *British Journal of Political Science* 3:Part 3 (July 1973):257-290. Reprinted in Mattei Dogan, ed., *The Mandarins of Western Europe: The Political Role of Top Civil Servants* (New York: John Wiley and Sons, 1975), pp. 87-126 at p. 89. See also C.H. Sisson, *The Spirit of British Administration* (London: Faber and Faber, 1959), p. 151.

Notes

The "Administrative State" is frequently referred to in writings on bureaucracy but very rarely defined and analytically discussed. Early writings on the subject tend to stress the societal changes which have brought about the growth of bureaucratic power: Is democracy more important than efficiency? Is the growth of bureaucratic centralization a grave danger to democracy? Or to put this question another way, as the administrative process grows in complexity, is it not true that the necessary powers devolved upon administrators leave a formal, and not a living content to democratic government? Is it legitimate to postulate the existence of a general process of administration distinct from the specialized administration of particular functions? These questions have informed much of the writings of Waldo, Mosher, Redford, Martin, Fritz Morstein Marx, Appleby and others. A sample of such is as follows:

Paul Appleby, *Big Democracy* (New York: Alfred A. Knopf, 1945).

Roscoe Martin (ed.), *Public Administration and Democracy* (Syracuse: Syracuse University Press, 1965).

Fritz Morstein Marx, *The Administrative State: An Introduction to Bureaucracy* (Chicago: The University of Chicago Press, 1957).

Frederick C. Mosher, *Democracy and the Public Service* (New York: Oxford University Press, 1968).

Emmette S. Redford, *Democracy in the Administrative State* (New York: Oxford University Press, 1969).

Dwight Waldo, *The Administrative State* (New York: Ronald Press, 1948).

Dwight Waldo (ed.), *Public Administration in a Time of Turbulence* (New York: Chandler Publishing Co., 1971).

Two books and an article should be mentioned as attempts to develop a "modified administrative state model" and to apply it to broad analyses of bureaucracy. These "models" exphasize the power aspects of administration leaving unexplored the other aspects which are of concern to us in this chapter.

(Comparative Government Studies)
Jean Blondel, *Introduction to Comparative Government*, (New York, 1969).

(Canadian Government)
T.A. Hockin, *Government in Canada*, (Toronto: McGraw-Hill Ryerson Ltd., 1976).

(United States)
Allen Schick, "Toward the Cybernetic State" in Dwight Waldo (ed.) *Public Administration in a Time of Turbulence* (New York: Chandler Publishing Co., 1971), pp. 214-233.

Only a few publications attempt to grapple with the genie image. The following we consider the best of a very slim selection:

**Reinhard Bendix, "Bureaucracy and the Problem of Power". *Public Administration Review*, Vol. V (1945): 194-209. Reproduced in Robert K Merton et al, *Reader in Bureaucracy* (New York: The Free Press, 1952): 114-135.

**Reinhard Bendix, "Bureaucracy", *International Encyclopedia of the Social Sciences* (New York: Macmillan and Free Press, 1968), II, 206-219. Reproduced in Reinhard Bendix and Guenther Roth, *Scholarship and Partisanship: Essays on Max Weber* (Berkeley: University of California Press, 1971): 129-155.

**Erik Damgaard, "The Political Role of Nonpolitical Bureaucrats in Denmark" in Mattei Dogan (ed.) *The Mandarins of Western Europe: The Political Role of Top Civil Servants*, (New York: John Wiley and Sons, 1975): 275-292.

The rest of the material listed below touches upon one or a few aspects of the administrative theme, but do not attempt to address the phenomenon as we have tried to do in this chapter.

**Alan C. Cairns, "The Governments and Societies of Canadian Federalism", *CJPS*:X:4, (December 1977): 695-725.

**Richard Chapman, "Official Liberality", *Public Administration* (London), Vol. 48, Summer 1970, pp. 123-136.

*Erwin A Jaffe, "Rearrangement of the Administrative State: Professor Lowi and 'The End of Liberalism.' " *Journal of Comparative Administration*, Vol. 1, #4, February 1970: 477-499.

*H.G. Thorburn, Canadian Pluralist Democracy in Crisis," *CJPS*, XI:4, December 1978:723-738.

CHAPTER FOUR

THE POLICY/ADMINISTRATION DICHOTOMY: BETWEEN SCYLLA AND CHARYBDIS*

As one who was involved for ten years in northern policy, I can hardly claim to be capable of complete objectivity. It would be easier to achieve such detachment if I could shelter behind the dictum so solemnly delivered from editorial pages and professorial podia that politicians, and not civil servants, make policy and civil servants, and not politicians, apply it. It is unfortunate that as clear and helpful a distinction should have so little truth about it.

R. Gordon Robertson,
Former Secretary to the Cabinet

Seek simplicity but distrust it.

Alfred North Whitehead

I. Introduction

The German philosopher Friedrich Nietzsche's lament that "God is dead and we have killed him" echoes in every aspect of twentieth century thought. Theories challenging and negating systems of norms, beliefs, and values abound in Western intellectual circles. In the theoretical vacuum left by this confusion and doubt, fragmentary behavioral theories rush in to fill the void, offering a "clearer construction of reality" and purporting to consign to the heap of super-

---

* Scylla in Greek mythology was a beautiful nymph whom Circe the sorceress turned into a sea monster. Scylla lived in a cave above the Strait of Messina opposite the dangerous whirlpool Charybdis and devoured sailors who came too close to her abode. Mariners who therefore sailed through the Strait tried to steer a middle course between Scylla and Charybdis. The analogy for the role of senior public servants should be apparent. Theirs is a middle course between the monster of adopting an open political role and the whirlpool of mere pencil pushing: to fall exclusively into either position is tantamount to bureaucratic suicide.

stitious nostrums many symbolic conceptions that constitute the basis of community and around which develop deep passions and strongly held values. The study and practice of public policy and administration is by no means exempt from this philosophical watershed: indeed nowhere is the problem more clearly demonstrated than in the conception of the relationship between public *policy* and public *administration.*[1] As we briefly demonstrated in Chapter Three, long before western societies evolved from absolute monarchies to liberal democracies, the view was firmly held and practised that bureaucracies were instrumental in nature.[2] We contend that this is an image of bureaucracy which has deep historical roots, and we have already demonstrated how this conception permeates every leading theoretical perspective on the interaction of *economy, state* and *society.*

Simply put, the theory known as the policy/administration dichotomy proclaims that policy and politics are closely interrelated, if not synonymous activities, and that they *are* and *should be* separated from administration. It is the legitimate duty of the politician to enunciate and formulate public choice. Administration, on the other hand, is the expediting of this choice, a necessary but nevertheless subordinate task devoted to clarifying the technical and other instrumental characteristics of policy. It is very important to note that this conception of the nature of bureaucracy embodies two images—that bureaucracy in historical precedent is a servile instrument and that because it has fulfilled this role in society so well in the past *it should continue to do so in the future.* Both *a fact* of historical accident merges with a *normative value* as to what should be. The policy/administration dichotomy is at once both *descriptive* and *prescriptive.*

A series of assumptions, which we will attempt to make explicit, relate to the above premises. The first is that the theory conveys a firmly held belief that seems to transcend most societies with bureaucracies, and that is, *the prescriptive concept of the primacy of political headship or legitimate domination* as Max Weber called it. Weber's comparative historical analysis of the relationship between legitimate domination and organizational forms outlined in Chapter Two conclusively demonstrates this fact. *The ghost of the absolute king, in the respectable disguise of the theory of sovereignty, still haunts us. The policy/administration dichotomy is really a theory of political accountability: it reaffirms the view that modern public organizations are first and foremost instruments of control to ensure predictable results.* They are artificially designed contrivances intended to achieve the purposes of the "owners" of public organizations, the people. Almost all modern-day writings conceive the bureaucracy as a tool with the people having ultimate sovereignty over their "public servants." The policy/administration dichotomy reaffirms this normative viewpoint in the strongest of terms by its emphasis on political supremacy.

The second assumption flows from the nature of the concept of sovereignty. The philosophical heritage underpinning the theories of sovereignty is a long, complicated and fascinating odyssey on the evolution of ideas which, unfortunately, cannot be our main concern here.[4] Briefly put, in the United States, government is based on the concept of popular sovereignty, that is, that citizens who were obliged to obey a government were also entitled to participate *directly* or through their representatives in the process by which the policies of that government were determined. *Sovereignty is not embodied in any one political institution or exclusively personified in the politician.* Popular sovereignty is expressed through such devices as the popular election of United States senators, the establishment of direct primaries, the initiative, referendum and recall, and the constitutional protection of home rule for regional and local areas of the country.

Thus such utilitarian phrases as "the public interest" and "the policy/administration dichotomy", although demonstrably English in philosophical origins, have been popularized in American literature and indeed have been made almost all-American in their usage in that they flow from the very nature of popular sovereignty.[5] During the Progressive reform era of the 1870s and 80s in the United States the dichotomy as a doctrine of accountability meant good government, businesslike management of the public accounts and the eradication of such "venal practices" as patronage in the filling of administrative positions. This meaning was synonymous with the concept of the public interest. According to Grant McConnell the public interest in America:

> . . . was self-evident in the Progressive era, when the promise of science in government and administration seemed brightest and "the greatest good for the greatest number in the long run" meant very simply that the people wanted what was good for them as revealed by the emerging administrative science.[6]

Canadian political traditions and institutions, although spasmodically influenced by the doctrine of popular sovereignty in the past, have been and continue to be based on the belief of parliamentary or legal sovereignty. As historian W. L. Morton expresses it: "Not life, liberty, and the pursuit of happiness, but peace, order and good government are what the national government of Canada guarantees."[7] The whole nature of the discourse on sovereignty in the two countries hinges on this difference. In the United States it is couched in the language of Rousseau, Locke, Tom Paine, John Dewey and the like. In

Canada, as Chapter Seven will demonstrate, the debate on the problems of accountability is carried on almost totally in the language of Jeremy Bentham, the Mills, Walter Bagehot, A. V. Dicey and others—that is, parliamentary sovereignty, ministerial responsibility and the conventions derived therefrom.

A third assumption of the dichotomy is inherent in the nature of prescriptions. While a description tells us about an observed uniformity in the past, a prescription includes the expectation that the uniformity both *should* and *would* continue in the future. Herein lies a fundamental problem, for a preference simply cannot authoritatively determine future behavior. *Human behavior is always in a state of flux and our institutions mirror this fact. Prescriptions are therefore more likely to imperfectly condition behavior,* to act as important guideposts against which actual behavior can be assessed from time to time by those who profess belief in those embodied values. Religious people cannot all be condemned as hypocrites simply because they do not fully live up to the precepts of their faith. In like manner the normative values inherent in this conception of responsibility and accountability cannot be dismissed as irrelevant simply because the conception does not exactly mirror all aspects of reality.

This point can be more clearly demonstrated from the following examples. It is ironic that few intellectuals understood the above fact more profoundly than some of the more notable scholars and essayists responsible for explaining and popularizing the liberal-democratic notions of ministerial responsibility and accountability. Walter Bagehot, the English essayist of whom we will have much more to say in Chapter Ten, attempted to show in *The English Constitution* (1867) how the social conditions of England at that time greatly influenced the political institutions of the day; how these institutions functioned, in part, behind the "smokescreens," of the formal political structures; how the "hidden political process," which could not be analysed in terms of the stated purposes of the political institutions, contributed to the maintenance of political and social stability. Five to six years later when Bagehot wrote an introduction to the second edition of his book he found himself wrestling with a major problem: how, if one is to go beyond the study of mere institutions, are processes—continually changing relationships—to be illustrated and at the same time made to seem more than quickly outdated vignettes of a political system at a particular point in time? The dilemma is posed but left unanswered:

There is a great difficulty in the way of a writer who attempts to sketch a living constitution—a Constitution that is in actual work and power. The difficulty is that the object is in constant change. . . . The difficulty is the greater because a writer who deals with a living government naturally compares it with the most important other living governments, and these are changing too, what he illustrates are altered probably in one way, and his sources of illustration are altered probably in a different way.[8]

This theme is again emphasized in the work of Professor Graham Wallas of the London School of Economics. Four decades after Bagehot, he too laid further stress on change by emphasizing the socio-psychological foundations of political behavior. In *Human Nature in Politics* he argued that often people thought in terms of images which remained with and had an influence upon them long after the original sources of these images had themselves changed. "The student of politics," he wrote, "must consciously or unconsciously, form a conception of human nature, and the less conscious he is of his conception the more likely he is to be dominated by it."[9]

Bagehot's and Wallas' contentions are extremely important. The policy/administration dichotomy in many aspects of its descriptive qualities has changed because society has evolved. These changes have in turn generated a controversy about the dichotomy's utility as a normative conception. Should we now develop new norms or refurbish old ones, and if so, how is this to be done? It has become fashionable in recent Canadian writings to dismiss our "images and influences" as anachronisms, fit only to be relegated to the ragbag of historical curiosities. Thus, one writer on ministerial responsibility claims that his paper "addresses the fundamental threat to our liberal constitutional state posed by the increasing vacuity of the traditional concept of ministerial responsibility,"[10] and others argue that "much of the constitutional and administrative theory derived from British tradition and still applicable to the executive and parliamentary processes lacks relevance in the context of Canadian federalism."[11]

We are not convinced that the norms inherent both in the dichotomy and in ministerial responsibility are irrelevant to our society today. We argue here that the "images" and historical events surrounding both these theories of accountability are important because they have profoundly affected the nature of many public bureaucracies and are likely to continue to do so for a very long time to come. Sociologists tell us that the direction of social change can only be understood within the context of historical precedent. That is, in the normal course of events it is highly unlikely that we will witness radical institutional change which would negate the constitutional and administrative theory derived from our past historical traditions.[12] Social change, nevertheless is occurring, and it is important for the student of government to detect and understand the nature and direction of such evolutionary trends.

There are thus two strings to the analytical bow needed to understand the policy/administration dichotomy. First, in keeping with our belief that ideas, like institutions, have consequences that are not always obvious at the time of their inception, we will describe the practical impact of the politics/administration dichotomy on both Canadian and American governments, and discuss why that impact is still of some importance today. Second, we will return to Nietzche's lament in discussing the challenges posed to the policy/administration dichotomy. These challenges have overshadowed the dichotomy by creating seemingly "new images" or norms through the doctrine of administrative pluralism. This doctrine has in turn, generated considerable controversy, and although the main features of that debate cannot fully concern us here, we will discuss a few salient aspects of it as we conclude by reflecting on the relevance of the dichotomy for present-day government.

II. Ideas Affecting Institutions: The Policy/ Administration Dichotomy In North America

A study of American administrative history informs us that between 1789 and 1828 there arose a debate between the Jeffersonians and the Federalists. At issue was the question of how the bureaucracy should be developed in the newly independent nation. The Federalists contended that effective government required a strong independent bureaucracy. The Jeffersonians, on the other hand, had learned their lessons from the English constitutional struggle only too well, and coupled with their fierce dislike of all central government, they countered that bureaucracy was at best a necessary evil to be kept weak and as a subservient tool of the politicians.[13] In the end the Jeffersonian point of view prevailed with the election of Andrew Jackson to the presidency, thus beginning a system of political dominance of the bureaucracy and widespread patronage which was checked only by the introduction of the merit system of appointment through the Pendleton Act of 1883.

The detailed history of this era of American porkbarrelling is of less concern to us here than an account of the forces which converged to rid American public life of the "venal practices of patronage." The American reforms of 1883 were backed with considerable support from academics and others in public life who wanted to rid public policy and administration of all forms of political interference. Chief among them was Woodrow Wilson, a political scientist at Princeton University who would later become Governor of the State of New Jersey and finally President of the United States. In 1887 Wilson, a contemporary of the Muckrakers and himself a major political beneficiary of the rise of reform sentiment, wrote an essay in which he distinguished between politics and administration.[13] Wilson observed that it "is getting harder to run a constitution than to frame one," and, quoting Bluntschli, called for the marshalling and employing of more intellectual resources in the management of the state:

Politics [Bluntschli says] is state activity "in things great and universal," while "administration, on the other hand," is "the activity of the state in individual and small things." Politics is thus the special province of the statesman, administration of the technical official. Policy does nothing without the aid of administration, but administration is not therefore politics."[14]

There has been considerable controversy among American scholars as to what this quote and others from Wilson's essay really meant, but to this writer Wilson's pronouncements simply asserted the fact that efficient administration is the key to better government.[15] Although ideas are undoubtedly catalysts to action they nevertheless must be accompanied by a technology for operationalization. Ideas associated with practical means to achieve them have profound consequences, and in the 1880s the American reformers were acutely aware of this fact. How was this then to be done? Reformers sought to improve administration by the adoption of practical "scientific" methods: merit and classification systems; reorganization of administrative structures by "scientific" principles; the call for increased professional specialization; and the ensuring of further protection against political interference or detailed intervention in the bureaucracy by creating gate-way structures such as public service commissions to oversee the application of the merit principle.

Most of these "scientific" trappings were closely associated with the theory of scientific management, developed by the engineer Frederick W. Taylor and his disciples for prior use in the American private industry. We will explore this theory in a little more detail later in this text. Thus a historical conception of government which views bureaucracy as instrumental in nature is reinforced by a theory of organization which at one and the same time emphasizes this instrumental characteristic but eschews, in the name of efficiency, the negative aspects of past servility (that is, the practice of patronage). Scientific management was a theory whose time had dramatically arrived even while it was still in its formative stages.[16] Its influence was pervasive. As one astute British observer, Sir Henry Bunbury expressed it, North American efficiency studies in administration had taken the place "which was previously occupied by the study of constitutional principles in administration. The efficiency engineer has become a formidable rival to the political philosopher."[17]

The policy/administration dichotomy, wedded to the theory of scientific management, was a powerful combination which any bureaucracy ripe for reform could not withstand. It showed the way to economy and efficiency which should be the most sought-after objectives of any administration, public or private. The Canadian federal government, like so many other administrations in North America, welcomed and adopted the dichotomy and its "scientific" trappings during the reform era (1918-1920). As E. O. Griffenhagen, a protégé of Frederick W. Taylor and himself the father of job classification, wrote to members of the Canadian federal cabinet:

[During our investigatory stay in Ottawa we became fully aware of] shortcomings in organization, [of] instances of duplication and of conflict, [of] examples of unnecessary work, of wasted effort, of extravagant practices, or of group and individual inefficiencies.[18]

There was, he argued, a need for "businesslike methods" in running the government of Canada:

The widespread demand for greater economy and more business-like methods of government has affected [even the] municipalities to a remarkable degree. Many cities have definitely accepted the idea that the administration of the local government should and can be managed in an efficient manner, and that public waste is as serious a matter of concern to every citizen as that of a private company is to the stockholder.[19]

The nature and extent of scientific management reforms in the Canadian government have been chronicled elsewhere, so we will confine ourselves to a few general observations on this remarkable convergence of technology (in the guise of efficiency and "scientific methods" of job structuring and organization), reform fervor, historical precedent and the beliefs in the classical free market economy.[20] In Canada and the United States:

1 The politics/administration dichotomy was assumed both as a self-evident truth and as a desirable goal. As such, pragmatism was wedded to theory. This union was reinforced by the common assumption made by public administration students at the time, that "Democracy is instrumental, a tool to achieve the Good Life, and its value lies in how it 'works' ".[21] Democracy was associated with efficient, "clean" rational administration not to be soiled by "dirty" politics. Administration was perceived to be a self-contained world of its own, with its own separate values, rules and methods. As such, administration was a realm of expertise from which politics could and should be excluded.

2 Organization theory was stated in "scientific management terms," that is, all aspects of public management were seen largely as problems in organizational technology. What most scientific management theorists held in common was that work could be studied in terms of the component parts of a task and that the most efficient method of work was that which involved the minimum necessary motions in the shortest possible time while accomplishing the given task. Work was largely conceptualized as a "mechanistic process," enabling the application of the scientific method of analysis to yield the "one best way" of accomplishing every possible task. Consequently every aspect of work could be conceptualized using a "scientific" method— a piece rate system which would allocate to each worker the precise market value of his productivity.

So ingrained is this philosophy in the work world of today that we take it as axiomatic in the work environment: component elements of a job which would enable a classification system of jobs to be built, and the devising of examinations to test the proficiency of candidates to meet these component elements. As the society became more "rational" by instituting these tests on its own—the proficiency of plumbers, architects, doctors, lawyers, electricians, foresters, chartered accountants, etc.,—the public organization has gradually phased out its administration of this entrance requirement[22] Moreover scientific management could also be extended to bureaucratic organization and procedures. This meant spelling out in explicit terms the necessity of a clear hierarchy in the bureaucracy, the use of staff agencies as opposed to line, the application of the span of control, and the scientific subdivision of work according to the principles of *purpose, process, place* and *clientele.*[23]

3 The budget was emphasized as an instrument of precise rational calculation, of coordination, planning and control. As one reformer puts it:

The problem of budget distribution is one of mechanics. The final appropriation is the resultant of all the forces in action just as truly as in an analogous case in physics. If . . . budgets . . . could be analyzed and compared, after variations due to peculiar political or geographical exigencies had been eliminated, certain tendencies would be apparent which would point the way for a norm of expenditures consistent with the state of progress at present achieved by society.[24]

Students of the policy/administration dichotomy tended to emphasize the "process aspects" of the budget rather than the parliamentary view of the budget as an instrument of executive control (the power of the purse).[25] The budget in Canada more so than in the

United States has always been historically viewed as an instrument of executive control rather than as a device geared largely for administrative "process" purposes. In recent years, particularly since the Royal Commission on Government Organization of 1965 (the Glassco Royal Commission), the government has increasingly emphasized "the process aspects" of the budget although the bias of executive control in the parliamentary tradition is still predominant.[26]

4 While the Rule of Law in both Canadian and American jurisdictions was extolled, scientific management added some legal realism to the "processes" of public policy and administration. Legal realism argues that while higher moral laws and *a priori* metaphysical beliefs about law in relation to society are all important as democratic myths, these must be tempered by a realism that processes of administration must be utilitarian (that is, to bring the greatest happiness to the greatest number of citizens), instrumentalist and pragmatic. Constitutional metaphysics must always be tempered by such concepts as "social advance" and the "general welfare" of members of society. Scientific management and legal realists thus joined forces in the firm belief that utility, practicality, objectivity and empiricism are the hallmarks of administrative law.[27] This body of law would be more precise and realistic in prescribing standards of due process in administrative conduct. There is considerable irony in the fact that this legal realism would eventually spawn the many administrative boards and tribunals whose operations in developing public policy would eventually lead to the challenging of the "correctness" of the politics/administration dichotomy.

These four central assumptions indicate that most of the problems singled out by the proponents of scientific management were concerned with making clear the distinction between *ends* and *means*. The objectives of society should be correctly visualized as a political process to be arrived at by those who legitimately exercise the trappings of state power. Administration, on the other hand, *is* and *should be* concerned with translating into practice those political decisions in the most efficient, effective and utilitarian manner as possible. To have any extensive intermingling between the two is inefficient and unethical. The two processes logically are and should be quite distinct. Or so it seemed. The recognition that these two processes are not and cannot be totally distinct came to North American practitioners and students of public policy and administration slowly but surely over the last four decades.[28]

Thus we have come full circle in North America: from a blatant intermingling of politics and administration; to an insistence that politics and administration are distinct fields of activity; to a ready acceptance today of the intricate, complex relationships between the two spheres. An example of the latter fact can be seen in the growth of Canadian government which took place in the 1940s during the crisis period of World War II, and continued into the 1950s, as government expanded into many areas of the economy providing leadership and finances for large public expenditure projects. Leading Canadian politicians, academics and bureaucrats readily admitted in their speeches and writings the powerful influences of the bureaucrat in the policy-making process. An excellent example of this point is the extremely influential role played by Dr. W. A. MacIntosh in the preparation and marketing of perhaps the most important economic policy proposals ever to have been prepared and instituted in this country, the White Paper on Employment and Income of 1945.[29] By the 1960s the power of the bureaucracy and attempts to hold such power to public account became one of the central challenges to face contemporary public policy and administration.

But what can we glean from all this? If it is true that senior bureaucrats are "political administrators," "closet statesmen" or "permanent politicians" as some of the literature on this subject describes them, then does this mean that there is a complete fusion between the two roles—that politics is administration and administration is politics? Is the politics/administration dichotomy both in its descriptive and prescriptive forms irrelevant to today's complex systems of public policy and administration?

III. Is God Really Dead? Reflections On An Ongoing Debate*

The concept of pluralism appeared at the turn of this century to express the increasing recognition by social scientists of the multiplicity of social forces, especially groups, in a complex industrialized society.

*The Marxist contribution to the ongoing debate on the politics/administration dichotomy has not been prominent in the American literature on the subject. Accordingly I have omitted specific reference to the sparse Neo-Marxist literature pertinent to the subject so as to emphasize the essentially American character of the debate. Although the work of Professor C. B. Macpherson of Toronto is not concerned with bureaucracy per se, his analyses of the dialectic between values and ideas in western liberal democracies can be fruitfully joined with the central arguments of social scientists Lowi, Thompson, Wagner, Buchanan and others explored in this chapter. I must however, leave this for the reader to pursue. For a Canadian Neo-Marxist contribution in this area, see Reginald Whitaker, "Scientific Management Theory as Political Ideology," Studies in Political Economy: A Socialist Review, No. 2. Autumn 1979, pp. 75-108.

The public is conceived as individuals and groups with specific interests which they urge upon government. Generally speaking pluralists deny the validity of monistic sovereignty because they assert that government is only one of the associations which shape our lives and direct our movements.[30]

Pluralist thought can also be divided into two categories; *ethical* pluralism and *empirical* pluralism. David Easton explains:

> In contrast to ethical pluralism, which speculated on the variety of political systems that became possible once the moral value of group life was acknowledged, empirical pluralism is practically coterminous with the notion of process. It leads on the descriptive level to the recognition of the multiplicity of causes, especially of a group nature, that influence social policy.[31]

An emphasis on empirical pluralism leads to the "discovery" that the public makes its influence felt in various ways, but chief among the devices used to influence policy are political parties, elections, the communications media, legislative bodies, chief executives, and, most crucial of all, access to all of these by organized associations of interested citizens.

Empirical pluralism inevitably led to some concentration on how governments respond to pluralistic demands. In the early 1930s E. Pendleton Herring, one of the key figures in developing pluralist political science in America, argued that the United States Congress to an increasing extent had escaped the onus of directly settling group conflicts, placing upon the shoulders of the bureaucracy "the burden of reconciling group differences and making effective and workable the economic and social compromises arrived at through the legislative process."[32] Carrying his analysis one step further he noted that public servants "in building 'public' support for their agency sometimes create a political machine of their own; the bureau builds a place for itself in the community and makes demands on Congress in the name of the 'public welfare'."[33] There is in Herring's book, significantly entitled *Public Administration and the Public Interest*, a dawning recognition of the *administrative state*, a discovery that the bureaucracy is both instrumental to political ends and powerful in its own right by virtue of its strategic position in the policy process. How does a liberal democrat confront this uneasy reality? A contemporary of Herring, Fritz Morstein Marx attempts some reassurance as he contemplates "big government":

> . . . the new liberals' faith in "positive government" is a far cry from the earlier liberal ideal of government restricted to the role of "night watchman".

But if the new liberal cannot be expected to take kindly to a loaded phrase such as "welfare state", he has come to make his peace with the more neutral concept of the "administrative state", especially with its practical realities.[34]

But perhaps the clearest recognition of the administrative state came in two books a decade after Herrings' publication. Immediately after World War II, Paul H. Appleby, a distinguished journalist, senior Washington administrator and Dean of the Maxwell Graduate School of Citizenship and Public Affairs, Syracuse University, published a book entitled *Big Democracy* (1945), to be followed by another small treatise four years later entitled *Policy and Administration* (1949). In *Big Democracy* Appleby makes an eloquent plea for the administrative state:

We have big government and clearly we are going to have bigger government. But with what spirit will it be motivated? On what terms and by what technique can we develop the unity our complexity demands and do it in a way that will harmonize with our history of freedom and our ideals of individual worth? Our hopes for genuine progress lie largely in the answers to these questions.[35]

While *Big Democracy* was aimed at reconciling the necessities of big government with the values of democracy in an industrial civilization, in *Policy and Administration,* Appleby explores the empirical reality between policy and administration. Appleby became for American public policy and administration what Walter Bagehot had been to the study of British institutions in the 1860s. Interestingly enough both came from journalistic backgrounds and wrote their empirical discoveries in journalistic style. Both were committed liberals dedicated to the ideals of individual worth and fascinated with the process as to how governments really work to achieve this aim.

In Appleby's work *descriptive* and *prescriptive* theory were virtually synonymous. In *Policy and Administration* he argues that in the pluralistic democratic industrialized society, policy constituencies tend to be administrative ones. Administrative organizations and activities have appeared in response to public policy needs—needs which could not have been fulfilled through the more traditional constitutional organs of society. As a consequence administrative activities combine the older functions of legislation and adjudication because these functions are the essence of the policy-making process. Administrative power is therefore political power. Reality demands that this be recognized, that we bury the old policy/administration dichotomy "myth," and that we come to terms with big government.[36]

Paradoxically what is fascinating is a reading of his normative theory of democratic governance as opposed to his view of how things work in practice. *It is for all practical purposes the old politics/ administration dichotomy.* In his third book, *Morality and Administration in Democratic Government* (1952), Appleby begins with the concept of the public interest, just as the Progressives had done some seven decades earlier. How is the public interest to be conceptualized given this new reality of democratic and administrative pluralism? The public interest, he argues,

> . . . is related to concern with consequences of private-association actions beyond the confines of the association. It is also related to concerns wholly outside the private field such as political freedom, foreign policy, and national defense. These two kinds of interest are tempered and modified by a third—regard for private concerns. From this enumeration it should be clear that the public interest is never merely the sum of all private interests nor the sum remaining after cancelling out their various pluses and minuses. It is not wholly separate from private interests, and it derives from citizens with many private interests; but it is something distinctive that arises within, among, apart from, and above private interests, focusing in government some of the most elevated aspiration and deepest devotion of which human beings are capable.[37]

Appleby's main preoccupation is determining what effect administrative pluralism *should have* on institutional arrangements. He argues that politics and hierarchy force public servants to refer special and private interests to the higher and broader public interests referred to above.[38] Politics achieves this aim by forcing both political executives and legislators to pay full regard to the attention of the majority as expressed through the ballot box. Hierarchy achieves the public interest by demanding from senior public servants both the responsibility and the necessity of homogenizing and moralizing the special interests represented through the lower levels of the organization. "The responsibility downward," he argues "is for positive leadership, for stimulation, for support, for guidance, for morale, and for assumption of one's own higher responsibility outward and upward."[38] For liberal democracy to work this is a necessary outcome of the process.

Appleby's views are consistent with the theory of popular sovereignty. Now that the "eighth political process,"[39] namely administration, had been unmasked as essentially a political process one must therefore fully recognize and come to terms with the political nature of the senior public servant's responsibilities. Secondly, one must fit such responsibilities into the overall theory of popular sovereignty by making senior public servants and their subordinates openly accountable both through politics and hierarchy. Administration is not a headless fourth branch of government. Under the doctrine of popular sovereignty it is held accountable through the primacy of political control which resides ultimately in the people and it is subjected, like all other poltiical institutions, to a process of accountability:

> Public administration is policy making. If admission that this is true seems to exalt administration, it must be seen that the emphasis on politics subordinates the administrator, exalts the politicians, and thereby exalts the citizen. Public administration, is policy making. But it is not autonomous, exclusive or isolated policy-making. It is policy-making on a field where mighty forces contend, forces engendered in and by the society. It is policy-making subject to still other and various policy makers. Public administration is one of a number of basic political processes by which this people achieves and controls governance.[40]

In this normative theory, hierarchy joins politics in the structural constellation of political responsibility. Popular sovereignty is in no way compromised. All heterogenous claims on the system simply have to come to terms with the realistic democratic system of American politics.

It is worth emphasizing three aspects of this then "new" theory of administrative pluralism. First, we have already made the point but it is worth reiterating that the theory's normative component is essentially the same as the "old" policy-administration dichotomy's. Control over the bureaucracy is still forcefully reaffirmed in the language of popular sovereignty. The public interest is achieved through the primacy of politics and the accountable hierarchy in public organizations.

Second, administrative pluralism is a sophisticated attempt to come to grips with the advent and recognition of the administrative state. The theory asserts its belief in bureaucratic rationality and openly admits the reality of administrative power. It however proclaims its sensitivity to the threatening implications of this new Leviathan in the domain of human values. The paradox of the administrative state is confronted by the "remedies" of politics and hierarchy.

Our third point returns us to the earlier arguments made by Walter Bagehot and Graham Wallas. How does one capture the essence of continually changing relationships? Max Weber attempted to do so for bureaucracy with his ideal types. Can the same be said for administrative pluralism which attempts to incorporate both a descriptive and prescriptive explanation of the administrative state? Many answer with an emphatic no. *The point to all this is that administrative pluralism has in its turn fallen victim to precisely the same criticisms its advocates once made about the policy/administration dichotomy. Many strongly contend that its descriptive aspects simply do not fit the facts.* Big bureaucracy is not big democracy; it is often a Leviathan to be feared. Many scholars in public policy and administration have come to view hierarchy in the administrative state not as a friend but as an enemy to open democratic government. The American literature on public policy and administration abounds with debates on the undemocratic consequences of the administrative state. We find a plethora of explanations, antinorms and new or refurbished public philosophies surfacing to compete in the gallery of ideas. Most of these purport to explain the new reality and to provide a new system of norms to deal with the "pathologies" inherent in the administrative state. Thus the prescriptive ghost of the policy/administration dichotomy continues to haunt us.

To do full justice to this literature is both impossible and indeed undesirable. We can, however, point to some of the more recent threads of thought which cannot be separated from the ideas already surveyed. Four of these threads will be briefly examined:
 (i) the theories of public choice advocating jurisdictional fragmentation and polycentricity in organizational forms;
 (ii) the juridical democracy of Theodore Lowi;
 (iii) the "new" public administration which generally advocates the doctrine of social equity; and
 (iv) the pluralism of Victor Thompson which vigorously rejects the criticisms made about authority relationships within organizations but reaffirms the need for smaller and more temporary organizational forms (see Figure I for illustrative diagram).

Public choice scholars are inclined to be suspicious of the concept of the public interest. They prefer to assume or base their analysis on the self interest maximizing of any political participant, including bureaucrats. For them the central problem with public bureaucracy, which tends to cause mismanagement, is the noncompetitive status of most public organizations. The growth of bureaucratic power and inefficiency is equated with administrative irresponsibility. Thus the administrative state is seen as a logical consequence of the monopoly positions which public bureaucracies enjoy. To best illustrate this view we can briefly describe the arguments put forward by one of its most outstanding proponents in public policy and administration, Professor Vincent Ostrom. In his book *The Intellectual Crisis in American Public Administration*, Ostrom emphasizes three concerns. First he presents a theory of change in ideas. Loosely borrowing from Thomas S. Kuhn's *The Structure of Scientific Revolutions*, Ostrom maintains that the "essential characteristics of normal science" is a general accep-

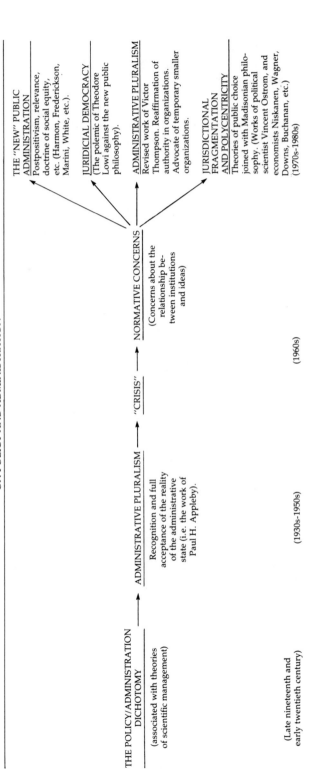

FIGURE I
DIAGRAM ILLUSTRATING THE ONGOING DEBATE
ON POLICY AND ADMINISTRATION

THE POLICY/ADMINISTRATION
DICHOTOMY

(associated with theories
of scientific management)

(Late nineteenth and
early twentieth century)

ADMINISTRATIVE PLURALISM

Recognition and full
acceptance of the reality
of the administrative
state (i.e. the work of
Paul H. Appleby).

(1930s-1950s)

"CRISIS"

(1960s)

NORMATIVE CONCERNS

(Concerns about the
relationship be-
tween institutions
and ideas)

THE "NEW" PUBLIC
ADMINISTRATION
Postpositivism, relevance,
doctrine of social equity,
etc. (Harmon, Frederickson,
Marini, White, etc.).

JURIDICIAL DEMOCRACY
(The polemic of Theodore
Lowi against the new public
philosophy).

ADMINISTRATIVE PLURALISM
Revised work of Victor
Thompson. Reaffirmation of
authority in organizations.
Advocate of temporary smaller
organizations.

JURISDICTIONAL
FRAGMENTATION
AND POLYCENTRICITY
Theories of public choice
joined with Madisonian philosophy. (Works of political
scientist Vincent Ostrom, and
economists Niskanen, Wagner,
Downs, Buchanan, etc.)
(1970s-1980s)

tance of a "basic theoretical paradigm or framework" amongst the community of scholars seeking enlightenment. This paradigm establishes certain important criteria:

The basic concepts establish the essential elements of analysis; and relational postulates and axioms specify the essential rules of reason. These rules of reason enable members of an intellectual community to pursue a structure of inferential reasoning where the work of one can be added to the work of others. Frontiers of knowledge can be extended with reference to the understanding shared by all members of the community.[41]

Ostrom then embarks on a highly *debatable* argument that American public administration is based on a paradigm derived from Woodrow Wilson's "invention" of the politics/administration dichotomy which emphasized perfection in the hierarchical ordering of sovereignty. According to Ostrom, this paradigm is created from the conjoining of the bureaucratic theories of Max Weber and Woodrow Wilson which "made an explicit paradigmatic choice in rejecting the political theory articulated by Hamilton and Madison in *The Federalist*."[42]

Secondly, Ostrom then emphasizes that the "crisis" in public policy and administration is created by a "recurrent problem in the history of scientific inquiry, "that is, the failure of an explanatory paradigm to account for "anomalies." Throughout the book Ostrom outlines this indictment. For example he argues that the dichotomy has no explanatory power in accounting for different forms of public organizations in differing political and social circumstances (p. v), and scientific management has failed to explain and to provide answers for the persistent failures of wartime control measures (p. 6). Ostrom's greatest salvos are reserved for the President's Committee on Administrative Management whose edicts represented the full embodiment of the politics/administration dichotomy. Luther Gulick's POSDCORB enunciated *the principle of unity of command*, a belief in the "iron law" of hierarchy.[43] Yet this principle directly contradicted another, namely the *principle of homogeneity* which led to different structural results. The result of course is "scientific confusion":

The principle of "a single structure of authority" (the principle of unity of command) had somehow dissolved into a "fabric of organizational interrelations" (the principle of homogeneity) with multiple networks of cross-departmentalization. The symmetry of a hierarchical pyramid was abandoned for the tangled lattice-work of a "jungle gym."[44]

Thirdly, Ostrom emphasizes the need for a new paradigm to permit renewed scientific progress. His solution is based on the tradition of democratic administration to be found in the writings of Alexis de Tocqueville and in the Federalist Papers and now being rejuvenated in the writings of public choice economists. Instead of the hierarchical ordering of the policy/administration dichotomy, public choice theory as applied by Ostrom emphasizes polycentricity and jurisdictional fragmentation. Its implications for public policy and administration are important but not always clear. Ostrom contends that administration should respond flexibly and willingly to the demands of all groups of citizens. Structure is irrelevant in this context since there should be as many shapes and sizes of administrative jurisdictions as there are publics. The key to democratic administration is political, in the sense that bargaining, cooperation and the veto power—all utilized according to the self interests of the various publics—would be arbitrated by a system of constitutional law. This descriptive and prescriptive amalgamation of public choice with "homegrown" American democratic theory is made explicit by Ostrom:

. . . a new theory of democratic administration will have to be fashioned from the works of Hamilton, Madison, Tocqueville, Dewey, Lindblom, Buchanan, Tullock, Olson, Niskanen, and many others. The theory of externalities, common properties, and public goods, the logic of collective action and public enterprise, the concepts of public-service industries, and fiscal federalism will have prominent places in that theory. Attention will shift from a preoccupation with the organization to concerns with the opportunities that individuals can pursue with the opportunities that individuals can pursue in a multi-organizational environment. Policy analysis will focus upon problems of institutional weakness and institutional failure inherent in any organizational structure or institutional arrangements. Policy recommendations will be presented with greater emphasis upon the opportunity costs inherent in different organizational arrangements.[45]

A second perspective which, like Ostrom, views constitutional law as an important element of its theorizing, but derives its critique of American society from altogether different premises, is to be found in the work of Professor Theodore Lowi. At the very beginning of his work Lowi spells out the urgent concerns which lie behind his enquiry into *The End of Liberalism: Ideology, Policy and the Crisis of Public Authority*:

The crisis [of our times] is at bottom a political crisis, a crisis of public authority. During the Depression, stability was regained after a spectacular but unrevolutionary turn to government. Confidence was restored long before economic conditions had returned to normal. But today government itself is the problem. Public morality has become involved. The institutions of the

State have become implicated. There is serious doubt about efficacy and justice in the agencies of government, the processes of policy making, leadership selection, and the implementation of decisions. The crisis deepens because its nature has not been discovered as yet.[46]

What then is the deep-rooted nature of the problem? According to Lowi capitalism has both shaped our institutions and given us a perspective of the world. Capitalist ideology, based as it is on the notions of a self-regulating market system, could not account for the mechanisms of adjustment made necessary by urbanization and industrialization:

Society did in fact adjust, but it did not do so in patterns remotely explicable in terms of self-regulating mechanisms. Quite the contrary; modern industrialized societies can be explained as an effort to make the "invisible hand" as visible as possible.[47]

The "visible hand" in this effort turns out to be "a trait essential to market economies—rationality," that is "differentation, which is simply rationality in the organization of conduct."[48] Thus the administrative state is born.

Capitalist ideology was also being transformed. The realistic doctrine of pluralism asserts the group fact of life in America. Government is transformed from the conception of an economic regulator to that of an initiator of social and economic activities. Thus emerges what Lowi calls "the new public philosophy" that is, an amalgam of the old capitalist ideology and pluralism commonly known as interest-group liberalism. *The administrative state comes into being because what has resulted is unlimited expansion of governmental activities and power due to market failure while at the same time we continue to see government as the handmaiden of society.* The bureaucracy is at once transformed into both faithful servant and indispensable ally in keeping the system afloat. Furthermore we have complicated the servile image by bureaucracy's allowing groups "a piece of the action" that is, by "parcelling out to private parties the power to make public policy."[49] We therefore face a crisis because a discussion of ends has been sublimated while we concentrate on means, that is, the process of bargaining among groups has become an end in itself. The interest-group process has been transformed into *our* government, *our* political process and even *our* state. This is the new American public policy, a conception which, in Lowi's view, denies legitimacy to formal institutions of popular control. The policy process has not become a free-for-all: every group becomes politically legitimate once it gains access to or is organized into the political process. "Interest group liberalism seeks pluralistic government, in which there is no formal specification of means or of ends. In pluralistic government there is therefore no substance. Neither is there procedure. There is only process."[50]

Lowi does not deny the reality of pluralism. The system in his view is simply not working in a just manner, for American ideology has abdicated politics and is now solely concerned with group activities. What is required, he concludes, is Juridical Democracy—a restoration of the rule of law; a return to administrative formality and a drastic reduction of the powers of the administrative state (i.e. discretion); restoration of the virtues of state government; the proper use and development of a senior bureaucratic elite; and the imposition of better fiscal policy as an instrument of central control. Lowi's work is in the true tradition of an academic polemic. Implicit in his argument is the view that the administrative state has, to return to an old analogy of Dwight Waldo's, become a rogue elephant. Curiously enough, what he calls for is a return to the old virtues implicit in the policy/administration dichotomy: cut the administrative state down to size by severely proscibing its discretionary powers and returning it to its largely servile role.

This is definitely not the position taken by those who share the perspective known as the "New Public Administration," a group hatched in the late 1960s. They would agree enthusiastically to reduce the powers of the administrative state; but not in the manner advocated by Lowi. Lowi's solution in their view would only serve to reinforce the values and practices inherent in the policy/administration dichotomy. As Robert Miewald has noted, those who share this perspective have felt that they inherited a barren intellectual legacy which can only be discarded by taking "the most drastic way to resolve the politics/administration problem: forget about the niceties of theory, which can only induce a debilitating sense of vertigo, and advise administrators to do whatever they feel is best—so long as it is "right." It is an impossibly dangerous approach, but one which indicates the frustration felt by younger scholars who cannot bear to be part of a perpetuation of an irrational rationality."[51]

This statement illustrates the difficulty of categorizing the "New Public Administration" as a group of people sharing an agreed-upon perspective. However this amorphous grouping includes a wide variety of interpretations of what is going on in the social sciences and how that applies to public policy and administration. We devote a little more attention to them here for despite their diffuse philosophy the "new" Public Administration has definitely affected the social movements in America calling for quota systems of minority representation and citizen participation in government. To illustrate what they represent, it is helpful to critically look at the "birth" of the perspective which took place at Minnowbrook, New York, in the late 1960s. The mood and statements of the Minnowbrook conference have been built upon in four major publications, and although we cannot summarize it all in a few paragraphs, the first publication, *Toward a New Public Administration* still stands as a good representation of the nature of the politics/administration dichotomy from this new perspective.[52]

It is important not to portray the Minnowbrook Conference as some sort of vast watershed for the study and practice of public policy and administration.[53] Yet Minnowbrook represented a prevailing mood about public policy and administration prevalent amongst a broader cross section of young people in North America and Western Europe at that time, and it is extremely important to place it in that context. It reflected a feeling that social decision-making had gone awry in both its *style* and its *relevance* to the problems of the latter part of the twentieth century. And the problems then, as many are still now, monumental: growing racial and economic inequalities in the richest areas of the globe, pollution on a scale which posed a threat to the existence of humanity, the proliferation of nuclear weapons and at the time a very unpopular war in Vietnam. Furthermore, bureaucracies purportedly in the form of the "military-industrial complex," a phrase made famous by a military hero and President of the United States, Dwight Eisenhower, had spawned and masterminded many of these problems. *What was disturbing to many was the reality of the administrative state:* bureaucrats were running the war in Vietnam, and the feeling, particularly amongst the young of America, was one of despondency. The slogan of American student revolutionaries sums up this frustration: "It is time to put our bodies on the machine and stop it."

Placed in perspective the Minnowbrook mood therefore represented something significant. This is the reason why some Canadian scholars saw it as "an important element of intellectual ferment . . . surrounding the reassessment of the theory, practice and teaching of public administration 'in a time of turbulence' . . ."[54] or holding ". . . considerable promise as a force for a new direction in the field."[55] The philosophy of the "new Public Administration" said something about administrative pluralism and its consequences, and could therefore be appropriately located within the context of the ongoing debate on the subject.

Reading and reflecting on Minnowbrook gives one a sense of the urgency of the times: the conference atmosphere seems to have been a close replica of the wider environment of "blooming buzzing confusion" and confrontation found in the cities of America and Europe that hot summer of 1968. From the very beginning it became an intellectual donnybrook at Minnowbrook as the participants signalled their commitment to confrontation by openly challenging the leadership of the conference itself. As Frank Marini, the informal chairman of the organizing committee of the conference puts it, "intense hours of discussion" were spent debating the very purpose of the meeting:

> . . . and the dynamics of the discussion became familiar to all: Why did we have to have formal papers? If we were really the young and the new, why were we so bound by the traditional in our conference arrangements? Who chose the topics? Weren't there more important topics? Shouldn't we break down into small groups?[56]

Given this state of anarchy, this rebellion against organization both inside and outside the conference, an effort to summarize or simplify the "new perspectives" is certain to be inadequate and even in some measure distorted. A basic theme, however, comes readily to mind as one surveys the problems and concerns voiced: responsibility in policy and administration is the key to unlocking the door for the *summum bonum*, the supreme good of democratic politics, namely, responsiveness to societal demands. And this responsiveness can only be realized in two ways: the recovery of *relevance* in the study of public policy and administration, and a critical examination and a call for new directions in *the style* in which it is practised.

In a critical analysis it is easy to fault anyone on the questions of normative criteria. Like the concept of the public interest, or the politics/administration dichotomy, the "new" Public Administration normative concerns were couched in symbolic language, a way of talking of human relationships. The primary normative premises of public policy and administration were expressed as "the purpose of public organization is the reduction of economic, social and psychic suffering and the enhancement of life opportunities for those inside and outside the organization"[57] or "simply put, new Public Administration seeks to change those policies and structures that systematically inhibit social equity."[58] A few attempts were made to operationalize these normative goals (the "politics of contract" versus the "politics of love")[59] but, such strivings hardly represented convincing efforts to the knowledgeable reader.

However, what was a disturbing element of this movement was the general propensity, displayed both at the conference and in scattered essays in public administration journals and books, to debunk previous knowledge and experience in the field. For example, in the area germane to our immediate concern, one proponent of the "new" public administration argued that previous discussions on the nature of the policy/administration dichotomy exhibited, "a fundamental negative stance on the nature of man in general and of public administrators in particular." Both viewpoints should be rejected for the new "humanistic and existential psychology" which stress "self-development" and "self-actualization."[60]

This type of rhetoric led one enthusiastic reformer to exclaim that "it appears that [the] new Public Administration is an alignment with good, or possibly God."[61] The general rhetoric seemed to lead to an unequivocal desire by the reformers to reject the past and start afresh under a new system of normative values—their own. Politicians who were largely to blame for the existing state of affairs were the ungodly sinners, while the reformers were to be found squarely on the side of the saints. This brings to mind a remark once made by York Willbern that the world was full of saints, each of whom knew the way to salvation, and the role of the politician was that of the sinner who stood at the crossroads to keep saint from cutting the throat of saint.

This "new" social gospel placed a tremendous amount of faith in humanity and administrative discretion. *By implication, the administrative state is the new utopia: in recent years it has been misdirected by those who stand to gain from its stagnation. More administrative discretion must be joined with less hierarchy, authority, and more decentralization.* The "new Public Administration" called for extensive refurbishing of the administrative state: first, reorganization to achieve the just-mentioned goals, and second, the application of the same general principles to the purposes and activities of bureaucracy in order to redress social misery and to improve the human condition. How precisely is this to be achieved? There are some tentative suggestions about "participation," "client-focus" agencies, "advocacy planning," "neighborhood initiative," "adaptive administration" and so on but nothing very concrete was proffered at that time. By implication there is a proctored withering away of the administrative state by extensive reorganization.[62] Again it is crucial to stress the American nature of this debate. The politician is seen by the advocates of the "new Public Administration" as just one of many pillars in the edifice of popular sovereignty. To them, it is not inconsistent with the doctrine of popular sovereignty to accord the bureaucrat—the "real" decision-maker in the administrative state—his rightful inheritance to make decisions and to accept full responsibility for so doing. We need not emphasize the fact that this assumption which bypasses the politician could hardly be seriously entertained by public administrators bred in the parliamentary tradition. The major thought the reader obtains from this philosophy is that Max Weber, Woodrow Wilson, Luther Gulick and others of like persuasion must be rejected, and the administrator is now to have a moral imperative to rid society of alienation and other ills through style and process of administration. However, for one participant who all along doubted the efficacy of solutions calling for more administrative discretion, and who thus preferred to remain amongst the sinners, the experience may still be of some value and consequence:

Insofar as Minnowbrook did not prescribe a rigid or logically consistent code of behaviour, but was merely a "perspective" involving predispositions toward greater administrative freedoms in policy formulation and implementation with certain values featured in rendering service to the public, then it may survive the intemperate and imprecise nature of its birth in upstate New York. If it does survive, then we should hope along with one of its advocates that it fosters a politics of love and not a politics of suppression. [63]

Finally we come to the "hard line" viewpoint on the subject posited by the organizational theorist, Victor Thompson. At the very beginning of his analysis, Thompson confronts the reality of the administrative state:

Rightly or wrongly, industrial societies increasingly channel the energies of their members through the large, purposive, rationalized organization that we have come to call bureaucracies. Not only productive or economic energies but much expressive energy is likewise so channeled . . . For many students, modernity is equated with organizations. Modern society has been called the "organizational society," modern man the "organizational man." [64]

Thompson makes his point clearly and concisely: *modern organizations are, above everything else, instruments of control.* Public "organizational tools," as he calls them, are designed to achieve the preference ordering of the owner, namely the sovereign people. To achieve their goals these "tools" hire "functionaries" who perform their duties in exchange for payment. "A screwdriver does not choose among goals or among owners," Thompson asserts, "It does what it is 'told'." [65] In this scheme of things it is irrelevant to see organizational compassion as a critical issue: ". . . in the likely case of conflict between goal and compassion, only one choice is possible; compassion must go unless it indeed is the goal." [66]

With relentless logic Thompson examines the different alternatives proposed to alleviate non-compassionate administration. He finds that such remedies as sensitivity training, organizational development programs, the ombudsman, areal administration and neighbourhood control are all palliatives lacking any real substance to mitigate the "pathologies"of administration. Thompson is least compassionate to the New Public Administration. He construes their effort as "a brazen attempt to 'steal' the public sovereignty." Stripping the philosophy of the New Public Administration down to a few paragraphs in his book, Thompson dismisses it all as "political absurdity and immaturity." The doctrine of social equity is construed as the most fundamental aim of this "new" philosophy: administration, through such devices as representative bureaucracy, is aimed at solving the problems of poverty and racial or ethnic prejudice. Thompson is unconvinced that this is any solution:

Compassionate treatment of the poor and downtrodden is often a kind of hoax whose principal function, really, is to reduce the neurotic sense of guilt in the "more fortunate" person. What is often needed by the "less fortunate" person is a painfully enforced readjustment and reformation of a failing personality and life style (e.g. psychiatric treatment, formal schooling) that will enable him to stand on his own feet.[67]

To Thompson, moral absolutism is definitely not the answer and in his final chapter, after he dismisses the new Public Administration, he turns to some solutions. First he makes an eloquent plea for the nature of present-day organizations:

To the extent that many people suffer either "in" our modern organizations or in dealing with them as clients, consumers, etc., we have a gap between the socialization of the individual and the technology of organization design—between the person and the institution. I feel rather strongly that this gap will be narrowed, if at all, not by gimmicks of the kind discussed in preceding chapters but by further evolution of the socialization process and further development of organization design—by evolving personalities and organization structures. The truly determining elements of the problem are changing families, socialization practices, motivations, personal orientations, and work, and the growing importance of creativity relative to productivity.[68]

New organizational designs should be characterized by bargaining and compromise among contending groups. Thompson is a firm believer in the pluralistic nature of society and he contrasts it continuously with the doctrine of social equity:

The old liberal pluralistic politics, with its interest associations, based so largely on the variable criterion of occupational interests, was a politics of achievement. People earned (or "slugged") their way to the top. The new "politics of love" is largely a politics of ascription. Demands issue from who you are, not from what you have achieved. The criteria for selection to the Democratic National Convention were mostly ascriptive: age, sex and race. Joe Smith helps select a presidential candidate because he is eighteen, not because he has earned the right to so do.[69]

In complex societies people tend to find their own niches by drifting towards reference groups they choose and interest associations they develop. Society in the end is like a free market place of preferences: in industrial societies achieved statuses and associations are much more important than ascribed or artificially contrived ones. This natural pluralistic grouping should be complemented by more organizational creativity (smaller organizations, task-force type structures) and an emphasis on such criteria as peer evaluation and more diffusion of norms of responsibility.

This book's conservative character inevitably creates intellectual controversy in public policy and administration. Thompson's relentless logic has placed him squarely on the side of organizational rationality and technology. If society desires organization because of its bountiful fruits in a complex environment, then society must come to terms with those fears associated with the Leviathan structure. Implicit here is the acceptance of the administrative state and a denial that we really need a new prescriptive theory to reaffirm humanity's mastery of the Leviathan. We already have it. Bureaucracy remains *our instrument* and we must come to terms, in a practical way, with what that machine demands of us in return. "Modern man needs to learn to be comfortable with impersonality," Thompson argues. "All this amounts to is giving a high value to instrumentalism, to the achievement of established goals."[70] The administrative state is therefore our own reality. Nothing stands in our way in reaffirming our mastery over machines. Thus the debate on the nature of administrative power continues, always returning to familiar normative overtones.

Conclusions

Has the ghost of the policy/administration dichotomy been laid to rest? About one hundred years ago it approximated both a philosophy of administration and a description of reality. It is fair to say that the description of reality was perhaps only realistic for a short time. Max Weber saw very clearly at the turn of this century that when rationality is applied to social relations, legal-rational bureaucracy is born. In his prophetic view Western society had given birth to an instrument which is at once servile and powerful, namely, the administrative state.

The policy/administration dichotomy embodied a philosophy of administration which aimed to keep rational bureaucracy servile. Half a century after it was first enunciated Appleby thought that he demolished the dichotomy, but what he really accomplished was to show that many aspects of its description of reality were no longer true. He demonstrated most convincingly that policy and administration are parts of a seamless web, and that administrative power is part of political power and part of our continuing collective ambivalence about power. But in the end his normative model of democratic governance was not different from the policy/administration dichotomy.

Today, the descriptive reality of administrative pluralism is under attack. We have presented four different perspectives of this debate. It is interesting to summarize their normative premises. Ostrom and the public choice theorists believe that too much bureaucratic monopoly (i.e. power) is at the root of our problems. We would do well to disperse it to ensure its efficiency and servility in "the public interest." Lowi would strip the administrative state of all discretionary (i.e. arbitrary) powers and subject it to the Rule of Law and ultimately the public interest. Boiled down to its essentials, the "new Public Administration" advocates the need for more servility in the bureaucracy. The doctrine of social equity is seen as a tool to ensure public awareness and sensitivity. Finally the refurbished pluralism of Victor Thompson is advocating the same ultimate goal of servility for public organizations. As he puts it: "In public organizations we often use the term "servant" instead of or in addition to "functionary." The owner of the public organization in the modern period is, of course, "the people" (it used to be a feudal king)."[71] All agree with the prescriptive aspects of the policy/administration dichotomy: *bureaucracy should be instrument and Caliban to its "rightful owner," the public despite its accretion of power. What they all essentially disagree on is the way this can be achieved.* With the exception of Victor Thompson's, the other perspectives are ambivalent about technology, one of the chief benefits of the administrative state. They all want its fruits (or at least some of it), but they reject the hierarchical ordering, the specialization, and the division-of-labor features of modern bureaucratic organizations.

So the prescriptive aspects of the policy/administration dichotomy are not dead. As we have already argued in Chapter Three, these aspects continue to condition the behavior of actors in the system. All view it as a normative goal to keep bureaucracy subservient to the "public interest." The beginning of wisdom in public policy and administration therefore lies in recognizing the continuing central importance of the debate inherent in the dichotomy. It was a philosophy which embodied the concept of rationality in organizations and much was done in its name: the introduction of the merit principle and the merit system and the legitimation of efficiency methods in public organizations.

If our standards of judgement are comparative, historical and realistic, we would recognize the fact that the dichotomy formed an accepted political/moral tradition in societies experiencing changes in institutional development and this fusion worked. It still lives on largely in its prescriptive aspects. Gordon Robertson's comment in the epigram of this chapter is therefore fundamentally true: the distinction is "clear" and "helpful" in understanding the still viable norms of our society, but it does not embrace reality in any total sense.

The dichotomy remains a powerful philosophy which, like Banquo's ghost, refuses to be banished, reappearing often in the guise of accountability. It has guided, and will continue to guide, many aspects of the actions and perceptions of politicians, public servants and the public, both in the United States and in Canada. If it is not yet apparent, the student will soon realize that the policy/administration dichotomy has a profound influence on just about every aspect of theory and practice in public policy and administration. The prescriptive liberal-democratic ideal which Woodrow Wilson enunciated close to a hundred years ago still remains central to our continuing debate on policy and administration:

The ideal for us is a civil service cultured and self-sufficient enough to act with sense and vigour, and yet so intimately connected with the popular thought, by means of elections and constant public counsel, as to find arbitrariness or class spirit out of the question. [72]

The Policy/Administration Dichotomy Revisited

Modern social science behavioralism had made fun of the policy-administration dichotomy because of the undeniable fact that administrators always incorporate values into their decisions different from or in addition to those laid down by the legislature and the chief executive. . . . However, pooh-poohing the politics-administration separation doctrine misses the point in a typically behavioral way. *The doctrine is a normative one, not a behavioral description.* To have democracy, and efficient and democratic administration, it is necessary to keep politics out of administration as much as possible—that is what the doctrine says.

Victor A. Thompson.

Footnotes

1. In this book the "policy/administration dichotomy" and the "politics/administration dichotomy" are used interchangeably. The former tends to be preferred by English authors while the latter is more prevalent in North American writings on the subject. They both mean the same thing.

2. The literature documenting this fact is rich and highly suggestive. We cite only a few examples:
   (i) Earnest Barker, *The Development of Public Services in Western Europe: 1660-1930.* (Oxford: Oxford University Press, 1945).
   (ii) Arnold Brecht, "How Bureaucracies Develop and Function," *Annals of the American Academy of Political and Social Science,* 292 (1954): 1-10.
   (iii) S.B. Chrimes, *An Introduction to the Administrative History of Medieval England.* (Oxford: B. Blackwell, 1959).
   (iv) S.N. Eisenstadt, "Bureaucracy and Political Development," in Joseph La Palombara (ed.) *Bureaucracy and Political Development.* (Princeton: Princeton University Press, 1963).
   (v) J.O. Lindsay, "Monarch and Administration: European Practice," *The New Cambridge Modern History* VII (1966): 141-160.

3. The late President of Ghana, Dr. Kwame Nkrumah had a catchy aphorism in his retort to those who argued that his nation building efforts should concentrate more on bureaucratic methods of modernization: "Seek ye first the political kingdom and all other things will be added unto you."

4. A.H. Birch, *Representative and Responsible Government: An Essay on the British Constitution* (Toronto: University of Toronto Press, 1964).

5. Peter Savage, "Dismantling the Administrative State: Paradigm Reformulation in Public Administration," *Political Studies,* Vol. XXII, No. 2 (147-157) at p. 149.

6. Grant McConnell, *Private Power and American Democracy* (New York: Alfred A. Knopf, 1966), p. 157.

7. W.L. Morton, *The Canadian Identity,* second edition. (Toronto: University of Toronto Press, 1972), p. 110.

8. W. Bagehot, *The English Constitution* (London: Cox and Wyman Ltd., 1963), p. 267.

9. Graham Wallas, *Human Nature in Politics,* third Edition (London: Constable and Co. Ltd., 1920), p. 15.

10. T.M. Denton, "Ministerial Responsibility: A Contemporary Perspective," in R. Schultz, Orest M. Kruhlak and John C. Terry (eds.), *The Canadian Political Process* Third Edition, (Toronto: Holt, Rinehart and Winston of Canada Ltd., 1979), p. 345.

11. Colin Campbell and George J. Szablowski, *The Super Bureaucrats: Structure and Behaviour in Central Agencies.* p. 241.

12. Schmuel N. Eisenstadt, "Institutionalization and Change," *American Sociological Review*, 29 (April 1964), pp. 49-59.

13. Paul P. Van Riper, *The History of the United States Civil Service* (New York: Harper and Row, 1958); L.D. White, *Introduction to the Study of Public Administration* Fourth Edition (New York: Crowell, Collier and Macmillan, 1965), p. 311 ff.

14. Woodrow Wilson, "The Study of Administration," *Political Science Quarterly*, Vol. II, No. 2, (June, 1887), p. 197-222. Reprinted in the same journal in Vol. LVI, (December, 1941), pp. 481-506, pp. 494-5.

15. Wilson *Ibid.*, pp. 494-5. There has been considerable controversy in the American literature about the importance of Wilson's contribution to this debate. The topic could be most fruitfully explored by any undergraduate student of public administration with an historical bent. Beginning with the original essay students will find additional information in the following publications:
    (i) Dwight Waldo, *The Administrative State: A Study of the Political Theory of American Public Administration*, (New York: The Ronald Press Co., 1948).
    (ii) W.J.M. Mackenzie, *Politics and Social Science*, (Middlesex, England: Penguin, 1967).
    (iii) M.E. Dimock, *The Philosophy of Administration* (New York: Harper and Row, 1958).
    (iv) Frederick C. Mosher, *Democracy and the Public Service*, (New York: Oxford University Press, 1968).
    (v) Fred W. Riggs, "Relearning Old Lessons: The Political Context of Development Administration," *Public Administration Review*, 25 (March, 1965).
    (vi) Richard J. Stillman, II, "Woodrow Wilson and the Study of Administration: A New Look at an Old Essay," *American Political Science Review*, Vol. 67 (June, 1973), pp. 582-88.

    All of these sources give different interpretations or varying interpretations of Wilson's contributions.

16. For one of the best critical discussions of the theory of scientific management see James G. March and H.A. Simon, *Organizations*. (New York: Wiley), 1958, pp. 12-22.

17. Sir Henry Bunbury, "Efficiency as an Alternative to Control," *Public Administration*, (London) Vol. VI, 1928, pp. 96-105.

18. Griffenhagen and Associates, "Report: Opportunities for Effecting Economies and Bettering Service in the Dominion Government Administration," April 28, 1920 Part I, p. 8. Borden Papers, vol. 265, 148990.

19. *Ibid.*,

20. For the most complete detailing of this historical event in Canadian public policy and administration see J.E. Hodgetts, William McCloskey, Reginald Whitaker and V. Seymour Wilson, *The Biography of an Institution: The Civil Service Commission of Canada, 1908-1967*. Montreal: McGill-Queen's University Press, 1972) especially Chapters 3 and 4.

21. Dwight Waldo, *The Administrative State,* especially ch. 4.

22. V. Seymour Wilson, "The Relationship between Scientific Management and Personnel Policy in North American Administrative Systems," *Public Administration* (London) Summer 1973, pp. 193-205.

23. A good example of the enduring influence of this classification can be found in J.E. Hodgetts, *The Canadian Public Service: A Physiology of Government 1867-1970* (Toronto: University of Toronto Press, 1973).

24. Mabel Walker, *Municipal Expenditures* (Baltimore: Johns Hopkins University Press, 1930), p. 47. © 1930 John Hopkins University Press.

25. Norman Ward, *The Public Purse: A Study in Canadian Democracy.* (Toronto: University of Toronto Press, 1951).

26. More accurately, since the 1930s the parliamentary control philosophy has been increasingly meshed with the internal administrative needs of planning and control. See J.E. Hodgetts et al., *The Biography of an Institution,* pp. 138-158.

27. One of the strongest advocates of legal realism in the United States was Mr. Justice Felix Frankfurter of the U.S. Supreme Court. See his *The Public and Its Government,* (New Haven: Yale University Press, 1930). Legal realists such as the late Professor A.J. Abel of Toronto and Chief Justice Bora Laskin of the Canadian Supreme Court have argued eloquently for such legal reforms as administrative tribunals and boards. For some further background reading on the legal realism tradition see the following:
    (i) Dwight Waldo, "Government by Procedure," in Fritz Morstein Marx (ed.), *Elements of Public Administration* (second edition) Englewood Cliffs, N.J.: Prentice-Hall, 1959.
    (ii) Robert H. Jackson, "The Administrative Process," in *Journal of Social Philosophy* 5 (January, 1940), pp. 143-149.
    (iii) John Dickenson, *Administrative Justice and the Supremacy of the Law in the United States.* (Cambridge, 1927).
    (iv) F.F. Blachly and M.E. Oatman, "Salvage of the Administrative Process," *Public Administration Review,* Vol. 6 (Summer 1946), pp. 213-227.

28. Paul H. Appleby, *Big Democracy,* (New York: Alfred A. Knoft, 1949),
    _____, *Policy and Administration* (Alabama: University of Alabama Press, 1949),
    V.O. Key, Jr., "Politics and Administration," Chapter VIII, *The Future of Government in the United States: Essays in Honour of Charles E. Merriam,* Leonard D. White (ed.), (Chicago, Illinois: University of Chicago Press, 1942).
    One year after the publication of *Big Democracy* another work with the same normative orientation was published. Charles S. Hyneman's *Bureaucracy in a Democracy* (New York: Harper and Brothers, 1950) is a much more formidable academic treatise than Appleby's but it is very long and detailed both in its theoretical and descriptive analyses. Part I is the most interesting section of the book. For two good reviews of Hyneman's study see J.R. Mallory, "The Rehabilitation of the Politician" *CJEPS* vol. xvii, no. 1, February 1951, pp. 93-97, and K.C. Wheare, "Bureaucracy in a Democracy," *Public Administration* (London) vol. xxix, Summer 1951, pp. 144-150. Wheare is particularly insightful in his remarks on American popular sover-

eignty as opposed to English parliamentary or legal sovereignty. As he puts it: "Nowhere does the deep and essential and far-reaching difference between the British and American governments . . . display itself so strikingly as in Professor Hyneman's exposition of his view of Congress's place in the direction and control of bureaucracy." (p. 150).

29. As Canadian examples the following is illustrative:
  (i) Dr. W.A. Mackintosh, "The White Paper on Employment and Income in its 1945 Setting," especially pp. 15-19 in *Canadian Trade Committee, Canadian Economic Policy Since The War* (A series of six public lectures in commemoration of the twentieth anniversary of the White Paper on Employment and Income of 1945), September-November, 1965.
  (ii) The Hon. Mitchell Sharp, "The Bureaucratic Elite and Policy Formation," in W.D.K. Kernaghan (ed.), *Bureaucracy in Canadian Government* (Toronto: Methuen, 1973). See also Mitchell Sharp, "Mitchell Sharp's Civil Service Recollections," *The Ottawa Journal*, December 12-13, 1958.
  (iii) The Hon. Paul Hellyer, "How They Killed Public Land Banking: A Political Memoir," *City Magazine*, Vol. 3, December, 1973, pp. 31-38.
  (iv) R. Gordon Robertson, "The Coming Crisis in the North," *Journal of Canadian Studies*, February, 1967.
  (v) John Meisel, *The Canadian General Election of 1957*, (Toronto: University of Toronto Press, 1962).
  (vi) R. MacGregor Dawson, "The Cabinet Minister and Administration", *Canadian Journal of Economic and Political Science*, Vol. IX, No. 3, February, 1943, pp. 1-38.

30. James C. Charlesworth, "Identifiable Approaches to the Study of Politics and Government", in James C. Charlesworth (ed.), *Contemporary Political Analysis* (New York: The Free Press, 1967), p. 9.

31. David Easton, *The Political System: An Inquiry into the State of Political Science* (New York: Alfred A. Knoft, 1965), p. 269.

32. E. Pendleton Herring, *Public Administration and the Public Interest* (New York: McGraw-Hill, 1936), p. 7.

33. *Ibid.*, p. 25.

34. Fritz Morstein Marx, *The Administrative State: An Introduction to Bureaucracy* (Chicago: The University of Chicago Press, 1957), p. 2. Reprinted from *The Administrative State: An Introduction to Bureaucracy* by Fritz Morstein Marx, by permission of The University of Chicago Press. © 1957. The University of Chicago Press. Marx's attempt to "neutralize" the term is not particularly helpful. He impresses the reader with size and efficiency considerations, but the obvious implications this has for the theory of democratic governance is not even discussed in the book.

35. Paul H. Appleby, *Big Democracy* (New York: Alfred A. Knopf Inc., 1949), p. 27.

36. _____, *Policy and Administration* (Alabama: University of Alabama Press, 1949).

37. _____, *Morality and Administration in Democratic Government* (Baton Rouge: Louisiana State University Press, 1952), p. 35.

38. *Ibid.*, pp. 219-258 at p. 235.

39. These were, according to Appleby, the following: "the presidential nominating process, the general nominating process, the party maintenance and operation process, the "agitational" process, and "the administrative or executive process involving everything done by agencies other than the legislative and judicial ones."

40. Paul H. Appleby, *Policy and Administration*, pp. 169-170.

41. Vincent Ostrom, *The Intellectual Crisis in American Public Administration* (Alabama: The University of Alabama, 1973), p. 13. Reprinted by permission of The University of Alabama Press.

42. *Ibid.*, p. 99.

43. See Chapters Five and Nine for a discussion of POSDCORB.

44. *Ibid.*, p. 39.

45. *Ibid.*, p. 132. A concise and very handy discussion of the utility of public choice in the study of public policy and administration is found in Vincent Ostrom and Elinor Ostrom, "Public Choice: A Different Approach to the Study of Public Administration," *Public Administration Review*, Vol. 31, March/April 1971, pp. 203-216.

46. Theodore J. Lowi, *The End of Liberalism* (New York: W.W. Norton and Co., Inc., 1969), p. xiii.

47. *Ibid.*, p. 19.

48. *Ibid.*, p. 20.

49. *Ibid.*, p. 58.

50. *Ibid.*, p. 97.

51. Robert D. Miewald, *Public Administration: A Critical Perspective* (New York: McGraw-Hill Co., 1978), p. 32.

52. The four publications are Frank Marini (ed.) *Toward a New Public Administration* (Scranton, Pa.: Chandler, 1971); Dwight Waldo (ed.), *Public Administration in a Time of Turbulence* (Scranton: Chandler Press, 1971); *Public Management* Vol. 53, No. 7, July 1971; *Public Administration Review* Vol. 34 (January/February), 1974, pp. 1-51.

53. See F. Marini's comments "The Minnowbrook Perspective and the Future of Public Administration Education," in F. Marini (ed.), *ibid.*, especially p. 367.

54. Kenneth Kernaghan, "Responsible public bureaucracy: a rationale and a framework for analysis," *Canadian Public Administration* 16:4 (Winter, 1973): 572-603 at p. 578.

55. A. Paul Pross, "Review Article: Public Administration texts: synthesizing, packaging and groping forward," *CPA* (Fall 1978): 450-451.

56. Marini (ed.), *Toward a New Public Administration*, p. 4.

57. Todd R. LaPorte, "The Recovery of Relevance in the Study of Public Organization," in Frank Marini (ed.), *Toward a New Public Administration*, p. 32.

58. H. George Frederickson, "Toward a New Public Administration," in F. Marini (ed.), *ibid.*, p. 312.

59. Orion F. White, Jr., "Social Change and Administration Adaptation," in F. Marini (ed.), *ibid.*, pp. 59-83.

60. Michael M. Harmon, "Normative Theory and Public Administration: Some Suggestions for a Redefinition of Administrative Responsibility," in F. Marini (ed.), *ibid.*, pp. 172-185.

61. Frederickson, "Toward a New Public Administration," in F. Marini (ed.), *ibid.*, p. 329.

62. Peter Savage, "Dismantling the Administrative State," *op. cit.*, p. 153. Another scholar in the New Public Administration movement summed this up rather well when he argued that "the faults in American society lie not with liberal values . . . but with political actions taken, or not taken, in the name of such values." See Richard S. Page, "The Ideological-Philosophical Setting of American Public Administration," in Dwight Waldo (ed.), *Public Administration in a Time of Turbulence* (New York: Chandler Publishing, 1971), p. 67.

63. Ira Sharkansky, "The 'New Public Administration" (Circa 1968): Minnowbrook Revisited," *Res Publica*, vol. 16, no. 2, 1974, pp. 221-232 at pp. 231-232.

64. Victor A. Thompson, *Without Sympathy or Enthusiasm: The Problem of Administrative Compassion* (Alabama: The University of Alabama Press, 1975).

65. *Ibid.*, p. 10

66. *Ibid.*, p. 13.

67. *Ibid.*, p. 67.

68. *Ibid.*, p. 88.

69. *Ibid.*, p. 84.

70. *Ibid.*, p. 91.

71. *Ibid.*, p. 10.

72. Woodrow Wilson, "The Study of Administration," p. 217.

Notes

1. There are four books by Paul H. Appleby:
   (i) *Big Democracy,* New York: Alfred A. Knopf, 1945.
   (ii) *Policy and Administration,* Alabama: University of Alabama Press, 1949.
   (iii) *Morality and Administration in Democratic Government,* Baton Rouge: Louisiana State University Press, 1952.
   (iv) *Citizens as Sovereigns,* Syracuse: Syracuse University Press, 1962.
   Of the four, *Policy and Administration* is the most fruitful. *Morality and Administration in Democratic Government* is a series of lectures which, on an individual basis, might be very helpful to dip into.

2. J.E. Hodgetts, W. McCloskey, Reginald Whitaker, V. Seymour Wilson, *The Biography of An Institution: The Civil Service Commission of Canada, 1908-1967* (Montreal: McGill-Queen's University Press, 1972).
   This book deals in part with the merging of scientific management and civil service reform in Canada. We recommend the first four or five chapters as supplemental reading to this chapter.

3. Theodore J. Lowi. *The End of Liberalism: Ideology, Policy and the Crisis of Public Authority* (New York: W.W. Norton and Co., Inc., 1969).
   This is an excellent polemic. Particularly useful is Lowi's first rate analysis of the causes of the administrative state (chapters 1, 2, and 3). His Part IV, "Beyond Liberalism" is highly debatable, but this should not mar the profitable reading of Part I of this book. It is a useful exercise to contrast and compare Lowi's "causes" with Ostrom's paradigm of ideas (which he contends leads to the intellectual crisis of public policy and administration) and the "New Public Administration" analysis of the factors leading to the societal crisis of the 60s.

4. Frank Marini (ed.) *Toward a New Public Administration,* (Scranton, Pa.: Chandler Publishing Co., 1971).
   This book represents the first "statement" of the New Public Administration movement. There are some very good pieces in this book expecially by Orion White, Michael Harmon and Todd LaPorte.

5. Grant McConnell, *Private Power and American Democracy* (New York: Alfred A. Knopf, 1966).
   In my judgement this is one of the best critiques of the pluralist doctrine in political science. It contains an excellent analysis of Progressive ideology and its contradictions as well as a first-rate analysis of the "public interest" in American political ideology. Unfortunately there is only tangential reference to administrative pluralism as such.

6. Vincent Ostrom, *The Intellectual Crisis in American Public Administration* (Alabama: The University of Alabama Press, 1973).
   A small book wedding public choice theory with American political philosophy. The book is significant in that Ostrom has been the leading public policy and administration scholar attempting to integrate economic thought in the mainstream of public administration. The book is worth reading as background for a good discussion on the current debate. Kuhn's paradigm of ideas is very central to Ostrom's analysis. Is Ostrom on safe ground here?

7. Victor A. Thompson, *Without Sympathy or Enthusiasm: The Problem of Administrative Compassion* (Alabama: The University of Alabama Press, 1975).
This book says something which much of the discipline of public policy and administration prefer to mute: *organizations are basically tools of control.* Thompson's logic is direct and at times "cast in cement." As the title implies there is hardly any room left for human initiative in his scheme of things (at one stage of the book he calls "functionaries" by the phrase "intellectual cripples.") Highly debatable book and very good reading. It is guaranteed to create a controversy in student discussions.

8. Dwight Waldo (ed.) *Public Administration in a Time of Turbulence* (New York: Chandler Publishing Co., 1971).
Another book in the New Public Administration tradition. Almost all the pieces are recommended, most of them for good reflective reading.

Articles recommended are the following:

1. H. George Frederickson, Symposium Editor. "Symposium on Social Equity and Public Administration," *Public Administration Review*, Vol. 34, January/February 1974, pp. 1-51.

2. H. George Frederickson, "The Lineage of New Public Administration," *Administration and Society*, Vol. 8, No. 2 (August 1976), pp. 149-174.

3. Michael Harmon, "Administrative Policy Formulation and the Public Interest," *Public Administration Review*, September/October 1969, pp. 483-491.

4. Erwin A. Jaffe, "Rearrangement of the Administrative State: Professor Lowi and 'The End of Liberalism'." *Journal of Comparative Administration*, Vol. 1, No. 4 (February 1970), pp. 477-499.

5. Vincent Ostrom and Elinor Ostrom, "Public Choice: A Different Approach to the Study of Public Administration," *Public Administration Review*, March/April 1971, pp. 203-216.

6. Volker Ronge, "The Politicization of Administration in Advanced Capitalist Societies," *Political Studies*, Vol. XXII, No. 1, pp. 86-93.

7. V. Subramaniam, "The Relative Status of Specialists and Generalists: An Attempt at a Comparative Historical Explanation," *Public Administration (London)* 46, Autumn, 1968.

8. Richard J. Stillman II, "Woodrow Wilson and the Study of Administration: A New Look at an Old Essay," *American Political Science Review* Vol. 67 (June, 1973), pp. 582-588.

9. Woodrow Wilson, "The Study of Administration," *Political Science Quarterly* Vol. II, No. 2, June 1887, pp. 197-222. Reprinted in *Political Science Quarterly* 55 (December 1941), pp. 481-506.

10. V. Seymour Wilson, "The Relationship between Scientific Management and Personnel Policy in North American Administrative Systems," *Public Administration* (London), Autumn, 1973, pp. 193-205.

CHAPTER FIVE

THEORIES OF COMPLEX ORGANIZATIONS: AN ELEPHANTINE PROBLEM*

> [The major problem with organizations is akin to] the fable of the blind men and the elephant. Each of the blind men . . . touched with his hands a different part of the elephant, and as a result, there was among them a radical difference of opinion as to the nature of the beast.
>
> Dwight Waldo, *Ideas and Issues*
> in *Public Administration.*

Each of the different conceptions of bureaucracy discussed in previous chapters has a corpus of both theoretical and popular writings to buttress its claims to credibility.

The Weberian view of bureaucracy has particularly been emphasized. Weber's model identified three aspects of the phenomenon which are crucial: those group of characteristics which relate to the internal structure and functioning of the organization; those aspects which are normative in concern such as the implications of fully rationalized bureaucracy for society and the individual; and finally the overriding view that organizational forms are deeply rooted in the social structure of our society. From this latter insight flows the whole notion of the administrative state and its implications for society.

There is, however, another intellectual tradition connected with the study of complex organizations which emphasize the first Weberian insight mentioned above, namely the internal structure and functioning of the organization.[1] This tradition is usually said to be structuralist in orientation and often associated with the "scientific quest" in

---

* *With apologies to Dwight Waldo whose article, "Organization Theory: An Elephantine Problem" in* Public Administration Review II *(Autumn 1961) remains an influential contribution to the literature on public policy and administration. This chapter also relies heavily on the theoretical perspective provided by Charles Perrow,* Complex Organizations: A Critical Essay *(Glenview, Illinois: Scott, Foresman & Co., 1972).*

the social disciplines for intellectual rigor, system and cumulation in knowledge gathering.[2] *Much of its theorizing, particularly during the first three to four decades of this century, was done in total ignorance or intellectually distinct from the Weberian tradition.* We wish to emphasize this distinction here because much nonsense has been written directly connecting, say, Weber's writings on bureaucracy with scientific management as one and the same. This chapter is concerned with giving *an overview* of this twentieth century quest, highlighting the major theoretical schools of thought and assessing the insights they provide against what we already know of the Weberian tradition.

Scientific Management or the Classical School of Organization Theory*

The origin of this school of organizational thought in North America provides one of the most fascinating aspects of the study of organizations. The great expansion of industrial enterprise in nineteenth century America brought with it in its wake a good deal of chaos and disorganization as well as a high rate of economic growth. The general societal strains caused by *laissez-faire* capitalism were widely recognized even at the time, but less generally noted was the organizational chaos within the capitalist units of production, created because of generally unplanned expansion. By the late part of the nineteenth century, it was becoming very clear that the old myth of freewheeling entrepreneur would have to give way to some form of bureaucratic reform of the structures of large-scale units of production if any approximation of organization efficiency were to be achieved. As businesses grew bigger the boss became more and more separated in the day-to-day routine from the workers, and new methods of control had to be invented.[3]

In this process the engineers and the cost accountants occupied strategic positions, the latter because their function was to measure and control costs, and the former because they were most closely associated with the day-to-day problems of organizing production in the factory. It was, therefore, hardly surprising that the first coherent managerial ideology to emerge from within American business arose out of the discussions of engineers. It was a paper read at the American Society of Mechanical Engineers in 1886 entitled "The Engineer as Economist" which first started Frederick W. Taylor, himself an engi-

* *The overview of organization theory presented in this chapter makes no pretense of even trying to cover substantive themes of each main area of organizational theorizing. This type of knowledge would be found in the many texts cited in our footnotes, and our annotated bibliography should be particularly helpful for beginners to this literature.*

neer, to think about management as a separate phenomenon, which eventually led to the elaboration of what became known as "scientific management" theory.

The genesis of scientific management among mechanical engineers is more than a matter of historical curiosity, for the assumptions of mechanics were in fact largely transferred to the study of people in organizations, thus establishing a very definite theoretical form of relationship between people within the industrial environment, a form which was in fact founded on a two-fold analogy between machines and people. The first level of this analogy was that the individual human being was, for the purposes of the factory at least, to be considered as a machine, whose specifications and performance could be quantitatively measured and rated, and whose efficiency as a machine could be improved through simple mechanical adjustments such as reducing the number of superfluous motions involved in any given action.

On the second level the entire factory structure was to be considered as a complex productive mechanism which combined actual machines with human workers in the process of transforming raw material into a finished product in the cheapest manner possible. *Rationalization, meaning the most efficient manner in achieving a stated objective,* was achieved by treating both machines and workers as standardized, interchangeable units, to be organized on the sole index of maximum productivity and minimum unit cost. *This view in organization theory of rationalization as efficiency is distinctly North American in theoretical emphasis and it remains the lodestone, the essential core of scientific management theory.*

What had happened was that the introduction of mechanization into enterprise had resulted in enormous growth, which in turn led to human organizational problems, and it was now proposed to solve these problems by treating humans as if they were themselves machines, thus solving the organizational question through the successful science of mechanical engineering. And the insights of Taylor worked! The logical organization of work was achieved—record keeping, typing pools established, specialization of tasks occurred, and delegation of some aspects of work began as a proper organizational norm.

However, the classical approach to the study of organizations contained both a theory of organizations and a theory of motivation.[4] The motivational concepts were in keeping with the general mechanistic analogy: the individual appeared as a sort of Hobbesian automation, directed by a fear of hunger and a drive for profit, and could thus be efficiently manipulated as a productive tool by a system of rewards and punishments. The relentless application of the machine analogy suggests Etzioni, led Taylor eventually ". . . to view human and machine resources not so much as mutually adaptable, but rather man functioning as an appendage to the industrial machine."[5]

In organizational terms, Taylorism looked to the division of labor as the basic principle, with extensive specialization of separate individual units, whether machines or workers, organized with reference only to the overall system, this complex meshing of disparate units to be controlled by a hierarchical pyramid of authority guided by the lodestar of efficiency. This latter aspect of Taylorism, the emphasis on the unity of authority working at a maximum, was a point which appealed strongly to American industrial managers in the early twentieth century, who were, as sociologist Reinhard Bendix points out, engaged in a bitter struggle for the "open shop" and the suppression of labour unions.[6]

Scientific management had, however, surprising implications beyond the merely obvious. Inherent in the entire approach is the assumption that there is a "one best way" of doing anything. It was widely believed at the time that once the laws describing the "one best way" were discovered and acknowledged, industrial conflict would be largely eliminated since nobody could complain about "unfairness" before such a government of impartial and universal laws.

Another factor to take into consideration was the consequent drastic limitation of the expectations of the worker for upward mobility within the enterprise. Before the introduction of scientific analysis, the loose unstructured nature of business organizations gave some credence to the myth of "office boy to president": such a rise at least seemed feasible. But scientific management theory, in switching focus from the person to the job, emphasized how the given human raw material might best be fitted to the capacities of the human beings. As March and Simon put it: "In general there is a tendency to view the employee as an inert instrument performing the tasks assigned to him. Second, there is a tendency to view personnel as a given rather than a variable in the system."[7]

It must be said that Taylor was vigorously consistent in his application of the scientific method to the factory, and his logic was largely unassailable, provided that is, that one is willing to accept his definition of people as appendages to—and somewhat poor copies of—machinery which they themselves have created.

It must also be recognized that the alleged scientific impartiality of the theory was widely accepted at the time, not only by the coldly realistic bent-on-profits capitalists but by "warm hearted" Progressive reformers intent on general uplift and even by hard-headed leaders of the vanguard of the proletariat! No less a personage than V. I. Lenin, the father of Russian Communism, thought highly of the "Taylor system" as "the last word of capitalism in this respect" indeed, one of its "greatest scientific achievements," and went on to assert that the Soviet Union "must at all costs adopt all that is valuable in the achievement of science and technology as part of the struggle to teach Soviet citizens to work more efficiently."[8]

This, in a nutshell, is the scientific management school of organizational theory. It was enormously influential in its heyday, because, first of all it worked; it made logical sense; and it appealed to all kinds of reformers—both public and private. Both Russian Communists and West European capitalists were keenly interested in the school's developments. The American movement of scientific management, it is fair to say, was much more influential in Europe than it was itself aware of the developments in European "administrative science." Whereas Frederick Taylor started with the individual worker at the bottom of the hierarchy and moved upward and outward to cover all factors that might affect the capacity of the worker to give his best, Henri Fayol, a French industrialist, started at the top with the general manager.

Fayol classified the function of major business operations and defined the administrative group as *organizing, coordinating, commanding, controlling and prevoyance* (a mixture of forecasting and planning). These ideas did not make the rapid impact across the Atlantic that "Taylorism" made in the other direction until the 1930s when Luther Gulick reinterpreted Fayol and spelt out the POSDCORB formula (the administrative process comprises: Planning, Organizing, Staffing, Directing, Coordinating, Reporting and Budgeting). It was alleged that the study of this formula could reveal universal principles with predictive value based on verifiable experience applicable to all administration.

Scientific management experts and moral reformers both argued for years that if North American capitalism did not reform its practices and conform to the principles of scientific management it would sooner or later suffer from economic bankruptcy. The advent of the Depression was seen as confirmation of this fact. Everything therefore seemed to point to the correctness of the outlook and method, and municipal reformers, both here in Canada and the United States, strongly advocated its adoption.[9] All these happenings or events, coupled with a most unanimous public approval made more relevant and urgent the cry for a reformed administrative technology, liberated from economic classes, ethnic or other social conflict.

We have spent some time outlining this major perspective in organization theory because of its enormous significance in governmental reform during the first three to four decades of this century. The philosophy's influence on government can be discerned by the drastic reorganization reforms of the Canadian federal civil service during 1918-19,[10] and the 1937 President's Committee on Administrative Management proposals to restructure the entire federal bureaucracy in the United States.[11]

These proposals led to the 1937 publication by one of the members of the Committee, Luther Gulick, along with the former Director of the Internal Management Institute of Geneva, the Englishman Lyndall F. Urwick of Papers on the Science of Administration containing eleven essays constituting now the *locus classicus* of the scientific management orthodoxy. In origin the essays were some American, some Western European, some concerned with public administration exclusively, most with business administration, all confident of a science of administration which transcends frontiers, time and purpose.

By the late 1930s, however, it was slowly being recognized that the reality of the practical environment was intruding more and more on the neat and tidy world of theoretical scientific management dicta. First, scientific management contained the seeds of its own questioning. As growth and complexity of organizations continued a pace, the charismatic one person leader became more and more remote from reality, and so did a clean mechanical structure with clear lines of authority to the top. A search for the qualities of leadership began with a frank admittance that something other than "sound principles" or "dynamic leadership" was required. The search for leadership traits implied that leaders were made, not just born, that the matter was complex and that several skills were involved in determining good leaership.[12]

Second, the rapid changes in technology required more adaptive organization. The scientific management school was ill-equipped to deal with change in the environment. It had presumed that once the proper structure was achieved, the organization could run forever without much adjustment. By the late 1930s, however, adaptation and change were, to put it mildly, forced upon any environment resisting these societal forces. Third, these political, social and cultural changes meant new expectations regarding the proper way to treat people. Labor, now aware of its powers, demanded organizational reforms. Strikes and labor disturbances became more common. Management adjusted by beginning to speak of a cooperative system of capital, management and labor. The machine model began to lose its relevancy.

Human Relations Theory

Even in its heyday scientific management theory had its share of doubtful Thomases. For example, Lillian M. Gilbreth, wife of the founder of "time and motion study," published *The Psychology of Management* in 1914, a study which was greatly concerned with the reactions of the worker to "scientific management." B. Seebohm Rowntree of the famous Rowntree chocolate family of British entrepreneurial fame, published *The Human Factor in Business* in 1921, and practised what he preached by working out profit sharing schemes with his employees. But these were exceptions to the rule. The majority of people sympathetic to the view of these early pioneers of human relations retained a limited view of the nature of the human being*, best exemplified by an animal psychology quote from Andrew Dunsire:

Paint your cowsheds green and play music to your milkers is apparently a proven recipe for higher milk yields, and the aim of most of the industrial psychology of the early twentieth century was undoubtedly higher productivity from contented workers, each worker being considered as a unit, independently responding to his individual environment, as is assumed of the cows in the cowshed.[13]

Thus no effective counterforce to scientific management developed until 1938 when a business executive from the New Jersey Bell Telephone Company, Chester Barnard, wrote an enormously influential book which, for the first time, gave coherence to the developing field of human relations. Barnard stressed that organizations are, *by their very nature*, cooperative systems and not the products of mechanical engineering. He emphasized such notions as upward communications, authority from below rather than hierarchical structuring, natural informal groupings in the organizational milieu and leaders who functioned as a cohesive force in the organization setting.

Barnard's volume, first published in 1938, gave a tremendous boost to the human relations theory of organizations which was by this time gaining momentum amongst students of organizations. The following year (1939), saw the final publications of a series of studies conducted between 1927 and 1932 at the Western Electric Company Hawthorne Works in Chicago. This was the study by F. J. Roethlisberger and William Dickson entitled *Management and the Worker*, the first empirical work conducted to test the relationship of productivity

---

* *This is an oversimplification of the state of affairs in the early beginnings of the human relations tradition. To obtain a more complete picture of early human relations we strongly recommend Reinhard Bendix and Lloyd Fisher "The Perspectives of Elton Mayo"; George C. Homans "Some Corrections to the Perspectives of Elton Mayo"; and William F. Whyte "Human Relations—a Progress Report"—all found in Amital Etzioni (ed.), Complex Organizations: A Sociological Reader (New York: Holt, Rinehart and Winston, 1961).*

and social relations. The research highlighted the important factors of work restriction norms, informal groups, the value of humane leadership, and the role of psychological manipulation of employees through the counselling system. More specifically, according to Amitai Etzioni, it discovered that:

1 The amount of work carried out by a worker is not determined by his physical capacity but by his social capacity.
2 Non-economic rewards play a central role in determining the motivation and happiness of the worker.
3 The highest specialization is by no means the most efficient form of division of labor.
4 Workers do not react to management and its norms and rewards as individuals but as members of groups. [14]

By the end of World War II the works of Barnard, and Roethlisberger and Dickson were given more coherence and substantiation by the pioneering works of Elton Mayo, William F. Whyte, George Homans and Kurt Lewin to name a few of the more notable scholars of this theoretical persuasion. For a while the assumptions underlying all this work was that the nature of human relations in the organizational setting was primarily determined by the human relations skills of the people in leadership positions. A good leader was kind, courteous, noble, loyal to the organization, and considerate of his employees' problems and so on.

Then came a series of disturbing questions to this philosophy. [15] Industrial sociologists Clark Kerr and Abraham Siegel started the ball rolling: If cooperation in industry depends primarily on the skill and understanding of the key people involved, why has there been consistent conflict in the longshoreman industry in the United States (substitute the Post Office of Canada or the Air Traffic Controllers in the Ministry of Transport), while industrial relations in the clothing industry (substitute the vast majority of administrative support unions in the federal public service) have been reasonably peaceful? Can it be that the key people in Industry A just happen to be skilled in human relations, whereas their opposite numbers in Industry B are a bunch of bunglers? If money or economic incentives are not important as the human relations advocates argue, why are there consistent intergroup problems in organizational settings created by incentive systems?

Studies then began identifying a crucial distinction between "consideration" or employee-centred aspects of leadership, and job-centred, technical aspects labeled "initiating structure." The latter was a clear indication that there are certain forces operating that are more powerful than the human relations techniques of individual leaders and motivation in organization. Kerr and Siegel's work, and the works of Leonard Sayles and George Strauss drew *attention to the powerful influence of job structure upon human relations on the job.* The structural aspects of organization were crucial after all in determining behavioral patterns. Most of this work signalling caution went unheeded for quite a while. Human relations theorizing led to a proliferation of studies of group processes which has had some influence on both private and governmental organizations. Noteworthy of these experiments are the widely acclaimed T-group programs, transactional analysis and encounter groups, utilized even by government agencies today.

English researchers of organization behavior were the first to sense the importance of job structure, that there was an intimate relationship among *technical, economic* and *social* aspects of organization. A study conducted by Eric Trist in the coal mines of North West Durham provided convincing evidence that job simplification and specialization did not work under conditions of uncertainty and non-routine tasks: the traditional technology of the mines ("single-place working"), where small teams of men worked their own part of the coal seam, had facilitated the formation of multi-skilled, self-selected, largely autonomous work groups. This allowed a great deal of independence within the work group, and generated a relatively high level of job satisfaction. Since the work groups did not compete with one another, their relations were normally harmonious.

Meanwhile, back on the North American continent, human relations theorists began to move from the micro aspects of work groups to the macro concerns of the organization. Organizations were disastrous to the environment when they insisted on routine tasks, ignorance of the goals of their employees, centralized decision-making, hierarchical leadership and so on. Researchers began to logically posit organizational alternatives which will, in the future, eradicate the problems of bureaucracy. In the private sector William G. Scott referred to "industrial humanism" of which he and others such as Douglas McGregor, Chris Argyris and Rensis Likert were leading exponents. Others, Warren Bennis being one of the chief among them, in spelling out the Valhalla of organizations of tomorrow, emphasized that,

The three main features of the environment will be interdependence rather than competition, turbulence rather than stability, and small rather than large enterprises. [16]

This strong humanistic theme, transferred to the level of global problems in both the developed and developing nations, had a direct appeal to an increasing body of adherents. [17]

In the public policy and administration literature Robert T. Golembiewski utilizes the term "man-centered organization" to refer to the increasing need to heed the individual in the organizational complex, and the 1965 reforms of the Glassco Royal Commission of Canada, argued for decentralization: "Let the managers manage."[18] Thus in public policy and administration, decentralization became one of the structural manifestations of the human relations school of organizational theory. It was a means for securing the participation and commitment of subordinates and a tool for reducing delays and red tape in decision-making.

Politicians have, however, never forgotten that administrative decentralization is a powerful manipulative tool which could aid in the achievement of certain political objectives. Governmental decentralization then is a much more crucial aspect of bureaucracy when viewed as a political device than as a human relations dictum. However, the human relations theory of organizations did help to sensitize both government and the public to the need to soften some of the harsher aspects of bureaucratic experience. Hence in the rhetoric and reasoned arguments advocating freedom of information, the ombudsman concept and participative administration we can detect philosophical positions strongly influenced by this view of the individual within complex organizations.

Nevertheless, some of the larger assumptions of human relations were being systematically assessed and called into serious questioning. In a path-breaking series of articles, George Strauss, himself one of the leading human relations theorists of the 50s and 60s, began to exhibit self-doubt. He started a methodological questioning of such assumptions as harmony, need hierarchy, conflict resolution and desire for participation—all central aspects of the school's philosophy.[19]

DR. DWIGHT WALDO
Professor Emeritus, The Maxwell School of Citizenship and Public Affairs, Syracuse University. Waldo's penetrating insights into politics and administration, organization theory and behavior, comparative administration and political philosophy inform this book throughout.

Theories of Conflict and Decision-Making

(i) The Contribution of European Thought: Marxian-Weberian Perspectives on Alienation

We have already discussed in the two previous chapters the intellectual traditions of classical Marxism and Weberian thought, but perhaps a further word is acceptable on where the two systems of thought converge. It is true that the early Marxism's position on the role of bureaucracy is not a distinct one, because the concept does not occupy a central position in Marxist thought. Marx analysed bureaucratic power in the context of the power structure of society—one can almost assert that he viewed bureaucracy as an epiphenomenon. The key to Marx's thinking on bureaucracy can be found in his trenchent criticisms of Hegel's philosophy of the state. As Mouzelis puts it:

> The Hegelian analysis conceives public administration as a bridge between the state and the civil society. The civil society comprises the professions, the corporations which represent the various particular interests, the state representing the general interest. Between the two, the state bureaucracy is the medium through which this passage from the particular to the general interest becomes possible.[20]

Although accepting this tripartite structure elaborated by Hegel, Marx rejected the view that the bureaucracy was some neutral bridge which converted particular interests to the public interest. The state, to Marx, represented the particular interests of the dominant class, and as such bureaucracy is the instrument by which the dominant class maintains its hegemony over the other social classes in society. The advent of true communism would mean the elimination of bureaucratic modes of organization by the "withering away of the state." This "withering away" concept, however, has remained an incomplete theoretical formulation of Karl Marx, and neo-Marxists in contemporary times have been attempting to grapple with the problems that it has posed for Marxist theory.[21] Suffice to state here that in his later writings Marx accepted that even in a communist society there will remain some social functions to perform analogous to the functions of the state in bourgeois society, but he stopped short of trying to spell out these functions. Perhaps in reference to the experience of the Paris commune, he argued that under true communism "the merely repressive organs of the old governmental power were to be amputated, its legitimate functions were to be wrested from an authority usurping pre-eminence over society itself, and restored to the responsible agents of society."[22]

Marx, however, gave no clues as to what state social functions might be needed under true communism, and beyond his comments about the Paris commune experience, he provided little direction as to what he regarded as the dictatorial element of proletarian rule. The state as the "hegemonic" instrument of class domination disappears under communism, but the state as the bureaucratic and economic implementer of public policy remains. As Oskar Lange once remarked, ". . . the real danger of socialism is that of bureaucratic organization of economic life . . ."[23]

Despite these incomplete formulations, Marx revealed some basic structural insights which would form the basis of conflict theory in later years. By emphasizing the impersonal characteristics of bureaucracy he identified most clearly the problem of alienation as a crucial variable: rationalization of structures had led to task specialization which in turn has created problems of repetition, monotony and lack of creativity and self-expression. In a word, the worker is alienated because he owns neither the means of production nor the products of his labor. Max Weber, according to Etzioni, added to this perspective by stressing that:

> . . . this basic estrangement exists not only between the worker and the means of production, but also between the soldier and the means of warfare, the scientist and the means of inquiry, etc. This is not just a legal question of ownership (e.g., that the gun belongs to the army and not to the soldier), but rather that with ownership goes the right to control, and that those that provide the means also define their use; thus the workers, soldier and researcher—and by implication all employees of all organizations—are frustrated, unhappy since they cannot determine what use their efforts will be put to since they do not own the instrument necessary to carry out independently the work that needs to be done . . . Alienation is a concept that stands for this sentiment and the analysis of its source in the Marxian-Weberian terms.[24]

While this is certainly not the appropriate forum to discuss differences in epistemological approaches it should be made clear that certain similarities of thought between Marx and Weber should nevertheless not mark the fundamental differences between them. As an example Weber firmly believed in the view that value systems greatly influenced human behavior while Marx did not, and their philosophies on the rationalization of ideas were sharply at odds with each other.[25]

(ii) The North American Input to the Conflict Perspective

One of the essential weaknesses of the early North American theoretical schools of organizational behavior was their inability to confront the problems of conflict in an organizational setting. There were isolated exceptions to this criticism, but more or less most in the scientific management or human relations tradition ignored conflict or treated it as a pathological manifestation of breakdowns in communication or the lack of effective leadership. The perspective of conflict as inevitable and indeed necessary for a liberal democratic society to function did find intellectual appeal among pluralist students of politics. Perhaps by accident more than by design, the analysis of conflict in political parties inevitably led to a concern for conflict in all complex organizations.

Inspired by Arthur F. Bentley's classic *The Process of Government*, social scientists began to analyze the balancing functions of struggle between political groups in party organizations and in the wider political arena. Describing the American political scene, James Burns waxed poetic: "Like dancers in a vast Virginia reel, groups merge, break off, meet again, veer away to new combinations."[26] The concept of conflict also influenced economists and revived an interest in the subject in sociology. This revival in sociology has led to the proliferation of conflict studies in the past decade dealing with conflicting goals of treatment and custody in mental institutions and prisons.[27]

The presence of legitimately conflicting goals and techniques of preserving and utilizing power was a very large pill to swallow for those whose organizational insights were dominated by the views of cooperation, humanism and employee-centered views on leadership. Legitimate conflicting goals were also very problematic for those who drew sustenance from the frameworks of efficiency derived from the scientific management tradition. After all, the distinguishing characteristics of such organizations pointed to effective ways of settling questions of power through organizational design and to keep conflict at bay by relying on systems of careers, span of control, expertise and hierarchy.

But conflict simply did not go away, and the contributions of the "conflict theorists" gradually gained acceptance and recognition in the study of organizations. The most extensive reformulations were done by the human relations students. What was crucial to them was the mode of resolution of conflict rather than its prevention.[28] Power became reconceptualized as "influence" and the distribution being conceived as less important than the total amount.[29] For students in the efficiency tradition (those who derived sustenance, implicitly and explicitly from scientific management) this meant less stress on bureaucracy's particular characteristics and more emphasis on its purpose. Thus analysis in the goal-setting tradition moved from a perspective dominated by efficiency-effectiveness considerations to a systems model approach which sought to balance the conflicting tensions generated by organization strain, flexibility needs and a concern for productivity.[30]

(iii) Decision-Making: The Impact of the American Behavioral Tradition

It is at this juncture that American social scientists studying organizational behavior made an important contribution to the study of complex organizations. We will introduce this tradition here, but a more detailed assessment of its contribution would be left for the next chapter, when we consider decision-making theory and public policy studies. In their book *Organizations*, which is slowly achieving the status of a classic, Herbert Simon and James G. March developed a concept which was to prove very illuminating. Human beings, they premised, are not all that rational, and their behavior, within limits, can be deliberately controlled. People are only "intendedly rational," because they are limited in intelligence, information at their immediate disposal, time available for considered deliberations, among other things—in a word, they have limited capacities and, compounded with the limitations of organizations, prevent any notion of complete rationality. Calling this phenomena "cognitive limits of rationality," they argued that reasonable decision-makers wishing to retain their sanity should and must "satisfice" rather than "maximize." To put it more simply, an individual ceases searching for proposals in decision-making when "satisfactory" alternatives present themselves. So stated, the satisficing concept expresses a significant, yet commonplace and neglected insight. Nevertheless, along with the works of another political scientist, Harold Lasswell, it is the core of the "decision-making school" and is concerned with the basic question of how people make decisions.[31] In the field of political science it has been more broadly conceived as the "public policy analysis" school, a categorization with which Herbert Simon disagrees.[32]

At any rate, this input into organizational theory had a very important and sustaining influence. It suggested that the organization can control in a number of ways the parameters of decision-making. In a word, it can define the situation or environment, an implication which has opened this school of thought to one of the charges levelled so often at the human relations school, namely that it was an exercise in "social engineering." These implications have never sat too easily with many of Simon's professional colleagues, to put it mildly.[33] Nevertheless, its manipulative insights were extremely revealing. It suggested to the hierarchy of an organization that what was necessary was not to give direct orders and expect effective implementation or even to leave subordinates to their own devices. It was necessary to control only the premises of their decisions. Left to themselves with those premises delineated, subordinates could, *on the aggregate*, be predicted to rely on precedent, professional values, keeping things stable, and smooth, and responding to signals that reinforce the behavior desired of them.[34] These aspects of Simons' insights have had some direct implications for topics dealt throughout the book (for example, administrative responsibility and control) and we will return to these from time to time.

March and Simon illustrated their thesis by a variety of devices so commonplace to seasoned bureaucrats that their contributions seem to border on truisms. In the traditional literature communication means clarity of orders, the authoritativeness of the source of orders and so on. However, communications for March and Simon means much more: information is specialized through specific channels, some key or stragetic positions in the organization can be bypassed intentionally by re-routing organizational information, and organizational vocabularies are developed which can blot out "some parts of reality and magnify other parts." For example, organizations develop vocabularies and myths which ensure that certain kinds of information are highlighted, selected within the organizational framework and disseminated in a variety of controlled ways. As a dramatic illustration of this in Canada we have the statement of a former solicitor-general of Canada, Warren Allmand, that the Royal Canadian Mounted Police has for years withheld selected bits of information from various solicitor-generals:

It seems that they did withhold information from me and from other solicitors-general. Some of them argued, and will argue, that they withheld it because it wasn't explicitly asked for. I wouldn't accept that in many cases.[35]

These insights into varying methods of manipulation and control are not totally dissimilar to a prevailing Marxist view as to how public organization levers are operated to arrive at policy choices.[36] An "unequal structure of representation" in the making of public policy is a tyranny in which government becomes the means of harnessing *almost all* but one class to the gratification of that one. These were new insights into human behavior which could prove to be a two-edged sword. While it gave leaders an opportunity to review in an insightful comprehensive way, their day-to-day strategies in organizations, it also provided to employees and to students of the social sciences the manner in which some people or, according to the Marxist almost all people, *have been, are* and *will be* manipulated in complex organizations.

What were the effects on the various organizational schools of thought? For the new diminishing band of scientific management disciples these new insights seem to be of no value or of very little impact, at any rate.[37] Students in the Weberian tradition absorbed these new insights in different ways. Some seemed confused by the contributions of Simon and March, producing books which gave no clear view of organizations.[38] Others, however, made the synthesis of Weber's insights with those of March and Simon. Control in organizations, they argued, can be effected by a number of mechanisms: by creating organizational myths and vocabularies to ensure selective and value infused information; monitoring performance through indirect means rather than direct surveillance. In essence, the "bloodless categories" of hierarchy, expertise, rules, offices and so on were now being clothed with sinews, veins and blood to obtain a realistic conception of organizational activity.

The human relations theorists, however, had some drastic overhaul in thinking to do at this venture. Theorists of this persuasion began to write about changing stimuli rather than changing personality. They had to concede that prestige, money and comfort were more important in changing attitudes rather than trust, openness and self insight.[39] They admitted that although leadership may be centralized, it can function best through indirect and unobtrusive means such as changing the premises on which decisions are made.

The English Contribution: Technology of Production and Organizational Variables

It is at this juncture that the English students of organization theory began to make a series of significant contributions to our understanding of organizational behavior. Joan Woodward, a teacher of management subjects, started a study of one hundred industrial firms in South-East Essex to substantiate the standard "classical theory" textbooks she used in the classroom. She found no clear relationship between business success and approved management structure. What she did discover was that principles of successful management change from one technological context to another: job shop firms, mass-production firms, and continuous process firms all had quite different structures because the type of task or "technology" was different in each case.[40] She showed in a most convincing manner that the sort of principles elaborated by scientific management theorists are *only* relevant in mass production factories. Three years later Tom Burns and G. M. Stalker researching certain aspects of innovations behavior, found that the most single determining factor of success in incorporating a capacity for innovation or planned change in an organization was, surprisingly, not the personalities of individual managers, or "industrial relations" in the firms, but the management and decision structure of the firm—the way jobs were distributed, the way information was channelled, the way problems were dealt with.

March and Simon were beginning to make a lot of sense and, despite some further elaborations and qualifications, Weber's original insight was still standing up to empirical testing. The 1960s saw a proliferation of empirical studies of hospitals, juvenile correctional institutions and industrial firms confirming Woodward's, Burn's, and Stalker's empirical research. What did it all add up to? Bureaucracy appeared to be the best form of organization for routine operations, whereas temporary work groups, decentralization and emphasis on interpersonal processes appeared to work best for non-routine operations. Thus the nature of the task can considerably affect the structure of the organization.[41]

The implications for earlier organizational theory were slowly being clarified. The students of Max Weber, despite the overwhelming evidence that structure loomed large as the most important criteria in the theory of complex organizations had a few lessons to learn. Structures must vary to accommodate variations in technology. Thus research and development units, for example, should obviously be managed differently from mass-production units.[42] Organizations vary considerably in their degree of routinization. But units within organizations also vary in their degree of routinization. A federal department such as Agriculture, for example, contains a research division of highly trained and world-renowned scientists, as well as a vast army of administrative support personnel whose jobs are to a large extent routinized. How should these be integrated into one organization?

It was once again substantiated that openness and trust, while being good humanist values, did not have much impact, or perhaps were not even possible in some kinds of work situations. What might be feasible and indeed desirable in a high status, challenging job performed by highly educated people might not be relevant or even beneficial for the vast majority of jobs and people. Where was the threshold, however? Much more work needs to be done in this area, but the most important to date has been the study by Paul Lawrence and Jay Lorsch, *Organizations and Environment*.[43] Lawrence and Lorsch argued that firms performed best when the differences between units were *maximized*, as long as the integrating mechanisms stood halfway between the two (being neither strongly bureaucratic nor non-routine). They noted that attempts at participative management in routine situations were counterproductive, that price, efficiency and cost reduction were trivial considerations in some firms and that the environments of some kinds of organizations were very stable, and as a consequence customers did not seriously entertain any suggestions of innovation and changes.[44]

Considerations of the Organic Nature of Organizations

While research in organization theory proceeded to clarify, qualify and, in some cases, nullify our previous conceptions of organizations, another school of organization theory continued to labor in the vineyard. This is the so-called "institutional school" or structural functionalism of organizations which emphasize the organic nature of organizations in three ways. First, an emphasis on the organization *as a whole* or what is called in sociology, functionalism. This emphasis on the whole organization gives a sense of the variety of differences in organizational types and goals, and in one sense emphasizes those studies and insights we have already referred to earlier on *leadership, technology* and *structure*. Functionalism forces another dimension on the researcher—an emphasis on the internal processes of the organization, indicating in what ways organizations take on lives of their own. This emphasis points the way to analysis on the conflict of goals in organizations and in what ways goal displacement takes place.

Structuralism on the other hand forces the researcher to speak of organizations in terms of system needs and the inculcation and reinforcement of values. Thus, the emphasis is and must be environmental. In many ways this emphasis dovetails with Max Weber's work. As has already been shown, Weber saw organizational forms deeply rooted in the social structure. He emphasized that the progressive rationalization of life had significant consequences for bureaucracies in that it allowed this type of organization to gradually penetrate all social institutions.

The institutional school has elaborated on this theme in a most dynamic and dialectic manner. Studies have detailed for specific organizations the very close interaction of organizations and their environments. Canadian sociologist S. D. Clarke has shown how religious sects in Canada, in responding to environmental changes, have also drastically changed their organizational philosophies.[45] These studies emphasized how unique organizations were in many respects; how organizations were embedded in their own history; how the stated goals of organizations were more often than not the subsidiary ones; how official leaders could be overshadowed by "eminences grises"; and how the sociological myths of the "public interest" and "efficiency and effectiveness" were important parts of organizational religion, but not necessarily organizational reality. We will return to a few of the insights of this school in section II of this book.

What did this all lead up to? Human relations theorists were once more placed on the defensive. These theorists had always assumed that problems created by organizations were largely limited to the psychological consequences of poor interpersonal relations rather than the impact of the environment on the organizational system. Autonomy and self-realization were no longer issues for members to decide; these issues were decided for them in actual practice. At least Weber and his students as well as the proponents of scientific management were right by the implications of their theoretical emphasis—organizations are not *by nature* cooperative systems.

But the issue was more complex than this. If the "institutional school" had shown that unofficial leadership, conflicting goals, "cooperation" of key personnel and a host of other "unintended" consequences did occur in organizations, to what extent can organizations be conceptualized as Weberian bureaucratic machinery? *Is it not equally conceivable to visualize them as the products of the strong interests which lay within their bosoms, having lives of their own which can drastically reshape their environments?*[46] As an example, is there not something to the basic thought behind the phrase "the military-industrial complex"? Thus, while we must acknowledge the insight that parts of the environment do affect organizations, *it is equally vital to recognize that complex organizations in turn can define, create and shape their own environments.*

To the extent that this is so, then the Weberian emphases had some reformulation to do, for it lacked a refinement of views on the interaction of organizations with their environment. Implicit in this reformulation is an acknowledgement that organizations should be conceived as systems. A sophisticated reformulation of the psychological literature on organizations is candid about this emphasis:

Psychologists have been characteristically unable or unwilling to deal with the facts of social organization and social structure. Societies and organizations consist of patterned behaviors, and the behavior of each individual is determined to a considerable extent by the requirements of the larger pattern. This context is not often incorporated into psychological theories.[47]

Similarly, sociologist David Silverman, who draws on the strengths of Weber in his organizational analysis argues that systems analysis:

. . . is concerned with the relative insights that may be derived by analyzing organizations from the transcendental view of the problems of the system as a whole, with human action being regarded as a reflection of the system needs, or from the view of interaction that arises as actors attach meanings to their own action and to the actions of others.[48]

In a sense, one could discover elements of systems analysis, either mechanical or biological systems, in just about every school of the theory of organizations. To a certain degree each school of organizational theory stresses some elements of interdependence. The *nature*, *quality* and *emphasis* of this interdependence are, however, treated differently in each school, and in the systems view it is all encompassing. In another sense, however, systems seem intellectually constipating because everything is related to everything else. As its critics have so eagerly pointed out, systems analysis seems incapable of generating theory because it is essentially a classificatory test. Others point to the fact that systems analysis denies a central fact which Simon has shown us so decisively a decade or two ago: the cognitive limits of our rationality.

What lessons have we learned over the last two to three decades? We will summarize, from our viewpoint, the lessons derived from all this, but a general philosophical point seems to stand out throughout this analysis. Theories of social phenomenon (and for that matter, physical phenomenon as well), can never be settled for all time, but are constantly open to validation, rejection or refinement. Those which are false must be rejected or reformulated in light of the new insights. This is certainly a messy business for the social sciences precisely because their verification methods are imprecise or subject to so many qualifications—hence the elephant image.

Students of the theories of complex organizations must nevertheless always be open-minded to new facts, theories and empirical testing of their most cherished views. This is not to say that one cannot reach certain conclusions based on available factual evidence (we have, for instance, argued that the Weberian tradition provides the best insights in organization theory), but total commitment which is blind to new substantive evidence is dangerous in all sciences—whether physical or social. The history of ideas is cluttered with the pathetic examples of noted individuals who have found it impossible to change the pristine purity of their philosophies despite the fact that the world of knowledge around them has progressed beyond their original insights.

Conclusions

It is twenty-five years ago that Dwight Waldo argued:

. . . that since administration is so large a subject, and still in many ways so dark, we should open upon it all the windows we can find; that all models and idioms have their virtues—and their vices; that as we proceed we exercise as much intelligence and good will as we can command in determining what any particular model can or cannot do for us.[49]

That is a very tall order to fill, particularly in a book which can only briefly summarize the literature on a subject as broad as this one. Authors, whether of textbook fame or of more specialized areas of study, therefore must unavoidably make numerous decisions as to what should be emphasized and what to leave out entirely.

This is particularly noticeable in North American textbooks on public policy and administration because of the general neglect of continental European writings on bureaucracy. Much more significant is the total disregard generally shown for Marxist writings on the nature of bureaucracies. This may have been due in part to the general neglect Marxists have shown towards the study of bureaucracy, but this state of affairs has been changing over the last three decades.

This "broad brush" eclectic approach, however, has highlighted certain significant facts about the theories of complex organizations which can be summarized under the following observations. In this century the voluminous development of research on theories of complex organizations has been almost exclusively a North American enterprise with significant but small contributions from the Marxian-Weberian tradition and from the so-called technological approach of English researchers. Conventionally, the development of these theories is viewed as divided into three periods: classical; human relations and modern or behavioral. We have presented an overview of all these historical stages and our conclusions are as follows:

1 All theories of organizations have been found wanting, some decidedly more so than others. It could not have been otherwise, for there is no theory known to humanity either in the social or physical sciences which can encompass total reality. Theories are more or less useful, and this can only be determined by the acid test of empirical testing.

2 Theorists in the scientific management tradition were too mechanistic in their assumptions of the individual. Their world of work was a smoothly functioning universe, mechanistic in its conception, and Newtonian in its regularity and predictability. As March and Simon put it: "First, in general there is a tendency to view the employee as an inert instrument performing the task assigned. Second, there is a tendency to view personnel as a given rather than as a variable in the system."[50] This notion of the individual as "given," and "inert," and all the implications attached to these assumptions had to be scrapped

as the complexity of human behavior revealed itself to social scientists in the twentieth century.

3 Theorists in the human relations tradition swing to the other side of the pendulum by focusing almost exclusively on the individual within organization. Their notions on good leadership, the production of change in an organization by managerial or hierarchical fiat (job enrichment, enlargement, sensitivity training, etc.) and their emphasis on interpersonal relations have been seriously qualified by empirical research. The various attempts to make work and interpersonal relations more humane and stimulating should be applauded as an inherent good value, but this should never have been confused with solving the problems generated by structural factors.

4 The writings of Karl Marx alerted us to the reasons behind alienation in organizations and the role of organizations as instruments of power relationships. The full implications of these two intellectual traditions have already been explored in two previous chapters.

5 We have also learned that a great deal of the variance in an organization's behavior can be attributable to its environment, but we have also gained the insight that an organization can in turn fashion or manipulate its own environment as well. In either case we must pay critical attention to structural consideration to uncover basic insights into organizational behavior. As an example of this, we have become more realistic about the limited range of change that can be induced through internal efforts. Good leadership must be supported by a whole range of other variables to effect change: available technologies, innovations, legislation, nature of the work force, and so on. According to this eclectic approach there are insights to be gained in learning how the reward structure of organizations are manipulated, how changes in the premises of decision-makers are effected, and how information within organizations is directed towards certain ends.

Above all, despite our strong desire and efforts to utilize theoretical insights in our descriptions and analyses of the institutions and processes of public policy and administration, we must realize that no theoretical insight in any field, be it either in the physical or the social sciences, can fully explicate total reality. Thus we would do well to heed the caveat of economists Buchanan and Tullock: "If our theory is capable of explaining all conceivable configurations, that might be observed in the real-world political process, then it is no theory at all."[54]

A Warning to Politicians about Policy Advice from Social Scientists

A political scientist is said to be a person who knows a great deal about very little and goes along knowing more and more about less and less until finally he knows practically everything about nothing.

An economist, on the other hand, is a person who knows very little about a great deal and keeps knowing less and less about more and more until he knows practically nothing about everything.

A politician, therefore, starts out knowing practically everything about everything, but ends up knowing nothing about anything due to having come to believe *political scientists* and *economists.*

Anon

Footnotes

1. In this book *bureaucracy* is considered a synonym for *complex* organization. We believe that the student, "hitting the beaches" of organizational theory and practice for the first time, can safely eschew as counterproductive the definitional niceties engaged in by more advanced scholars.

2. The experienced reader might well raise an eyebrow to our assertion that the wide disparity of writings summarized in this chapter can all be classified as "scientific." We use the term to categorize all the literature represented here as having the following common traits:

   . . . the idea (has) appeared that social phenomena have a regular character, and are therefore subject to natural laws more or less analogous to those which govern the physical universe: the conception of social laws marks a decisive step forward as the purpose of science is to look for laws which can be tested by experiment.

   Maurice Duverger, *Introduction to the Social Sciences,* translated by Malcolm Anderson, London: Allen and Unwin, 1964, p. 15.

3. See V. Seymour Wilson, "The Relationship Between Scientific Management and Personnel Policy in North American Administrative Systems," *Public Administration* (London), Vol. 51, Summer 1973, pp. 193-205, for a concise discussion of scientific management and a good representative bibliography on the subject.

4. Amitai Etzioni, *Modern Organizations* (Englewood Cliffs, N.J.: Prentice-Hall, 1964), pp. 21-29. Reprinted by permission of Prentice-Hall, Inc., Englewood Cliffs, N.J.

5. *Ibid.,* p. 21.

6. Reinhard Bendix, *Work and Authority in Industry: Ideologies of Management in the Course of Industrialization* (New York: John Wiley and Sons, 1956), p. 274.

7. James G. March and Herbert A. Simon, *Organizations* (New York: John Wiley and Sons, 1958) p. 29.

8. Quoted in Bendix, *op. cit.*, pp. 206-107.

9. See John C. Weaver, *Shaping the Canadian City: Essays on Urban Politics and Policy, 1890-1920* (Toronto: The Institute of Public Administration of Canada, 1977).

10. J.E. Hodgetts, *et al.*, *The Biography of an Institution: The Public Service Commission of Canada, 1918-1967* (Montreal: McGill-Queen's University Press, 1972), especially Chapters 3 and 4.

11. *Ibid.*, Chapter 4.

12. This statement may seem to be a contradiction in terms because the main aim of scientific management was to demystify organizational relationships, and hence the several skills of leadership should have been made evident by "science." However, while demystifying the cult of charisma in organizations, it reinforced the notion that the organization is a great hierarchy of superior-subordinate relations in which the person at the top issues the general order that initiates all activity. Scientific management said very little about the human relationships and roles which are so imperative to good leadership. See V. Seymour Wilson, *op. cit.*, pp. 197-198.

13. Andrew Dunsire, *Administration: The Word and the Science* (London: Martin Robertson & Co. Ltd., 1973), p. 103.

14. Amitai Etzioni, *op. cit.*, pp. 32-39.

15. Some of this questioning is summarized in William F. Whyte, "Human Relations— A Progress Report," in Amitai Etzioni, *Complex Organizations: A Sociological Reader* (New York: Holt, Rinehart, and Winston, 1961), pp. 100-112.

16. Warren G. Bennis, *Changing Organizations: Essays on the Development and Evolution of Human Organization* (New York: McGraw-Hill, 1966), p. 10.
    Elaborating on his futuristic theories of bureaucracy Bennis argues that changes must include:
    (i) A new concept of *man*, based on increased knowledge of his complex and shifting needs, which replaces an oversimplified, innocent, push-button idea of man;
    (ii) A new concept of *power*, based on collaboration and reason, which replaces a model of power based on coercion and threat;
    (iii) A new concept of *organization, values*, based on humanistic/democratic ideals, which replaces the depersonalized mechanistic value system of bureaucracy.
    Warren Bennis, "Organizations of the Future," *Management of Organization Development*, University of Bradford, United Kingdom, 1971, p. 16.

17. As a good illustration of this theme, see the appealing thesis of E.F. Schumacher, *Small is Beautiful*, London: Blond and Briggs, 1973.

18. Canada, *Report of the Royal Commission on Government Organization* Queen's Printer, 1962, Vols. 1-5.

19. George Strauss, "Notes on Power Equalization," in *The Social Science of Organizations*, Harold J. Leavitt, ed., (Englewood Cliffs, N.J.: Prentice-Hall, Inc., 1963), pp. 39-84; and item "Human Relations, 1968 Style," in *Industrial Relations*, 7, No. 3 (May 1968), pp. 262-276. Another good overall criticism is found in Sherman Krupp, *Patterns in Organizational Analysis* (New York: Holt, Rinehart and Winston, 1961).

20. Nicos P. Mouzelis, *Organisation and Bureaucracy, op. cit.,* p. 8.

21. Acknowledging this lack of clarification, Marxists have, over the years, sought to reformulate aspects of this concept. Considerable intellectual energies have gone into exposing the nature of the present state in capitalist societies. Beginning with the notions of "hegemony" and "managers of legitimation" the outstanding Italian communist theorist, Antonio Gramsci, has led the way in emphasizing the significance of ideological orientations in capitalist state action. His work has been expanded by, among others, Ralph Miliband in Britain, and by Leo Panitch and others in Canada. To fully explore this theme we recommend the following:
    (i) Ralph Miliband, *The State in Capitalist Society* (London: Weidenfeld and Nicolson, 1969).
    (ii) _____, *Marxism and Politics* (London: Oxford University Press, 1977), especially Chapter 3.
    (iii) Leo Panitch, *The Canadian State: Political Economy and Political Power* (Toronto: University of Toronto Press, 1977).

22. K. Marx, *Critique of the Gotha Programme 1875: Selected Works*, Vol. II, p. 577. During the French Revolution the Paris Commune was organized, and one of its major aims was to destroy the class-oriented French bureaucracy. During its brief existence the commune, in revolutionary fervor, abolished all hierarchical rank and accorded equal rights and responsibilities to all members of the community: to serve in the militia and to elect all state officials as well as commune members, thereby abolishing the standing army and the "bourgeoise" bureaucracy. Marx considered the brief Commune experience as a practical model for true communism.

23. Oskar Lange and Fred M. Taylor, *On the Economic Theory of Socialism* (Minneapolis: The University of Minnesota Press, 1948), p. 109.

24. Amitai Etzioni, *op. cit.,* p. 42.

25. The literature on the significance of Max Weber and his ideas for the sociology of knowledge is both rich and prolific. As an introduction we refer the student to two short articles:
    Talcott Parsons, "Max Weber 1864-1964" *American Sociological Review*, Vol. 30, No. 2 (April, 1965), pp. 171-175.
    Reinhard Bendix, "Max Weber and Jakob Burckhardt," *American Sociological Review*, Vol. 30, No. 2 (April, 1965), pp. 176-184.

26. James M. Burns, *Congress on Trial* (New York: Harper Bros., 1949), p. 33.

27. See Robert A. Gordon, *Business Leadership in the Large Corporation* (Berkeley: University of California Press, 1961). Jessie Bernard, "Where is the Modern Sociology of Conflict?," *American Journal of Sociology*, LVI, (1950), pp. 11-16; N.J. Demerath III,

Richard A. Peterson (eds). *System Change and Conflict* (The Free Press, New York, 1967); Lewis Coser, *The Functions of Social Conflict* (Glencoe, Ill.: The Press Press, 1956; Ralf Dahrendorf, *Class and Class Conflict in Industrial Society* (Stanford: Stanford University Press, 1959).

For a comprehensive overview of conflict studies, see: Charles Perrow, "Hospitals: Technology, Goals and Structure," in James March (ed.), *Handbook of Organizations* (Chicago: Rand McNally & Co., 1965), pp. 901-971; Sykes Gresham, *The Society of Captives: A Study of Maximum Security Prisons* (Princeton: Princeton University Press, 1958); Mayer N. Zald, "Power, Balance and Staff Conflict in Correctional Institutions," *Administrative Science Quarterly*, 7, (June 1962), pp. 22-49.

28. Melville Dalton, *Men Who Manage* (New York: John Wiley & Sons Inc., 1959).

29. A.S. Tannenbaum and R. Kahn, *Participation in Union Locals* (White Plains, N.Y.: Row, Peterson and Co., 1958); A.S. Tannenbaum, "Control in Organizations," *Administrative Science Quarterly*, 7, 1962, pp. 236-257; Idem, *Control in Organizations* (New York: McGraw-Hill, 1968).

30. Amitai Etzioni, *Modern Organizations*, especially Chapter 2.

31. For an early classic, see Harold Lasswell, *Politics: Who Gets What, When, How* (New York: McGraw-Hill Book Co., Inc., 1936) where sketches of this approach already could be discerned. For the most thorough and sophisticated criticisms of both Lasswell's and Simon's works, see Herbert J. Storing (ed.), *Essays on the Scientific Study of Politics* (New York: Holt, Rinehart and Winston, Inc., 1962), pp. 63-150; pp. 225-304.

32. See his warnings in "A Comment on the Science of Public Administration," *Public Administration Review*, VII, 3 (Summer 1947), pp. 200-203.

33. "Simon teaches fundamentally that the manager is free to engineer any kind of equilibrium, to use any kind of inducements, and to demand any kind of contributions that he can get away with—and to do this with the aim of gratifying whatever desires he chooses. The manager will not be permitted to get away with anything too raw, that the equilibrium of the organization will not be the equilibrium of terror and brainwashing of 1984, is part of Simon's unexamined political faith." Herbert J. Storing, "The Science of administration," in H.J. Storing (ed.), *Essays on the Scientific Study of Politics* (New York: Holt, Rinehart and Winston, Inc., 1962), p. 106. Storing's critique is the most thorough criticism of Simon's work so far published.

34. Simon has enlarged on this theme in Herbert A. Simon, "The Changing Theory and Changing Practice of Public Administration," in Ithiel de Sola Pool (ed.), *Contemporary Political Science: Toward Empirical Theory* (New York: McGraw-Hill, 1967), pp. 86-130.

35. "RCMP deceived him, former solicitor-general says," *The Globe and Mail*, Thursday, November 17, 1977, p. 1.

36. Rianne Mahon, "Canadian Public Policy: The Unequal Structure of Representation," in Leo Panitch (ed.), *The Canadian State, op. cit.*, pp. 165-198.

37. See, for example, T.E. Stephenson, "The Longevity of Classical Theory," *Management International Review*, Vol. 8, No. 6 (1968), pp. 77-83.

38. See Theodore Caplow, *Principles of Organization* (New York: Harcourt, Brace, and World Inc., 1964).

39. For an interesting article on this "problem" see Amitai Etzioni, "Human Beings are not very easy to change after all: An unjoyful message and its implications for social programs." *The Saturday Review*, June 3, 1972, pp. 45-47.

40. Joan Woodward, *Management and Technology* (London: Department of Scientific and Industrial Research), *Problems and Progress in Industry,*[3] HMSO, 1958.

41. See Donald Ralph Kingdon, *Matrix Organization: Managing Information Technologies* (London: Tavistock, 1973). It must be conceded that there are sharp differences of opinion among theorists about the impact of technology on organizational structure. There is, however, general agreement that different structures and leadership techniques are required for varying situations.

42. An excellent synthesis of the work done in this area could be found in Charles Perrow, "A Framework for Comparative Organizational Analysis," *American Sociological Review*, 32, No. 2, (April, 1967), pp. 194-208.

43. Paul Lawrence and Jay Lorsch, *Organizations and Environment* (Boston: Division of Research, Graduate School of Business Administration, Harvard University, 1967). See also the earlier pioneer effort of James Thompson, *Organizations in Action* (New York: McGraw-Hill Book Co., 1967).

44. A series of studies, taking their cue from Lawrence and Lorsch have since appeared in social science publications. Samples are: (Public health departments) Dennis J. Palumbo, "Power and Role Specificty in Organization Theory," *Public Administration Review*, 29, No. 3, (May/June 1969), pp. 237-248. (Welfare organizations) Jerald Hage and Michael Aiken, "Routine Technology, Social Structure, and Organizational Goals," *Administrative Science Quarterly*, 14, No. 3, (September, 1969), pp. 366-377.

45. S.D. Clark, *The Church and Sect in Canada* (Toronto: University of Toronto Press, 1948).

46. As an illustration of this thesis see Seymour Melman, *Pentagon Capitalism: The Political Economy of War* (New York: McGraw-Hill, 1970).

47. Daniel Katz and Robert L. Kahn, *The Social Psychology of Organizations,* (New York: John Wiley & Sons, 1966), p. 12.

48. David Silverman, *The Theory of Organizations* (London: Heinemann, 1970), p. 41.

49. Dwight Waldo, *Perspectives on Administration* (Mobile: University of Alabama Press, 1956), p. 49.

50. J.G. March and H.A. Simon, *Organizations*, p. 29.

51. James M. Buchanan and Gordon Tullock, *The Calculus of Consent: Logical Foundations of Constitutional Democracy* (Ann Arbor: University of Michigan Press, 1962), p. 299.

Recommended Readings

As the detailed footnotes to this chapter indicate, the literature on complex organizations is voluminous and very technical in certain areas. There are, however, some very good readable analyses which we would recommend to the uninitiated. The following is a representative sample:

Amitai Etzioni, *Modern Organizations* (Englewood Cliffs, N.J.: Prentice-Hall, Inc., 1964).
Chapters 3, 4 and 5 present brief overviews of the main schools of organizational theory. Developments are, however, not presented in chronological sequence as we have done here.

Joseph Massie, "Management Theory," in James March (ed.), *Handbook of Organizations* (Chicago: Rand McNally & Co., 1965) pp. 387-422.
This is an excellent overview of scientific management and its development over time. Another work which is useful, because it discusses many of the personalities whose works are discussed in this chapter, is D.S. Pugh, D.J. Hickson and C.R. Hinings, *Writers on Organizations* (London: Penguin, 1971). The student would obtain short, crisp discussions of Max Weber, Joan Woodward, Simon, the Hawthorne experiments, Frederick W. Taylor and others in the classical school and the Human Relations Movements as represented by such luminaries as Likert, Argyris, Blake and Mouton and so on.

Amitai Etzioni (ed.) *Complex Organizations: A Sociological Reader* (New York: Holt, Rinehart and Winston, 1961).
There are several pieces in the above which are recommended for the Human Relations perspective: William F. Whyte, "Human Relations—A Progress Report"; Reinhard Bendix and Lloyd H. Fisher, "The Perspectives of Elton Mayo"; and Chester I. Barnard, "Organizations as Systems of Cooperation." One of the source books which is also very helpful is Rensis Likert, *New Patterns of Management* (New York: McGraw-Hill, 1961).

For books which provide a good introduction to the role of technology in the organizational theory literature see James Thompson, *Organizations in Action* (New York: McGraw-Hill, 1967) and Paul Lawrence and Jay Lorsch, *Organizations and Environments* (Cambridge, Mass.: Harvard University Press, 1967). A useful introduction is also provided by Joan Woodward. See her book, *Industrial Organization: Theory and Practice* (London: Oxford University Press, 1965).

Suitable readings for the modern or behavioral period will be provided in the next chapter (Chapter 6) but a good, although somewhat difficult introduction, is provided by Richard M. Cyert and James March, *A Behavioral Theory of the Firm* (Englewood Cliffs, N.J.: Prentice-Hall, Inc., 1963), especially Chapters 1, 2, 3 and 6.

The two best books on the relationship between the organization and its environment are written by the American sociologist Philip Selznick. See his short volume,

Leadership in Administration (Evanston. Ill.: Row, Peterson, 1957) for an excellent theoretical and simple discussion of this perspective. Another of his books which develop the perspective in terms of a case study of an organization see *TVA and the Grass Roots* (Berkeley and Los Angeles: University of California Press, 1949).

Although there are literally hundreds of books now proclaiming the virtues of systems analysis, the best and most careful exposition is provided in the section of the book by Daniel Katz and Robert Kahn, *The Social Psychology of Organizations* (New York: John Wiley & Sons, Inc., 1966).

Finally, for a critical perspective of the whole gamut of organizational theory—a first rate theoretical and critical overview—see Charles Perrow *Complex Organizations: A Critical Essay* (Glenview, Illinois: Foresman and Co., 1972). The latest edition (1979) contains a new chapter developing the organizational-environmental perspective to which Perrow is committed.

CHAPTER SIX

DECISION-MAKING THEORY AND PUBLIC POLICY STUDIES*

Public policies are like the two-headed Janus, looking in different directions. One is in the direction of principle, of fundamental values, in so far as values are fundamental; the other is in the direction of the processes (and their institutions) by which the policies are put into action. It is not always clear what is principle, or policy, or process; and many, many difficulties are caused by the confusion, because a principle is not easily compromised; a process is but a means to an end; and a policy, the pig in the middle, has qualities of both. Public policy research cannot therefore concentrate on policy questions without looking at *principles* and *processes*.

A. W. R. Carrothers

Why worry about contradiction? You'll never write about feelings if you do.

Nobel Laureate Saul Bellow

I. Introduction

In the preceding chapter dealing with the theories of complex organizations, we briefly attempted to show how decision theory has partly influenced the corpus of theoretical knowledge on organizations. Our broad-brush treatment of this complex subject of necessity precluded any detailed assessment of decision theory. However, as one strand of the theories of complex organizations decision theory has in turn spawned a variety of decision-making models; a proliferating body of knowledge now fashionably called policy analysis, and a growing lit-

---

The classification which is presented here (and incidentally, the one in the previous chapter also), is not self-evident in academic textbooks on public policy and administration. To claim such would be, as Hugh Heclo once put it in another context, "donning crimson in the bullpen." It is simply this author's way of attempting to show the important connections between the theories of complex organization and decision theory and policy studies. Too many authors on "public policy" or "policy analysis" start a consideration of the policy literature (or parts of it) without really knowing, or for that matter caring, about the basic roots of their intellectual preoccupation. If they do not, a case could be made for the fact that this book should.

erature on case studies, examining either single decisions or policy in specific areas (taxation, pollution control, social services, etc.). Literally hundreds of books now exist on the subject and its outgrowths, so one chapter cannot even vaguely hope to give a satisfying treatment of synthesizing the literature.

However, there is some merit in attempting a taxonomic classification of the scattered voluminous body of knowledge so that the student can make some sense of it all before delving into specialized areas of decision-making theory as preference dictates. Taxonomy is, after all, the "cornerstone activity" of every field of knowledge in the physical and biological sciences. Taxonomic classification helps to categorize knowledge, to provide a "road map" for direction in orderly study, and to make sense out of a seemingly confused, contradictory body of knowledge. In the social sciences such an orderly classification is not fully attainable. After all, as Saul Bellow reminds us in one of this chapter's epigrams, we are dealing with human beings with emotions and unpredictable whims—aspects of life that can never be neatly classified or categorized. Nevertheless, the attempt can and does bring some semblance of intellectual order to the literature, hence it is presented here for the reader.

Thus to the message. The chapter will first concentrate on the early contribution of Herbert A. Simon, a public administration scholar who first popularized the concept of decision theory.[1] Simon's early work subsequently led to the blossoming of other contributions from various fields in the social sciences, all taking their initial cues from his seminal writings, but moving into new vistas of intellectual activity. We will outline these contributions and some of the criticisms which have been made of them. Secondly, we will then concentrate on one of the offshoots of decision theory, namely, policy studies. However, basically this discussion will be taxonomic in nature, leaving the more detailed assessments of this literature to more specialized texts.

II. The Contribution of H. A. Simon and Others: Decision Theory in its Early and Contemporary Stages

Simon's contribution to the social sciences can begin with his now famous critique of the concepts of PODSCORB first popularized by Gulick and outlined in Chapter 5.[2] Such "principles of scientific management" he argued in his critique are really proverbs in the sense that "it is not that the propositions expressed by the proverbs are insufficient, it is rather that they prove too much. A scientific theory should tell what is true but also what is false."[3] Using this criteria Simon argued that PODSCORB was basically homilectics, and new theoretical guidance had to be sought "to substitute rational decisions for . . . snap judgments":

When I attempted twenty years ago to find answers to some questions of municipal organization—e.g., whether a recreation department should be administered by the school board or the city government, or how the city planning function should be organized . . . —I discovered that no theory existed that could provide the answers, and I was forced into an analysis of the ways in which organizations affect human choice. Finding no better answers to this new stratum of questions, I thought it necessary to reexamine the theory of rational decision-making. The latter task required me, in turn, to settle in my own mind some basic problems of logic.[4]

In his major work, *Administrative Behavior,* Simon tackles these problems of logic by conceiving of administrative organizations primarily as decision-making structures:

What is a scientifically relevant description of an organization? It is a description that, so far as possible, designates for each person in the organization what decisions that person makes, and the influence to which he is subject in making each of these decisions.[5]

Decisions, according to Simon who initially accepts the logic of the logical positivists, are based on two types of premises: factual premises, which are subject to empirical validation in order to assess their falsity or truth, and value premises which cannot be tested because they deal with normative consequences, that is what "ought to be" rather than what "is." This relationship between fact and value is spelt out clearly by Simon:

A decision is a sentence in the imperative mode. It is a direction to the self or to some other person or persons. In order for a decision to appear as a conclusion in a valid logical proof, one of the following must be the case: (1) it is possible by the rules of logic, to derive imperative sentences from assumptions that are all in the indicative mode or (2) among the assumptions are one or more sentences in the imperative mode. Logical positivists reject the first alternative on the ground that no one has shown by what sleight of hand it can be accomplished. Hence they conclude that a decision can be logically validated only if at least some of the unproved assumptions from which it is derived are sentences in the imperative mode. These unproved imperatives they call value premises. Moreover, they argue that these value premises cannot be derived solely from empirical observations, since empirical observations establish sentences of the form that "such and such is the case"—i.e., declarative sentences.[6]

Rational behavior is viewed as a means-end hierarchy. Given certain ends (ethical propositions) appropriate means (several relevant facts) are selected for their attainment. Once the ends are reached, however, these "certain ends" often become intermediate, that is, "the ends" often become the means to attain further ultimate ends. Thus a means-end chain or hierarchy gets established.[7] Simon argues that this logic of means-ends becomes crucial to the organization because the administrative hierarchical structure allows all decisions, except those defining ultimate ends, to rest on factual rather than on value premises. Means rather than ends are therefore crucial in this structural set-up. Organizations are established with specific purposes in mind. These purposes serve as a framework for the means-end hierarchy, for the ends of members of the organization are thereby defined by the directives of their superiors. The main responsibility of subordinates is to find the best means of attaining these directives. Thus, we have an interesting combination: subordinates find that (1) their value premises are supplied by superiors and (2) their search for the best means of attaining these premises is proscribed by procedural regulations in the organization. The combination of these two limitations permits rational decision-making in an organization.

At this point of his analysis Simon gently drops his excursion into logical postivism. Many reasons can be speculated for this, but one most likely explanation is the tremendous amount of criticism which was engendered by his means-end schema.[8] At any rate, well into the book Simon mildly warns the reader that "this analysis of rational behavior in terms of a means-end hierarchy may lead to inaccurate conclusions unless certain cautions are observed."[9] Three dangers are pinpointed: "(1) the ends to be attained by the choice of a particular behavior alternative are often incompletely or incorrectly stated through failure to consider the alternative ends that could be reached by selection of another behavior [selecting one end may mean overlooking others equally crucial]; (2) in actual situations a complete separation of means from ends is usually impossible, for the alternative means are not usually valuationally neutral [means-end terminology may not truly separate facts from values in decision-making]; (3) the means-end terminology tends to obscure the role of the time element in decision-making [it may not be fully appreciated that the realization of a particular end at a given time limits the ends that can be realized at that and other subsequent occasions]."[10] He seems to finally make the break with logical positivism by arguing that the means-end language fails to make a complete separation of factual and value questions, which is "the only valid distinction."[11] He further buttresses this viewpoint (or conclusion) by his assertion that:

Sociology has been forced to treat of human behavior (at least in its rational aspects) in terms of "ends" and "means"; for example, these are fundamental categories in [Talcott Parsons'] *The Structure of Social Action*. It could easily be shown that these two terms complicate rather than simplify the analysis of human rationality, and it is to be hoped that they will now be discarded, both in sociology and in ethics, in favor of the schema of "alternatives," "consequences," and "values" attached to "consequences." . . . This schema quite obviously owes its origins to the utility calculus of economics, but in its generality it can be applied, at least descriptively, to all behavior, whether rational or not.[12]

This question of rationality therefore remained central to Simon's concerns just as it was a prime concern to the scientific management experts Simon had criticized in his previous works. But having eschewed the means-end hierarchy Simon also argued that it is equally futile for a theory of organizational behavior to divorce itself from human reality by adopting the rationality of "economic man"—always armed with the full facts of the situation, knowing all and shifting all the known facts to arrive at the best solution to the problem. In a word, "the economic individual" *maximizes* in every decision made. On the other hand, "the administrative individual" making administrative decisions has his/her rationality limited for various reasons: all the facts and consequences of a particular course of action cannot be humanly predicted and realistically assessed; and because rationality requires a choice among every possible alternative, this becomes an impossibility and many alternatives will of necessity be excluded in the actual making of the decision. The organization serves to limit the scope of decisions by supplying the administrative individual with overall organizational objectives and limiting the choice of means by regulations. In a word, rationality in an economic sense is eschewed. The organization member must forego a search for the best of alternatives and be content with finding satisfactory choices:

The central concern of administrative theory is with the boundary between the rational and the non-rational aspects of human social behavior. Administrative theory is peculiarly the theory of intended and bounded rationality—of the behavior of human beings who satisfice because they have not the wits to maximize.[13]

Simon's basic interest in the limits of rationality has taken him, over the past three-and-a-half decades, into the realm of psychology and the processes of thinking. He has pursued this further through his studies on information theory and cybernetics, to computer models seeking to plumb the depths as to *how* human beings make choices.[14] His contributions have been monumental, and almost all studies in decision theory or policy analysis usually begin by paying homage to his path-breaking contributions.[15] Whatever one thinks of his efforts, for Simon is not without his numerous critics, it must be conceded, nevertheless, that this social scientist remains one of the most remarkable Renaissance men of our age: first starting out in political science, public policy and administration and economics, he has continued to straddle these "fields" and more. His interest in psychology had led to his earlier appointment as a senior professor in psychology at Carnegie-Mellon University, and finally during 1978, the bestowing of the Nobel Prize as a crowning glory to a most brilliant academic career.

Why was Simon's contribution so important and considered to be so path-breaking? After all, the concern for rationality in organizations was not a "Simonian invention," for it was also a central concern of the earlier scientific management "efficiency experts."[16] V. Subramaniam suggests three essential reasons why Simon's contribution to administrative studies was so vitally important during the last three decades.[17] The first is an academic one, that is Simon's subsuming of Fayol's POCCC or Gulick's POSDCORB into the single all-embracing one of decision-making:

DR. HERBERT A. SIMON.
Nobel Laureate (1978)

In doing this, he was satisfying the deepest craving among the followers of any single discipline to find a single focus or a single fundamental concept. Many philosophers have sought a focus for philosophy in the concept of substance in the West or in different types of relation with God in the East. Physics found it in the interaction of matter and energy and Chemistry in the reactions of elements and compounds. As for Biology, a great biologist like Julian Huxley regretted such lack of focus and suggested the concept of evolution and the basic living cell as the focus of biological studies. Simon's ideal of decision or "decisional premise" seemed to him to provide such a fundamental basis for administration and drew much support from students and teachers who yearned for such a single basis.[18]

A second reason was the rise in popularity of the philosophy known as Existentialism in the immediate postwar years. The existentialists glorified the agony and activity of choice as the ultimate redeeming feature of the human condition. This agony is principally, although partly, a by-product and symptom of the obligation to exclude certain choices from others. This existentialist glorification ultimately leads to a concentration on actual decision-making processes, emphasizing the mechanisms of choosing or problem solving in terms of its steps, such as search and comparison and the ultimate need to "maximize or satisfice"—areas which Simon concentrated his intellectual efforts.

Thirdly, Simon was the first to catch the subtlety and nuances of choice. Decision-making was simply not a question of commanding and doing, but all actors were intimately bound up in a subtle nuance of ethical (value) and factual propositions. There is much credence to the fact that the former (value) is validated in accordance with the rules and behavior of democratic procedure and the latter in accordance with the process of scientific investigation and verification. Simon was the first to recognize this subtlety while at the same time helping to strengthen the prevailing criticism that politicians choose while administrators expedite. The politics-administration dichotomy is neither right nor wrong because it is an intricate mixture of democratic values and factual propositions. Very few students of administration caught this subtlety in Simon's arguments.[19] Subramaniam, however, puts this thought very well:

. . . the climate of opinion had changed in regard to the relation between decision and administration. Others were only vaguely aware of it but *Simon understood it more deeply.* The old description of administration as doing things or getting things done had a modest as well as an assertive connotation and both connotations had become obsolescent by the nineteen forties. In the first sense, it meant that people's representatives and leading statesmen made decisions while the public administrator loyally carried them out. In the second sense, it sneered at those politicians who talked airily and prescribed vaguely as against those (administrators) who really did things. *Both interpretations were fast becoming irrelevant in the post-Second World War period. Critics and defenders of administrative discretion, administrators and academics had all realized for some years that the public administrator was making at least as many important decisions as the politicians in office.* [20] [italics are mine]

Simon was confident enough to predict that decision-making theory would revolutionize the theory of organizations. In *Administrative Behavior* he declared that "the construction of an efficient administrative organization is a problem in social psychology" and by the end of the book he prognosticated that the "science of administration" would take perhaps two paths. On the one hand it might pursue knowledge "as to how men would behave if they wished their activity to result in the greatest attainment of administrative objectives with scarce means." On the other hand it might simply describe and analyse "the way in which human beings behave in organized groups."[21] These alternatives, he argued, were similar in other scientific studies such as economics:

First, economic theory and institutional economics are generalized descriptions of the behavior of men in the market. Second, business theory states those conditions of business behavior which will result in the maximization of profit.[22]

Administrative Behavior had dealt with both aspects because it was the rivulet from which greater streams will spring: its building block, the decisional premise, was "the central concern of administrative theory."[23]

Simon turned out to be right in his prognostications as shown in Figure I. Many of Simon's disciples and admirers developed certain descriptive-analytical aspects of decision theory by concentrating on socio-psychological modelling. Socio-psychological studies concentrate clearly on personality characteristics of individuals rather than on the social structure. In analyzing the processes of decision-making psychological criteria are traced back to the past social experiences that produce them: what are the past experiences and characteristics of decision-making participants which lead to produce decision X as opposed to decision A or Z?[24] Other disciples developed mathematical tools and techniques to help in the formulation of clear, quantified alternatives.[25] A competent description of this literature is now well beyond the abilities of this author. However, from a general knowl-

FIGURE I
A TAXONOMIC CLASSIFICATION OF DECISION THEORY EMPHASIZING ITS
RELATIONSHIP TO
THEORIES OF COMPLEX ORGANIZATIONS

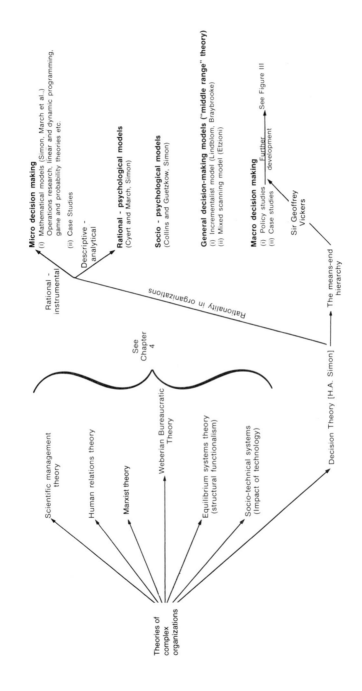

edge of the literature it is clear to the intelligent reader that mathematical tools are advocated for mostly evaluating *known* alternatives by processing information. To put this another way, it seems that the rightful place for mathematical tools and techniques (operations research, network analysis etc.) is to help in the delineation of choices more clearly *after some alternatives have been roughly settled upon by the decision-makers*. Mathematical tools are therefore aimed at those hoping for greater certainty in decision-making, those concerned with the definition of a problem either econometrically or for engineering purposes, and those others concerned with single value business decisions in contrast to multivalued public decisions.

A third group has developed "middle range theory" by concentrating on simplified general decision-making models. These researchers argued that advanced mathematical techniques remain largely the province of those concerned with relatively small-scale problem-solving where the total number of variables were small and precise and value-problems restricted. Economist Charles Lindblom, one of the leading exponents of "middle range theory," quotes approvingly Charles Hitch, an expert in quantitative techniques:

I would make the empirical generalization from my experience at RAND and elsewhere that operations research is the art of suboptimizing, i.e. of solving some lower-level problems, and that difficulties increase and our special competence diminishes by an order of magnitude with every level of decision-making we attempt to ascend. The sort of simple explicit model which operations researchers are so proficient in using can certainly reflect most of the significant factors influencing traffic control on the George Washington Bridge, but the proportion of the relevant reality which we can represent by any such model or models in studying, say, a major foreign-policy decision, appears to be almost trivial.[26]

In contrast, "middle range theory" is not "greedy for facts" and can be constructed simply and not through an extensive elaboration and collection of observations.[27]

Yet a fourth group has criticized socio-psychological and mathematical models in particular by contending that these models have simplified and rarefied decision-making. Policy making, they contend, is too complex and too full of uncertainties and imponderables for precise mathematical calculations. *Policy making to them involves several conflicting values, a multifarious number of actors in the decision process and an undefined time perspective—a conception of policy, incidentally, which coincides with our definition of policy in Chapter One.* After a prolonged study of the British National Health Service, one well-known British political scientist emphasized this perspective in a way highly reminiscent of Simon's means-ends hierarchy:

[There is a need] to develop a way of conceptualizing policy-making as a sort of multidimensional chess. . . . In a field like health services, it is the *interrelatedness* of areas and issues which seems to be the norm. If the medical profession adopts a particular stance on issue X, it may well be because section A of the profession wants to enlist the support of section B on issue Y. Similarly, government may well give in to the demands of the medical profession on issue Z, because it wants to conserve its political and administrative resources for the coming conflict over issue W.[28]

Others were asking some practical questions of all this intellectual activity: how is this new knowledge about decision-making to be taught to students in our universities and colleges? It did not take long for the case study method to be popularized both in business and public administration programs. Case material developed typically involved a decision that had been made, or that needs to be made, thus offering the student opportunities for learning from another's experience as well as for constructive guessing. The proliferation of intellectual activity is shown by Figure I. The classification is by no means a detailed one, but it indicates the main taxonomic outline in the growth of decision theory in the past three-and-a-half decades.

For our purposes we will concentrate on three aspects of this growth. First, we will make some comments on the utility of case studies both in the micro- and macro-decision categories outlined in Figure I. Secondly, we will concentrate on the development and use of "middle range theory" in decision-making by describing the early "general models" of incrementalism and mixed scanning, both devised also in reaction to the rational model criticized by Simon. Finally, we introduce our exploration of the growing field of policy studies by concentrating briefly on the important contribution of Sir Geoffrey Vickers, a retired British public servant, whose excellent analytical work in decision-making and policy studies gives us further insights into that Byzantine human activity we know as policy making.

III. Case Studies, General Decision Theories and Policy as Multivalued Choice

At around the same time that Simon's contribution to decision theory was receiving widespread attention, R. A. Dahl of Yale also wrote an article in *Public Administration Review* complaining of "putative efforts" which then existed to make a "science" of public administration from the principles of Gulick, Urwick and others. As such, Dahl joined ranks with Simon in attacking the then conventional knowledge of administrative principles and action. What was needed, Dahl concluded, was a set of middle range, analytically relevant, scientifically verifiable propositions for the task:

No science of public administration is possible unless: (1) the place of normative values is made clear; (2) the nature of man in the area of public administration is better understood and his conduct is more predictable; and (3) there is a body of comparative studies from which it may be possible to discover principles and generalities that transcend national boundaries and peculiar historical experience.[29]

In North America the response was to write case studies of particularly interesting decisions with the hope that out of these narratives would spring "principles and generalities that transcend national boundaries." One social scientist argued that the failure of theory to emerge was due to this lack of case study material and as more cases are written this defect will be then rectified.[30] The case study method, in the 1940s and '50s, became the dominant formal technique used in public policy and administration and in other areas of the social sciences where studies of both public and business policies were conducted (for example, case studies in social work and in business administration).[31]

For those whose primary interest is pedagogical rather than theoretical this development of cases provided an adequate vehicle to give students "a feel" for the practical operations of policy development. As Robert T. Golembiewski argued:

. . . the cases in the aggregate should direct attention to common managerial processes and dynamics, within the context of public employment. These processes and dynamics cover a mammoth range: the causes and effects of managerial actions; the motivation and morale of employees; the structure and policies that define a work site; the good and bad consequences of specific managerial styles, and far more besides that is intended and unintended in organizational life.[32]

The use of case studies as a pedagogical tool has gained widespread acceptance both in Europe and North America. In Britain, the British Civil Service College uses cases extensively in its training programs and in the United States the Inter-University case program has grown significantly in the past thirty years.[33] In Canada the use of cases has been sanctioned both by the Institute of Public Administration in Canada (IPAC) and the Committee of Schools and Programs in Public Administration. As a result, a project aimed at developing more cases in Canadian public administration has been launched, and thus far over twenty cases have been prepared and utilized by the public administration community.[34] These cases have little pretention of building cumulatively toward theory. A. D. K. Kernaghan, the first Director of the Case Program of IPAC, is careful to emphasize its pedagogical strengths and to argue that "the use of the case method [enables] teachers and students [to] experience vicariously the complexities, difficulties and opportunities of decision making in government."[35]

Some scholars, particularly those engaged in the study of decision-making in international relations, argue for the full acceptance and further development of the case method as an analytical tool.[36] Others have criticized the use of cases, but remain unequivocal about them,[37] and still others have rejected them altogether as nontheoretical and unscientific, contributing little, if at all, in the cumulative building of theoretical insights into decision-making.[38] Perhaps the most balanced assessment of the role of case studies has been presented by Professor Hugh Heclo, who, while critical of past efforts in the development of the case method, argues that, "there appears to be nothing about the case study technique which is inherently nontheoretical or unscientific; the problem lies in assuming that theoretical contributions will emerge automatically from narrative."[39] He further amplifies this point at length, and it is crucial that we quote him because Heclo seems to have struck upon a reasonable position on this controversy:

Case studies may in fact have unique advantages for theory construction. Perhaps the greatest area of promise in case studies concerns their ability to "move" with the reality of dynamic factors. If the earlier points are accepted concerning policy as a moving course of action or inaction (rather than as a discrete decision, enactment, or program administered at a moment in time), then attention to changes *through* time is crucial. Again it does not seem any inherent deficiency in policy case studies which has created their curiously ambiguous treatment of change. On the one hand, the approach seems particularly well suited to the delineation of dynamic forces in the sense of concentrating on "how things work." On the other hand, most case studies have been unnecessarily static by failing to investigate how "the working of things" changes. Another way of saying the same thing is that case studies have attended to motions far more than to transformations. Thus, the popular decision-making approach in policy case studies has typically led to analyses which stop at the point of decision rather than more broadly and more realistically considering the decision sequences which constitute an on-going policy. . . . Thus for example the "case," rather than concerning an individual action or decision event, may in the future treat policy in terms of a cohort of decisions and decision makers, i.e. aggregates through time which experience significant events in certain chronological intervals. Here too there seems to be great scope for a qualitative expansion of the case study approach to public policy.[40]

In Figure I we have attempted to show some of the different ways in which the use of case studies have been found useful. Mathematical and empirically oriented models are geared to be used with data from both individual case studies where only a few variables are involved and objectives are fairly explicit (micro-decisions) and more complex cases or combination of cases using aggregate data drawn from comparative sources.[41] Also, case studies are utilized to demonstrate a decisional process involving several conflicting values, many groups and/or institutions and an undefined time series. Under this heading we can group the variety of non-mathematical or descriptive case studies to which we have referred in our discussion.

Those who have argued for more "middle range theory" in decision-making contend that precise mathematical models and the use of case studies as such fail to capture an analysis which is more realistic of the decision-making environment. Analysis, they contend, should proceed on two levels simultaneously: first, *a concentration upon the participants in the decision-making process,* the actors, roles, institutions and so on, and second, *a concern with how the process interacts with the larger political system so that patterned interaction among certain relevant participants occur to generate public policy or decision-making*—a dual emphasis on the individual engaged in the decisional process and on the systematic properties of the process as a whole.

These scholars have not got themselves embroiled in the sterile debate about the futility or non-futility of utilizing case studies. As a matter of fact they have quietly used the case study method to help in the generation of certain general observable patterns of behavior—the first step in the more precise formulation of general hypotheses for further testing.[42] Added to this "scientific concern" this group purport to be jointly involved in ways to improve the quality of decision-making in a democratic context. Put in another way, they contend that they are normative in their research thrust, "scientific" in orientation, and very much concerned with providing a basis for improving rational efficient methods of policy formulation. The works in the so-called "policy sciences" of Lasswell and Lerner, Yehezkiel Dror, Braybrooke and Lindblom, and Dahl and Lindblom, are good illustrations of this category. We cannot discuss in any detail the major concerns of these scholars, but it is sufficient to point out that their explicit goals have opened up a whole Pandora's box of criticisms: from the argument that the "expert" observer should refrain at this stage from being involved with policy advice (given his imprecise tools),[43] to the charge that this school of thought is either manipulative in intent or really sophisticated advocates of the status quo.[44]

There is one common orientation which brings together the general models of decision-making advocated by this grouping. They view policy making as a complex multivalued choice exercise *for the whole system,* and in so doing they tend to concentrate their analysis on how the individual policy maker operates within that on-going political system. By stressing the parameters of individual choice the assumption is made that the political system demands an approach to policy making which is both *continuous* and *gradual* in nature. The best illustration of this thrust of analysis is illustrated by the very popular general model of "disjointed incrementalism" espoused by the political philosopher David Braybrooke and the economist Charles Lindblom in their book, *A Strategy of Decision.*[45] This approach, like the earlier Simon's contributions, begins by criticizing the rationalist decision model:

It assumes intellectual capacities and sources of information that men simply do not possess, and it is even more absurd as an approach to policy when the time and money that can be allocated to a policy problem is limited, as is always the case. Of particular importance to public administrators is the fact that public agencies are in effect usually instructed not to practice the first method. That is to say, their prescribed functions and constraints—the politically or legally possible—restrict their attention to relatively few values and relatively few alternative policies among the countless alternatives that might be imagined.[46]

Stripped to its essentials, the disjointed incrementalist model is a matter of making small changes and basing sequential action after these changes upon an evaluation of the incremental results.[47] This incrementalism is dubbed "a strategy of decision." It has a normative side to it in that it calls for us to continue this type of incremental strategy, perceived to have yielded satisfactory results on previous occasions in decision-making. People decide to repeat what is reinforced in their past behavior. By acting incrementally one gets away from all this theoretical emphasis on grand strategy. [Incrementalism,] write Braybrooke and Lindblom, *"can adapt itself to the absence of theories; it is a way of getting along without theory when necessary."*[48]

Schoettle gives one of the best descriptions of the disjointed incrementalist model by briefly enumerating its eight essential characteristics:

1 Choices are made in a given political universe, at the margin of the status quo.
2 A restricted variety of policy alternatives is considered, and these alternatives are incremental, or small, changes in the status quo.
3 A restricted number of consequences are considered for any given policy.
4 Adjustments are made in the objectives of policy in order to conform to given means of policy, implying a reciprocal relationship between ends and means.
5 Problems are reconstructed, or transformed, in the course of exploring relevant data.
6 Analysis and evaluation occur sequentially, with the result that policy consists of a long chain of amended choices.
7 Analysis and evaluation are oriented toward remedying a negatively perceived situation, rather than toward reaching a preconceived goal.
8 Analyses and evaluation are undertaken throughout society, that is, the locus of these activities is fragmented or disjointed.[49]

Despite its popularity in the literature as a general "middle range" theory of decision-making, the disjointed incrementalist model has been subjected to extensive criticisms by various authors. We can perhaps very briefly mention three general criticisms made of the model: 1 The model fails to indicate what would count as an incremental intervention and what would not; 2 decision-makers are left in the dark as to when they should interpret and act upon the results of their incremental adjustments; and 3 a corollary of 1 and 2 namely that the decision-maker has absolutely no clear indication from the model as to when it would be safe to intervene in the process.

In brief, the criticisms point to the central fact that all public policies generate feedback data. The incrementalist model ignores this feedback in an explicit way by not exploring how inputs translate into outputs. The model will apparently demonstrate that such and such can work or will not work *but is completely incapable of distinguishing the intervening variables which will account for why it does or does not work.* This is a crucial point to which we will return later. Robert K. Merton has identified this important point by asserting that "unless the crucial theoretical variable . . . can be identified there is no basis for assuming that the same results will be obtained on other occasions."[50] Not identifying the crucial variables for understanding leads us nowhere in determining what counts as an incremental decision and what is not. This is so because we have no way of determining this fact: step no. 7 in our disjointed incrementalist model becomes no step at all because we have no criteria for analysis and evaluation of "perceived situations."

Moving on to the general plane of societal decision-making where this model also is applicable, it is pointed out by critics that incrementalist strategy clearly recognizes the theory's inadequacy in accounting for "large" or fundamental decisions, such as a decision to go to war.[51] As such, it is therefore a partial theory and needs supplementing by other partial "middle range" theory. As Amitai Etzioni puts it:

(a) most incremental decisions specify or anticipate fundamental decisions, and (b) the cumulative value of the incremental decisions is greatly affected by the related fundamental decisions. . . . Thus while actors make both kinds of decisions [fundamental and incremental] the number and role of fundamental decisions are significantly greater than incrementalists state, and when the fundamental ones are missing, incremental decision-making amounts to drifting—action without direction. A more active approach to societal decision-making requires two sets of mechanisms: (a) high-order, fundamental policy-making processes which set basic directions and (b) incremental processes which prepare for fundamental decisions and work them out after they have been reached. This is provided by mixed scanning.[52]

Mixed scanning, advocated by Etzioni as a "middle range" general theory, incorporates aspects of both the rationalist and incrementalist models. Fundamental decision-making requires a more thorough search of alternatives. The scanning of such requires adequate time, resources, personnel and effort. It is, however, not an extensive search as in the rationalist model for only a few problem areas are selected for a fundamental scan. This kind of scan is analogous to a spot-check audit whereby areas to be thoroughly audited are selected by whatever process for a fundamental analytical inspection:

Having selected one or more high-priority policy areas, it is hypothesized, the policy-maker will then be found making a significant effort to evaluate alternatives in an orderly fashion. The process is less encompassing than that suggested by the rationalist model but, unlike the incrementalist model, it does involve decision-points where "reversibility declines," that is, decisions are made of sufficient importance to make equally important alterations difficult (without returning to the original starting point). The mixed scanning model thus includes major hypotheses from both the rationalist and the incrementalist models, and insofar as these are linked together, it does constitute a third alternative model rather than being simply a middle ground position.[53]

The critique remains, however, that in both general models the questions raised as to *why* incremental or mixed scanning interventions are capable of working or not are not raised. Were these models saying that public policy decision-making is basically incrementalist as a matter of definition or as a matter of contingent experience? Were they advocating this style of decision-making as a political program or were they designing models to implement these particular biases in the decision-making process?[54] These questions remain and continue to provide critical evaluations and re-evaluations of the general middle range theories.[55] Anderson sees no clear way out of this and warns that in the use of models one should in the end use a little common sense:

Each [of the models] focuses attention on different aspects of politics and policy making and seems more useful for some purposes or some situations than others. Generally, one should not permit oneself to be bound too rigidly or too dogmatically to a particular model. . . . It is my belief that the explanation of political behavior, rather than the validation of a given theoretical approach, should be the main purpose of political inquiry and analysis.[56]

Interestingly enough this is the same viewpoint of a British lawyer-administrator and man of letters, Sir Geoffrey Vickers, who has been leery of some of the specialized theoretical expositions in decision theory and policy studies:

I have spent my life practising the law and helping to administer public and private affairs; and I have thus had opportunity to observe and take part in the making of policy. The more I have seen of this, the more insistent has been the challenge to understand it both as a mental activity and as a social process, for it seems strange and dangerous that something so familiar and apparently important should remain so obscure. My enquiry into it has led me further than I expected. I have had to question sciences in which I am not professionally qualified and sometimes to supply my own answers, when theirs seemed ambiguous, inconsistent or absent. I present the result with humility but without apology. Even the dogs may eat of the crumbs which fall from the rich man's table; and in these days, when the rich in knowledge eat such specialized food at such separate tables, only the dogs have a chance of a balanced diet.[57]

What follows is a remarkable and brilliant book, an analytical treatment of public policy which is yet to see its theoretical import fully incorporated into the corpus of the theory of organizations. As V. Subramaniam has remarked, Vickers' "major work on decision making [is] so much admired and [yet] so little followed up."[58] We can only

SIR GEOFFREY VICKERS
Intellectual, retired lawyer—senior administrator and man of letters.

summarize its broad outlines here and indicate why Vickers' contribution is an important one.[59]

Vickers' point of departure is making quite clear to his reader his fundamental belief as to what policy is: "I have described policy making as the setting of governing relations or norms, rather than in the more usual terms as the setting of goals, objectives or ends. The difference is not merely verbal; I regard it as fundamental."[60] What this means is that policy making is seen as a continuous interaction between individuals, organization systems and the wider environment. Unlike H. A. Simon who concentrated on "the decision" or "the premise of the decision" as the central nucleus and all-pervading activity of an organization,[61] Vickers argues that systems maintenance rather than perpetual goal seeking is the norm of human activity. Rather than focus on "the purpose ridden 'man'," a fallacy of the psychological textbooks, we should concentrate on the norm-maintaining person wielding what power or influence possessed by maintaining a set of relations in time and space:

> The objects of our desires and aversions are not objects but relations. No one "wants an apple." He may want to eat it, sell it, paint it, admire it, conceivably even merely to possess it—a common type of continuing relation—in any case to establish or change some relation with it. *The goals we seek are changes in our relations or in our opportunities for relating; but the bulk of our activity consists in the "relating" itself.*[62]

Given this constant need for norm-maintenance rather than constant goal seeking, "facing a particular problem" and "searching for alternatives" (the logical requirements of continuous goal-seeking activity), is replaced by an "appreciative system," in Vickers' terminology. Vickers' analysis here is excellent, for instead of getting into the logical-positivist distinction of facts and values separation which Simon quickly abandoned in his earlier work, Vickers shows how the appreciation system is an inevitable feature of the human condition—appreciating facts and values operate as *a single system* at all times. Vickers in a discursive chapter describes the appreciative system as "the evolution and modification of the course, the norm, the standard, the governing relation which is inherent in every policy and the selection and ascertainment of the facts relevant to it."[63] A succinct description is proffered by Subramaniam:

This is the continuous (system of) interaction in the individual mind between reality judgments and value judgments. Reality judgment, of course, means one's estimate of present and past events, future probabilities and also other people's unspoken opinion (value judgments) and probable reactions. *A value judgment* is what one believes to be good or right; it is seen as an act of oneself but is a fact or a part of a reality judgment of another. *The appreciative judgment* of the appreciative system sees or poses a problem as soon as it spots a particular combination of realities and values; the better one system is, the earlier it poses a problem over a long time perspective and then, instrumental judgment searches for a solution. Both judgments are essential to policy making but the former is clearly held to be more important.[64]

Vickers then places this individual appreciative system, with its capacity to integrate facts and values continuously; its feedback learning process; and its conflict dealing and innovative mechanisms, within an organizational context. What then follows is a highly analytical description as to how the appreciative system integrates with institutional processes to produce policy. Vickers builds a triangular system (see Figure II) of both external and internal indices: (a) the organization's external controllers, (b) the metabolic and functional criteria of the organization's managers, and (c) the actual direction of policy.

He first distinguishes individual decision-making (considered a "market" decision) from decisions made on behalf of others (a "political" decision). The organizational elite and chosen others are really in the business of making "political decisions"—the latter mode of decision completely eclipsing "market" decisions in our modern societies. Vickers then gives important dimensions of "political" decisions which we need not detail here (the self-perpetuating nature of organizations, the division of tasks among units, the accountability issue, motivational characteristics and so on).[65] Among "political" decisions the most important is the manner in which the outside organizational controllers determine objectives for the organization. However, this is usually not a big problem on the average. As Subramaniam points out: "Different controllers apply different vague organizational suc-

FIGURE II
SCHEMATIC DIAGRAM OF SIR GEOFFREY VICKERS'
"HUMAN-ECOLOGICAL" SYSTEM

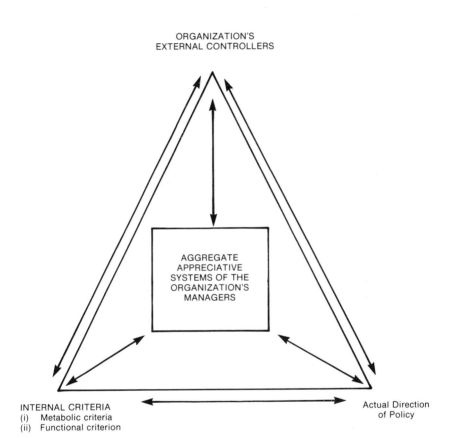

ORGANIZATION'S
EXTERNAL CONTROLLERS

AGGREGATE
APPRECIATIVE
SYSTEMS OF THE
ORGANIZATION'S
MANAGERS

INTERNAL CRITERIA
(i)   Metabolic criteria
(ii) Functional criterion

Actual Direction
of Policy

In his summary chapter (ch. 20) Vickers describes the system as
"our self-maintaining and self-exciting system" (p. 228).

cess criteria such as growth or annual profit, depending on the nature of the controllers and the characteristics of the organization. As these criteria are generally vague and as the controllers' criticism is intermittent, the ultimate criterion is the amount of trust vested by the latter in the internal decision makers."[66]

The responsibility of organizational maintenance is thus usually relegated to the managers who possess internal criteria which is broadly divisible into metabolic and functional criteria. Metabolic criteria is concerned with balancing income with expenditure, "optimizing" the value obtained for resources spent on the quality of organizational self-maintenance and to maximize incoming resources to enhance the level of self-maintenance.[67] The functional criterion of the organization (profit, or service or crime prevention etc.) is emphasized as a proper justification of the organization's existence—its *raison d'être* in a word. This organizational context and its internal controls are overwhelmingly important whenever the external controllers are too busy or uninformed to set up detailed guidelines and specific objectives—which is most often the case. *Thus the metabolic criteria based on the internal machinations of the organization (survival, growth, etc.) dominate most organizations both in the public and private sphere. This is why public-sector and private-sector organizations begin to look alike. It is not the nature of their tasks which bring on this resemblance; rather it is their metabolic criteria which so approximate each other.*

There is much, much more to Vickers but it is hoped that enough is said here to whet the appetites of our readers to continue further study of this first rate exposition of decisional theory and public policy making. First, Vickers had made a significant contribution to the literature by his "appreciative system." His analysis of the interdependence of reality and value judgement in the appreciative system gets the fact-value distinction earlier made by Simon out of the dead-end alley it had fallen into. Furthermore, the appreciative system is an important complement to all the step-by-step methods of policy making so popular in North America, because it begins to give the decision-maker or observer of decisions some clues as to *why* such and such an intervention is capable of success or not—an earlier criticism of general decisional models. Secondly, he has successfully enlightened us about the external and internal factors which account for norm maintenance (and changes in these norms) in the organization. His analytical description of the workings of external control, internal metabolic criteria and the direction of policy fills an important gap in the literature. Subramaniam has glowing praise for this work: "Vickers' total picture is harmonious, explains the limitations of men and organizations, puts decision in proper perspective in the total context of human activity and is a valuable corrective to assumptions about discrete decision situations, unlimited rationality and unlimited organizational capacity to achieve external goals."[68]

As a partial model of decision-making Vickers' model definitely complements those micro- and macro-decision models previously described which completely disregard realistic assumptions as to how the "responsible" human mind operates towards a decision, and how some organizational "givens" circumscribe the courses of action open for choice.[69] The reader also begins to appreciate the basic distinctions involved in making a decision as opposed to the more complex norm-maintenance integral to policy making. To repeat once more, policy making is an activity incorporating several conflicting values, involving many institutions and groups and operating usually on an undefined time perspective. As such, it is usually qualitatively categorized as "complex decision-making."[70] It is to a categorization of this theoretical literature that we now turn.

Policy Studies

Without giving it a second thought most people think of public policy as goals enunciated by political parties and leaders during electioneering time or as the public pronouncements of politicians from time to time after executive deliberations. These goals are then carried out by administrative means (that is, the bureaucracy) whose input is usually viewed as instrumental in character. This perception is reinforced in the academic literature where students of public policy have tended to separate the study of behavior and institutions (politics and policy formulation) from that of administration and implementation *without making it conceptually clear that any analytical or normative distinction is not or should not be equated with a total perception of reality.* As Andrew Dunsire puts it:

[The rationale of the policy/administration dichotomy] is a separate matter from the appropriateness of any particular labels one might choose for the two aspects (although names must be given or there is no way of talking about it); and that in turn is a separate matter from the success or failure of the instrumental use that someone may have tried to make of it. Though the policy/administration dichotomy may not satisfactorily discriminate between the work of politicians and the work of officials, that does not necessarily mean that there is no policy/administration dichotomy; and even if we found that, indeed, a policy/administration dichotomy is a false one, that would not mean that a command/execution dichotomy was also false.[71]

What Dunsire is in effect arguing is that public policy is conditioned by a mix of ideas, ideologies, interests and institutions. It is this mix which gives birth to such ideological formulations as the politics/ administration dichotomy, which if it is not a reflection of total reality, nonetheless strongly conditions our behavior and attitudes to our political leaders and bureaucratic actors in the system. And what is even more important these political and bureaucratic actors are in turn conditioned by these ideologies as well.

Thus, any attempt to comprehend the formulation and implementation of public policy is made all the more complex by the intermingling of the inseparable characteristics of the *factual situation, normative or value considerations* and *the complex network of processes* surrounding policy. As one of our epigrams indicates, it is not always altogether clear what is principle, process or policy and "many, many difficulties" are caused by this confusion. However moving from the realm of ideas to the more practical concerns of making some taxonomic sense of the theoretical literature there is some logic to the distinctions made so long as one does not view such distinctions as water-tight compartments of thought, but only as helpful tools in the task of clearing away some conceptual cobwebs in policy analysis.

In Chapter Three we argued that Western political thought has never broken from the Aristotelian tradition of assuming that the nature of the polity is greatly influenced by the non-political bases of social and economic life. It should therefore come as no surprise that most studies of public policy would therefore emphasize the policy process as the most crucial factor in the formulation of public policy. Marxists for example would contend that the capitalist state can only be fully understood in relation to its structures and processes and that there is a very close connection between "the organizational dynamics of the state" and "the contradictions of the capitalist society as a total system."[72] While other students would place a lesser emphasis on economics and relatively more on social aspects, the Aristotelian bias nevertheless remains the same: policy is dependent on both the social and economic realities of our society.

Figure III is an attempt to come to grips with a classification of the different conceptions. It can be readily seen that most studies emphasize policy process rather than policy content. Furthermore there is some doubt as to whether those studies which proclaim the emphasis on content actually do so in practice, but that is a problem which we will leave for another platform. As Figure III indicates there are at least five subcategories of the theoretical literature which emphasize policy process. These are studies in the Marxist tradition, systems analysis and its progeny, public choice, the technological literature, and, for want of a better term, the neo-institutional school of public policy (successor to the descriptive/institutional approach in political science before the behavioral movement of the 1950s). We have identified only two of the subcategories emphasizing policy content, namely, the policy content typology of Theodore Lowi and the nondecision elitist theories of Bachrach and Baratz and their followers.

It is only recently that Marxist studies have emphasized the "organization dynamics of the state" and have paid more than a passing attention in examining its importance. Within the last two decades Marxist research has attempted to rectify this imbalance by first concentrating on studies of economic elites, focusing especially on interinstitutional relationships and the interpenetration of economics and politics. This orientation is particularly evident in the work of Ralph Miliband who has emphasized the personal links of kinship, education and other socialization patterns between the state (the bureaucratic and political elites) and corporate elites.[73] Louis Althusser and Nicos Poulantzas carry the concept of the state one step further by emphasizing its all-inclusive characteristics which allow it to permeate all institutions of society as the "organizer of hegemony":

> . . . the system of the State is composed of several apparatuses or institutions of which certain have a principally repressive role, in the strong sense, and others a principally ideological role. The former constitute *the repressive apparatus of the State* . . . (government, army, police, tribunals and administration). The latter constitute *the ideological apparatuses of the State,* such as the Church, the political parties, the unions (with the exception, of course, of the *revolutionary* party or trade union organizations), the schools, the mass media (newspapers, radio television), and, from a certain point of view, the family. This is so whether they are *public* or *private.* [The State is therefore] . . . the instance that maintains the cohesion of a social formation and which reproduces the conditions of production of a social system by maintaining class domination.[74]

As the "organizer of hegemony" the state does not act always in the full short term interests of the dominant class. After all, it must "keep the peace" over *all* classes in *the long term interests* of the dominant class. This is why the state apparatus is conceived by Neo-Marxists as independent from individual interests, in order to allow it to act *on behest of* the dominant class in society, namely, the capitalists:

> For Marxists the function of the state in a capitalist society is to serve the *long-term* interests of the *whole* ruling class. The state is understood to serve the interests of the bourgeoisie not so much in its day-to-day activities as to ensure the continuity of capitalist relations of production, and not only in the face of the fundamental challenge potentially posed by the proletariat but also, at times, against short-term threats posed by fractions within the bourgeoisie

FIGURE III

POLICY PROCESS (Policy assumed to be a dependent variable)	POLICY CONTENT (Policy assumed to be an independent variable)
I Neo-Marxist studies (i.e. Poulantzas, Miliband)	I *Lowi's policy content typology.* (i.e. Lowi, Salisbury).
II *Systems Analysis* (i) Bureaucratic politics. Inclusion of some psychological factors to account for organizational routines and standard operating procedures (i.e. Simon, Cyert, March, Allison). (ii) Socio-economic development analysis. Forces outside political system having important roles in shaping policies. (i.e. Dye, Hofferbert.) (iii) Heavier reliance on systems of constraints and consideration for actors (i.e. Crozier, Gouldner, Silverman).	II *Elitist theories, especially the concept of non-decision.* (i.e. Bachrach, Baratz).
III *Structural technological aspects stressing the sociology of organizations.* Policy affected by organizational structure which is contingent on environment, technology, capacity to cope, size, etc. (i.e. Burns, Woodward).	
IV *Public choice* (i.e. Buchanan, Olson, Niskanen, Hartle).	
V *Interplay of ideas, interests, and institutions.* Single country examples or comparative case study approach (i.e. Heclo, King, Doern, Aucoin).	

whose immediate interests put them against the global interests of their class. Consequently, the actual form of the role of the state will differ under different conditions of capitalism, though the ultimate content remains unchanged. [75]

Whether one takes the narrower view of the state (Miliband) or this all-inclusive view by Poulantzas and his followers really does not matter much, Neo-Marxists insist. What matters is "the conceptual clarity all Marxists possess to explain the functioning of capitalist institutions generally."[76] As a consequence of this understanding of the state Neo-Marxists have of late concentrated in roughly four theoretical areas to indicate the main forces shaping the formation of public policy: 1 the labor theory of value,[77] 2 the forces and relations of production,[78] 3 historical analyses regarding capitalism as a continually developing system simultaneously resolving old contradictions and creating new ones,[79] and 4 a concentration on the class structure and class struggle.[80]

We will not attempt to describe in any detail those Neo-Marxist studies of public policy which have incorporated some or all of these theoretical areas. It is sufficient to state here that all of these studies incorporate these theoretical concerns when they contend that: (a) public policy studies are usually ahistorical with little attention given to the ways in which the state has moulded both elite attitudes and institutions.[81] (b) the study of public policy has generally been isolated from issues of social stratification, social class and social conflict;[82] (c) almost all the literature on the theory of organizations, including decision-making and policy studies, are elitist oriented because of their bias in studying managerial behavior as more important, variable and worthy than that of the workers;[83] (d) in general, public policy studies are undialectical, seldom identifying the societal contradictions of tomorrow in the reality of today.[84] But above all, Neo-Marxists almost overwhelmingly argue that their contributions must not just be narrowly critical of existing theory or geared to "intellectualizing" in order to increase the understanding of political reality.[85] Rather, it should include all these things and more: Marxist public policy studies should be geared to human practical activity, or praxis, in order to achieve the desired changes needed in society:

Needless to say, a discussion of Marxian concepts is either absent in organizational textbooks, or badly distorted, or focusing only on Marxian or Neo-Marxian theories of the state. . . . Important as it is, a merely critical posture has certain limitations and pitfalls. For example, the negation of mainstream theory or orthodox methodology may serve as common ground for a variety of unorthodox, deviant, or critical positions. But negation is only one aspect of a larger process of posing, counterposing, and resolving problems—that is, transcending and superseding contradictions. In the language of dialectics, negation is but one moment within praxis. Thus, while we are negating certain rigid, reified methodological procedures, we also need to move toward transcending them *and* our own counterposition. Concretely, this means that we will not make theoretical and methodological progress if we merely counterpose new methods to old ones, hermeneutics against causal-explanatory empiricism, interpretation against the technical-rational mode of scientific method, detached analysis against evaluation, intervention, and social action. We may have a chance of developing a broader methodological praxis if we retain the interpretive mode together with the "objectifying" scientific mode as natural phases of the process of inquiry—that is, if we develop a method that becomes *practical*, in the sense that it changes the object of inquiry or, at least, indicates how the object can be changed. Praxis does not replace interpretation but includes it.[86]

By their theoretical orientation Marxists can be thus categorized as very much concerned with the policy process, that is, the various processes by which public policy is actually formed.[87] Liberal-democratic students of the behavioral persuasion at least agree with this emphasis but they have contended that the explanation of public policy can best be helped by the construction of models which portray the relationships between policy outcomes and the forces which shape them. Generally one conceptualizes outcomes as a result of forces brought to bear upon a *system* and causing it to make particular *responses*. Thus a model which builds on this insight would stress the relationships between socioeconomic inputs (the forces), political system characteristics (systems) and policy outcomes (responses). Much of this systems analysis has been built from the theoretical works of David Easton and the "policy sciences" prescriptive and empirical model theorizing of Harold Lasswell.[88] While there are many variations to systems analysis in its general form, Figure IV is a very good representation of system links between environment, system behavior and input/output characteristics. In this model is identified:

1 **Policy inputs:** demands for action (and inaction) arising from both inside and outside the political system.
2 **Policy outputs:** levels of services and goods provided in tangible ways by the system. These services could also be identified as regulative or symbolic in character.
3 **Policy outcomes (or impacts):** the effect (either intended or unintended) a level of service has on the population.

The first of the systems model we would note is the so-called bureaucratic politics model best characterized by the work of Graham Allison, and it concentrates and builds upon Allison's case work on the Cuban missile crisis using a paradigm of "governmental (bureaucratic) politics."[89] Briefly, Allison argues that policy input/output studies should concentrate on policy processes which emphasize the notion of bureaucratic politics (the output of bargaining amongst a variety of actors) or the output of organizational processes (organizational routines and standard operating procedures). Organizational structures within the political system, together with the vested interests of political actors, act on the decisional processes to mould the emerging output. As Allison puts it: "Governmental behaviour can be understood . . . less as deliberate choices and more as outputs of large organizations functioning according to standard patterns of behaviour."[90]

Drawing heavily on the pioneering decisional studies of Simon, March and Cyert, Allison's approach argues for treating organiza-

FIGURE IV

AMENDED SYSTEMS MODEL OF THE POLICY PROCESS

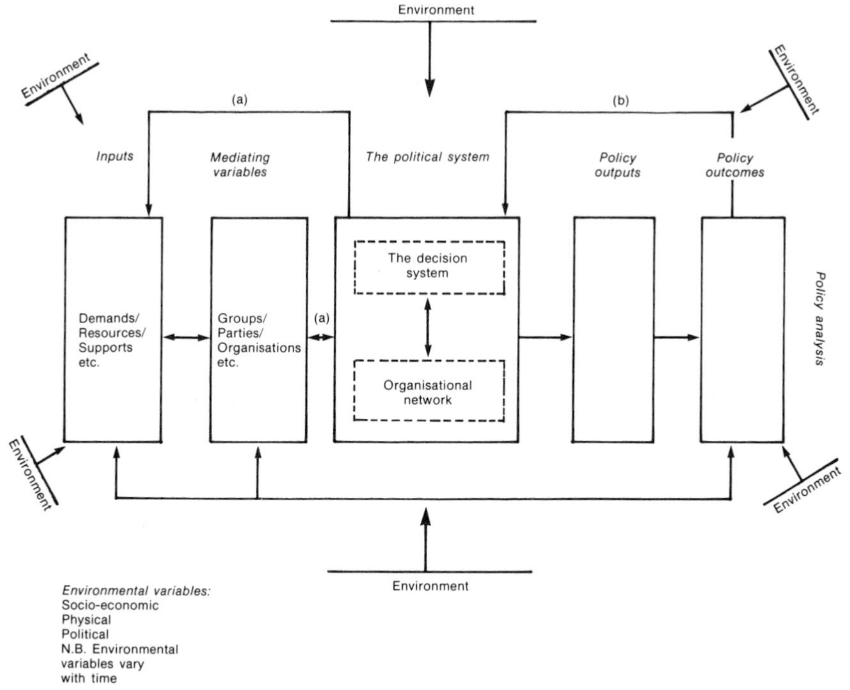

Adapted from W.I. Jenkins **Policy Analysis: A Political and Organisational Perspective** (London: Martin Robertson, 1978)

tions as unit entities with goals. These goals constrain organizational behavior, turning rationally enunciated objectives into "satisficing" activity. Thus, considered over time, organizational structure and routine procedures do affect the development of goals and the procedures of choice. As W. T. Jenkins argues:

Organizations avoid uncertainty; the more complex their activities, the more important standard operating procedures become and the more likely it is that organisations will aim at acceptable performance which "maximises" their own particular position. Hence as the political system is, over and above all, an organisational network, a policy analyst adopting this perspective would examine organisational interests, demands and actions, since these are seen as key determinants of policy.[91]

In brief, any real understanding of the policy process must take into consideration the infrastructure from which policy arises: administrative influences are central in explaining governmental outcomes.[92]

This thesis is not accepted by all input-output studies. Defining policy as "the level or amounts of taxes, expenditures or service" some scholars have argued that these aggregate data offer "methodological and theoretical promise" for a "systemic empirical study of policy."[93] Furthermore, "interesting questions can be asked in a scientifically respectable manner about substantive outputs."[94] These output studies, therefore, concentrate on economic development analyses, which examine national and cross-national aggregate data on levels of government spending, taxing and service. These are correlated with such variables as levels of wealth, industrialization, adult education, population density, capita income and so on. The works of Richard I. Hofferbert and T. R. Dye are in this category.[95] From "systemic studies" comparing empirical data from the American States Dye, for example, argues that it was socio-economic rather than political variables which were much more significant in explaining the levels of expenditure and service. In his own words: "Economic development variables were more influential than political system characteristics in shaping public policy in the U.S. states."[96]

A Canadian study utilizing this genre of systems analysis was attempted by Professors David Falcone and M. S. Whittington some years ago.[97] The authors sought to examine "the extent to which political factors are predictors of temporal variations in political system outputs in Canada". Thus, such variables as, the party in power, party competition, the background and recruitment patterns of Members of Parliament, turnout at elections and others were analysed to determine, in aggregate statistical terms, whether they are reliable predictors of output. The study concluded that political variables did not seem to matter much and that socio-economic factors appear to be better predictors of policy output. The authors did however candidly acknowledge that their findings may have been predetermined more by their methodology than by "reality."[98]

Considerable criticisms have been generated by those opposed to both the methodology and conceptualization of the "number-crunching" perspective of Hofferbert, Dye and their followers. Aggregate studies fail to account for the redistributive effects and the measure of conflict in the system. As one critique pointed out, such detail had generally been provided by case studies, but the abandonment of this focus for more "systemic comparative data" veiled the extreme significance of the effects of elites, the ideological antecedents of policy, and the influence of intervening institutions in the political system. Another critic argues that the output studies of Dye, Hofferbert and others ". . . are primarily pitched at a level where much is eliminated, where the detail of the political process or implementation is lost, where perceptions and behavior are downgraded and where issues such as conflict disappear behind the smokescreen of correlation analysis."[99] Such criticisms have led to subsequent modifications and amendments of "systemic" studies. Dye has subsequently argued that too much has been read into "systemic" studies: "Results obtained in analysing levels of government activity may not be the same as those obtained in analysing *distributional* policies or *qualitative* policies."[100]

For these reasons and more, many students of policy studies concentrate their research efforts on the bureaucratic input/output model previously described, but with a heavier concentration on organizational actors to account for a better understanding of variation in organizational behavior and performance. The work of sociologists Michel Crozier, Alvin Gouldner, Tom Burns and David Silverman are in this category.[101] Arguing for a more dynamic approach to organizational and societal variables these sociologists stress: (a) a detailed understanding of the operation of the organizational system and the political system in which it is found;(b) a consideration of changes over time in the internal structures of the organizations; and (c) the relationships of organizations with each other and with their wider environment. In such an environment different actors pursue different ends under different constraints, and the researcher must have a clear understanding as to what these constraints are: "To understand such patterns one must explore the changing perceptions of such groups and the variety of attachments that they have. . . . One is led, therefore, to explore actor's perceptions and, particularly in this instance, a world of internal politics which is clearly more than a bargaining process within the political system."

Another partial model of the policy process in part closely related to the work of Crozier, Gouldner and others mentioned above, is the so-called contingency theory of organization which eschews psychological considerations and concentrates on the theme that *activities within organizations may be constrained by the nature of the organizational structure itself.* Jenkins points out that the specific nature of this orientation pinpoints how variation in organizational internal structures may be significant for factors such as: (a) the rate of organizational innovation; (b) attitude and morale within the organization; and (c) behavior within and between departmental units in the organization. If the correlation is significant "then one needs to know what causes structural differences, and their relevance for governmental action."[102] Jenkins' description is excellent for he explains to the reader how from contingency theory come the ideas "that there may be links between technology and structure, that certain structures are most appropriate for certain technologies, that changes of technology without changes of structure usually lead to problems and tensions within organizations,"[103] and so on. A "logic of analysis" is thereby generated in the following manner:[104]

Contextual Variables	Organizational Structure	Organizational Performance
e.g., size, rate of environmental change, political sensitivity, etc.	e.g., degree of centralization, formalization of rules and procedures, etc.	Performance, e.g., attitudes, efficiency, adaptability, etc.

This preoccupation with the links between technology and structure has led some critics to charge that contingency theory ignores to a large extent the actors in the system—their behavior, actions and perceptions. As a partial model of public policy its defenders however contend that such deficiencies can be corrected by widening and rethinking many aspects of the model.

A fourth subcategory of the theoretical literature, essentially economic in nature, also makes the assumption that the processes of policy are most significantly correlated to the inner dynamics of political and administrative organization, and that this comprehension is crucial if one wants to understand and/or reform the political system. This body of knowledge is collectively known as public choice. Traditionally, economists have devoted a considerable amount of energy on such topics as income distribution, unemployment, inflation, the operation of markets and so on. In other words, economics can be defined by its subject matter (substantive policy areas), this being linked with the distributive and allocative mechanisms through which goods are apportioned—a definite emphasis on policy content.[105] As a science of choice, economics can be construed as an approach which emphasizes the individual as a rational (at least in his terms), self-interest maximizing actor. "This individual," explains Maslove, "when placed in an environment defined by its institutions, rules of behaviour and a set of prices (incentives) will maximize his perceived self-interest, and will respond to changes in this environment in a predictable fashion.[106] In other words, the decisional structure, the processes of policy can also be considered extremely significant to the final outcome. Economists therefore bring to the study of public policy an orientation which stresses both process and content but with an added emphasis:

What is relatively new . . . is the examination of the public decision-making process and its outcomes (such as policies, programs, budgets) taking into account the motives of all the actors and the incentives facing them. The novelty and the promise of this approach is its emphasis on individuals rather than institutions as the primary actors in the system.[107]

Most of the public choice theorists are economists and their work, although significant and highly suggestive as partial theory, will not be reviewed here.[108] We will, however, mention one public administration scholar, namely Vincent Ostrom, whose normative assumptions we have already explored and who applies public choice to the understanding of problems of public policy and administration. Ostrom is heavily critical of centralized control in administration which characterizes our public institutions of today. In their search for "efficiency" the conventional theorists of bureaucratic politics have overlooked the fact that different decision-making structures may be suitable for different policy circumstances. Viewed in this way organizational "arrangements can be thought of as nothing more or less than decision-making arrangements."[109] The gist of his argument is that a plurality of structures is the only efficient way of allocating public goods. Making a strong plea for his concept of democratic administration Ostrom concludes that the successful reform of our present institutions "would point to the conduct of policy and administration via a decision framework that was multi-organisational in form and style of operation."[110]

The core of public choice theory is the notion of methodological individualism which has come in for its share of criticisms. There is much doubt that people behave in the many roles they happen to occupy as if they were impersonal market conditions. In many life situations individuals, when they must act, take much more than self-interest into account before making their decisions.[111] Public choice is silent on this fact. Furthermore, the organizational framework of decision-making has been criticized as somewhat fuzzy in conception. W. I. Jenkins, for example, points out that this lack of an organizational perspective "demands that legislators and administrators respond solely to preferences expressed outside the organisation; in general terms, it denies the possibilities of organisational attachments, attachments which, if absent, may raise questions concerning organisational survival. Thus the model may be useful in an economic sense but in practice has low potential for capturing the complexity of behaviour unless fundamental changes occur."[112]

Despite the severe criticisms that public choice is in reality a new guise for the continuing "conservative, non-interventionist, anti-administration" biases of conventional economics,[113] some enthusiasts of this partial theory remain undaunted about its possibilities. For example, it is clear from Maslove's critique of Hartle's public choice paradigm that these "biases" are viewed as obstacles which the individual researcher must confront and solve rather than inherent problems which cannot be eradicated from the research methodology. Despite its youth,[114] public choice theory has an impressive and increasing body of literature to its credit: the role of the bureaucracy in policy formulation (Niskanen), voting behavior (Downs), pressure group activity (Olson), coalition formation (Riker), conflict (Boulding) and the nature of democracy (Buchanan and Tullock).[115] There seems no doubt that this prolific contribution to public policy studies will continue.

Finally we consider a fifth theoretical perspective in the policy process category, namely the interplay of ideas, interests and institutions. It would not be entirely correct to argue that this interplay perspective is a new one entirely or for that matter a well-formulated theory. It however points to characteristics which tend to be deemphasized in other partial theories, and which advocates of the interplay perspective argue are the most crucial ones. These are the interplay of structures of political institutions, the social and physical settings which affect the policy environment and the ideology of the social system.

Students of political institutions are well acquainted with the older tradition of the study of political institutions. The interplay perspective reaffirms this tradition in arguing that such areas of intellectual interests as the nature of federalism, the differences in the functions and perspectives of the legislature and its executive, the role of the court system, the absence or presence of disciplined national political parties and so on are important determinants both to the substance and quality of public policy. Added to this is of course the social conditions of the polity under consideration. "Institutionalists" of the 1940s amd 50s certainly began to stress such variables as the geographical setting, the racial, religious, class and even age differentials as crucial determinants in policy formulation.

The role of ideas in this interplay has been receiving the most attention recently because advocates have been fascinated with the relationship of thought to political behavior. Some have even gone to the extreme by arguing that ideology outweighs all other political factors in the formulation of public policy. Anthony King, commenting on the development of American public policy is emphatic on this score:

The pattern of American policy is what it is, not because . . . the demands made on government are different from those made on governments in other countries; not because American interest groups have greater resources than those in other countries; not because American institutions are more resistant to change than those in other countries (though they probably are); but rather because Americans believe things that other people do not believe and make assumptions that other people do not make . . . Ideas constitute both a necessary and sufficient condition of the American policy pattern.[116]

Anthony King's stance on ideology is however more the exception rather than the rule among those advocating this theoretical perspective. A more modest claim for ideas is made by Ronald Manzer in the development of his "policy paradigms" which help to "express the current assumptions from which specific policy making can proceed, . . . limit the appropriate set of policy instruments, and . . . summarize the world view of the policy-making community."[117] According to Manzer these paradigms are unlike ideology for they do not claim to portray a world-view of reality. Rather they are more or less restricted either to "specific fields of public policy or to dimensions of public policy that cut across policy fields but are not the entire substance of public policy."[118] As examples in Canada Aucoin gives for the former the policy paradigm of the health field where public support for professional curative care has been, until very recent times, the dominant mode. This dominance has of course been challenged by a competing school of thought stressing the need for personal preventive care. An example of the latter would be economic policy in Canada where, until very recently Keynesian economics was dominant.[119]

Doern and Aucoin contend that the "trio of categories" (ideas, interests and institutions) are a flexible mode of analysis in that they lend themselves to be combined in any manner appropriate to the researcher's taste. Thus they argue that "the study of public policy is greatly influenced by the eye of the academic beholder."[120] This flexibility allows Doern and Aucoin to emphasize much neglected "processes" internal to governments: the overall priority-setting process; the economic-policy and management process and its often conflicting struggle with social-policy processes and redistribution; the expenditure-budgetary process; the regulatory process; and the federal-provincial relations process.

This flexibility of being all things to all people seemed to be both the greatest weakness as well as strength of the interplay perspective. Relating such fuzzy notions as "policy paradigms" or "ideas" and "ideology" to actual specific behavioral aspects of policy formulation, and assigning causal weights to these notions, seem, to say the least, a rather imprecise exercise open to all sorts of speculative far-fetched theorizing. Yet the same can be said of any theory. At least it can be said that the interplay perspective if handled competently by any public policy scholar has tremendous potential for enlightening us on public policy issues both comparatively and on a single case study basis.[121]

We now move to the classification of those studies which concentrate on policy content (see Figure III), and the genre of studies most often quoted and widely referenced are those of the political scientist Theodore Lowi. Lowi began his contribution many years ago by being critical of the state of the art in policy studies. He was generally very dissatisfied with the case-study approach or the issue-oriented studies commonly researched by his fellow social scientists. Issues and cases are "too ephemeral." Politics is a continuous activity, thus "it is on the basis of established expectations and the history of earlier government decisions of the same type that single issues are fought for.[122]

Lowi argues that input-output studies in the policy process category very badly distort the reality of policy content and policy making. Studies of this ilk make the questionable assumption that "policy is simply the output of any decision maker, whether it be an individual or collectivity, a government or a non-government." In short, "policy making is policy making is decision making."[123] Why is this so? Lowi traces this attitude to the 1950s and '60s when the behavioral revolution was in full swing:

Behavioral social science is primarily a focus on socially microscopic phenomena of interpersonal relations, small groups, and opinions; the larger phenomena have been taken as aggregates of the microscopic or as environmental factors that interact with the microscopic. What was neglected, albeit not entirely abandoned, were those more macroscopic things within which individual behavior takes place. This includes rules and norms, institutions and other social structures and any individual or interpersonal behavior must presuppose. This context is the public and formal, which is distinct from, yet the correlative to, the private and informal or behavioral.[124]

Lowi argues that the most important dynamic concept uniting all these "structural variables" is "governmental coercion"—a factor which makes government distinct from any other form of organization. To obtain a further insight into public policy, Lowi argues that one must examine the character of the choices made by governments and ask questions about the impact of these choices or the processes themselves to get a proper perspective on what these policies are all about. In other words, instead of starting with the inputs, as in systems analysis, one should start with outcomes, the other way around, and then work one's way to the input side of the equation. *By examining policy content first, one is making a basic assumption that policy can and does affect politics; that is, policy can be construed as an independent variable.* Lowi's work in public policy becomes very important for students because it enables us to understand and to differentiate what part of political behavior (dependent variable) is structured by the policy (independent variable) and what remaining variation of policy may be due to other factors such as resources, goals and tactics. Thus we will have isolated that part of the variation due to policy. However, Lowi argues that to understand fully the reality of the policy process, we should encompass both aspects of the policy-politics equation (politics ⟶ policy, and policy ⟶ politics).[125]

Furthermore, if politics encompasses the notion of coercion, therefore differing ways of using coercion would imply differing types of policy content and also differing processes to arrive at output and outcomes. As he puts it, we must define our study of public policy ". . . in terms of these aggregative characteristics—meaning state, public, coercion, and real policy—rather than in terms of the muscular movements of components of that system."[126] Thus, for every type of "real policy" there is likely to be a type of political relationship which is distinct, which in turn leads to a categorization of policies in ways which identify their impact or expected impact on the political process. Lowi thus categorizes policies as *distributive, redistributive, regulative* and *constituent*.

1 Distributive policies help to disaggregate resources into individual units, each of which may be dispensed in isolation from the others. With these policies conflict is low or totally absent and it is extremely difficult to identify if any one loses because of the gains of others. The dispensation of patronage is a good illustration of this category of policy. "When a billion-dollar issue can be disaggregated into many millions of nickel-dime items and each item can be dealt with without regard to others, multiplication of interests and of access is inevitable and so is reduction of conflict."[127]

2 Redistributive policies do not apply to individual behavior directly as distributive policies. These policies work through large groups or classes within which individual behavior takes place. Furthermore, they are created to ensure a transfer of resources within a society and are characterized by centralized decision making. The progressive income tax laws of Canada are a good illustration of this category.

3 Regulative policies are specific, direct and individual in their impact, and encourage a multiplicity of participants. Regulative decisions involve direct choices resulting in direct winners and losers on any particular issue, and the regulative process is characterized by bargaining among tangential interests in their struggle to influence policy through conflict and compromise.

4 Constituent policies are indirect or remote forms of coercion and are aimed at fairly large groupings of people. Such governmental actions as the symbolic uses of politics (playing of the national anthem), the issuance of propaganda or policy "balloon" statements and the creation of new agencies to represent particular constituents' interests are illustrative of this type.

Lowi's analysis leads him to clearly assert that *no one model of policy studies is sufficient to explain policy formation*, a point which has already been emphasized by our use of the term "partial models" for all the various contributions already described. This new focus which Lowi advocates has produced many critical analyses, chief among them being: (a) that Lowi has offered concepts which cannot be easily tested empirically; and (b) that these concepts, at any rate, inevitably draw the researcher back to a full preoccupation with inputs and outputs, the variables so easily dismissed by Lowi.[128] Be that as it may, it nevertheless remains true that the student of public policy has been given a new perspective by Lowi which has proved intellectually useful in analysing some facets of public policy. For example, for the first

FIGURE V

TYPES OF COERCION, TYPES OF POLITICS AND TYPES OF POLICY

(AFTER T. A. LOWI*)

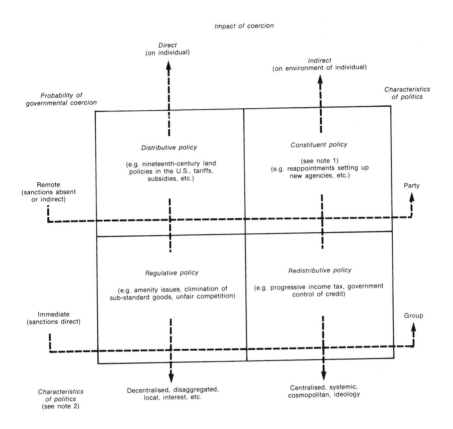

Adapted from W.I. Jenkins **Policy Analysis: A Political and Organisational Perspective** (London: Martin Robertson, 1978)

time an analytical tool in public policy studies treats *the regulatory function of government as a basic form of governing device involving very direct coercive activity on groups affected by or involved with such activity.* As Bruce Doern indicates:

The "other" half of the reality of government has recently been rediscovered. Regulatory functions and regulatory and adjudicative agencies, boards and commissions are of course a major part of governmental policy and organization, but unlike expenditure outputs and regular departments, the regulatory arena of political activity does not go through a process or cycle of assessment analogous to the budgetary process. . . . Hence this "other" half of the reality of government can be easily ignored in an aggregate sense.[129]

While political science is well known as a discipline with a *policy process bias*, the "behavioralist revolutionaries" of the '50s and '60s argued, among other things, that this policy process bias needed a fundamental correction in that by concentrating on "the authoritative allocation of values" rather than on the "State," a much clearer focus as to what the discipline is all about will be achieved.[130] The implication of this focus is clear to William Riker:

> Now if, as Easton asserts, politics is the authoritative allocation of values and if, as I interpret it, "allocation" refers not to a physical process but to the social process of deciding how a physical process shall be carried out, then the subject studied by political scientists is decision-making.[131]

In other words, if politics is visualized as a process of allocating values by the making of decisions, then the political process must be construed as the central axis around which a number of lesser processes revolve. Process is seen as the "how" of making decisions as distinct from "who" decides, "under what conditions or upon what occasion . . . in what organizational context . . . or what results of the decision might be." This concern for the linkages between *policy process* and *policy content* therefore becomes a central focus for those studying public policy making.

These concerns ultimately led to the flourishing of research and the ensuing debate in political science and sociology concerning the nature of societal power. From small beginnings (a case study analysing community power in Atlanta, Georgia), this area of intellectual activity has spread to basic philosophical concerns about the nature of liberal democracy itself.

The first study of community power concentrated on those members of the city of Atlanta having a "reputation" for power. Power and influence were measured by attribution in the eyes of knowledgeable individuals rather than by any more direct method of their determination. This method has become known as the "elitist model" of power. C. Wright utilized this type of material to make his wider generalizations about American society: power in America is permanently concentrated in the hands of an elite few immune from the pressures and concerns of the masses in the majority.

The debate which these conclusions have engendered has gone on for years, and to this day it still continues in one form or the other.

Here we can hardly hope to capture the main aspects of this intellectual quarrel. The most sustained criticisms of Hunter, Mills and others from the reputational school have come from the so-called "Yale pluralists" who argued with the underlying philosophical assumptions of the reputational approach rather than with the research procedure utilized. Robert Dahl, Raymond Wolfinger and Nelson Polsby argued, through their case studies, that the political system is composed of a series of competing groups with differing power bases. Unlike the elitists they argued that the channels to the system were opened to all. This is the so-called normative theory of democracy which implicitly asserts that pluralism is diffuse power—a power which is never concentrated permanently in the hands of a single elite. Instead, political power is always issue-based and subject to being used in the same manner as one uses money: it is fleeting, at times elusive and most of the time fractionated.[132] The assumption is also made that most of the time this reality of democratic pluralism is the best of all possible worlds. "Mass democracy has, through its very nature," opined E. H. Carr, "thrown up on all sides specialized groups of leaders—what are sometimes called elites. Everywhere, in government, in political parties, in trade unions, in co-operatives, these indispensable elites have taken shape with startling rapidity."[133] R. A. Dahl adds to this sentiment, "It is difficult—nay impossible—to see how it could be otherwise in large political systems."[134]

The point of all this is that the pluralist model has in turn engendered a tremendous amount of criticism. One of the most important for our purposes comes from E. E. Schattschneider: "The flaw in the pluralist heaven is that the heavenly chorus sings with a strong upper class accent. Probably about 90 per cent of the people cannot get into the pressure system . . . All forms of political organization have a bias in favor of some kinds of conflict and the suppression of others because organization is the mobilization of bias. *Some issues are organized into politics while others are organized out.*"[135] What Schattsneider and others were in effect saying is that the pluralist vision is limited because it tends to concentrate only on those issues which seem to generate open conflict. Pluralists ignore the other reality of political power, namely, the mobilization of bias in the system to suppress or ignore certain issues. Thus power and policy can only be understood by examining the two faces of Janus: decisions and non-decisions. Taking the world for granted is to become ensnared in a "false consciousness" which assumes that the one-dimensional face of power which is presented is the only reality. The debate on this issue continues with undiminished fervor. The content of policy, the anti-pluralist contend, must be analysed from a "three-dimensional view" which conceives power as being (1) exercised through collectivities, (2) may involve inaction rather than observable action, and (3) may be exercised unwittingly. W. I. Jenkins, an enthusiast for the non-decision perspective on policy analysis, explains:

A focus on non-decisions therefore links with, and extends a focus on, policy content or policy area by posing wider questions regarding actions and inactions within the political system, such as the extent to which process and content influence each other to establish ongoing constraints. . . . The message for policy analysis is therefore two-fold: first, broaden the scope of the activity; second, realise that values and moral issues are of paramount importance. Thus a realization of the process-content interaction linked with a focus on issue areas, demand patterns and decision structures—can permit a more comprehensive policy analysis to be developed, if tempered with the realization that the bias of the investigation need not and should not be the same as the bias of the system being studied.[136]

This is perhaps as clear a statement as any indicating that conceptual approaches to the study of public policy serve one purpose only, and that is to provide useful insights into the subject matter under study. We have implicitly argued that terms such as "models," "paradigms," "perspectives" and "conceptual approaches" serve chiefly to enlighten us about the reality we live and observe. The emphasis either on *process* or *content* in the study of public policy and administration is a further statement of this assertion. No one approach is sacrosanct: different approaches are helpful to the extent that they prove to be powerful in explanatory power.

How then do we conclude this overview of decision theory and public policy studies? It is patently obvious that much has been left unsaid, and so we choose to conclude on an apologetic note which emphasizes the complex nature of our subject matter and the "impossibility" of dealing with this corpus of knowledge in any one volume. We have presented here a taxonomic survey of the main areas of this burgeoning and important literature. This survey approach was chosen because it gives the student a panoramic view of the corpus of knowledge, a glimpse of the forest rather than a detailed study of a few of the trees. The notes which follow this chapter will identify the important areas and readings in this narrative which could now be studied more intensely.

To return once again to the fable of the blind men and the elephant, the epigram of Chapter Five. To describe the elephant in the sketchiest of details took six chapters. At times the reader may have doubted whether we were really discussing the anatomy of that enormous pachyderm, but we were. In reality, it is the story of people in all their awesome complexities and contradictions coming together to pursue certain aims and aspirations. If that central theme is grasped from the complex theories of organizations then these chapters would have served some useful purpose.

The Complexity of Human Existence

We spend the first year of our lives learning that we end at our skin, and the rest of our lives learning that we don't.

Saul Gorn

Footnotes

1. Despite his now prolific publications Simon's earliest book *Administrative Behavior: A Study of Decision-Making Processes in Administrative Organization* (New York: Macmillan, 1947) remains his most widely read and influential publication. The student will find that to understand Simon more deeply one must begin with this publication. There have been several editions of this book, the cheapest being a Free Press paperback, 1968. The second edition is cited here.

2. See also our further comments in Chapter Nine. A large proportion of English publications write the acronym as POSDCORB; see, for example, A. Dunsire, *Administration: The Word and the Science* (London: Martin Robertson, 1973). Most American publications write it as PODSCORB. For additional information and exposition of these principles, see Luther Gulick and L. Urwick, et al., eds *Papers on the Science of Administration* (New York: Institute of Public Administration, Columbia University, 1937) and L. Urwick, *The Elements of Administration* (New York: Harper and Brothers, 1945).

3. Herbert A. Simon, "The Proverbs of Administration," *Public Administration Review* 6 (Winter 1946):53-67. Cited here is the reproduction in D.C. Rowat, ed., *Basic Issues in Public Administration* (New York: Macmillan, 1961), pp. 57-64 at pp. 57-58.

4. Herbert A. Simon, *Administrative Behavior*, 2nd ed., pp. xiii-xiv.

5. Ibid., p. 37.

6. Herbert A. Simon, "Development of Theory of Democratic Administration," and "Replies and Comments," *American Political Science Review* 46:2 (June 1952):495.

7. For a good but too brief exposition of this, see V. Subramaniam, "Fact and Value in Decision Making," *Public Administration Review* 23:4 (December 1963):232-237.

8. The earliest criticisms are Norton Long, "Public Policy and Administration: The Goals of Rationality and Responsibility," *Public Administration Review* 14:1 (Winter 1954):22-31; Dwight Waldo, *The Study of Public Administration* (New York: Random House, 1955) especially Chapter 6; Philip Selznick, *Leadership in Administration*

(White Plains, New York: Row, Peterson and Coy, 1957), pp. 79-82. Dwight Waldo, "Development of Theory of Democratic Administration," *APSR*, Vol. XLVI, No. 1, (March 1952): pp. 81-103 and "Development of Theory of Democratic Administration: Replies and Comments," pp. 500-503. Edward C. Banfield, "The Decision-Making Schema," and Herbert A. Simon, " 'The Decision Making Schema': A Reply," *Public Administration Review* Vol. XVII: No. 4, (Autumn 1957): 278-285 and (Vol. XVIII: No. 1) (Winter 1958):60-63. The best theoretical critique of Simon's work is by Herbert J. Storing, "The Science of Administration: Herbert A. Simon", in H.J. Storing, ed., *Essays on the Scientific Study of Politics* (New York: Holt, Rinehart and Winston, Inc., 1962), pp. 63-150. For serious students of Simon's work this critique is an absolute must.

9. Simon, *Administrative Behavior*, p. 64.

10. Ibid., p. 65.

11. Ibid., p. 184.

12. H.A. Simon, "Review of John von Neumann and Oskar Morgenstern, *Theory of Games and Economic Behavior*," *American Journal of Sociology* Vol. L, No. 6, (May 1945):559-560. Reprinted by permission of The University of Chicago Press. © 1945 The University of Chicago Press.

13. Simon, *Administrative Behavior*, p. xxiv. A full exposition of the satisficing model is found in James G. March and Herbert A. Simon, *Organizations* (New York: John Wiley and Sons, Inc., 1958), Chapters 6, 7. The model is foreshadowed in *Administrative Behavior*, pp. 96-100.

14. For students interested in following the Simon of the late '50s, '60s and '70s, see the following:
    (a) A. Newell, J.C. Shaw and H.A. Simon, "Chess-Playing Programs and the Problem of Complexity," *IBM Journal of Research and Development* 2:4 (October 1958):320-335;
    (b) H.A. Simon, "A Behavioral Model of Rational Choice," *Quarterly Journal of Economics* 69:1 (February 1955):99-118;
    (c) _____, "From Substantive to Procedural Rationality" in S.J. Latsis, ed., *Method and Appraisal in Economics* (Cambridge: Cambridge University Press, 1976): 129-148.
    (d) _____, "Rationality As Process and as Product of Thought," *American Economic Review* Vol. 68, No. 2, (May, 1978):1-16.
    (e) H.A. Simon and A. Newell, "Heuristic Problem Solving: The Next Advance in Operations Research," *Operations Research* 6 (January/February 1958):1-10;
    (f) H.A. Simon, *The New Science of Management Decision*, (New York: Harper & Row, Publishers, 1960).

15. A few pages in an introductory textbook cannot even begin to describe and assess Simon's contribution to decision theory and his most successful effort in insisting that it is an integral part of the theory of organizations. The best place to start with Simon, however, remains *Administrative Behavior* and the criticisms this book engendered from political theorists, and well-known students of public administration.

16. See, for example, Dwight Waldo, *The Administrative State* (New York: The Ronald Press Co., 1948), especially Chapter Ten "Economy and Efficiency." Also, it can be convincingly argued that it was Simon's mentor Chester I. Barnard who really began decision-theory by seeking the origins of organization in the limited effectiveness of individual choice. Simon has clearly indicated his early debt to Barnard in his writings, but as he developed his ideas in this area, Simon's work has spread chiefly on its own accord. For Barnard's early contribution, see C.I. Barnard, *The Functions of the Executive* (Cambridge, Mass.: Harvard University Press, 1938).

17. V. Subramaniam, "The Place of Decision Theory in Administrative Studies," *International Review of Administrative Sciences* XXXVII:4 (1971):395-402.

18. Ibid., p. 397.

19. For an exception, see Martin Landau, "The Concept of Decision-Making in the 'Field' of Public Administration," Sydney Mailick and Edward H. Van Ness, *Concepts and Issues in Administrative Behavior*, (New York: Prentice-Hall, Inc., 1962) pp. 14-22; for a later publication of Norton Long's which finally caught this nuance, see Norton E. Long, "The Administrative Organization as a Political System" in Sydney Mailick and Edward H. Van Ness, eds., *Concepts and Issues in Administrative Behavior* (New York: Prentice Hall, Inc., 1962), p. 112.

20. Subramaniam, "The Place of Decision Theory in Administrative Studies," p. 396.

21. Simon, *Administrative Behavior*, pp. 2, 253.

22. Ibid., p. 253.

23. Ibid., p. 240.

24. For good illustrations of this genre of socio-psychological studies in decision-making, see Barry E. Collins and Harold Guetzkow, *A Social Psychology of Group Processes for Decision-making* (New York: John Wiley and Sons, Inc., 1964); W.T. Edwards, *Social Psychology: Theories and Discussions* (London: Longman Group Ltd., 1974).

25. For an example of this emphasis on mathematical tools and techniques, see Lawrence A. Welsch and Richard M. Cyert, eds., *Management Decision Making* (Middlesex, England: Penguin Books Ltd., 1970). For an overview of the mathematical literature to the mid-1960s, see Julian Feldman and Herschel E. Kanter, "Organizational Decision Making" in James G. March, ed., *Handbook of Organizations* (Chicago: Rand, McNally, 1965), pp. 614-649.

26. Quoted in Charles E. Lindblom, "The Science of Muddling Through," *Public Administration Review* XIX:2 (Spring 1959):79-88 at 80. Reprinted from *Public Administration Review* © 1959 by The American Society for Public Administration, 1225 Connecticut Avenue, N.W., Washington, D.C. All rights reserved.

27. Ibid., p. 87.

28. Rudolf Klein, "Policy Problems and Policy Perceptions in the National Health Service," *Policy and Politics* 2:3 (March 1974):235

29. R.A. Dahl, "The Science of Public Administration: Three Problems," *Public Administration Review* 7:1 (Winter 1947):11. Reprinted from *Public Administration Review* © 1947 by The American Society for Public Administration, 1225 Connecticut Avenue, N.W., Washington, D.C. All rights reserved.

30. Howard S. Becker, "Observation: Social Observations and Social Case Studies," *International Encyclopedia of the Social Sciences* 11 (1968):232-238.

31. The profession of law has, of course, used the case method for ages in the training of young lawyers in faculties of law.

32. Robert T. Golembiewski and Michael White, *Cases in Public Management* (New York: Rand McNally & Co., 1973), p. xi.

33. See *Index and Summary of Case Studies of the Inter-University Case Program, Inc.*, The Inter-University Case Program, Inc., Syracuse, 1971; see also, the introduction to Harold Stein's *Public Administration and Policy Development* (New York: Harcourt, Brace, and Co. 1952); Edwin A. Bock, "Case Studies about Government: Achieving Realism and Significance" in Edwin A. Bock, ed., *Essays on the Case Method* (Syracuse: The Inter-University Case Program, 1962), pp. 89-119.

34. For an early description of this program, see Kenneth Kernaghan, "Case research in Canadian public administration," *Optimum* 6:2 (1975):5-20.

35. Ibid., p. 15.

36. James Rosenau, "Moral Fervor, Systematic Analysis, and Scientific Consciousness in Foreign Policy Research" in Austin Ranney, ed., *Political Science and Public Policy* (Chicago: Markham Publishing Co., 1968), pp. 201-205.

37. Richard Simeon, "Studying Public Policy," *Canadian Journal of Political Science* IX:4 (December 1976):550-551.

38. Robert H. Salisbury, "The Analysis of Public Policy: A Search for Theories and Roles" in A. Ranney, ed., *Political Science and Public Policy*, p. 153.

39. Hugh Heclo, "Review Article: Policy Analysis," *British Journal of Political Science* Part 1, Vol. 2 (Cambridge: Cambridge University Press, January 1972):83-108 at 93.

40. Ibid., pp. 93-94.

41. Examples are: Richard M. Cyert and James G. March, *A Behavioral Theory of the Firm* (Englewood Cliffs, New Jersey: Prentice Hall, Inc., 1963); Erik Johnsen, *Studies in Multiobjective Decision Models* (Sweden: The Economic Research Center in Lund, 1968). Those readers interested in a general overview of empirically oriented organization theory should read two articles: Kalman J. Cohen and Richard M. Cyert, "Simulation of Organizational Behavior" and William H. Starbuck, "Mathematics

and Organization Theory" in James G. March, Ed., *Handbook of Organizations,* pp. 305-334 and 335-386 respectively.

42. Examples of this genre are Robert Dahl's community case studies which attempt to elucidate the distribution of power by examining actual cases, and the case study work of Edward Banfield examining informal power relations in a decentralized political system. Banfield's work has led to considerable controversy concerning its manipulative ends, but Heclo notes the following about his contribution: "Banfield draws out the theoretical implications by showing how the distribution of influence creates an 'informal centralization' leading to social choices rather than deliberate decisions and how this process affects the adoption of new proposals." See H. Hugh Heclo, "Review Article: Policy Analysis," p. 90. See also, H. Lasswell and Daniel Lerner, eds., *The Policy Sciences* (Stanford, Calif.: Stanford University Press, 1951); Yehezkiel Dror, *Public Policy-Making Re-examined* (San Francisco: Chandler Publishing Co., 1968); R.A. Dahl and C.E. Lindblom, *Politics, Economics and Welfare* (New York: Harper and Row, 1953); Daniel Lerner, ed., *The Human Meaning of the Social Sciences* (New York: Mendian Books, 1959); D. Braybrooke and C.E. Lindblom, *A Strategy of Decision* (New York: Free Press, 1963).

43. Richard Simeon, "Studying Public Policy," pp. 549-550; Randall Ripley, "Review of Ranney and Dror," *American Political Science Review* 83 (September 1969): pp. 918-921. This genre of criticism also adds another by implication: the task of the social scientist should not be muddled with the second or lower order priority of policy analysis (advice on the choosing of alternatives). Rather, his/her main preoccupation should be with "policy theory" (the explanation of why certain alternatives are chosen and others are not).

44. For an extensive critique of this manipulative theme in policy sciences, see Robert Horwitz, "Scientific Propaganda: Harold D. Lasswell" in Herbert J. Storing, ed., *Essays on the Scientific Study of Politics,* pp. 225-304. This critique is quite extensive and detailed, covering all of Lasswell's contributions to the social sciences to the early 1960s. Horwitz, however, contends that ". . . Lasswell's social science, taken in its entirety, has always had the character of what he has in recent years identified as the 'policy science of democracy' " (p. 300).

45. David Braybrooke and Charles E. Lindblom, *A Strategy of Decision* (New York: Free Press, 1963), especially pp. 62-65 where the "model" is outlined.

46. Charles E. Lindblom, "The Science of 'Muddling Through'," *PAR* XIX:2 (Spring 1959):80. Reprinted from *Public Administration Review* © 1959 by The American Society for Public Administration, 1225 Connecticut Avenue, N.W., Washington, D.C. All rights reserved. Also see Charles E. Lindblom, *The Policy Making Process* (Englewood Cliffs, New Jersey: Prentice Hall, 1968), especially Chapters Three and Four.

47. Some readers would no doubt disagree with my broad categorization of the works of such different writers as Dror (advocating more optimal use of available knowledge for policy sciences), Braybrooke and Lindblom (who argue for more cautionary steps in policy formulation), Lasswell (who seems to advocate everything for better decisions) and Etzioni (who seems to argue a little bit of everything in his view of "mixed scanning"). A careful reading of the works of all these authors, despite their differences and at times varying emphases, are the following:

(a) All of these authors specify that any theory of the process stress attributes of the individual policy maker and the overall system in which he operates.

(b) They require that the theory relate variables which intervene between the individual and the system (roleplaying, interest group behavior etc.).

(c) The theory further focuses attention on how to change or improve the policy product.

For a further elaboration of this orientation, see Enid Curtis Bok Schoettle, "The State of the Art in Policy Studies" in Raymond A. Bauer and Kenneth J. Gergen, eds., *The Study of Policy Formation* (New York: Free Press, 1968), pp. 149-179. Thus Dror stresses better institutions and elite training for policy sciences, Lindblom and his admirers, such as Aaron Wildavsky, stress elite analysis and the cautionary use of such dynamic models of modern technology for feedback as cybernetics, and Lasswell's lasting preoccupation with elite profiles (which he calls "developmental constructs") and testing to identify or determine their capacity to play given specialized roles. For further extension of these remarks, see in particular:

(1) Y. Dror, *Public Policymaking Reexamined*, especially Chapter 19 "Changes Needed in Structure and Process Patterns."

(2) Aaron Wildavsky, *The Politics of the Budgetary Process* (Boston: Little, Brown and Co., 1964) especially pp. 126ff.

(3) Harold D. Lasswell, *Psychopathology and Politics* (New York: Viking Press, 1960); and "Agenda for the Study of Political Elites" in D. Marvick, ed., *Political Decision Makers* (New York: Free Press, 1961), pp. 264-287.

48. Braybrooke and Lindblom, *A Strategy of Decision*, p. 118.

49. Schoettle, "The State of the Art in Policy Studies," p. 151. See also, for a succinct description, Peter C. Aucoin, "Theory and Research in the Study of Policy Making" in G. Bruce Doern and Peter Aucoin (eds.), *The Structures of Policy-Making in Canada* (Toronto: Macmillan of Canada, 1971), pp. 10-17.

50. Robert K. Merton, "The Role of Applied Social Science in the Formation of Policy" in R.K. Merton, *Sociology of Science* (Chicago: University of Chicago Press, 1973), pp. 70-98 at p. 96.

51. Amitai Etzioni, "Mixed Scanning: A 'Third' Approach to Decision-Making," *PAR* XXVII:5 (December 1967):385-392 at 387. Reprinted from *Public Administration Review* © 1967 by The American Society for Public Administration, 1225 Connecticut Avenue, N.W., Washington, D.C. All rights reserved.

52. Ibid., p. 388.

53. Aucoin, "Theory and Research in the Study of Policy-Making," p. 18.

54. See B.B. Schaffer, "Review Article: On the Politics of Policy," *Australian Journal of Politics and History* XXIII:1 (April 1977):146-155 at 147.

55. See Y. Dror, "Muddling Through: 'Science' or Inertia," *PAR* 24:3 (September 1964): 153-157; Robert Goodin and Ilmar Waldner, "Thinking Big, Thinking Small, and Not Thinking at all," *Public Policy* 27:1 (Winter 1979):1-24, and Norman Beckman, Symposium Editor, "Symposium on Policy Analysis in Government: Alternatives to 'Muddling Through' "presented in *PAR* 37:3 (May/June 1977):221-263.

56. J. Anderson, *Public Policy Making* (New York: Praeger, 1975), p. 25.

57. Sir Geoffrey Vickers, *The Art of Judgment: A Study of Policy Making* (London: Chapman and Hall, 1965), p. 11.

58. V. Subramaniam, "A Disposition Towards Decision Theory," *Indian Journal of Public Administration* XVIII:1 (January/March 1972):6.

59. What follows is our own understanding of three of Vickers' works read over the years: *The Art of Judgment*; *Making Institutions Work* (London: Associated Business Programmes Ltd., 1973) and *Value Systems and Social Process* (New York: Basic Books, Inc., 1968). The latter presents many of his more important ideas in synopsis form, particularly in Parts Two and Three of the book. For our narrative, however, we will use the main analytical work, *The Art of Judgment*, and the excellent summary by V. Subramaniam, "Two Complementary Approaches to Macro-Decision Making," *Public Administration* (Sydney) XXX:4 (December 1971):337-347.

60. Sir Geoffrey Vickers, *The Art of Judgment*, p. 31.

61. Subramaniam protests that Simon attempted "to portray all organizational activity as decision-making . . . Fortunately, this effort made in March and Simon *Organizations*, did not catch on" (Subramaniam, "A Disposition Towards Decision Theory," p. 2).

62. Vickers, *The Art of Judgment*, p. 33.

63. Ibid., p. 39.

64. Subramaniam, "Two Complementary Approaches to Macro-Decision Making," p. 339. Vickers, in his treatment of this appreciative system, gives cases to illustrate how it operates. He also has a theoretical discussion to indicate how the appreciative system accommodates conflicting values, deals with the capacity to innovate, and the learning "building blocks" of the appreciative system based on the experience of past decision situations. Chapters Three to Eight essentially cover these themes.

65. This is covered in Chapters Nine to Twelve.

66. Subramaniam, "Approaches to Macro-Decision Making," p. 340.

67. Ibid.

68. Subramaniam, "A Disposition Towards Decision Theory," p. 6.

69. Professor Subramaniam criticizes Vickers' contribution on two grounds: (1) for not paying more attention to the individual micro-decisional unit, and (2) for a disregard of the more normative and optimistic criteria incorporated (for better decisions) in the works of Dror, Simon, March and others. See Subramaniam, "Approaches to Macro-Decision Making" and "A Disposition Towards Decision Theory."

70. V. Subramaniam, "The Place of Decision Theory in Administrative Studies," *International Review of Administrative Studies* XXXVII:4 (1971):395-402 at 402.

71. Andrew Dunsire, *Implementation in a Bureaucracy, The Execution Process:* Vol. I. (Oxford: Martin Robertson & Co. Ltd., 1978), p. 7.

72. Erik O. Wright, "To control or smash bureaucracy: Weber and Lenin on politics, the state and bureaucracy," *Berkeley Journal of Sociology* Vol. XIX, 1974-75: 69-108.

73. Ralph Miliband, *The State in Capitalist Society* (London: Weidenfeld and Nicolson, 1969).

74. Nicos Poulantzas, "The Problem of the Capitalist State" in R. Blackburn, ed., *Ideology in Social Science* (London, 1972), pp. 251, 246.

75. Henry Milner, "The decline and fall of the Quebec Liberal regime: contradictions in the modern Quebec state" in Leo Panitch, ed., *The Canadian State: Political Economy and Political Power* (Toronto: University of Toronto Press, 1977), p. 101.

76. Ibid., p. 105.

77. Briefly, the *labor theory of value* attempts to explain the genesis of a commodity's value in relation to the human labor involved in its production. The worker sells his labor to survive, the capitalist, in order to survive, must obtain and reinvest surplus value as a necessary condition to retain his hegemony.

78. The forces of production include such factors as physical implements used in production (tools, technical innovations etc.) and the human abilities to perform labor.

79. The historical approach to Marxism continually points out the internal contradictions of the capitalist system: capitalists *must* continue to generate production despite the potential hostility of the labor force.

80. The class approach emphasizes how the class structure and struggle are endemic to this internal contradiction.

81. Mostly good Canadian illustrations will be used in footnoting the following #81 to #85. See the contributions of Leo Panitch, "The Role and Nature of the Canadian State" and Reg Whitaker "Images of the State in Canada" in Leo Panitch, ed., *The Canadian State: Political Economy and Political Power* (Toronto: University of Toronto Press, 1977); H.V. Nelles, *The Politics of Development* (Toronto: University of Toronto Press, 1974). The latter is a first rate historical study of the development of natural resources (forest, mines and hydro-electric power in Ontario between 1849 and 1941). It should be read in its entirety, but if pressed for time I would highly recommend Chapters Ten, Eleven and Twelve as superb reading.

82. See the contributions of Denis Olsen, "The State Elites"; Wallace Clement, "The corporate elite, the capitalist class, and the Canadian state"; Hugh Armstrong, "The labour force and state workers in Canada"; Alvin Finkel, "Origins of the Welfare State in Canada"—all in Leo Panitch, ed., *The Canadian State: Political Economy and Political Power* (Toronto: University of Toronto Press, 1977).

83. Paul Goldman and Donald R. Van Houten, "Managerial Strategies and the Worker: A Marxist Analysis of Bureaucracy." Reprint from Department of Sociology, University of Oregon, OR 97403.

84. Ibid.

85. Among Marxists there is some difference of opinion on this point. Leo Panitch, in the preface of his edited book, argues for close association of Marxists with the working class, "for without a working class helping to identify the 'significant problems' by its own actions, and taking up cultural as well as political and economic struggle by re-examining its history and developing a theory and practice for future change, Marxist theory will lack a social base, which is finally the *sine qua non* for the sustenance of any body of ideas" (p. x). Reg Whitaker, however, contends that: "At this stage in our history there is little point in discussing a Marxist revolutionary critique as a dominant aspect of mass working-class politics. Marxism exists more importantly as an analytical tool and an academic mode of interpretation . . ." (p. 65).

86. Wolf Heydebrand, "Organizational Contradictions in Public Bureaucracies: Toward a Marxian Theory of Organizations" in J. Kenneth Benson, ed., *Organizational Analysis: Critique and Innovation*, Sage Contemporary Social Science Issues 37 (Beverly Hills, California: Sage Publications,) pp. 85-109 at p. 86.

87. Here it might be useful to make a distinction between an *institutional process* (such as the legislative process) and the *patterns of interaction* which would tell us something about how policy problems develop, who is involved in policy formation, on what kinds of issues, under what conditions, in what ways and to what effect. For a good discussion on this score, see Charles O. Jones, *An Introduction to the Study of Public Policy* (Belmont, Calif.: Wadsworth, 1970), pp. 4-5.

88. See Daniel Lerner and Harold D. Lasswell (eds.), *The Policy Sciences* (Stanford: Stanford University Press, 1960). The early policy science scholars accepted the logical distinction between empirical and normative models of policy, but they argued that the relationship between instrumental policies and end values were really empirical questions. See specifically the arguments of Harold D. Lasswell, "The Policy Orientation" in Lerner and Lasswell, pp. 3-15.

89. For the evolution of the bureaucratic model, see the account by G.T. Allison and Morton H. Halperin, "Bureaucratic Politics: A Paradigm and Some Policy Implications" in R. Tanter and R.H. Ullman, eds., *Theory and Policy in International Relations* (New Jersey: Princeton University Press, 1972).

90. Graham T. Allison, *The Essence of Decision* (Boston: Little, Brown, 1971), p. 67.

91. Jenkins, *Policy Analysis*, p. 34.

92. *Ibid.*, p. 6. For a Canadian study arguing for the suitability of Allison's model in the analysis of external affairs policy see Kim Richard Nossal, "Allison through the (Ottawa) Looking Glass: bureaucratic politics and foreign policy in a parliamentary system." *Canadian Public Administration* Vol. 22, No. 4, Winter 1979, pp. 610-626.

93. R. Hofferbert, *The Study of Public Policy* (New York: Bobbs-Merrill, 1974), pp. 258-259.

94. Ibid., p. 7.

95. See T. R. Dye, *Understanding Public Policy* (New Jersey: Prentice Hall, 1972).

96. Ibid., p. 245.

97. David Falcone and M.S. Whittington, "Output Change in Canada: A Preliminary Attempt to Open the 'Black Box' " A paper presented to the Annual Meeting of the Canadian Political Science Association, Montreal, June, 1972.

98. *Ibid.,* pp. 50-51.

99. For these criticisms see W.I. Jenkins, *Policy Analysis* pp. 56-57.

100. Quoted in ibid., p. 56.

101. Michel Crozier, *The Bureaucratic Phenomenon* (Chicago: University of Chicago Press, 1964); Alvin Gouldner, *Patterns of Industrial Bureaucracy* (Glencoe, Illinois: Free Press, 1954); Tom Burns and G.M. Stalker, *The Management of Innovation* (London: Tavistock, 1961); David Silverman, *The Theory of Organisations* (London: Heinemann, 1970).

102. Jenkins, *Policy Analysis,* p. 73.

103. Ibid., p. 74.

104. Ibid., p. 75.

105. For an excellent review of these approaches, see Douglas G. Hartle, *A Theory of the Expenditure Budgetary Process* (Toronto: University of Toronto Press for the Ontario Economic Council, 1976).

106. Allan M. Maslove, "Review Article: A Theory of the Expenditure Budgetary Process," *CPA* 21:1 (Spring 1978): 125-129 at 125.

107. Ibid., p. 126.

108. See Hartle, *A Theory of the Expenditure Budgetary Process,* pp. 1-55, for a comprehensive review.

109. Vincent Ostrom, *The Intellectual Crisis in American Public Administration* (Tuscaloosa: University of Alabama Press, 1973), p. 3.

110. Jenkins, *Policy Analysis,* p. 136.

111. Thomas R. De Gregori, "Caveat Emptor: A Critique of the Emerging Paradigm of Public Choice," *Administration and Society* 6:2 (August 1974):205-208.

112. Jenkins, *Policy Analysis*, p. 144. Also see R. De Gregori, ibid.

113. De Gregori, "Caveat Emptor," pp. 205-208.

114. By late 1968, this particular economic orientation did not even have the name of public choice. See the interesting article by James M. Buchanan, "An Economist's Approach to 'Scientific Politics' " in M.B. Parsons, ed., *Perspectives in the Study of Politics* (Chicago: Rand, McNally & Co., 1968), pp. 77-88. Also see Vincent and Elinor Ostrom, "Public Choice: A Different Approach to the Study of Public Administration," *Public Administration Review* XXXI:2 (March/April 1971):203-216.

115. All of these works and more are competently reviewed by Hartle in *A Theory of the Expenditure Budgetary Process*, pp. 11-24.

116. Anthony King, "Ideas, Institutions and the Policies of Governments: A Comparative Analysis" *British Journal of Political Science*, Vol. 3, No. 4 (Cambridge: Cambridge University Press, October 1973), p. 423.

117. Ronald Manzer, "Public Policies in Canada: A Development Perspective" a paper presented to the Canadian Political Science Association, Edmonton, June 1975 and quoted in G. Bruce Doern and Peter Aucoin (eds.) *Public Policy in Canada: Organization Process, and Management*, (Toronto: MacMillan, 1979) p. 15.

118. Peter Aucoin "Public-Policy Theory and Analysis" in G.B. Doern and Peter Aucoin (eds.) *Public Policy in Canada*, p. 15.

119. *Ibid.*, p. 15.

120. *Ibid.*, p. ix.

121. For an excellent example of this see Arnold J. Heidenheimer, Hugh Heclo and Carolyn T. Adams, *Comparative Public Policy: The Politics of Social Choice in Europe and America* (New York: St. Martin's Press, 1975).

122. T.A. Lowi, "American Business, Public Policy, Case Studies and Political Theory," *World Politics* 16:4 (July 1964):677-715 at p. 688.

123. T.A. Lowi, "Decision Making vs Public Policy: Toward an Antidote for Technocracy," *Public Administration Review* 30:3 (May/June 1970):314-325 at p. 318. Reprinted from *Public Administration Review* © 1970 by The American Society for Public Administration, 1225 Connecticut Avenue, N.W., Washington, D.C. All rights reserved.

124. Ibid., p. 314.

125. Lowi, "American Business, Public Policy, Case Studies and Political Theory," pp. 688-689.

126. Lowi, "Decision Making vs Public Policy," p. 324.

127. Lowi, "American Business, Public Policy, Case Studies and Political Theory," p. 692.

128. Charles O. Jones, *An Introduction to the Study of Public Policy*, 2nd ed. (Massachusetts: Duxbury Press, 1977), pp. 224-225.

129. G. Bruce Doern, "The Concept of Regulation and Regulatory Reform" in G. Bruce Doern and V. Seymour Wilson, eds., *Issues in Canadian Public Policy* (Toronto: Macmillan of Canada, 1974), p. 8.

130. David Easton, *The Political System: An Inquiry into the State of Political Science* (New York: Alfred A. Knopf, 1965), pp. 106-148.

131. William Riker, *The Theory of Political Coalitions* (New Haven: Yale University Press, 1962), p. 10-11.

132. Robert Dahl, *Who Governs?* (New Haven: Yale University Press, 1961); Nelson W. Polsby, *Community Power and Political Theory* (New Haven: Yale University Press, 1963); Raymond E. Wolfinger, *The Politics of Progress* (Englewood Cliffs, New Jersey: Prentice-Hall, Inc., 1974).

133. E.H. Carr, *New Society* (Boston, 1951), p. 72.

134. Robert Dahl, "Power, Pluralism and Democracy: A Modest Proposal," a paper delivered at the 1964 annual meeting of the American Political Science Association, Chicago, p. 3.

135. E.E. Schattschneider, *The Semisovereign People* (New York: Holt, Rinehart and Winston, 1960) p. 35.

136. Jenkins, *Policy Analysis*, pp. 115-116.

Notes

The essential readings for this chapter are prolific and in many instances not easily accessible (in obscure, highly specialized journals, etc.). The footnotes to the chapter have already given the reader some commentary on important books and articles, but a little amplification on some of the recommended readings is necessary.

Books and Monographs

1. Michel Crozier, *The Bureaucratic Phenomenon* (Chicago: University of Chicago Press, 1963).
   This is an important case study of bureaucracy in modern organizations and its cultural setting in France. As a review of theory, Chapters Six and Seven are first rate. Recommended for advanced students.

2. D.G. Hartle, *A Theory of the Expenditure Budgetary Process* (Toronto: University of Toronto Press for the Ontario Economic Council, 1976).

Hartle's review of public choice theoretical literature is the best we have so far as an overall review. Highly recommended.

3. Carl J. Friedrich, ed., *Nomos VII: Rational Decision* (New York: Atherton Press, 1964).
   There are some excellent pieces in this book. The piece by Judith N. Shklar, "Decisionism," is a good complementary piece to Subramaniam's articles on decision-theory. The articles by Eulau, Kaplan, Sir Isaiah Berlin, and Friedrich are particularly good, especially for advanced students.

4. W.I. Jenkins, *Policy Analysis: A Political and Organisational Perspective* (London: Martin Robertson, 1978).
   This book was used extensively in this chapter. It is a very good review of the policy studies literature. Recommended for both students and teachers. Jenkins' bibliography is a very useful addition to the book.

5. Herbert A. Simon, *Administrative Behavior* (New York: Macmillan Company, 1964).
   There are about thirteen printings to this book, possibly more. With the exception of some changes in the preface, the original text remains the same. A must for anyone who really desires to understand Simon and his later contributions. I recommend that students be given bits and pieces of the book from time to time.

6. Sir Geoffrey Vickers, *The Art of Judgment: A Study of Policy Making* (London: Chapman and Hall, 1965).
   As stated in the chapter, I consider this book a brilliant work. For the uninitiated, however, there is some need for interpretation. Certain sections could be used as readings for discussion ("The Appreciative System," "Institutions as Dynamic Systems," "The Human-Ecological System," etc.).

Articles

Articles marked with double asterisks (**) are highly recommended, while those with one asterisk (*) can be read lightly for introductory purposes. A few articles are also listed (*) because of their availability but are not recommended for the beginner.

** James M. Buchanan, "An Economist's Approach to Scientific Politics" in M.B. Parsons, ed., *Perspectives in the Study of Politics* (Chicago: Rand McNally & Co., 1968), pp. 77-88.
   A good descriptive piece on public choice for the beginning student.

** Thomas R. De Gregori, "Caveat Emptor: A Critique of the Emerging Paradigm of Public Choice," *Administration and Society* 6:2 (August 1974):205-228.
   A better than average critique of public choice.

* Paul Diesing, "Noneconomic Decision-Making," *Ethics* Vol. LXVI No. 1, Part I, October 1955, pp. 18-35.

** Amitai Etzioni, "Mixed-Scanning: A 'Third' Approach to Decision-Making," *Public Administration Review* XXVII:5 (December 1967):385-392.

** Robert Goodin and Ilmar Waldner, "Thinking Big, Thinking Small and not Thinking at all," *Public Policy* 27:1 (Winter 1979):1-24.
   This article is an advanced, but excellent critique of incrementalism.

** Hugh Heclo, "Review Article: Policy Analysis," *British Journal of Political Science* Part 1, Vol. 2. (1972):83-108.
   This is an advanced review of public policy studies up to the early '70s. Heclo's article is thorough, balanced and perceptive. Highly recommended particularly for professors and advanced students.

** Charles E. Lindblom, "The Science of 'Muddling Through'," *Public Administration Review*, XIX:2 (Spring, 1959):79-88.

** Theodore Lowi, "Decision Making vs Policy Making: Toward an Antidote for Technocracy," *PAR* 30:3 (May/June 1970):314-325.
   This is essentially a review of books on public choice, incrementalism, policy sciences and an amalgam of readings. Lowi puts forward his own analysis of public policy and his public policy content typology. Good reading.

* Vincent Ostrom and Elinor Ostrom, "Public Choice: A Different Approach to the Study of Public Administration," *PAR* XXXI:2, (March/April 1971):203-216.
   This article is a good review of public choice but its linkage to a critique of public administration is somewhat dubious. Recommended reading for teachers in particular.

* Richard Simeon, "Studying Public Policy," *Canadian Journal of Political Science* IX:4 (December 1976): 548-580.
   This is a big review of the policy literature attempting to carve a place for what political science *should* study in public policy. The piece is reference-studded but is marred by a hyper critical stance to just about every approach to public policy which does not concentrate on the supposedly "vital elements" and "independent variables of *power, conflict* and *ideology.*" This piece should have been subjected to a severe critique in turn, but in typical Canadian style we have had only silence from the academic community studying public policy at our universities. Not recommended for introductory reading, but recommended for teachers and advanced students.

   Articles by Subramaniam are all highly recommended (**) for their ability to elucidate the reader on the highlights of the major works on decision theory and policy studies.

V. Subramaniam, "Fact and Value in Decision-Making," *Public Administration Review* 23:4 (December 1963):232-237.

———, "The Place of Decision Theory in Administrative Studies," *International Review of Administrative Sciences* XXXVII:4 (1971):395-402.

———, "The Fact-Value Distinction as an Analytical Tool," *Indian Journal of Public Administration* XVII:1 (January/March 1971):1-9.

———, "Two Complementary Approaches to Macro-Decision Making," *Public Administration* (Sydney) XXX:4 (December 1971):337-347.

———, "Dror on Policy Making," *Indian Journal of Public Administration* XVI:1 (January/March 1970):84-96.

Some Canadian Environmental Concerns

Perhaps the element of the social system least reducible to simple models and a trustworthy information process is the symbolic, i.e., the symbols, ideas, ideologies, theologies, myths, etc., that constitute the basis of community and around which develop deep passions and strongly held values.

Kenneth E. Boulding

The struggle with the riddle of history is difficult, but not impossible. History offers us no vantage point, no Archimedean point from which a panoramic view of its topography would yield automatically the truth of its inner structure—its essence, our essence. History must be interrogated from within. We are immersed in history. We are nothing outside history. We are our history, but we are also more than any historical actuality.

Alkis Kontos

CHAPTER SEVEN

OUR PARLIAMENTARY HERITAGE: MINISTERIAL RESPONSIBILITY AND ITS DERIVATIVES

The concept of ministerial responsibility helps to define and determine how power is and should be exercised in the Canadian political system and who is or should be held responsible for the exercise of that power. It provides a major frame of reference for the allocation of power and responsibility among ministers, legislators and public servants.

Kenneth Kernaghan

Giving lip service to such myths as "ministerial responsibility" may have some salutary psychological effect on the ministers and civil servants who are charged with a degree of discretionary authority. . . . But for serious commentators . . . to use such terms with the intent of describing actualities is at best anachronistic and at worst entirely misleading.

F. F. Schindeler

I. Introduction

Canadians, as historian Kenneth McNaught once reminded us, have "produced a unique sense of ideas, structure and custom that defies the model maker."[1] We have relied heavily on our British heritage for our customs and ideas but we have also borrowed American institutions and customs when this borrowing has been appropriate to our needs. The result is sometimes a curious mélange of "ideas, structure and custom" which, if not understood by the contemporary analyst, would make him "about as secure as a goose on shell ice."[2] As Chapter Four has demonstrated we have learned and borrowed much from the manner in which Americans have conducted their debate on responsibility and accountability. Thus, although our discourse on the subject has been carried out almost entirely in the language of our

British heritage, the perceptive contemporary analyst would detect certain elements of an American heritage as well.

In addition to the language, the tone of the Canadian discourse on accountability is also different from that of the American. On the whole, political commentators in the United States have never taken kindly to the administrative state and, as we have already seen, they debate its advent rather vigorously. Indeed, Americans enjoy the singular distinction among the English-speaking peoples of debating issues in terms of fundamental principles. American concern about the administrative state has been dominated by the themes of bureaucratic growth and rigidity and the implications these themes have for the institutions of popular sovereignty and the rights of individual Americans.

In contrast, Canadians have been much more pragmatic about the administrative state. Using the state machinery as an instrument for economic development was never fundamentally debated in Canada. In the nineteenth century it was assumed as a necessity if we were to achieve the higher goal of responsible government. Harold Innis has argued that from Canada's early beginnings active state intervention was a mandatory requirement if the combined resources of the community were to be successfully mobilized to foster economic growth, prosperity and nationhood.[3] Today, this fundamental assumption is still accepted by Canadian analysts. Thomas A. Hockin, for example, argues that:

Thanks to its growth in Canada, and its ability to identify itself with national development and local particularisms, the state took on a life of its own . . . [Thus] the whole movement of the state has been from a mere mechanism separate from society, to part of the organism of society, so that the two are inextricably intermeshed . . . Canadians have not, from the early years of its conservative tradition, been greatly adverse to the use of the state; and herein may lie Canada's hopes for plotting a more independent course in North America.[4]

The administrative state in Canada has been accepted with greater equanimity, if not with unanimous approbation, by the majority of our social and political commentators. Some attention has been centered on the implications this growth has for the principle of parliamentary sovereignty and what measures, if any, can be adopted to restore parliamentary control and more openness in the conduct of government business.

Mr. Justice Felix Frankfurter once wrote that "The history of liberty has largely been the history of observance of procedural safeguards."

Canada's constitutional tradition and parliamentary heritage recognize two means of limiting the exercise of governmental power. The rule of law is one of these procedural safeguards.[5] The other is the notion of ministerial responsibility to Parliament for the conduct of government. As this chapter's two epigrams demonstrate, commentators differ widely as to the utility of the latter concept. While Kernaghan argues that "it provides a major frame of reference for the allocation of power and responsibility" in our liberal democracy, Schindeler dismisses it as an "anachronistic" and "misleading" myth. Kernaghan and Schindeler appear to represent two diametrically opposite perspectives on the ideological spectrum of this issue. We recognize that the labelling of ideological perspectives can be very misleading on occasions but for purposes of this chapter we will describe those who hold to the Kernaghan's point of view as "constitutionalists" while others approximating Schindeler's viewpoint we would categorize as "pragmatists." This distinction will, however, break down when we argue that both points of view are really much alike in normative terms, the differences between them hinging on questions of behavioral emphasis.

While it is true that Canadians have not debated the advent of the administrative state in terms of fundamental principles of democracy, political commentators during the 60s and 70s have nevertheless raised the state issue in tangential ways. For example, voting analyst Peter Regenstreif has concluded that the extensive policies of social legislation enacted by the Canadian Parliament during the 40s "were not manifestations of the demands made upon the political system by specifically identifiable groups as was the case in the United States. Instead these programs were instituted as part of a general scheme for dealing with the catastrophe of the Depression and the dislocations of war."[6] Regenstreif's views have been confirmed by the senior economic adviser to the Canadian government at that time.[7] In 1965, J. E. Hodgetts argued that the creation of regional units of administration were not "part of the demand inputs entering the system" but rather "a creation of the political system itself." Thus the system had created both its own demands and supports by "manipulating the regional environment."[8] Frank MacKinnon has argued that provincial politics in the province of Prince Edward Island has been dominated by big government, and Alan Cairns has extrapolated the argument of MacKinnon and Hodgetts for his analysis of Canadian society and government:

The impact of society on government is a common theme in the study of democratic politics. Less common is an approach which stresses the impact of government on the functioning of society. I have chosen the latter for the guiding theme of my remarks, because I am convinced that our approach to the study of Canadian politics pays inadequate attention to the capacity of government to make society responsive to its demands.[9]

But while these commentators have raised the issue of the administrative state and have even mildly suggested some negative implications if its growth continues unabated, they have not proffered any grand designs for administrative change as has been done in the American case. This is all the more interesting given the fact that during the 1960s and 70s we have had a proliferation of constitutional designs for a renewed Canadian federalism.[10] Canadian ambivalence about administrative power remains somewhat different to its American neighbour. Our instrumentalist attitude towards bureaucracy is reflected in our assumption that as we settle the greater issues of constitutional reform the problems of the administrative state would, by implication, be solved also. As we saw in Chapter Four, many American writers of the 70s and 80s do not assume this. Thus, perhaps as a result of the Canadian historical past of active state intervention in the economy, Canadians seem only mildly worried about administrative power.

Canadian discourse on administrative power continues to be dominated by the doctrine of ministerial responsibility. Our first task is to describe in its barest essentials the doctrine of ministerial responsibility and its conventions. In doing so we will sketch out what we have called "the hierarchical responsibilities paradigm"—a perspective which outlines the main institutions in our democracy which are given shape by the ministerial doctrine. Secondly, we will describe the disparate collection of ideas identified here as the pragmatist perspective outlining an accompanying "pragmatic paradigm."[11] Thirdly, we will critically examine both paradigms indicating to what extent the two of them are helpful in comprehending the nature of administrative power in Canada.

II. Ministerial Responsibility and Accountability: A General Discussion

J. E. Hodgetts starts us off on our discussion by emphasizing that as a "fixed feature" of our environment, the concept of ministerial responsibility has left "deep imprints on our public service,"[12] a statement with which the English constitutional expert, Sir Ivor Jennings, would wholeheartedly agree. According to Jennings, "the essential feature" of the Westminster model of responsible government are two aspects: the clear division of roles between politicians and public servants and the historical and structural manifestations of the relationships between policy and administration. The buckle which binds both of these essential aspects is the doctrine of ministerial responsibility. Ministerial responsibility, in the words of the late John P. Mackintosh, is "the main principle moulding the structure and outlook of the senior civil service."[13]

Exactly how does one define ministerial responsibility? The English constitutional scholar Geoffrey Marshall asserts the following:

Ministers, as the Crown's servants, carry on the executive government of the country. They accept *legal responsibility* for the use made of the royal prerogative and for the advice which they give to the Crown. They are *politically accountable* to the House of Commons both collectively and individually. They must by convention resign if defeated in the Commons on *an important policy issue*. A Minister as head of a department *should resign* if he is found to be at fault in the running of it or if important errors are made by civil servants under his control which are of such a kind that they imply inadequate supervision by the Minister.[14]

In its pristine form this doctrine describes the reality of liberal democratic government as its creators envisaged it. It is essentially a nineteenth century feature of British constitutional and administrative theory. It was formulated during the period of British history when the House of Commons had considerable direct control over the everyday details of governmental activity. The doctrine was devised to ensure that parliamentary dominance and scrutiny was maintained over the "servants" of the public, namely the members of the bureaucracy.

But a second look at the doctrine as stated above leads to some further reflection. What is implied by legal responsibility as opposed to accountability? What is the distinction between individual and collective responsibility? Do these responsibilities not contradict each other? How is an important policy issue determined in the judging of ministers? "A minister . . . should resign," the definition reads; why not "must resign"? Civil servants can make "important errors . . . which are of such a kind that they imply inadequate supervision by the Minister." Hence the minister is called upon to answer for errors about which he may have no direct knowledge, given today's complex and sprawling bureaucracies. Is this answerability criteria either fair or realistic? We have immediately complicated the issue by introducing a series of questions replete with both factual and normative implications. As with the policy-administration dichotomy, the philosophical assumptions inherent in ministerial responsibility have both descriptive and prescriptive qualities which we must explore.

Some of the conceptual subtleties inherent in the doctrine can be made clearer if we examine the distinction between the interrelated concepts of *responsibility, accountability* and *answerability.** The concept of responsibility is an umbrella term used for integrating a set of ideas in which the administration is responsive to public demands and public opinions. It is a liberal democratic term which attempts to define and circumscribe governmental power to prevent arbitrary excesses in the use of such powers. Flowing from these philosophical ideas we have such notions as the rule or sovereignty of law, government under the law, the separation of powers among judicial, executive and legislative parts of government, the distinction between public and private law and so on. The concept of responsibility also asserts that social relations in our community are irreducibly moral relations. Decision-making in our community will unavoidably be concerned with ethical questions, since ethics is the art of making wise choices. Therefore such an expression as "administrative responsibility" which is derived from the more generic term "political responsibility" is coined to assess public judgements of consistency: administrative acts being judged by an ultimate standard of goodness.[15] Herbert Spiro emphasizes the overarching central importance of the concept by his contention that "responsibility is the central problem of government and, indeed, of life today."[16] It is, as Kernaghan also concludes, "a frame of reference for the allocation of power."

While responsibility is more prescriptive in its implications, the notion of accountability is a more practical or descriptive term in that it embodies the relationship of agency, that is, the manner in which political responsibility is given practical expression. *Accountability emphasizes the structures, either formal or informal, devised to ensure political responsibility.* In the philosophical debate on responsibility, accountability is often subsumed under the concepts of *subjective* and *objective* responsibility, for both sets of "responsibilities" are really concerned with Frankfurter's observation concerning procedural safeguards to

---

* *A full discussion of the subtle distinctions involved here is best given in Herbert J. Spiro,* Responsibility in Government: Theory and Practice. *New York: Van Nostrand Reinhold Co., 1969. We have, however, further simplified Spiro's excellent theoretical analysis for purposes of our own. His* responsibility as obligation *is roughly equivalent to our umbrella term of responsibility; we forego the subtleties of Spiro's explicit and implicit accountability and utilize the term to mean regularized channels of structures of responsibility; and his rigorous analysis of* responsibility as cause *is subsumed under our notion of answerability.*

enhance and preserve responsible government (see Figure 1). Kernaghan is correct in pointing out that "accountability involves concern for the legal institutional and procedural devices by which public servants [and ministers also] may be held accountable or answerable for their actions."[17]

FIGURE I

A SCHEMATIC DIAGRAM OF THE VARIOUS "RESPONSIBILITIES"

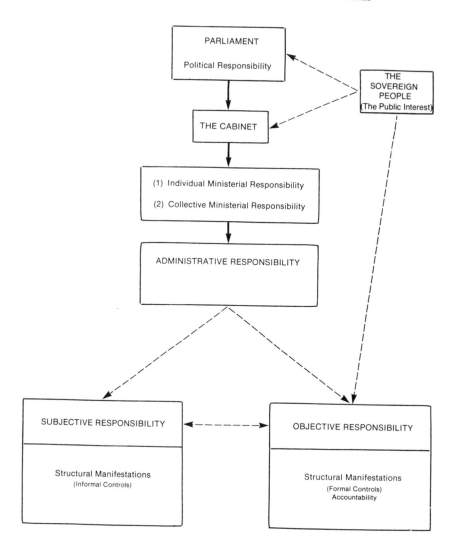

Answerability is a term often used synonymously with accountability (indeed it is used that way in the Kernaghan's quote above), but it is much more precise in that it seeks to express responsibility and accountability in day-to-day situations. Answerability is analogous to the classical judicial procedure of weighing *the facts* of the case (specific time, place, other factual considerations) against *a legal code or established rules of law* (eternal verities of justice). Thus answerability not only identifies the *locus* of responsibility but it seeks to determine the facts of a situation and apply such facts in making a judgment on responsibility. Should minister X be held accountable given the facts (A, B, C and D) of the situation? Answerability places a direct spotlight on behavioral realities. In law changing factual situations in society bring about changes in the legal code. Likewise answerability measures quickly expose any glaring discrepancy between *prescriptive* and *descriptive* criteria. Society seems to generally opt for either of two choices: discard the prescriptive criteria altogether for new criteria, or rearrange description to be more in harmony with prescription. The Lambert Commission recognizes this subtlety of distinction between responsibility and answerability by reaffirming the doctrine of ministerial responsibility while calling for changes in the system of answerability.[18] Kernaghan reinforces this interpretation by his argument that "while the focus of responsibility in government continues to be primarily the minister, the *locus* of actual responsibility [that is, answerability] lies increasingly in the public service . . . It is likely that direct administrative answerability to the legislature and the public will increase."[19] Paul Thomas concurs in arguing that the pragmatic relaxation of the traditional vow of silence for senior public servants to enable them to testify on administrative matters before parliamentary committees means that deputy ministers are *answerable* before Parliament but only ministers are *responsible* ". . . The distinctions involved in the two positions," he adds, "are subtle."[20]

These distinctions mirror significant evolutionary changes which have always been recognized by informed observers of our parliamentary heritage. For at the very time when ministerial responsibility was becoming fully acceptable as constitutional doctrine, some of its descriptive aspects were changing rather quickly and dramatically. What were these changes? The first has been the advent of the administrative state, which accompanied the familiar explosion of the scope and complexity of the activities of bureaucracy. It soon became apparent that neither parliament nor the informed public could reasonably expect ministers of the Crown to be fully cognizant of every action taken by their public servants. Indeed, academic commentators were emphasizing that official independence was a necessity for the smooth functioning of effective democratic government. Early constitutionalists began the argument for "the principle of official independence," that is, the bureaucracy must be entrusted with a measure of independence, particularly in technical and specialized matters, thus freeing it from too much political surveillance and day-to-day interference. At the turn of this century, the views of Professor Graham Wallas of the London School of Economics were illustrative of this evolution. "If we read history," he reminded us, "we see for how short a period men have accepted from thinkers like Bentham, and Jefferson, and Gambetta, the doctrine of the all-sufficiency of representative government."[21] Thus we must recognize that society is in a constant state of flux and always adapting: "the most striking political tendency of our time is a movement away from the simple optimism of nineteenth century parliamentarianism."[22]

R. MacGregor Dawson concurs with this analysis. "The size of the modern state and the complexity of our civilisation" he contends, have forced changes in the pristine doctrine of ministerial responsibility. Taking issue with Sir Sidney Low's graphic descriptions of ministerial responsibility in practice, Dawson argues that the complexity of government has forced evolutionary changes in some of the conventions of the doctrine, and in order to ensure efficient and effective government we must recognize and encourage "the principle of official independence." Implicit in Dawson's argument is the view that technical rationality in bureaucracy is a "new" measure to ensure probity, integrity and responsible government. Indeed the principle of official independence is a new standard to ensure answerability. We need not resurrect Dawson's argument in any more detail, but perhaps the following quote would serve to illustrate his views on the issue:

. . . modern experience has confirmed that the use of skilled officials is an essential condition of a democracy's existence. It is clear that to ascertain the will of the people is not sufficient; there must also be the means to ensure that what they desire will be carried out in the best possible manner. The real democracy demands a subtle combination of election and appointment, of non-expert minds and expert minds, of control and trust, of responsibility and independence. The size of the modern state and the complexity of our civilisation may make it extremely difficult to attain this combination; but the survival of democratic government nevertheless depends on its attainment.[23]

A quarter of a century after writing these words, Dawson again reaffirms his raison d'etre for this point of view: ". . . no minister . . . can hope to make even the major decisions for the five or ten or twenty thousand employees who may be nominally under him."[24]

The increased scope and technicality of government operations is only one of two factors accounting for evolutionary changes in the conventions underpinning ministerial responsibility. The second is the politics of collective accountability. A series of compelling reasons have forced this evolutionary change. The most important is the growth of party discipline and cabinet power making any attack on ministerial responsibility an assault or challenge of prime ministerial government. As Professor S. E. Finer documented so conclusively for Britain, no Parliament can penalize a minister for departmental actions so long as the Prime Minister views such a frontal attack as a serious challenge to the integrity of his government or a damaging reflection on the managerial capabilities of his ministry.[25] Allied to this notion of party government in Canada is the corollary need to consolidate financial control of the public purse and the compelling demands to ensure cabinet regional representation. Hodgetts thus notes:

First, the convention that the cabinet should provide adequate regional representation could make sense only if most matters were brought before the cabinet for final decision . . . [thus] the necessity of obtaining collegial decisions on a wide range of relatively unimportant matters has, in a sense, forced the Canadian cabinet, like the individual minister, to concern itself with detailed problems of management often at the expense of its broader task of acting as a co-ordinating board of directors in settling the main policy goals of the nation.[26]

And on financial management, the Privy Council's submission to the Lambert Commission puts it this way:

Collective responsibility [has become] the cement of our system of government. Its three key elements are Treasury control and the allied convention that the government alone and as a single entity may ask the Commons to approve ways and means and vote supply, and the *de facto* powers of appointment over ministers and other holders of high office that are exercised by a prime minister that emanate from his historic role as the arbiter of Treasury control and patronage. These are the elements that make possible the cabinet, which exists to bring together the individual responsibilities of ministers so that they may be exercised by each minister in a manner that is acceptable to all ministers.[27]

As Kernaghan has thoroughly documented, the doctrine also has consequences for internal public service relations.[28] First is the interrelationships of political accountability to the conventions of neutrality, secrecy, anonymity and hierarchy and the consequences which flow from these conventions. Second is the debate on the structural manifestations of political accountability. Must accountability for public servants be clearly defined in readily discernible structural forms or is it best manifested in the internalization of professional norms and ethical considerations? We will examine both of these areas in turn.

III. Derivatives of Accountability and Answerability

The conventions of neutrality, anonymity, secrecy and hierarchy are directly related to the accountability and answerability components of responsibility. It is in this area of concern that the constitutionalists point to the likelihood of changes, but they agree with Kernaghan that such changes will not radically alter the umbrella concept of ministerial responsibility: ". . . rather it will be complemented by new procedures and practices which will expand administrative responsibility."[29] *Constitutionalists are therefore implicitly arguing that the prescriptive aspects of the doctrine will remain intact while certain descriptive aspects of it are subject to slow evolutionary changes.* But what are the consequences of these conventions of internal civil service relations? First, all the departmental actions are issued in the name of the minister, and his responsibility for such actions to Parliament is concretely manifested in the British North America Act and the preambles to most, if not all, departmental acts.[30] Thus J. E. Hodgetts concludes that "the phraseology of the British North America Act is in complete accord with the constitutional doctrine of parliamentary supremacy. Thus the locus of *ultimate* authority over the public service seems to be clearly settled in parliament."[31] And T. M. Denton, after a comprehensive review of "the statutes governing the organization of the federal public service" is led to the conclusion that "Parliament is not at the periphery but at the centre of the Canadian constitution and that the entire public service is subordinated to the principle of democratic accountability."[32] Because of these facts it is only through the sufferance of the ministers, either individually or collectively, that public servants are given permission to appear before Parliament or any outside body to defend their views and administrative activities.[33] This cloak of anonymity leaves the doctrine of ministerial responsibility formally unchallenged, but it also accords public servants considerable freedom in dealing with the various interests jostling for policy advantages without having to bear the ultimate responsibility of either policy success or failure. There is, however, a dilemma for responsible government here for as the administrative state becomes more clearly identified this convention is being increasingly challenged even by the constitutionalist. J. E.

Hodgetts, for example, has argued that "the shift from laissez-faire to collectivism has been accompanied by an unprecedented shift in the balance of real power, discretion and initiative—away from courts, legislatures and even cabinets to public servants." "The public," he further warns, fears the administrative state (*power* in the hands of "faceless" people and mandarins) and suspect "that their rights are being invaded even as they are ostensibly being *served* by [these] public employees."[34]

Given this reality does one deny the prescriptive aspects of ministerial responsibility or does one seek remedies within its broad framework so as to correct some imbalances in the shift of decision-making power? Should we have more ombudsmen or deputy ministerial accountability or both? The dilemma is clearly posed, but what do we do?[35] In matters of financial management the Lambert Commission has clearly opted for deputy ministerial accountability. This recommendation is by no means universally accepted by academic critics and parliamentary governments.[36] Ministerial responsibility retains its legitimacy but it is still far from clear as to what changes should occur in the convention of public service anonymity as we approach the twenty-first century.

The second constitutional convention of internal public service relations deals with administrative secrecy which shrouds both minister/public servant and public servant/pressure groups relationships.

DR. W. D. K. KERNAGHAN
Professor of Politics and Administration, Brock University, and Editor, *Canadian Public Administration*. Kernaghan's contribution to Canadian public policy and administration has been significant in the area of administrative responsibility and control. Some of his writings have formed the basis of a number of ethical codes and conflict-of-interest guidelines for various levels of Canadian government.

This is a most confused and complex debate and we will attempt to discuss only a few aspects of it in the next chapter. Stated simply, the constitutional convention requires that a public servant cannot have a public identity apart from the responsible minister s/he advises. If the public servant cannot accept this convention because of values which are so fundamentally different from that of the minister's, then public service neutrality is invalidated and the public servant must resign. [37] Because this convention is so firmly held it is assumed that public service advice can only be channelled within the bowels of the bureaucracy, and public servants are rarely allowed to explain any but official departmental views in public forums. The same shroud of secrecy which envelops collective cabinet responsibility is spread over the public service. Because the minister is ultimately responsible, secrecy allows the minister to control the facts of the situation, a monopoly which renders the task of the opposition very difficult indeed. According to J. P. Mackintosh, the consequences of discarding the convention has certain implications for ministerial government:

> If the doctrine were broken and officials could explain their views freely in public, then ministers would have the much more formidable task of making their case against men who were seized of the key counter points and who knew their arguments were accepted by many in the ministry. It is clear why ministers, who lose only a little and gain a great deal from the doctrine, should want to keep it going. [38]

The issue is further complicated by the negotiations which go on between interest groups and public servants at various levels of government. Thus, the problems of interaction between interest groups and public servants and between public servants of different levels of governments, pose dilemmas for democratic governance which are summarily stated by S. E. Finer:

> Increasingly, what the minister presents to the Commons is a package arrangement agreed between his civil servants and the representatives of the outside groups [or between civil servants of different levels of government]. In the House, party discipline inhibits backbenchers from challenging their government; even if it did not, the information and evidence on which the package depends are confidential and have not been disclosed; and even if it had been, the nature of the package is so well balanced a set of compromises that if any one part were overturned in the House, the entire deal would have to be re-negotiated. [39]

In Canada, D. V. Smiley has argued that "executive federalism" (that is, federal provincial negotiations between public servants of different levels of government) has increased secrecy in government and has also contributed to the lack of understanding and minimal citizen participation in federal-provincial affairs. Pointing to secrecy and the "extra-ordinary complexity of the process," he asks:

. . . how can one reasonably expect intelligent public or even parliamentary debate on the Federal-Provincial Fiscal Arrangements and Established Programs Financing Act of 1977—perhaps one of the most important enactments of the Canadian Parliament in recent decades? And I would also defy anyone without specialized training to make sense of the national dimension and emergency doctrines as these were argued in the Anti-Inflation reference of 1976. [40]

Serious critics of this secrecy in government—commentators like D. C. Rowat and former parliamentarian Gerald Baldwin, argue that the only way to prevent this secrecy convention from denying us democratic government is to "open up the windows" and allow as full access of information as possible. Usually this means "adequate" access to information both for the press and members of the public capable of interpreting this information, much of which, as Smiley has stated, is very complex. But exactly how much opening of the windows can be allowed without infringing upon the rights of others? Much information which governments possess has been given in confidence. Despite this obvious need for some secrecy, what kinds of information must remain private and what can now enter the public domain? In cases of dispute as to the release of certain kinds of information, who has the final say, the minister or the courts? The issues here are complex and there are no simple answers as we confront the thorny problems of dismantling some features of the administrative state.

Finally we come to the role hierarchy plays in reinforcing ministerial responsibility. Normally hierarchy is not included among the conventions of secrecy, neutrality and anonymity, but hierarchy nevertheless plays a significant role in preserving the doctrine of ministerial responsibility by channelling control from above. The full implications of departmental hierarchy in parliamentary government and its place in the order of things will be dealt with in Chapter Ten. But how much hierarchical authority can be retained in a sprawling administrative state, particularly when it is readily acknowledged by informed observers that bureaucratic centralization is the chief ingredient of organizational rigidity? Hodgetts poses this dilemma succinctly: "A *responsive* bureaucracy clearly ought to be concentrating on transferring authority to the administrators down the hierarchy and out in the field; yet the historical claims for a *responsible* bureaucracy can best be met by retaining authority close to the top where it can be used by the minister and scrutinized by parliament."[41] The Lambert Commission considered this dilemma and opted for centralization, a choice which has caused much adverse criticism in the public service.[42]

IV. The Structural Manifestations of Accountability: The Hierarchical Responsibilities Paradigm

How are these conventions made manifest? In what concrete ways do we make bureaucracy accountable and answerable? Is it best to place an overlay of controlling structures on the bureaucracy or can control be achieved informally by relying on bureaucratic socialization of certain desirable norms and professional values which will tend to guarantee predictability and professional integrity? We can begin to explore these questions by focusing on the distinction between *objective* and *subjective* responsibility. Frederick Mosher gives a good definition of both concepts:

Responsibility may well be the most important word in all the vocabulary of administration, public and private. But it has a confusing wealth of different meanings and shades of meanings, of which I here identify two. The first, *objective responsibility,* connotes the responsibility of a person or an organization *to* someone else, outside of self, *for* something or some kind of performance. *It is closely akin to accountability* or *answerability.* If one fails to carry out legitimate directives . . . Responsibility is also essential to predictability; if a person does not behave responsibly, his behavior cannot be predicted.[43]

On the other hand, *subjective responsibility* focuses:

. . . not upon to whom and for what one is responsible (according to the law and the organization chart) but to whom and for what one *feels* responsible and *behaves* responsibly. This meaning is more nearly synonymous with identification, loyalty, and conscience than it is with accountability and answerability.[44]

To help sort out the various "responsibilities" we have already referred to Figure I which outlines in rough classificatory form our discussion thus far. It is somewhat difficult to place subjective responsibility in a system which emphasizes hierarchical ordering, but when it is realized that most of these informal controls reinforce the legitimacy of constitutional government, then the problem is not so conceptually difficult to handle.

The fundamental distinction between these two "responsibilities" lays at the heart of the most important philosophical debate on the subject between Carl Joachim Friedrich and Herman Finer during the period 1935-1941.[45] The debate centered, as most subsequent discussions of the concept of administrative responsibility, on the most effective means of guarding against the abuse of administrative power and discretion, and ensuring responsible administrative conduct.

Certainly the writings of Friedrich and Finer can be thought of as book-ends—they are diametrically opposed to each other in their basic approaches, and the detail of their debate covers the entire spectrum of ideas that should be considered. To oversimplify, Finer does not trust human nature and Friedrich does. Finer believes that *objective rules* must be established to control the activities of public administrators. These rules should be formulated and enforced by the political representatives of the people because only in this way is responsibility assured:

. . . the servants of the public are not to decide their own course: they are to be responsible to the elected representatives of the public, and these are to determine the course of action of the public servants to the most minute degree that is technically feasible.[46]

Friedrich, on the other hand, feels that public administrators can be trusted to follow the dictates of their own consciences, and therefore to behave correctly, which means a consistent behavior attuned to the norms of the organization and of society. As he puts it, "Responsible conduct of administrative functions is not so much enforced as it is elicited."[47] Finer thus pins his faith on *objective standards* determined by the political arm of government, while Friedrich is convinced that only *subjective standards*, determined largely by the administrators themselves, remain the best solution to the problem.

What are some of these standards? In Friedrich's view, only lip service is still being paid to what he sees as an outmoded principle, and the public administrator really reports to himself/herself or to the immediate superior. He proposes to by-pass the political function almost completely and to establish a direct responsibility of the administrator to the citizen. Friedrich argues:

. . . we have a right to call such a policy irresponsible if it can be shown that it was adopted without proper regard to the existing sum of human knowledge concerning the technical issues involved . . . [and] if it can be shown that it was adopted without proper regard for existing preference in the community, and more particularly its prevailing majority. Consequently, the responsible administrator is one who is responsible to these two dominant factors: technical knowledge and popular sentiment.[48]

Thus Friedrich embraces human nature as being basically good and worthy of trust.

Herman Finer is having none of this Jean Jacques Rousseau's "natural man" philosophy. For him nature is easily corrupted, and it therefore must be subject to a set of written rules, and their enforcement must be rigorous. The elected representatives of the people should, to repeat part of a quote made earlier, "determine the course of action of public servants to the most minute degree that is technically feasible."[49] In assuming this position, Finer's stance should become readily obvious to the reader: he is strictly maintaining the constitutionalist position of political accountability.

The "book-ends" nature of this debate could be further discerned by Herman Finer's own summary of both his and Friedrich's positions:

First, responsibility may mean that X is accountable for Y to Z. Second, responsibility may mean an inward personal sense of moral obligation. In the first definition the essence is the externality of the agency or persons to whom an account is to be rendered and it can mean very little without that agency having authority over X, determining the lines of X's obligation and the terms of its continuance or revocation. The second definition puts the emphasis on the conscience of the agent, and—if he commits an error it is an error only when recognized by his own conscience, and—the punishment of the agent will be merely the twinges thereof. The one implies public execution; the other hara-kiri.[50]

The debate settled nothing in a conclusive way for each protagonist was correct in pointing to the strengths of his arguments and the deficiencies in his opponent's. As Kernaghan points out, Friedrich has lived to see many of his predictions on the topic coming to fruition: the rapid growth of professionalism in almost every area of the public service; the massive delegation of powers of a legislative and judicial nature; and the extension of collective bargaining rights to public employees, to name a few developments.[51] Nevertheless, Finer was also correct on many points he made. Despite all the progressive advances, we have seen continuous official corruption both at home and abroad; the extensive delegation of legislative and judicial powers have led to some celebrated abuses in recent years; professionalism has had to be monitored by governments appointing lay observers "in the public interest," to many of the self-governing professional councils; and, of course, there has been Watergate and all its significant consequences for morality in liberal democratic governments. While Finer's argument was accurate in the recognition of the continuing need for political controls over the bureaucracy, its weakness lay

FIGURE II

THE HIERARCHICAL RESPONSIBILITIES PARADIGM: DERIVATIVES AND STRUCTURAL
CONSEQUENCES

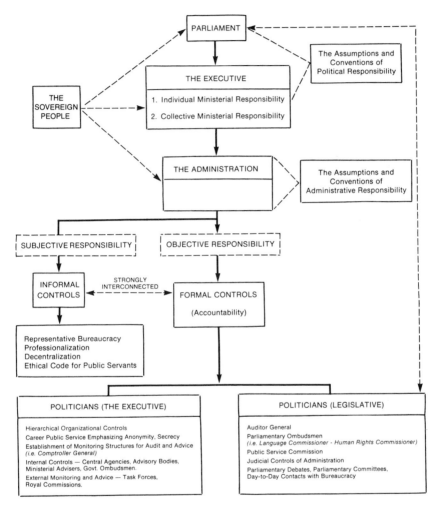

as Kernaghan puts it, "in the failure to anticipate the inadequacy of
[political] controls to ensure administrative responsibility in a period
of ever-accelerating political and social change."[52] Kernaghan has
correctly indicated both sets of controls have been relied upon in liberal democratic societies and Figure II is an attempt to categorize in
our hierarchical responsibilities paradigm the many measures so employed. In enlarging on Figure I we have simply filled out the "empty
boxes" of *subjective* and *objective* responsibilities. As the reader can

readily see, objective responsibility has received most of the attention because this classification mirrors the popular insistence of concretizing all aspects of reality. In a complex bureaucratic structure public servants must, after all, be held responsible for their actions, and the only concrete way this is done is to erect institutions to do the task. A discretion which allows subtle decision-making choices between good and good, or choices tinged with sympathy or compassion irrespective of clearly delegated rules and regulations, must be treated as highly suspect. Moreover, unlike *objective responsibility*, notions of *subjective responsibility* are more difficult to pin down: one cannot easily bring to account the concept of professionalization, or point to an ethical code for public servants which is comprehensive and all-inclusive for all times.[53]

Nevertheless all of these considerations are included in the hierarchical responsibilities paradigm because the liberal democrat in the constitutional tradition relies on all of them to help in controlling the administrative state. Corry and Hodgetts made this point many years ago:

If government is going to perform many positive services for the community, there must be greater concentration and less dispersion of power than that which marked the age of laissez faire. But wherever power is lodged, devices are needed to ensure that it can be called to account. The more power is concentrated, the more nicely calculated the means of controlling it must be. The elaboration of new and more effective controls has not kept pace with the growing concentration of power. More thought must be given to such controls in the immediate future.[54]

V. The Pragmatist View of Ministerial Government: The Pragmatic Paradigm

The pragmatist view of ministerial government is a forthright attempt to come to grips with the reality of the administrative state. The initial impression one gets from reading this literature is that this viewpoint eschews the intricacies of ministerial/public servant relationships described in the hierarchical responsibilities paradigm. The question is asked: Who has real power in the system? Descriptions are given which tend to end in fuzzy generalizations about the pluralism of actors and forces. However, the answers they seek and the reality they wish to explore are very real concerns in a consideration of the dynamics of political power.

The literature on the pragmatic view is very diffuse and it is impossible to attempt a concise summary of it in a few pages of a chapter.

The empirical work of these pragmatists, however, points to certain general conclusions. First there is an impressive unanimity amongst students of Canadian government that the linkages between political decision-makers and their environment (that is, the general public) are weak. "Canada" argues Richard Simeon, "combines the British tradition of a strong executive and centralized leadership with a *relative* freedom from mass pressure and popular constraint."[55] This is the general conclusion of D. V. Smiley on federal-provincial relations,[56] J. R. Mallory on mass citizen participation,[57] Bruce Thorardson and Peter Dobell on Canadian foreign policy,[58] and R. Van Loon and M. S. Whittington on the Canadian political system as a whole.[59] In their first edition to the *Canadian Political System*, Van Loon and Whittington confront this reality by asking the rhetorical question: "How is it that, in spite of rather weak input processes which should keep them marginally in touch with the environment, decision makers often make satisfactory decisions?"[60] Their main conclusion is that:

. . . decision makers make "right" decisions for the majority of Canadians because they are socialized to a set of values which are congruent with or similar to those held by that majority. For this reason their "gut reaction" to information is likely to be much the same as that of most Canadians. Their reactions are "right" for most of us because they are people just like most of us.[61]

Who are these decision-makers with 'gut reactions'? Are they to be found in Parliament? Pragmatists overwhelmingly argue that your average Member of Parliament is not the "decision-maker" alluded to above. Parliament is first and foremost a "talking shop" and not the key decision-maker in the process.[62] Some commentators consider Parliament to be irrelevant, while others take the position that if it is not irrelevant at least it is close to becoming so.[63] As one disgruntled Member of Parliament puts it: "The key issues today are not being settled in Parliament. Federal-provincial conferences settle the price of oil and gas as well as apportion the cost of social progress. The federal bureaucracy settles the big spending questions in defence and CIDA."[64]

The contemporary literature on parliamentary government suggests that members of the House of Commons and the Senate perform five essential functions in the political process (a) they have the *formal* responsibility for assenting to new legislation and *influencing* its content; (b) they fill a recruitment function by providing a pool of talent from which leaders are drawn; (c) they reflect public opinion and help to educate the public and one another; (d) they undertake scrutiny of government action; and (e) they look after the particular interests of their constituents.[65] Nowhere in these five functions do we have listed a parliamentary role of actual policy making. Faced with these critical analyses of Parliament's actual role in the policy process some commentators have argued that it is more our expectations of what the House of Commons *ought to be doing* which are at fault rather than the institution itself. For example, Gerhard Lowenberg declares that it is primarily our faulty expectations which have fostered the familiar argument that Parliament is declining in quality and influence. Such conclusions, he declared are ". . . often the result of applying the standards of a previous age of institutional development to the parliamentary behaviour of the moment."[66]

Given this parliamentary "decline," what then is the role of the courts? Are they not there to curb the excesses of political power and guarantee the rule of law in our democratic society? Again the prognosis of the pragmatic commentators is mixed. Empirical evidence points out that the judiciary is held in very high regard in Canada.[67] This is no doubt due to the prestige of the profession, but part of it is also due to the traditional perception the populace has about the neutrality and impartiality of the judicial process. However, as the courts are called upon to increasingly exercise discretion in the interpretation of public policy, there is a growing recognition of the power of decision-making left to the courts. Commentators suggest that this increasing recognition of the public policy powers of the courts will tend to weaken its traditional neutral image as a technical interpreter of previously established rules of law.[68]

Courts are also called upon by parliament to scrutinize and check the actions of administrators. But as administrative discretion is increased it has become exceedingly difficult for the courts to accomplish effective limitations on bureaucratic power. Furthermore, the traditional role of the courts in safeguarding the rights of one individual against another or against the state has been curtailed because the courts were not designed to adjudicate matters not found in pre-established law. "In essence, the traditional courts are incapable of playing a constructive part in the newly developing functions of government, where exercise of discretions is required."[69]

The most important locus of political action is what Doern and Aucoin call "the executive-bureaucratic arena,"—the sphere of interaction between the bureaucratic mandarins, the members of the cabinet, and the powerful interest groups who have access to the corridors of power.[70] The literature and range of topics considered here are extensive and we have attempted to analyse and summarize some of it in successive chapters on central agencies (Chapter Nine), the

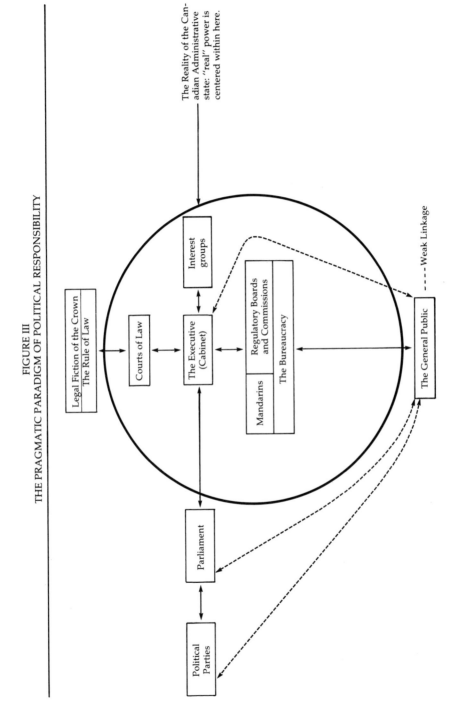

FIGURE III
THE PRAGMATIC PARADIGM OF POLITICAL RESPONSIBILITY

ministerial profile (Chapter Ten) and interest groups (Chapter Twelve). Suffice to point out here that political power is viewed by the pragmatists as a relational concept: it is unlike currency because it cannot be located spatially or spent conceptually. "Political power" as Jackson and Atkinson put it, "links together two or more actors, with different political resources, in a situation involving a multitude of influences, including severe losses for non-compliance."[71] Viewed in this way, policy formulation is thus conceptualized as a mandarin to mandarin process. Bureaucratic factions are viewed as having "competitive, not homogenous interests; priorities and perceptions of policy issues are shaped by positions; and the management of piecemeal streams of decisions is more important than steady state choices."[72] Figure III is an attempt to depict these various relationships in a very broad fashion. Some pragmatists have conceptualized the process in terms of sociological role theory,[73] while others have conceived it in terms of "coalitions, log-rolling, and full-line forcing at the timing of elections." An advocate of the latter viewpoint sums it up in the following way:

What is the role of government? Is it nothing more than a highly complex means of resolving, through an endless series of compromises, the conflicting interests of those subject to its authority in such a way to avoid the open use of force: "the war of all against all," to use Hobbes' phrase? The answer is usually yes, but occasionally no. There is a role for government leadership by which we mean the adoption of policies that are unpopular in prospect but come to be accepted perhaps even with enthusiasm and pride, after they have proven themselves.[74]

And another pragmatist makes a global judgment of what policy really is, given this "unmasking" of the deployment of political power:

It is not possible for ever to evade questions about "the right kind of society," the purposes of the state, the basis and justification of government business. The determination of ends, the choice of means, the balance of social forces, are the stuff of politics. In these terms, it is clear that some civil servants are engaged in politics. The word "policy" is a recognition of this, it is a way of describing what civil servants do when they play a part in determining ends, choosing means and fixing priorities. It is distinguished from politics, which is limited strictly to the activities of political parties, and from administration which is the maintenance of the status quo. "Policy" is then nothing more than the political activity of civil servants.[75]

VI. The Two Paradigms: Implications for Ministerial Responsibility and its Derivatives

We have outlined here two paradigms of political responsibility, which, at first glance, seem to be miles apart from each other: one accentuating the norms and values of liberal democratic society and the manner in which governing institutions are affected by these norms, and the other emphasizing the subtle interplay of political power among politicians, bureaucrats and interest groups. The first viewpoint seems to be preoccupied with devising ways and means of channelling and circumscribing the use of legitimate state power, while the second seems to argue that much of these constitutional ideas are really "ghosts" which act to cement systems of philosophies or academic thought. Thus, such concepts as "the public interest" and "subjective and objective responsibility" really obscure the issue of the use of power and should be disrobed to show that they have no more authority over the exercise of state power than an unfrocked priest has over the faithful. This may be stating these two perspectives in the baldest of terms but it concisely summarizes them for purposes of this chapter.

The pragmatists have contributed immensely to the study of political and bureaucratic power by their emphasis on behavioral criteria. The more knowledgeable amongst them view power as a relational concept, and this has helped to analyse bureaucratic power in more meaningful ways as we will attempt to show in Chapters Nine and Twelve. There is a tendency, however, for the pragmatists to view the constitutionalists as "myth makers" and "students of anachronisms," when they mistakenly view the firmly expressed values of the constitutionalists as both *prescriptive* and *descriptive* in content. Furthermore, some constitutionalists encourage this interpretation by not clarifying the distinction in their writings.

What is, however, immediately obvious is that the true constitutionalist view does not contend that the institutions and conventions of liberal democracy are somehow engraved in stone and immutable to change. There is no doubt that the constitutionalists have a firm commitment to the democratic principles of liberty, fraternity, responsible government and so on. It is also their firm belief that the normative values inherent in ministerial responsibility are inviolate. But to keep this principle alive may require a number of accountability measures, some of these unchanging because they have stood the test of time, others constantly being refurbished, and yet others created and/or abolished as changing circumstances dictate. As already indicated, this is why in the early part of this century, Graham Wallas argued that the institutions of liberal democratic government were not "all sufficient," and R. MacGregor Dawson contended that there was a need for a new "principle of official independence" to meet the changing circumstances for democratic governance. It can therefore now be fully understood why J. A. Corry and J. E. Hodgetts have argued that "more thought must be given to [democratic] controls" because "the elaboration of new and more effective controls [of responsible government] has not kept pace with the growing concentration of power."[76]

Accountability measures therefore can and will change to continuously confront the reality of the administrative state. The problem becomes even more acute for answerability measures. We earlier argued that answerability is a more precise formulation of accountability: democratic responsibility and accountability measures are given further practical expression by the weighting of specific facts and circumstances. It therefore follows that as government grows in complexity and size some answerability measures will fall into desuetude and others will be created to meet changing circumstances. One such answerability measure judged to be an anachronism is the assumption that a minister will automatically resign when, through no direct fault of the minister in question, it is brought to public attention that senior officials have misappropriated their powers through intentional misdeeds or faulty judgments. In an article written during the mid 50s, S. E. Finer makes the clear distinction between the *prescriptive values of ministerial responsibility* and the *descriptive aspects of answerability*. The latter, he argues, had been subject to signficant changes through the decades:

Now in its first sense, that the Minister alone *speaks* for his Civil Servants to the House and to his Civil Servants for the House . . . ministerial responsibility has both the proleptic and the compulsive features of a "rule." But in the sense in which we have been considering it, that the Minister *may be punished, through loss of office* for all the misdeeds and neglects of his Civil Servants which he cannot prove to have been outside all possibility of his cognisance and control, the proposition does not seem to be a rule at all . . . All it says (on examination) is that if the Minister is yielding, his Prime Minister unbending and his party out for blood—no matter how serious or trivial the reason—the Minister will find himself without Parliamentary support. *This is a statement of fact, not a code.*[77]

Without perhaps realizing it, this is precisely the point which the pragmatists have been attempting to make, but in doing so their arguments tend to confuse the two issues correctly identified by

Finer. Quite rightly they point to the fact that the liberal democratic principles which we cherish so highly today only came to fruition during the last century. Quite rightly they point to the conventions which have been derived from the doctrines of political and ministerial responsibility, reminding us that conventions are *mere practices and not inviolate truths*. Quite rightly in their adversarial descriptions of political power they loudly announce the advent of the administrative state, pointing to the fact that the arrival of such a phenomena has created considerable havoc to the conventions of anonymity, secrecy and neutrality. It is no accident that pragmatists make frontal attacks on all the above conventions. Pragmatists are behavioralists and conventions purport to be behavioral descriptions of certain governmental practices accepted over time. Thus with the advent of the administrative state secrecy is questioned because of its threat to open government; anonymity for its placing of a shroud on the "real power actors" in the system; and neutrality for its presumption that policy advice to politicians is proffered by a collection of well paid and highly intelligent political eunuchs.

However, conventions are too often grouped together or mistaken for principles and doctrines, and what we have is the discarding of both conventions *and* doctrines. Moreover, there is no realization that even "conventional conventions" take on a subtlety of meaning which recognizes changing reality:

What neutrality *does* mean is that the relation between minister and civil servant is not that of patron and client, the minster is not responsible for the appointed official's tenure, he has few if any powers to discipline him and, by rules of conduct which are conventionally accepted rather than explicit, the civil servant keeps enough distance both from the minister as a person and from the more crassly partisan aspects of public affairs that he can transfer the same kind of loyalty to another "political master" either of the same partisan complexion or otherwise . . . Civil servants are not anonymous in the sense that members of the covert element of the Central Intelligence Agency are anonymous . . . What anonymity *does* mean is elected executive officials rather than appointed persons are made *answerable* for the conduct of government.[78]

The pragmatist viewpoint is most revealing in that its discourse on ministerial responsibility is devoid of any distinct normative alternatives. If we discard the doctrine, what will we put in its place? Serious pragmatists are stumped in arriving at any meaningful answer to this question. Either they remain conspicuously silent on the issue or they declare in vague terms that "the future of democracy rests upon principles of accountability." Exactly what these principles are remains open to questioning. Most pragmatists are "closet constitutionalists" at heart, for they implicitly believe in the prescriptive aspects of ministerial responsibility. Where they part company with the constitutionalists is in their sweeping behavioral criticisms of the conventions of accountability and answerability.

Constitutionalists who adopt the hierarchical responsibilities paradigm in their descriptions of government tend to measure evolutionary changes against Canadian constitutional and political theory. Their analyses have sought to emphasize that many of the supporting pillars of ministerial responsibility—anonymity, neutrality, disavowance of open partisan activity by public servants, confidential advice tendered to ministers, and the loyal implementation of government decisions irrespective of the public servant's personal views—are still viable concepts which not only condition public service behavior, but remain essential components of legitimate government in Canada. Changes are inevitable in these concepts, but such changes must be accompanied by a clear vision as to what they imply for democratic governance. In insisting on measured change constitutionalists are often labelled as obstructionists to much needed reform. The evidence we have gathered points to the fact that the "conservative" constitutionalist viewpoint on change is the prevailing consensus in the Canadian political system on the subject.

The nature of the discourse of political responsibility and accountability in Canada has always been couched in "conservative" tones. As Seymour Martin Lipset once expressed it "Canadians [are] more prone to identify liberty and democracy with legal traditions and procedures than with populism, the right of the people to rule or with the freedom of business and enterprise."[79] As an example, the report of the Royal Commission on Financial Management and Accountability appraises the debate that Parliament is in danger of losing control of the public purse and concurs, but in recommending certain structural changes the Commission is careful to point out that these changes are "in the spirit of our constitutional evolution to date and do not represent radical departures from it."[80] Perhaps this is to be expected from an officially commissioned report, but it is significant that both the public discourse on the matter and the published debates on the Commission's recommendations did not challenge this frame of reference. It is therefore realistic to forecast that the continuing Canadian debate on responsibility and accountability will be conducted in the constitutional language and traditions of legal sovereignty. Ministerial responsibility and all its trappings will continue to be around for a long time to come.

The "Pragmatist/Constitutionalist "Viewpoint—Is it Really that Confusing?

It is almost trite to say that [the] traditional doctrines of ministerial and cabinet responsibility are now under question as being misleading or inoperative or impossible to attain. *My own views on the matter are confused.* The pristine doctrines of ministerial and cabinet responsibility cannot be applied without some significant modifications to governments with the scope of activity which prevails today. Yet to reject these doctrines completely is surely indefensible for without them we appear to have no guides to the most fundamental of political relations between governments and legislatures, among members of the political executive, between elected politicians and bureaucrats, between governments and those whom they govern.

Donald V. Smiley

Footnotes

1. Kenneth McNaught, "History and the Perception of Politics," in John H. Redekop (ed.), *Approaches to Canadian Politics* (Scarborough: Prentice-Hall of Canada, 1978), p. 108.

2. *Ibid.,* p. 108

3. H.A. Innis, *Political Economy in the Modern State* (Toronto: University of Toronto Press, 1946), p. 188.

4. T.A. Hockin, *Government in Canada* (Toronto: McGraw-Hill Ryerson Ltd., 1976), pp. 94-96. It is worth reading Hockin's Chapter Three, "The Growth of Government in Canada" for a full exploration of this theme.

5. J.A. Corry, "The Prospects for the Rule of Law" *CJEPS*, Vol. 21, 1955, pp. 405-415.

6. Peter Regenstreif, *The Diefenbaker Interlude: Parties and Voting in Canada* (Toronto: Longmans, 1965), p. 17.

7. W.A. Mackintosh, "The White Paper on Employment and Income in its 1945 Setting," in S.F. Kaliski (ed.), *Canadian Economic Policy Since the War* (Ottawa: The Canadian Trade Committee, 1966), pp. 9-21.

8. J.E. Hodgetts, "Regional Interests and Policy in a Federal Structure," *CJEPS*, XXXII (February 1966), pp. 3-14.

9. Alan C. Cairns, "The Governments and Societites of Canadian Federalism," *CJPS* X:4 (December 1977), pp. 695-725, at p. 695; Frank Mackinnon, "Prince Edward Island: Big Engine, Little Body," in Martin Robin (ed.), *Canadian Provincial Politics* (Scarborough: Prentice Hall of Canada, 1972), p. 272.

10. A striking exception to this statement is the unpublished doctoral dissertation of the late Donald Gow. See his "Canadian Federal Administrative and Political Institutions: A Role Analysis" unpublished Ph.D. thesis, 1967, Queen's University, Kingston, Ontario.

11. Two terms need a little clarification (i) the institutionalization of government (or the creation of structures) and (ii) the concept of paradigm. (i) By instutionalization we mean the following:

    Institutionalization is the process by which organizations and procedures acquire value and stability. The level of institutionalization of any political system can be defined by the adaptibility, complexity, autonomy, and coherence of its organizations and procedures."

    Samuel P. Huntington, "Political Development and Political Decay," in Norman J. Vig and Rodney P. Stiefbold (eds.), *Politics in Advanced Nations* (Englewood Cliffs, N.J.: Prentice-Hall, 1974) p. 115. (ii) Strictly speaking, a model implies a conceptual tool with predictive capacity. A paradigm is simply a framework of codification. It claims no predictive value and its use is simply to classify disparate ideas and concepts on a specific topic, so as to present some logical consistency on the subject. For an excellent discussion on the use of paradigms in sociology, see Robert K. Merton, "On Sociological Theories of the Middle Range," in R.K. Merton, *On Theoretical Sociology: Five Essays, Old and New* (New York: The Free Press, 1967), pp. 39-72.

12. J.E. Hodgetts, "Challenge and Response: A Retrospective View of the Public Service of Canada," *CPA*, VII, 4, (December, 1964), pp. 409-421 at p. 413.

13. Sir Ivor Jennings, *Cabinet Government*, 3rd ed. (Cambridge: Cambridge University Press, 1969), p. 133; John P. Mackintosh, *The Government and Politics in Britain* (London: Hutchinson U. Library, 1970), p. 144.

14. Geoffrey Marshall, "Ministerial Responsibility," *Political Quarterly*, 34 (1963), p. 256.

15. For further clarification, see Carl Joachim Friedrich, *Constitutional Government and Democracy* (New York: Ginn and Co., 1950) especially pp. 25-28, on "the essence of constitutionalism"; Herbert J. Spiro, *Responsibility in Government* (New York: Van Nostrand Reinhold, 1969).

16. *Ibid.*, p. vii.

17. Kernaghan is referring to some accountability measures (see Figure 1) when he argues that:

    The source of administrative responsibility on which there is a substantial measure of agreement in scholarly writings include political executives, legislators, judges, administrative superiors, members of the general public and interest group and mass media representatives.

    Kenneth Kernaghan, "Changing concepts of power and responsibility in the Canadian public service," *CPA*, Fall 1978, Vol. 21, No. 3, pp. 398-399, p. 580.

18. Canada, Royal Commission on Financial Management and Accountability. *Final Report* (Ottawa: Supply and Services, March 1979), pp. 56-57. We intend to be

much more detailed in our discussion of answerability when we address that question in Chapter Nine.

19. Kenneth Kernaghan, *Freedom of Information and Ministerial Responsibility*. Research Publication No. 2, Commission on Freedom of Information and Individual Privacy, Ontario, September, 1978, p. 28.

20. Paul G. Thomas, "The Lambert Report: Parliament and accountability," *CPA*, Vol. 23, No. 1 (Spring 1980), p. 50.

21. Graham Wallas, "Introduction," in R. MacGregor Dawson, *The Principle of Official Independence* (Toronto: University of Toronto Press, 1921), p. xiii.

22. *Ibid.*

23. *Ibid.*, p. 27.

24. R. MacGregor Dawson, *The Government of Canada*, 4th ed. (revised by Norman Ward) (Toronto: University of Toronto Press, 1964), p. 256.

25. S.E. Finer, "The Individual Responsibility of Ministers," *Public Administration*, journal of the Royal Institute of Public Administration, (London), vol. 34, 1956, pp. 377-396.

26. J.E. Hodgetts, *The Canadian Public Service: A Physiology of Government 1967-1970* (Toronto: University of Toronto Press, 1973), p. 51.

27. Canada, Privy Council Office, Submissions to the *Royal Commission on Financial Management and Accountability* (Ottawa: Minister of Supply and Services, 1979), p. 16.

28. Kenneth Kernaghan, "Responsible Public Bureaucracy: A Rationale and a Framework for Analysis," *CPA*, vol. 16, Winter 1973, pp. 581-588; _____ "Policy, Politics and Public Servants: Political Neutrality Revisited," *CPA*, vol. 19, Fall 1976, pp. 432-456; _____ "Power, Parliament, and Public Servants in Canada: Ministerial Responsibility Reexamined," *Canadian Public Policy*, vol. 3, Summer 1979, pp. 383-396.

29. K. Kernaghan, *Freedom of Information and Ministerial Responsibility*, p. 28.

30. For an excellent short review of the legal aspects of ministerial responsibility in Canada, see T.M. Denton, "Ministerial Responsibility: A Contemporary Perspective" in R. Schultz, Orest M. Kruhlak and John C. Terry (eds.), *The Canadian Political Process*, 3rd Edition, (Toronto: Holt, Rinehart and Winston of Canada Ltd., 1979), pp. 344-362.

31. J.E. Hodgetts, *The Canadian Public Service*, p. 58.

32. T.M. Denton, *op. cit.*, p. 353.

33. For a recent debate about this convention as it is applied to the Clerk of the Privy Council see J.R. Mallory, "The Two Clerks: Parliamentary Discussion of the Role of the Privy Council Office," *CJPS*, X:1, March 1977, pp. 3-19.

34. J.E. Hodgetts, "Challenge and Response: A Retrospective View of the Public Service of Canada," *CPA*, VII:4 (December 1964), pp. 409-421. Reproduced in Kenneth Kernaghan (ed.) *Public Administration in Canada: Selected Readings* (Third Edition) (Toronto: Methuen Publications, 1977), pp. 41-53, at p. 53.

35. Paul Pross, for example, implies a challenge to this convention, but the implications such a challenge has for ministerial responsibility are not followed up in his article:

> It is sometimes agreed that it is the duty of the senior public servant "to support his Minister by giving him the best advice of which he is capable and by ensuring that the decisions ultimately reached are put into proper effect." Practice falls far short of this ideal because the public agency, possessing organizational drives similar to and just as powerful as any possessed by the various bodies with which it must deal, modifies the intelligence it transmits.

A. Paul Pross, "Input Versus Withinput: Pressure Group Demands and Administrative Survival" in A. Paul Pross (ed.) *Pressure Group Behaviour in Canadian Politics* (Scarborough: McGraw-Hill Ryerson Ltd., 1975), p. 166.

36. See Paul Thomas, "The Lambert Report: Parliament and accountability," *op. cit.*

37. S.M. Lipset, *Agrarian Socialism* (California: University of California Press, 1967). For a good discussion of this theme, see Ch. XII, "Bureaucracy and Social Change," pp. 255-275.

38. John P. Mackintosh, *The Government and Politics in Britain*, p. 143.

39. S.E. Finer, *Comparative Government* (London: Allen Lane the Penguin Press, 1970), p. 157.

40. Donald V. Smiley, "An Outsider's Observations of Federal-Provincial Relations Among Consenting Adults," in Richard Simeon (ed.), *Confrontation and Collaboration—Intergovernmental Relations in Canada Today* (Toronto: IPAC, 1979), p. 106.

41. J.E. Hodgetts, *The Canadian Public Service*, pp. 237-238.

42. For an implied critique of this centralization in one "super-agency" see T.H. MacLeod, "The Special National Seminar on Financial Management and Accountability: an appraisal," *CPA*, Spring 1980, Vol. 23, no. 1, pp. 71-100, especially pp. 94-96.

43. Frederick C. Mosher, *Democracy and the Public Service* (New York: Oxford University Press, 1968), p. 7.

44. *Ibid.*, p. 8.

45. The philosophical debate between Friedrich and Finer took place over a seven-year period, and there were many interveners on both sides. We supply here the main articles between the two friendly protagonists. Carl J. Friedrich, "Responsible Government Under the American Constitution," in *Problems of The American Public Service* (New York: McGraw-Hill, 1935), pp. 3-74; "Public Policy and the Nature of Administrative Responsibility," in Carl J. Friedrich and Edward S. Mason (eds.), *Public Policy: A Yearbook of the Graduate School of Public Administration* (Cambridge:

Harvard University Press, 1940), pp. 3-24. Copyright © Harvard University Press, 1940. Reprinted by permission of John Wiley & Sons, Inc. Herman Finer, "Better Government Personnel," *Political Science Quarterly* (1936), pp. 569ff; and "Administrative Responsibility in Democratic Government," *Public Administration Review*, 1:4 (1941), pp. 335-350. Reprinted from *Public Administration Review* © by The American Society for Public Administration, 1225 Connecticut Avenue, N.W., Washington, D.C. All rights reserved.

46. Finer, "Administrative Responsibility in Democratic Government," p. 336.

47. Friedrich, "Public Policy and the Nature of Administrative Responsibility," p. 19.

48. *Ibid.*, p. 12.

49. Finer, "Administrative Responsibility," p. 336.

50. *Ibid.*

51. Kenneth Kernaghan, "Responsible public bureaucracy: a rationale and a framework for analysis," p. 577.

52. *Ibid.*, p. 577.

53. J.E. Hodgetts, "The Civil Service and Policy Formation," *CJEPS* 23 (1957), pp. 467-479 at p. 479.

54. J.A. Corry and J.E. Hodgetts, *Democratic Government and Politics*, Third Edition, Revised, (Toronto: University of Toronto Press, 1964), p. 649.

55. Richard Simeon, "The 'Overload Thesis' and Canadian Government," *Canadian Public Policy* 2 (1976), p. 550.

56. D.V. Smiley, *Canadian in Question: Federalism in the Seventies* (Toronto: McGraw-Hill Ryerson, 1980), pp. 91-119.

57. J.R. Mallory, "Responsive and Responsible Government" *Transactions of the Royal Society of Canada*, Fourth Series, XII (1974), p. 208.

58. B. Thordardson, *Trudeau and Foreign Policy: A Study in Decision-Making* (Toronto: Oxford University Press, 1972); Peter C. Dobell, *Canada's Search for New Roles: Foreign Policy in the Trudeau Era* (Oxford: Oxford University Press, 1972) especially chapter 2.

59. R. Van Loon and M.S. Whittington, *The Canadian Political System: Environment, Structure and Process* (Toronto: McGraw-Hill Ryerson, 1971), pp. 491-495.

60. *Ibid.*, p. 495.

61. *Ibid.*, p. 495.

62. Roman March, *The Myth of Parliament* (Scarborough: Prentice-Hall, 1974); R.L.

Stanfield, "Ottawa Power Upsets the System," *The Globe and Mail,* Tuesday, February 8, 1977, p. 7; _____ "The Present State of the Legislative Process in Canada: Myths and Realities" in W.A.W. Neilson and J.C. MacPherson (eds.) *The Legislative Process in Canada: The Need for Reform* (Toronto: Butterworth & Co. (Canada) Ltd., 1978), pp. 39-72.

63. A close approximation of this point of view is given by Geoffrey Stevens, "The Influence and Responsibilities of the Media in the Legislative Process" in W.A.W. Neilson and J.C. MacPherson (eds.) *Ibid.,* pp. 227-247.

64. Douglas Roche, *The Human Side of Politics* (Toronto: Clarke Irwin & Co., 1976), p. x.

65. Two excellent attempts to spell out some of these functions are J.A.A. Lovink, "Parliamentary reform and governmental effectiveness in Canada," *Canadian Public Administration,* Spring 1973, vol. 16, no. 1, pp. 35-54; and W.A. Matheson, "Canadian Political Structures: Twenty-Five Years of Change," paper presented to the Conference on Political Change in Canada: The Last Quarter Century," University of Saskatchewan, Saskatoon, March 17-18, 1977.

66. Gerhard Loewenberg, "The Role of Parliaments in Modern Political Systems," in G. Loewenberg (ed.) *Modern Parliaments: Change or Decline?* (Chicago: Atherton, 1971), p. 19.

67. Sociologist Blishen ranked male judges first of 343 groupings in an occupational class scale combining name, years of schooling, sex, etc. See his "The Construction and Use of an Occupational Class Scale" in Bernard R. Blishen et al., (eds.) *Canadian Society* (Toronto: Macmillan of Canada, 1961), pp. 477-485.

68. Peter Russell, "Judicial Power in Canada's Political Culture," in M.L. Friedland (ed.) *Courts and Trials: A Multidisciplinary Approach* (Toronto: University of Toronto Press, 1975), pp. 78-79. I am also indebted to the excellent analysis of D.V. Smiley in his *The Freedom of Information Issue: A Political Analysis,* Research Publication I, (Toronto: The Commission of Freedom of Information and Individual Privacy, September 1978), pp. 52-58.

69. Eric Hehner, "Growth of Discretions—Decline of Accountability" in Kenneth Kernaghan (ed.) *Public Administration in Canada: Selected Readings* (Third Edition) (Toronto: Methuen, 1977), pp. 323-333 at p. 325; J.E. Kersell, "Statutory and judicial control of administrative behaviour" *CPA,* Summer 1976, vol. 19, no. 2, pp. 295-307.

70. G. Bruce Doern and Peter Aucoin (eds), *The Structures of Policy Making in Canada* (Toronto: Macmillan, 1971).

71. Robert J. Jackson and Michael M. Atkinson, *The Canadian Legislative System* (Toronto: Macmillan, 1974), p. 52.

72. Graham T. Allison, Morton H. Halperin: "Bureaucratic Politics: A Paradigm and Some Policy Implications." *World Politics,* Vol. XXIV, Spring 1972, p. 44. This is also the general conclusion I have arrived at after reading the excellent study of pressure group behaviour edited by A. Paul Pross. See A. Paul Pross (ed.), *Pressure*

Group Behaviour in Canadian Politics (Toronto: McGraw-Hill Ryerson, 1975), especially the chapters by Aucoin, Pross, Barry and Bucovetsky.

73. Donald Gow, *Canadian Federal Administrative and Political Institutions: A Role Analysis* (unpublished Ph.D. dissertation, Queen's University, 1967).

74. Douglas G. Hartle, *Public Policy Decision Making and Regulation* (Toronto: Butterworth & Co (Canada) Ltd., 1979), p. 34.

75. Brian Chapman, *The Profession of Government* (London: Unwin University Books, 1966), pp. 274-275.

76. J.A. Corry and J.E. Hodgetts, *Democratic Government and Politics*, p. 649.

77. S.E. Finer, "The Individual Responsibility of Ministers," p. 394.

78. D.V. Smiley, *The Freedom of Information Issue: A Political Analysis*, pp. 51-52.

79. Seymour Martin Lipset, "Revolution and Counterrevolution: The United States and Canada," in O.M. Kruhlak et al., (eds.) *The Canadian Political Process: A Reader* (Revised edition) (Toronto: Holt, Rinehart and Winston of Canada Ltd., 1973), pp. 3-29 at p. 24.

80. Canada, Royal Commission in Financial Management and Accountability, *Final Report* (Ottawa: Supply and Services, March 1979), p. 419.

Notes

Few books are recommended for this chapter, for the best readings are in article form. The following books or book length publications are, however, highly recommended.

1. A.H. Birch, *Representative and Responsible Government* (Toronto: University of Toronto Press, 1969), especially Chapters 10-13, 17.

2. Canada. Royal Commission on Financial Management and Accountability, *Final Report* (Ottawa: Supply and Services, March 1979).

3. Canada, Privy Council Office. *Submissions to the Royal Commission on Financial Management and Accountability* (Ottawa: Supply and Services, 1979).
   This is an excellent summary of the conventional literature and the constitutional trappings around ministerial responsibility.

4. Douglas Hartle. *Public Policy Decision Making and Regulation.* (Toronto: Butterworth & Co. (Canada) Ltd., 1979).
   Hartle's book presents an adversarial approach, a good basis for our pragmatic paradigm. He claims no predictive powers for his perspective or "conceptual framework." See especially Chapters 2 and 3.

5. T.A. Hockin (ed.) *Apex of Power* (Toronto: Prentice-Hall of Canada, 1977).
   Almost all the pieces are highly recommended.

6. J.E. Hodgetts, *The Canadian Public Service: A Physiology of Government 1967-1970* (Toronto: University of Toronto Press, 1973).

7. Kenneth Kernaghan, *Ethical Conduct: Guidelines for Government Employees* (Toronto: Institute of Public Administration of Canada, 1975).

8. Kenneth Kernaghan, *Public Administration in Canada: Selected Readings* (Third Edition) (Toronto: Methuen, 1977), especially selected pieces in Chapters 6 and 7.
J.R. Mallory, *The Structure of Canadian Government* (Toronto: Macmillan of Canada, 1971).
A solid treatment of the basic elements of constitutionalism and the nature of parliamentary and representative government. The knowledge here is based on accurate and discriminating research and it is well written. The book remains this author's "bible" on representative and responsive Canadian government. I recommend the reading of the whole book to all senior students, and a further recommendation to return to it from time to time for its insights.

All of the articles listed are highly recommended:

1. J.A. Corry, "The Prospects for the Rule of Law," *CJEPS*, vol. 21, 1955, pp. 405-415.

2. T.M. Denton, "Ministerial Responsibility: A Contemporary Perspective," in R. Schultz et al. (eds.) *The Canadian Political Process* (Third Edition) (Toronto: Holt, Rinehart and Winston of Canada Ltd., 1979), pp. 344-362.

3. Rowland Egger, "Responsibility in Administration: An Exploratory Essay: in Roscoe C. Martin (ed.) *Public Administration and Democracy* (Syracuse: Syracuse University Press, 1964), pp. 299-329.

4. H.V. Emy, "The Public Service and Political Control." Published by the Royal Commission on Australian Government Administration as Appendix B, Volume One. Canberra, Australia, A.G.P.S.

5. There are a series of articles comprising the Friedrich-Finer debate of the 1930s and 40s. They are all listed in footnote #24.

6. S.E. Finer, "The Individual Responsibility of Ministers," *Public Administration* (London), vol. 34 (1956), pp. 377-396.

7. J.E. Hodgetts, "The Civil Service and Policy Formation," *CJEPS*, 23 (1957), pp. 467-479.

8. ———, "Challenge and Response: A Retrospective View of the Public Service of Canada" *CPA* VII:4 (December 1964), pp. 409-421.

9. Kenneth Kernaghan, "Responsible public bureaucracy: a rationale and a framework for analysis," *Canadian Public Administration* 16:4 (Winter 1973) pp. 572-603.
This is an important article. It has been used in this chapter to put together the basic ideas and assumptions of the hierarchical responsibilities paradigm.

10. ———, "Policy, Politics and Public Servants: Political Neutrality Revisited," *CPA*, vol. 19, Fall 1976, pp. 432-456.

11. Gerhard Loewenberg, "The Role of Parliaments in Modern Political Systems," in G. Loewenberg (ed.) *Modern Parliaments: Change or Decline?* (Chicago: Atherton, 1971).

12. J.R. Mallory, "Responsive and Responsible Government," Presidential Address, Section II, *Transactions of the Royal Society of Canada,* Series IV, volume XII, 1974.

13. _____, "The Two Clerks: Parliamentary Discussions of the Role of the Privy Council Office," *CJPS,* vol. 10, March 1977, pp. 3-19.

14. Geoffrey Marshall, "Minister Responsibility," *Political Quarterly,* 34 (1963).

15. Paul Thomas, "The Lambert Report: Parliament and Accountability," *Canadian Public Administration,* Vol. 23, No. 1 (Spring 1980).

16. Donald V. Smiley, "An Outsider's Observations of Federal-Provincial Relations Among Consenting Adults" in Richard Simeon (ed.), *Confrontation and Collaboration—Intergovernmental Relations in Canada Today,* (Toronto: IPAC, 1979).

CHAPTER EIGHT

LIVING WITH LEVIATHAN: SOME STRUCTURES OF BUREAUCRATIC ACCOUNTABILITY IN CANADA

Students of the Canadian Parliament tend to be pessimistic that the changes in the machinery and attitudes of government needed to increase significantly Parliament's power over the public service will be made. In any event, Parliament is a potentially important but far from a sufficient instrument to ensure a responsible public bureaucracy. In the search for an appropriate balance between administrative power and administrative responsibility, the role of parliament must be supplemented by a broad range of controls and influences exercised by other actors in the political system.

Kenneth Kernaghan

I. Introduction

To almost anyone in contemporary society power is a patently real concept. Our concerns on the issues of the day, whether social, political or economic are funnelled into a debate as to who possesses real power, a little power or no power at all. Likewise our interpretations of bureaucratic life, particularly with the advent of the administrative state, are based on who possesses power within the hierarchy and who does not. "I take it for granted that in every human organization some individuals have more influence over key decisions than do others."[1] How one conceptualizes the various dimensions of power is far from a settled matter, but just our everyday perception of its exercise gives us some very good clues as to how complex the concept really is.

The most obvious example is the wielding of excessive coercive powers (in the form of administrative discretion), a use which has been traditionally viewed by many as an illegitimate function of bureaucrats. We have already discussed this conception at length in previous chapters. The advent of the administrative state has how-ever given birth to another power dimension, that is, bureaucracy may suffer not from "excessive zeal" in the pursuit of its goals, but from "inadequate enthusiasm" in performing its assigned tasks. Max Weber recognized this when he argued that duties may be performed by the modern functionary *sine ira ac studio*, that is, without passion or enthusiasm. Thus goals or *ends* can be either intentionally or uninten-tionally thwarted in a quagmire of *means*. Indeed the concept that bu-reaucrats emphasize the means of administration more than they do the ends—the "inversion of means and ends"—has been posited as the "sociological theory of bureaucracy" by some authors.[2] For a mul-tifarious number of reasons administration is defined by some as the triumph of technique over purpose.

A third dimension of administrative power is that the mere exercise of such power has frightening implications for those interacting with the bureaucratic phenomenon. In the words of the vernacular, bureaucracy can be "damned if it does and damned if it doesn't." For example, just being omnipotent, bureaucracy has created a problem for itself. More than a hundred years ago, author Charles Butler, a critic of the British colonial administration, wrote a classical descrip-tion as to how this is brought about. The ideal colonial administrator is satirically named, Mr. Mothercountry, and he does everything *with* enthusiasm and diligence. According to Butler, Mr. Mothercountry:

. . . is familiar with every detail of his business and handles with unfaltering hands the piles of papers at which his superiors quail. He knows the policy which previous actions render necessary, but he never appears to dictate. A new Secretary [equivalent to a Canadian Minister] . . . intends to be indepen-dent, but something turns up that obliges him to consult Mr. Mothercountry. He is pleased with the ready and unobtrusive advice which takes a great deal of trouble off his hands. If things go well, his confidence in Mr. Mother-country rises. If badly, that official alone can get him out of the colonial or parliamentary scrape; and the more independent he is the more scrapes he falls into.[3]

Mr. Mothercountry's behavior is impeccable. He performs his legit-imate duty by using his influence as an adviser, doing so unobtru-sively and humbly. He knows everything there is to know about the right action at the right time. And yet we have a classic situation where the power of a bureaucrat has grown to such enormity that the stage of bureaucracy as an objectionable form of government has been reached.

Max Weber visualized all these dimensions of the bureaucratic phe-nomenon. He was deeply concerned that this indispensable instrument of Western technological and industrial achievement should be subjected to strong political control. And why? First, bureaucracy legitimized the relationship between the ruler and the ruled: every system of legitimacy is accompanied by a system of procedural correctness. According to Weber, those subject to authority, whether of a person or of a law, only accept it as legitimate if proper procedural rules are instituted and followed. Secondly, bureaucracy must be rational. To be rational meant that "it involved control on the basis of knowledge, in particular specialized knowledge; because of its clearly defined spheres of competence; because it operated according to intellectually analysable rules; because of the calculability of its operation; finally, because technically it was capable of the highest level of achievement."[4]

And yet there was a striking ambivalence to rationality. On the one hand, the bureaucratic type of administration opened up the possibilities of an extension of human capacities never before unleashed in the history of mankind. Yet on the other hand, this rationalized "human machine" with Draconian logic, contained the inevitable seeds of alienation in that, as a social force with powers and values of its own making, it subjected humanity to the inexorable iron logic of these powers and values. In other words, people, in becoming masters of their environment, have created a Frankenstein which some commentators feel is capable of turning on its creators. So, "where through the rationalization of life men sought to bring their external circumstances more under their control and so increase their freedom, at the same time this also increased the powers to which they were subject."[5] These examples demonstrate some of the ambivalences of power. How does one, in a complex industrialized society, keep a measure of control? To Weber, there was only one solution. "Bureaucracy" he argued, "could be *controlled* from above by a democratically elected politician, but could not be *replaced* by an election from below."[6] How is this control to be accomplished? Weber never supplied us with clear answers to this question, an inadequacy in his work no doubt due to his early and untimely death. But since Weber our experience with liberal democratic government has made it obviously clear that there is no one answer to the question as the politician walks the tightrope of instituting and inteposing control and other monitoring devices to ensure both *subjective* and *objective* responsibility. How this is done, as Kernaghan has argued in this chapter's epigram, depends to a great extent on the perceptions and the ingenuity of democratic political leadership, and it is to an analysis of these methods that we will presently turn.

The argument we are attempting to make about bureaucratic power and the need for accountability measures can also be stated in the analytical terms introduced by Herbert Simon in his study of administrative decision-making. In *Administrative Behavior*, Simon argued that we must conceptualize "the process of human choice as a process of drawing conclusions from premises." It is therefore the *premise* (and a large number of these are combined in every decision) rather than the whole *decision* that serves as the smallest unit of analysis."[7] Throughout his seminal work Simon argued that many public decisions are, in the first instance, factual but many others, if not the most important ones, are evaluative also. Simon therefore concluded that:

Democratic institutions find their principal justification as a procedure for the validation of value judgments. There is no "scientific" or "expert" way of making such judgments, hence expertise of whatever kind is no qualification for the performance of this function . . . *Since the administrative agency must of necessity make many value judgments, it must be responsive to community values far beyond those that are explicitly enacted into law.*[8]

It is perhaps now clearer why liberal democrats believe that Parliamentary controls of the bureaucracy must of necessity be supplemented by a very broad range of other controls and influences. These run the gamut from direct executive control measures to such subjective control devices as ethical codes and civil service traditions, including anonymity, secrecy and neutrality. We will obviously not try to discuss the whole range of devices used to ensure subservience in the bureaucracy, but our discussion will attempt to mirror the above perspective as much as possible by discussing at least two devices of informal control not explicitly amenable to legislative enactment (political sensitivity and professional conduct). Two measures of formal control (the ombudsman and freedom of information legislation) are also discussed because of their importance in the accountability debate in the 1970s and 80s. Such other methods as financial and judicial controls must be left to another publication dealing specifically with administrative processes and performance.

As argued previously, both the formal and informal controls of bureaucracy are inextricably linked and in our discussion here this linkage is assumed. For example, the informal control of political sensitizing is accompanied by some rather explicit formal measures (order-in-council appointments of political sympathizers, regulations regarding the minister's office staff and so on). Secondly, we also argued that administrative responsibility and its conventions of anonymity, neutrality and secrecy flowed from the fundamental principles inherent in political and ministerial responsibility. However, the pragmatist arguments for controls on ministerial responsibility have always implied that in the majority of cases this meant controls on bureaucrats, who, operating on behalf of their ministers, find umbrage under the political system's conventions. Thus in keeping with our arguments in the previous chapter we make the assumption that those who advocate controls on ministerial responsibility or "Crown privilege" are, in the majority of instances, seeking control over the bureaucracy also.

II. Sensitizing the Bureaucracy

Apart from two small-scale studies of the 1970s, top-level officials in the Canadian federal bureaucracy whose positions are not covered by career public service regulations have not been extensively studied in Canada.[9] Yet this personnel is important because its members are central to the problem of obtaining intelligent and effective management and policy direction in the federal government. Through them the Prime Minister and cabinet direct and control the bureaucracy and establish lines of defence and political support for the government's programs. It therefore follows that any government would be vitally interested in sensitizing this grouping to the political realities demanded of its bureaucratic position. Max Weber would most likely have approved the customary practice in Canada of the cabinet appointing all deputy ministers and heads of federal commissions, boards and tribunals. The appointment of deputies and public servants of like status is vested, under Section 2 of the Public Service Employment Act, in the Governor-in-Council. This prerogative has always been defended as a tested method of sensitizing bureaucracy to the political realities of its environment.

Another well-known method used in Canada is that of "parachuting" outsiders to senior positions in the public service. In Canada this means employing a lateral recruit from outside the public service to fill a senior post over the heads of aspiring career individuals in the lower ranks of the public service. There is little statistical evidence to indicate on an on-going basis how widespread this practice is, but Campbell and Szablowski point to this career phenomenon in their study of central agencies and an earlier study for the Royal Commission on Bilingualism and Biculturalism explores an interesting aspect of the question. In trying to determine the salary levels of Francophones in the Public Service, the survey showed that by 1965 the under-$6,000-a-year salary group contained 23.1% Francophones, a strong proportional presence in comparison with the rest of the population. However, as one moved up the salary scale, the Francophone presence gradually diminished, reaching a low point of 5.00% at the $18,000-$18,900 level. Then a most revealing reversal occurs: *at the $20,000 and over level, the percentage increased to 16.5% Francophone representation.* (See Figure 1.) This is because of the "parachutist phenomenon," a phrase perhaps deserving some recognition in the lexicon of Canadian public policy and administration.[10]

In his book, *The Vertical Mosaic,* John Porter reported the same phenomenon. He discovered, in the late fifties and early sixties, that French Canadians held only 27 or 13.4% of 202 "elite" positions, but most of these 27 cases were clustered in the highest categories of these elite positions: "It is perhaps significant that about one-half of them were outsiders at the time of their appointment. Of the five at the deputy minister level, three were outsiders." By the mid-1960s all the evidence suggests that recruitment *at the very top* had been much more accessible to outsiders of the public service than at the level *just below the top.*[11] Some Canadian commentary on this phenomenon has claimed that "parachuting" is one way of keeping the bureaucracy responsive and responsible to the general public and its elected representatives.[12] Others, particularly in the journalistic profession, view this practice simply as outright patronage, having nothing to do with the need for political sensitivity. As in so many instances, the truth seems to lie somewhere between, but no Canadian analysts, of which we are aware, have attempted to decipher the complex reasons for the phenomenon. As Professor D. C. Corbett of Flinders University, Australia, has argued, the reasons in Canada seem to be partly sensitivity needs, partly blatant patronage, and partly pressing recruitment realities spanning over the last two decades.[13]

There are two other areas in which sensitizing the bureaucracy is said to take place. One particular strategic point is at the "focus and fulcrum of politics," namely the cabinet, and another is located at or around individual ministers in the ministerial departments of government. Let us examine the latter so-called strategic level first. The evidence we have on the public record thus far is that political appointments around individual ministers are not a particularly effective means of monitoring the administration in a department. In one particular example, when a Finance minister in the Pearson government, the Hon. Walter Gordon, attempted to bring in temporary political help to advise him on various aspects of budgetary policy, the political and administrative storm which ensued forced the minister to dismiss his "whizz kids" entourage.[14]

General housekeeping political appointments to minister's offices in Canada, however, are a traditional feature of our system. Since the civil service reforms of 1918, ministerial staff members have been

FIGURE I

PRESENCE BY SALARY LEVEL WITHIN THE FEDERAL PUBLIC SERVICE
OF THOSE OF FRENCH MOTHER TONGUE IN 1965

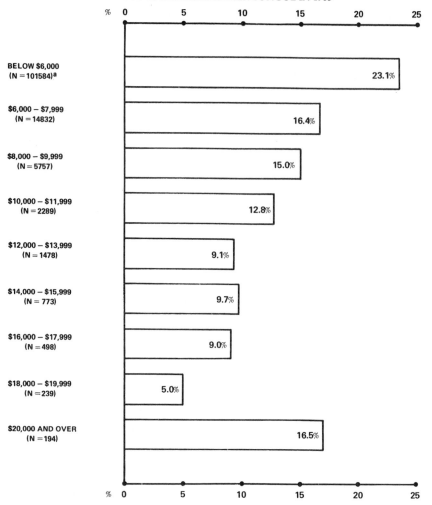

Source: J.W.C. Johnston et al., "Public Service Survey" a study prepared for the
R.C.B. and B (a) These are weighted case bases.

exempted from the provisions on appointments contained in our civil service legislation. Moreover, civil service regulations provided that after three years service in a minister's office, personnel were entitled to be transferred to a permanent position in the public service. J. R. Mallory has grudgingly conceded this practice: "This exception to the merit-based and non-political structure of the public service has a long history and may represent, in part, the price that had to be paid to persuade ministers to give up their right to nominate candidates to the public service."[15] This, however, seems hardly a strong argument when, on the average, there are only ten or eleven positions involved, and given the increasing practice of ministers selecting "bright young men and women" from within the public service to be seconded to these positions for a period of their careers. Their duties seem innocuous enough, being in the nature of speech writing, improving the Minister's contacts with the press gallery, and keeping the Minister in the public eye and sufficiently responsive to the politically importunate.[16] Indeed, the argument could be made that this "political sensitivity" grooming of young, promising career bureaucrats is a necessary and logical measure in keeping with the needs of liberal democratic government. Nevertheless, these appointments have created concern in some quarters in Canada, partly because of scandals involving executive assistants,[17] and partly because political voices have been strongly advocating reforms which would make these positions strategic gateposts between the politicians and their senior public servants. In other words, many Canadian advocates of reform see these positions as potential "control funnels" through which politicians can screen policy advice given to them by their non-partisan bureaucrats.

J. R. Mallory is definitely against any such proposals. He argues that, "It is clearly undesirable that a considerable number of persons not a part of the civil service should be interposed between a Minister and his department."[18] This, he feels, could encourage serious abuses of public office as exemplified by the Rivard affair of 1964 by these political appointees and it could also dangerously insulate the Minister from his senior public servants. Paul M. Tellier disagrees with this argument: "Les bureaux des ministres ne sont pas organises aussi efficacement qu'ils devraient etre. . . . Le personnel actuel des bureaux de ministres n'est pas suffisant. A quelques exceptions pres le directeurs de cabinet n'ont ni la formation, ni les connaissances approfondies, ni l'experience necessaire pour remplir le role de conseiller decrit plus haut."[19] The implication being, of course, that more experienced personnel are really needed to fill these positions. What this reform could mean to ministerial/senior public servant relationships is not explicitly spelled out by its advocates.

By contrast with the unreconstructed state of ministers' offices, Prime Minister Trudeau since 1968 has done a considerable amount of refurbishing of politically important advisory positions around his office. While it seems somewhat farfetched to compare the PMO's functions to those of the office of the Presidency and other structural trappings of the American executive, it nevertheless remains true that these advisers do perform some strategic control functions for the Prime Minister.[20] In the first place, the advisory role in policy making was a prime reason in 1968 and thereafter for the recruitment and assembling of a motley collection of political experts, social scientists, mathematicians, journalists and operations research experts in the PMO. Doern wrote that the role of the reconstructed Prime Minister's Office was derived from the logic of its "functional input into policy." Furthermore:

The PMO's role as the strategic source of political advice and the PCO's role as the source of overall governmental advice flow from their position as the only organizations that can maintain an overview of strategic governmental activity in a total sense.[21]

But the heady presumptions of the PMO's "new" strategic role in policy making slowly but inevitably gave way to the pragmatic every-day realities of running such an enormously complex machine as the federal bureaucracy. Richard French notes that through these reforms many of the "budding technocrats" had high hopes of succeeding the "classic mandarins," but there is a tone of implicit skepticism as to whether they had indeed accomplished this goal.[22] The evidence seems to point to a much more modest assessment as to what had been achieved by this strategic planning activity.

By 1971, Marc Lalonde, the then principal secretary to the Prime Minister, was openly admitting that political advisers were mainly fulfilling a service role to the Prime Minister, with an advisory role being a by-product only. Thomas d'Aquino concurs: policy advice was being given on an "ad hoc trouble shooting basis" and did not normally "generate policy initiatives or in-depth policy analysis."[23]

Following the near defeat of the Trudeau government in the 1972 general election, the Prime Minister's political advisers seem to have settled into this service role, but a cloudy grey eminence image of these advisers persisted.[24] The PMO still contained a highly visible policy adviser and trouble shooter in the area of international relations. Furthermore, the "service functions" of the Prime Minister's political advisers included monitoring discussions in cabinet committees for the Prime Minister, performing "a political clearance process"[25] on persons being considered for senior appointments in government service, and collecting policy ideas from backbenchers and middle level civil servants.

These are all strategic, political functions. However, the debate as to how strategic the PMO has been is far from settled, and it is guaranteed to raise further academic commentary in the 1980s as the

Privy Council/Prime Minister's Office continue to evolve. As an example, a further merging of the political and senior administrative roles was demonstrated by the Trudeau changes of 1980: a former Clerk of the Privy Council who had been fired by the short-lived Conservative administration apparently for his overt political role, is reinstated in his old position, and a former assistant principal secretary in the Prime Minister's office is coopted to be the new Secretary to the Cabinet for Federal-Provincial Relations. Exactly how one measures the importance of these changes and the power relationships involved is a matter for further conjecture, keen observation and academic scrutiny.*

III. The Professional Conduct of Public Servants: Relationships to Loyalty, Anonymity, Neutrality and Secrecy in Job Performance

The British tradition of a strong government which is dominated by the Executive basically hinges on the doctrine of ministerial responsibility. Thus, while in theory the doctrine makes much of parliamentary control over the decisions and actions of Ministers and their servants, in practice it works out to a heavy reliance on various accountability measures over most of governmental administration with overall political responsibility exacted in a periodic basis at the time of general elections. From these central practices of responsible government flow an assortment of theoretical and practical assumptions and conventions which guide liberal-democratic governments. Those germane for our purposes so far are the politics-administration dichotomy; the career public service recruited by open competitive examinations; and the loyalty, anonymity and neutrality of public servants to their Ministers. Other measures include the budgetary system of yearly estimates and parliamentary appropriations and the evolution of the ministeral department in the machinery of government.

The catholicity of the doctrine of ministerial responsibility for democratic government should therefore be obvious. We should, however, give some further indication why such assumptions as neutrality, loyalty and anonymity have become integral parts or by-products of the doctrine. The exact meaning and implications of these assump-

---

*In November 1980 the Institute for Research on Public Policy (IRPP) released its advertising brochure for seminars on government operations to be held from January to May 1981. The IRPP document identifies the PMO as one of "the key central agencies" which constitute "the nerve centre of public policy formulation and administration" in the Canadian federal government.

tions are not easy to decipher but certain pieces of information are available as clues to the puzzle.

The first clue is the manner in which confidentiality in the cabinet process is reflected in the oath taken by all incoming members of the Council. Indeed, as Gordon Robertson has pointed out, the very name Privy Council is derived from the French *privé* which "stresses the privacy that has, from the origins of the body, been regarded as fundamental." This practice of the privacy of deliberations of the monarch's advisers is steeped in European history long before the concept of a bureaucratized public service ever came into being:

> The antique phrases of the oath, dating from at least Elizabethan times, require each new Councillor to swear that he "will keep close and secret all such matters as shall be treated, debated and resolved on in Privy Council, without publishing or disclosing the same or any part thereof, by Word, Writing or any otherwise to any Person out of the same Council, but to such only as be of the Council." Throughout the history of Cabinet government, whether in England or in any of the countries that have adopted the English style of executive, the privacy of personal ministerial opinion, and the secrecy of collective discussion have been fundamental. It was, in fact, the fear that confidentiality might not continue to have the same rigid and unalterable observance that stood in the way of having a Cabinet Secretary, an agenda or any minutes through several centuries of Cabinet operation.[26]

Yet one cannot point to any particular moment in history when the practice of secrecy and confidentiality became widespread as a permanent feature of cabinet government and administration. Kitson Clark has discovered statements in English historical records which show that the concept of neutrality was already being popularized by both politicians and civil servants in the period between 1830 and 1860. The significance of these dates is readily discerned by the fact that it was not until 1870 that the British government finally established a non-political career public service based on the Northcote-Trevelyan reforms, to which the doctrine of neutrality is commonly attributed.[27]

The Northcote-Trevelyan reforms in England sought to concretize these assumptions by socializing new and young recruits to a professional sense of pride in service, yet subordinating them to the political realm. The Report envisaged:

> An efficient body of permanent officers, occupying a position duly subordinate to that of Ministers . . . yet possessing sufficient independence, character, ability and experience to be able to advise, assist, and to some extent, influence those who are from time to time set above them.[28]

Three structural manifestations gradually evolved to ensure ministerial hegemony. The first was that the machinery of government had to be refashioned to ensure the orderly coordination of administrative work by responsible ministers of the Crown. As the academic commentaries of Willson, Finer, Clark and others have shown, up to the 1870s much of the British machinery of state "had been created as need from time to time demanded and then heaped together without much thought of ministerial control," or as to how these varied collections of autonomous boards, commissions and departments should be linked to Parliament. The coordination of administrative work under ministerial departments which occurred *simultaneously both in Canada and Britain in the second half of the nineteenth century,* was a necessary step for effecting ministerial responsibility, "the basic principle on which the necessity for the neutrality and anonymity of the civil servant is grounded."[29] In Chapters Ten and Eleven we shall address ourselves to the evolution and contemporary manifestations of governmental machinery, both in the theoretical context of ministerial responsibility, and in the more practical context of getting the day-to-day tasks of contemporary administration accomplished.

Another structural manifestation was the code enunciating the politics-administration dichotomy. We have already dealt with this aspect in full detail, giving the reader a sense as to how it became manifest in both American and Canadian governments. However, a historical illustration from the Parliamentary tradition would serve here to indicate how deeply ingrained the normative implications of the dichotomy remains in our system of government. Historically, in Britain many administrators held seats in the British Parliament, and, as to be expected in such circumstances, publicly advocated their own policies sometimes in open conflict with those of their ministers. By the 1840s this practice was slowly abandoned as ministerial responsibility began evolving and a new set of accompanying conventions took hold. The political activity of civil servants gradually became a prohibition, public comment by officials about government policy became anathema, and the confidentiality of information gathering and discussion prior to decision-making, previously a condition clearly applicable in the law to Privy Councillors only, became standard modes of conduct for all civil servants.

A third structural manifestation was the Northcote-Trevelyan reforms themselves which inculcated the well-known socialization pattern of recruiting young, well-educated public servants at the beginning of their careers and conditioning them by lifetime service to the limitations of their roles. In England, this socialization process could not have been accomplished overnight as subsequent historical evidence has shown,[30] but there is ample empirical evidence that, once within the bureaucracy, the socialization patterns known there are much more crucial as controlling variables of bureaucratic conduct compared to the pre-entry socialization patterns of school and even home.[31] This is one reason why the notion of representative bureaucracy espoused by the "new" Public Administration" as a means of making bureaucracy more responsive and responsible to the public interest is held in doubt by many commentators.

The idea of representative bureaucracy is that the public service should be democratized, and that this can be accomplished by including in the composition of the bureaucracy, "representatives" from the major social groups in proportion to each group's numerical size within the total society.[32] Thus the notion of representative bureaucracy gains much of its persuasiveness from the assumption that if a bureaucracy is "representative" in a numerical-proportional sociological sense (a "representative sample") it will therefore be "representative" in the normal sense of political agency. But the evidence gathered on this assumption cast serious doubts as to its validity. It is, for example, highly questionable whether persons continue, in their mature lives, to be dominated by early group experience.[33] The inherently unique features of individual personality, and the variability of individual psychological-intellectual development, undermine the validity of generalizations which attempt to explain individual adult behavior according to early group influences.[34] It is therefore doubtful that a bureaucracy which is a miniature, or representative sample, of the larger society, will automatically or even probably, represent the interests, values and attitudes of society's groups.[35]

In the past decade, hypotheses and empirical evidence by students of bureaucratic behavior point to the fact that when we use the term "neutrality" in describing the actions of public servants, we are partly inferring "predictability."[36] The concept of predictability in turn means that the public service leadership has a fairly good grasp on the general value premises of recruits to the public service. There are several ways by which this is achieved, but perhaps the most prominent method in recent years is through the device of professional controls over value premises. In his study, *The Forest Ranger*, Herbert Kaufman argued how the claims of professional socialization and those of rational bureaucracy reinforced rather than conflicted with each other. Herbert Simon, in his analysis of these findings, sums up the evidence thus:

Any profession engaged in administration necessarily exercises power. It applies its knowledge and technique, but it applies them to some end. The forest ranger is not simply someone who knows about the growth and harvesting of trees and how to extinguish forest fires. He *fosters* the growth and orderly harvesting of trees, and he *fights* forest fires. His specialized knowledge is perhaps a necessary condition to society's granting him a measure of autonomy, but it is not a sufficient condition. He will enjoy freedom only to the extent that the values he serves are non-controversial. *The forest ranger's autonomy rests not on his being a neutral instrument, but on his being a reliable instrument whose values are pretty well known and widely accepted.*[37]

This is a highly controversial hypothesis linking professional conduct with predictability and control. But Simon's thesis has a definite ring of credibility:

The professionals, far from being neutral, identify with characteristic professional values; and this identification increases their predictability and reliability as instruments of policy—hence the feasibility of delegation to them. The power of professionals over policy relates less to their possession of esoteric knowledge that protects them from lay scrutiny than it does to their advantageous position for innovating and initiating new programs.[38]

This is precisely what both Graham Wallas and R. MacGregor Dawson were attempting to say at the turn of this century in their declaration of "the principle of official independence."

However, predictability achieved through extensive delegation of decision-making powers to professionals will remain, at best, only one measure among a series of others aimed at the ultimate control of administrators engaged in the making of public policy. The government has at its ready disposal a series of governing instruments which run the gauntlet from measures of gentle persuasion to some of the most Draconian laws on the Canadian statute books aimed at those engaged in flagrantly leaking confidential or top secret information, or caught in acts of sedition against the nation.

Conflict of interest is one area in which the government uses both gentle persuasion and coercive methods to effect control. The term covers a whole multitude of sins and has been defined as "a situation in which a public employee has a private or personal interest sufficient to influence or appear to influence the objective exercise of his official duties."[39] According to Kernaghan, this covers the gambit from (i) influence peddling; (ii) financial transactions which conflict with the official's responsibilities; (iii) gifts and entertainment from those with whom the official must transact official business; (iv) outside employment during after-duty hours which has the potential of creating a conflict with the public servant's duties; (v) future employment with a business concern with which the public servant is transacting or has transacted official business; (vi) the exercise of discretionary control over applications relating to business practices or other activities of one's relatives; (vii) or straight corrupt practices such as the acceptance of bribes, committing fraud, perjury, or the fabrication of evidence to obstruct the normal course of justice.[40] All of these situations are first covered in general terms in the *Conflict of Interest Guidelines* which forms the basis of Order-in-Council of 18th December 1973 (P.C. 1973-4065), followed by more elaborate rules and regulations in the Treasury Board circular (1973-183) entitled *Standard of Conduct for Public Service Employees.*

Another area where the government for over fifty years maintained stringent statutory restrictions is the sphere of political activity.[41] With the revision of public services legislation in 1967, however, section 32 of the Public Service Employment Act now allows public servants to seek nomination or stand as candidates in a political campaign after the express permission of the Public Service Commission of Canada has been sought and received. Evidence to date shows no great rush of public servants applying for such leave, hence allaying any fears that there would be a heavy influx of party political activity in the ranks of the federal bureaucracy with the relaxation of restrictions.[42]

We come now to the last aspect of the "professional" conduct of public servants. Perhaps it is the most important of all the aspects because of its all-embracing quality of control, namely the issue of confidentiality. Conflicts of interests, political commentary by bureaucrats and even the political activity of public servants become serious public policy issues because bureaucrats handle or are in possession of confidential government information used in the formulation of public policy.

No serious commentator will deny the need for some secrecy in government. There are documents in government files which will prejudice the security or integrity of the state. This is so axiomatic to everyone (with the exception of the seditionist or conspirator) that we need not elaborate further on the necessity for secrecy in the withholding of this kind of information from public consumption. The political executive is given the ultimate responsibility to judge this criteria of secrecy. Secondly, there is a motley collection of matters in trade or military agreements which can create potential difficulties for a country's bilateral or multilateral relations with other countries.

These international agreements may be of crucial importance not only to the country in question but to a host of other countries directly or tangentially involved.

Finally, there are a variety of assorted matters such as health records, insurance numbers, and statistical information supplied in confidence to government departments or agencies by both private individuals and businesses, and records or information that concern trade secrets. Most of this type of information is readily adaptable to computer storage, leading to real fears that computerized information systems can become a menace to the traditional liberal-democratic "right to Privacy." Thus, according to Hugh Lawford, in recent years the Canadian "villain of piece" has not been the government official suppressing publication of information, but the operator of a computerized information system seeking "broader dissemination of information."[43] For all of these reasons, D. C. Rowat, long a student of administrative secrecy and strong advocate of more openness in government concedes that:

There will always be the problem of drawing the line between the government's need to deliberate confidentiality and the public's need of information. It is simply a question of emphasis.[44]

The problem is, whose emphasis? The debate on secrecy of information in Canada has unfortunately been conducted on the grounds of polar opposites with both sides arguing in the extreme. As to be expected, the federal government refuses to move in, "opening up the windows of information" with what it considers to be "undue haste." As the former Secretary to the Cabinet puts it:

. . . this is not to say that public access to federal government documents in Canada is satisfactory, not that progress cannot be made. We must move forward with a complete assessment of the manifold implications—constitutional, administrative, financial, ethical—of increased public access. We must not allow ourselves to accept superficial arguments in the defence of either confidentiality or openness. We must accurately understand the systems of so-called "freedom of information" which are so glibly evoked. We must recognize that those systems have their origins and play their role in political and cultural situations radically different from our own.[45]

However, academic commentators as distinguished as Carl J. Friedrich have pointed out that *both* propaganda and secrecy are common characteristics of *all* political systems, and that these two ways of manipulating the ruled by the ruler and of influencing the ruler by the ruled resemble other "pathologies" of politics. Secrecy becomes "a pathology" because all states have a tendency to view most of their actions as secret, thereby developing an inclination to keep "under cover" documents and positions of policy that are already widely known.[46]

The nature of this debate on confidentiality has all the potential for developing into one of diametrically opposite positions. This is perhaps needed to force some changes in assumptions and conventions that are by no means sacrosanct and which seem particularly unnecessary in a modern democracy.[47] However, one of its disadvantages is that the debate tends to obscure the slow but progressive changes which have been made towards greater access to government information. At one extreme are the proponents of reform, some advocating grand design changes to the cabinet system of government.[48] As these reformers see it, all "professions" in the public service are, to paraphrase George Bernard Shaw, "conspiracies against the laity," and left to their own designs the bureaucracy would continue to display a "conspiracy of silence."

At the other end of the debate are those defenders of the *status quo* who are most eager to demonstrate with impeccable syllogism how any changes in the conventions of ministerial responsibility, particularly in the area of confidentiality or openness, would be prying loose a brick that would ultimately bring down the whole system of liberal democratic government. If we wish to have a better comprehension of the problem it seems necessary to shed some of the emotional and biased aspects of the debate evinced by both sides, and to approach the subject somewhat dispassionately.

The doctrine of ministerial responsibility is related to the conventions of anonymity, secrecy and neutrality. Though these conventions have given meaning to the doctrine in the past there is no guarantee that they will continue to do so in meaningful ways forever. Indeed, advocates of change strongly contend that they do not even give meaning to the doctrine at present. Though their arguments on ministerial responsibility are somewhat muddled, lawyers John Swift and Murray Rankin of the Freedom of Information Legislation Committee of the Canadian Bar Association are correct when they argue that changes in the convention of secrecy need not destroy the doctrine of ministerial responsibility.[49] Indeed, Rankin argues that changes in secrecy may even enhance ministerial responsibility rather than proscribe it. The formidable task ahead for advocates of change is to convincingly show how recommended changes in these conventions would eliminate their undesirable features while retaining their strong aspects.

Already one convention, that of automatic resignation of a minister for all the misdeeds and neglects of his officials, has fallen into desuetude. Neither Parliament nor the public realistically expect ministers to be in full control of every decision made within their departments, and to resign automatically upon the discovery of administrative malfeasance. Both paradigms discussed in the previous chapter have

already made the point clear to us. But if this convention on resigna-
tions can change why not other related conventions? The biggest
problem in making reforms is to ensure that changes in one area do
not damage or destroy important features or characteristics of another
area.

By way of illustration let us look at a recent British case on the subject although Kernaghan has supplied us with some interesting Canadian examples.[50] During 1971-72 a case of glaring administrative error
in the insurance section of the Board of Trade became public knowledge. During 1971 one of Britain's main auto insurers (the Vehicle
and General Company) went bankrupt, and in the course of a public
inquiry, the major share of the blame for this state of affairs was
placed on an Under Secretary and two Assistant Secretaries in the
division. The report of the inquiry argued that public servants failed
to take decisive action when there were clear signs of impending financial catastrophe for the company.[51] The storm which broke in the
House of Commons was rather revealing. The minister quite rightly
made no moves to resign his position, but he also refused to accept
responsibility for the debate. Furthermore, he made it clear that he
was prepared, as a general principle, to "throw senior public servants
to the wolves" to defend themselves publicly when they are criticized
by tribunals.[52] If this precept and its full implications were accepted
by any British governments, it would mark a drastic and revolutionary change in government, with far reaching implications for liberal
democracy as we now know it.[53] What are some of these implications?

We list three of them here but undoubtedly there are many more.
First, although public service anonymity and silence have worked to
increase the political advantage and dominance of the executive,
these conventions have also afforded the government's advisers considerable leeway in dealing with interest groups and collecting all
sorts of confidential material needed for policy purposes. "Throwing
public servants to the wolves" when policy goes wrong would mean
that the whole information and advisory processes of government—
including even cabinet documents—would now be liable for full disclosure, legal or otherwise. It is also possible that policy can go wrong
because public service advice was not followed. Why then should the
public servants involved "take the heat" in silence when documents
exist to exonerate them as being right in the first place?

Second, the information process in government or indeed in all
complex organizations requires position papers outlining various
potential scenarios on policy issues. These documents do not represent policy by any means and in most instances they are subjected to

heavy criticisms internally before any policy position emerges victorious. Position papers are therefore devices used for outlining options open to governments. With the possibility that these documents will now be open to public scrutiny, no public servant with an eye to a safe career in government would be prepared to risk enunciating potentially unpleasant or unpopular options which a government might well have to face. The information process would have been successfully laundered. Confidential information would be increasingly transmitted by word of mouth thus creating tremendous problems in policy misrepresentation, uncertainty in policy formulation and certainly an increase in dishonest policy formulation.

Third, if public servants now have the veil of secrecy and anonymity lifted from their daily deliberations then it logically follows that they would have the right to explain their views freely in the public forum. Ministers would now have the formidable task of making their case against members of the Opposition who would now be armed with the information that their arguments were acceptable to many of the minister's policy advisers. It should be readily apparent from this example "why ministers who lose only a little and gain a great deal from the doctrine [of ministerial responsibility] should want to keep it going."

There is no doubt that despite these complications the system can be changed to mitigate some of its undesirable features, especially in the area of secrecy. But exactly how and in what direction should change occur? What new systems of accountability need to be instituted to replace some conventional structures? How would such replacements improve on the present inadequacies and pathologies in the administrative process? These are tough questions, and it is clear from the policy literature that no advocate for change has many answers to them. It may also be true that this is how it must be inevitably because changes of this kind can only occur incrementally. No one is clear on the potential side effects significant changes might have on the integrity and stability of the system.

IV. Towards Opening Up the Windows: Some Beginnings

Earlier it was noted that the laws governing administrative secrecy in Canada do have certain Draconian characteristics. The most important of these laws is the Official Secrets Act which is supplemented by certain provisions of the Criminal Code that define related offences such as treason, sabotage, sedition and so on. The intent of the Act seems clear enough: it is designed to cover spying with punishment which befits the crime. However, as Maxwell Cohen has pointed out, section 4 of the Canadian Official Secrets Act embraces in intent almost any form of information obtained in the course of service or contract of employment or otherwise, and then passed on without authority to any other person:

> . . . whatever his status and whatever the purposes of the transfer of information may be, however unclassified the information may be (and) if obtained from sources available because of holding a government position or having a government contract.[54]

In this widesweeping net aimed at catching conspirators many small and even "innocent" offenders can be trapped. The severity of the Act is further emphasized by the fact that the onus of proof of innocence is on the accused if a limited case on the facts has been made out by the Crown. Doern illustrates how wide the scope of this Act can be:

> . . . under present Canadian legislation it is not clear that a journalist or a scholar speaking to a civil servant is not in breach of the Official Secrets Act in the ordinary exchange of any confidence at all between them, and this may apply to civil servant and Cabinet minister as well. When are journalists or scholars persons "authorized" to receive confidential information within the meaning of the Canadian Act? . . . In practice some disclosure to journalists and scholars is tolerated up to a point, and indeed encouraged in some cases; yet the civil servant or adviser to the Executive is generally on his own in trying to assess the propriety of any particular disclosure he might make.[55]

The "winds of change" seem to be slowly blowing over this state of affairs. Both the Royal Commission on Security in 1969,[56] and the Wall Report prepared in the Privy Council Office in 1974,[57] advocated complete revisions of the Official Secrets Act to reflect this dire need for change. In 1969, the government announced a new policy of transferring to the Public Archives of Canada all government documents over thirty years old to be made available for public perusal. However, this would not include records "whose release might adversely affect Canada's external relations, violate the right of privacy of individuals, or adversely affect the national security."[58] In 1970, Parliament approved a Federal Court Act which gave the courts certain powers to compel the production of official documents, thereby curbing the wide-ranging concept of Crown privilege somewhat.[59] In 1971, Parliament passed the Statutory Instruments Act which made the publication of all Government regulations and many related statutory instruments mandatory. In 1973, the government continued this step-by-step cautionary approach to confidentiality by issuing guidelines to the departments which stated that as a general principle departments should make public as much information as possible. This directive was referred to a standing joint committee on Regulations and Other Statutory Instruments, and by 1975 a report was issued by the committee approving in principle the concept of legislation relating to freedom of information. Prior to the introduction of specific legislation the government issued a Green Paper entitled *Legislation on Public Access to Government Documents* which put forward certain lists of exemptions, proposed the establishment of an Information Commissioner, who would be an advisory ombudsman, as to which documents can be released, and opposed a right of appeal to the courts.[66] These proposals have been severely criticized by the Canadian Bar Association and by the joint committee on Regulations and Other Statutory Instruments for the lack of appeal provisions. In support of a final appeal to the courts, the Committee agreed with a research study prepared for the Canadian Bar Association by lawyer Murray Rankin, that:

no constitutional, legal, or practical impediment stands in the way of judicial involvement in the adjudication of freedom of information questions," and that the argument that ministerial responsibility precludes it is a time-worn dogma that collapses upon an examination of English and Canadian constitutional precedents . . . to hand the final decision on disclosure of information to the unreviewable discretion of a Minister "who is hardly a disinterested party" would make a sham of any system of access to Government documents.[61]

Ministerial responsibility would simply not go away, despite all the criticisms that it is a "time worn dogma" of yester-year. By the autumn of 1978, the Liberal administration had made it abundantly clear that while it is prepared to go along in advocating and legislating further reforms in the area of confidentiality of information, it was definitely not going to allow any legislation which would, in its view, jeopardize the doctrine of ministerial responsibility. Formal controls of information must belong in the final analysis to the responsible government. Thus ministers rather than the courts would continue to have the final word as to which documents can or cannot be released to the public. As the then Secretary of State, Mr. John Roberts opined, appeals to the courts are extremely cumbersome and costly to the public purse, and "it is to my mind something to be avoided."[62]

With the defeat of the Liberals in early 1979 those proposals were cast aside by the minority Conservative government of Joe Clark. In its place the government proposed a new bill which was distinguished by its appeal provisions to an information commissioner and ultimately to the Federal Court. But with the defeat of the minority government on December 13, 1979, this bill also "died" on the order paper of the House of Commons. In the throne speech during the opening of Parliament in April 1980, the newly elected Liberal government signalled that its former position on appeals had softened and that some system of judicial appeals will be allowed in pending legislation.

V. The Ombudsman and Political Responsibility

"The ombudsman concept writes Walter Gellhorn, "is very simple. It means only that a citizen aggrieved by an official's action or inaction should be able to state his grievance to an influential functionary empowered to investigate and to express conclusions."[63] This is a very disarming definition which accentuates the ombudsman concept as a control institution against arbitrary and inhuman bureaucracy. Early advocates of the ombudsman scheme both in Canada and the United States emphasized this bureaucratic control function as the main *raison d'etre* of an ombudsman's office.[64] As the concept increased in popularity, it became apparent, particularly in countries with a British parliamentary tradition, that in principle the concept can challenge the central core of parliamentary government, the dominance of the Executive.

To many, the implications of this challenge became clearer after the New Zealand government in 1962 adopted the institution. Adapted

DR. DONALD CAMERON ROWAT
Professor of Political Science, Carleton University, and former President of the Canadian Political Science Association (1975-76). Rowat has had a lifelong scholarly interest in the methods of administrative control in liberal-democratic societies. He was the first Canadian academic to popularize the ombudsman concept for this country, and he remains an untiring advocate for freedom of information legislation for all levels of government.

from the original Scandinavian model to suit New Zealand's needs, the institution was given the statutory right to do two things: to pare down the common law doctrine of privilege; and to give the ombudsman the potential power to examine any departmental recommendations to Ministers, although in practice it was hoped that he would not go so far. The net result of this is that much depends on the person holding the office who must not only be a consumate diplomat, but a tightrope dancer as well, attributes generally conceded to the first holder of that office, in New Zealand, Sir Guy Powles. The broad intent of the original legislation, explained Sir Guy:

> . . . is as the Attorney-General said in introducing the Bill, that "matters of policy would be outside the Ombudsman's jurisdiction, because, for those matters, the Government must be solely responsible to Parliament." The actual wording of the Act, however, confers jurisdiction if a matter relates to administration, which could conceivably occur in the case of some matters of policy. Nevertheless, difficult jurisdictional decisions do from time to time have to be made in the Ombudsman's office. In New Zealand, the system of government organization, including the powers, duties, and functions of ministers, is almost wholly the creation of statute—indeed of a multiplicity of statutes. A good general principle is that the statutes lay down policy and what the departments do pursuant to their statutes is administration. [65]

This aspect of the scheme, namely its potentiality for interfering with political responsibility, set off a series of academic and popular articles critical of the ombudsman for parliamentary government settings. In Canada, A. S. Abel contended that the ombudsman was not in "the Commonwealth style," a style of governing which revolves around "a Holy Trinity" of three great concepts: parliamentary supremacy, the rule of law, and ministerial responsibility. [66] The Ontario Royal Commission Inquiry into Civil Rights (commonly known as the McRuer Report) reported a generally negative stance towards the ombudsman concept because of its interference with ministerial responsibility. Traditionalists of the common law advocated instead a strengthening of the reviewing power of the traditionally independent judiciary. [67]

In Britain, a Conservative administration rejected the scheme out of hand in 1962 on the ground that it would interfere with ministerial responsibility. When the ombudsman was finally re-introduced, it became known as "our parliamentary ombudsman" to members of Parliament because the scheme "had been deliberately devised as a wholly parliamentary instrument, under the control and at the disposal only of MPs, to be used by them as and when they saw fit." [68]

Furthermore, a minister of the Crown can halt any parliamentary ombudsman's investigation if, in the Minister's opinion, such investigation interfered with ministerial responsibility.

It is this fear of curbing in unknown ways the doctrine of ministerial responsibility which has prevented a wholesale acceptance of the ombudsman scheme at the federal level. From the record, what seems clear is that the federal government has generally adopted a cautionary attitude towards the scheme, preferring to learn from experience of the nine of our ten provinces which have introduced it to their individual jurisdictions (the one exception being the province of Prince Edward Island).[69] Instead of one ombudsman with potential powers to make a frontal challenge to ministerial responsibility on a whole range of politico-administrative issues, the federal administration has opted for a series of "specialized ombudsmen" confined to investigating and reporting on administrative malfeasance and inaction in specific jurisdictions. Thus we have a Commissioner of Official Languages, a Prison Ombudsman, a Transportation Ombudsman, a Human Rights Commissioner and a Privacy Commissioner.[70]

A description of events surrounding the creation of the latter position does give some indication of the trend of governmental thinking and legislation on the ombudsman concept. In 1972 the federal Minister of Justice announced the government's intention to create a commission for the protection of human rights which would include the power of a parliamentary ombudsman, as in Britain, to investigate complaints against the bureaucracy. In 1975 when the commission was finally created, no such ombudsman scheme was proferred.

Instead the law gave Canadian citizens the right to inspect personal files that the government may be holding on them, and to file a correction or counter-statement to what is presently on the file. This has been a particularly significant change in Canadian law, for citizens have always been denied any right of access to personal information on them collected by the police or by other agents of either the federal or provincial governments.[71] This federal legislation is one of the first in Canada to make changes in the law to permit access to personal information. There is a long series of exemption to this open access, but any individual wishing to challenge these exemptions can appeal to a Privacy Commissioner who, like an ombudsman, can make an appropriate recommendation on the case. This law came into effect as the Canadian Human Rights Act in March 1978. By the following month (April 1978), changes to the legislation were already proposed. Following the recommendations of a committee of senior officials on an ombudsman scheme, the government proposed Bill C-43, proposing that the Privacy commissioner become an assistant ombudsman with strong powers of access to information. In the case of a minister's refusal to allow a document to be perused, the Commissioner could apply to the Federal Court for a ruling on the case. However, as Donald Rowat has indicated, there are still strong restrictions to the assistant ombudsman's powers of investigation:

> . . . (the assistant ombudsman and his officers) would be bound to confidentiality during the course of an investigation, and they would not be allowed to disclose information in a list of categories similar to the exemptions in the 1973 guidelines on the release of documents to Parliament. This list, too, introduces each category with the broad words "might" or "would be likely to" rather than "would" (e.g., "might be injurious to . . . federal-provincial relations").[72]

The Canadian government has therefore allowed Crown privilege to be pared in some very significant ways by the federal courts. However, in so doing, the government refused to accept the argument that the doctrine of ministerial responsibility, upon which the whole concept of Crown privilege rests, is a "time-worn dogma that collapses upon an examination of . . . Canadian constitutional precedents."

VI. Conclusions

We have tried to demonstrate how the theories and conventions of liberal-democratic government have had such practical consequences for the ongoing business of bureaucratic performance. The key to the understanding of the whole "edifice" is the notion of Executive dominance, a notion which finds its theoretical roots in political responsibility in a parliamentary system of government. From this notion of Executive dominance flows a virtual cornucopia of conventions which are considered important in controlling the bureaucracy and ensuring executive hegemony. These are: the Executive control of all parliamentary business; the direct responsibility of the Executive in deciding matters of war and peace and the conduct of foreign relations; the Ministerial monopoly of financial proposals; Ministerial discretion in answering parliamentary inquiries; and one which we have repeatedly stressed, the Executive's dominance over the machinery of government which includes control over all government documents, and the allegiance of all public servants.

All these trappings of Parliamentary government are summed up in one concept, "Crown privilege," an ancient doctrine of government which allows the Executive the ultimate discretion in deciding what constitutes the public interest. Crown privilege is therefore an absolute reserve of political power which allows the Executive to decide what Parliament, the public, or even the independent judiciary should know about the internal processes of government. It is this Crown privilege which was wrested from the monarchy reducing that institution, in Walter Bagehot's words, to a dignified and ornamental impotence. It is also this Crown privilege which bothers many commentators today, and if wrested from the Executive must finally reside in some other institution of democratic society. Some would attempt to restore it to Parliament. Others are not too sure or are downright skeptical about Parliament's ability to wield such power. And there actually is where the matter rests, for executive dominance continues to be one of the power realities in our society. To fail to understand this is to fail to comprehend the doctrine of ministerial responsibility. It has been a powerful weapon in controlling the bureaucracy, and from it flows the motley collection of control measures, both formal and informal, which we have briefly considered here. In addition, the internal consistency of the doctrine has also benefited those it seeks to control, for bureaucrats have found permanence, professional satisfaction, and protection from abuse under its umbrage. Therefore, to argue that ". . . the whole doctrine of Ministerial responsibility is only a convention, an unwritten rule that tends to shift and change over time and recent events have demonstrated this convention is now but a myth."[73] is to seriously muddle the issues involved by "throwing the baby out with the bathwater." The doctrine is not just a convention for it embodies both *prescriptive* and *descriptive* elements. As a prescriptive doctrine it was made operable in the past in parliamentary democracies by conventions which "tend to shift and change over time." At least one of these conventions has already been discarded as both Finer and Kernaghan so persuasively show. Conventions are not immutable principles: they *are* and *should be* subject to change. But such changes should proceed with due care and caution because of the interrelationships between conventions and fundamental principles. The problem is a difficult one to solve for our politicians who must be constantly concerned with an appropriate balance in the bureaucracy between firm control and unfettered discretion. Robert Putnam does us all a service by pointing out the inherent dangers in making such choices:

. . . any trend toward a more "political" bureaucracy is not without dangers: the danger that party patronage might gradually reduce the level of competence of the administrative elite and thereby its technical ability to be responsive on larger matters; the danger that growing political commitment on the part of administrative officials might encourage the intrusion of partisanship into those activities of the state which can and should be governed by essentially objective criteria; the danger that politicization of the higher civil service might lead over time to fragmentation and demoralization and thus in turn to a reduction in overall effectiveness; the danger that beyond some point a more political bureaucracy might be less innovative and hence less able to respond creatively to changing social needs; the danger that, as a politically aware bureaucracy comes to play a more active role in the policy-making process, the ability of the representative institutions of government to control that bureaucracy may be weakened. These dangers call attention to the fact that bureaucratic attitudes are not the only determinant of government responsiveness, that conditions for responsiveness interact with one another, that progress along one dimension may bring difficulties along others.[74]

A Canadian economist view of the continuing accountability debate

In my view, the reform of Parliament and a drastic reduction in government secrecy are desperately needed whether or not they improve government policies. Our individual liberties are vulnerable because the present parliamentary system with its obscene secrecy rules and absolute party discipline gives too much power to the Executive Branch under majority government. *Uncontrolled power concerns me more than uncontrolled expenditures.*

> Dr. Douglas Hartle,
> Former Deputy Secretary,
> Treasury Board of Canada

Coming from an economist, the whole quote, but in particular the last sentence, is quite a mouthful!

Footnotes

1. R.A. Dahl, "A Critique of the Ruling Elite Model," *American Political Science Review,* LII (1958).

2. James G. March and H.A. Simon, *Organizations* (New York: John Wiley and Sons, Inc., 1958), p. 36ff.

3. Charles Butler, *Responsible Government for Colonies,* London, 1840, quoted in A. Lawrence Lowell, *The Government of England,* 2nd edition, (New York, 1912), Vol. I, p. 178. For a fascinating account of the same phenomenon occurring in the twentieth century, see Bruce J. Berman "Bureaucracy and Incumbent Violence: Colonial Administration and the Origins of the 'Mau-Mau' Emergency in Kenya," *British Journal of Political Science,* 6, 1976, pp. 143-175.

4. David Beetham, *Max Weber and the Theory of Modern Politics* (London: George Allen and Onwin Ltd., 1974), pp. 68-69.

5. *Ibid.*, p. 71.

6. *Ibid.*, p. 70. For an excellent synopsis of Max Weber's political views as distinct from his academic sociology, see Robert D. Cuff, "Wilson and Weber: Bourgeois critics in an organized age," *PAR*, May/June 1978, Vol. 38, No. 3, pp. 240-244. And for a rare perceptive Canadian comment on the fundamental distinction between American scientific management and Weberian concepts of bureaucracy see the review by Ken H. Cabatoff of Frederick C. Mosher (ed.), *American Public Administration: Past, Present, Future,* in *CPA*, Vol. 19, No. 2, Summer, 1976, pp. 328-331.

7. Herbert A. Simon, *Administrative Behavior.* Second edition (New York: The Free Press, 1965), p. xii.

8. *Ibid.*, 56-58.

9. P.J. Chartrand and K.L. Pond, *A Study of Executive Career Paths in the Public Service of Canada* (Chicago Public Personnel Association, 1970); Colin Campbell and George J. Szablowski, *The Super Bureaucrats* (Toronto: Macmillan, 1979).

10. See D.C. Corbett, "The Politics of Bureaucracy in Canada," *Public Administration* (Sydney), Vol. XXXII, No. 1, March 1973, p. 54.

11. This mushroom type representation had, however, changed drastically by the efforts of the Public Service Commission over the last decade to rectify this problem. For a further amplification of this theme as it was then, see C. Beattie, Desy and Longstaff, *Bureaucratic Careers: Anglophones and Francophones in the Canadian Public Service,* Vol. 1, pp. 120-124 (Study prepared for the Royal Commission on Bilingualism and Biculturalism). As it is now, see the articles by V. Seymour Wilson and W.A. Mullins, Kenneth Kernaghan and J.J. Carson in *Canadian Public Administration,* Winter 1978.

12. D.C. Rowat, "On John Porter's Bureaucratic Elite," *Canadian Journal of Economics and Political Science,* XXV, No. 2 (May 1959), pp. 204-207.

13. See D.C. Corbett, "The Politics of Bureaucracy in Canada," pp. 53-55.

14. Judy LaMarsh, *Memoirs of a Bird in a Guilded Cage* (Toronto: McClelland and Stewart, 1969), pp. 65-66.

15. J.R. Mallory, *The Structure of Canadian Government* (Toronto: Macmillan of Canada, 1971), pp. 116-117.

16. *Ibid.*, p. 117.

17. J.R. Mallory, "The Minister's Office Staff: An Unreformed Part of the Public Service," *CPA,* X, No. 1 (March 1967), pp. 25-34.

18. *Ibid.*, p. 32.

19. Paul M. Tellier, "Pour une Reforme des Cabinets de Ministres Federaux," *CPA*, Vol. XI, No. 4, Winter 1968, p. 426.

20. Dennis Smith, "President and Parliament: The Transformation of Parliamentary Government in Canada," in Thomas A. Hockin (ed.), *Apex of Power*, 2nd ed. (Toronto: Prentice-Hall, 1977), pp. 308-325. The reader should also digest the excellent reply to Smith by Joseph Wearing, "President or Prime Minister," in T.A. Hockin (ed.), *Ibid.*, pp. 326-343.

21. G. Bruce Doern, "The Development of Policy Organizations in the Executive Arena," in G. Bruce Doern and Peter C. Aucoin (eds.), *The Structures of Policy Making in Canada* (Toronto: Macmillan, 1971), p. 41.

22. Richard D. French, "The Privy Council Office: Support for Cabinet Decision Making," in R. Schultz et al., *The Canadian Political Process* (Third edition), (Holt, Rinehart and Winston, 1979), p. 387.

23. Thomas d'Aquino, "The Prime Minister's Office: Catalyst or Cabal?" *CPA*, 17 (1), Spring 1974, p. 71.

24. Jack Pickersgill, a former Cabinet minister in various Liberal administrations over the last three decades, sums up this image rather neatly by describing these advisers as occupying ". . . a never-never land between politicians and proper bureaucracts. . ." See The Hon. J.W. Pickersgill, "Bureaucrats and Politicians," *CPA*, XV, No. 3 (Fall 1972), p. 421.

25. In explaining this "political clearance process" of the PMO, the then Senior Assistant Secretary of the Privy Council was somewhat cautionary about this role:
    That does not mean by any stretch of the imagination that everybody who is appointed is a member of the governing party. It is, however, an entirely legitimate function it seems to me of a government to want to ensure that people being appointed, all things being equal, are sympathetic to it and its policies. I say this because there are some people who seem to feel there is something improper about this part of the operation.
    Gordon S. Smith, "Relationship to the Privy Council Office and the Cabinet" in *Speakers' Remarks: Report on a Seminar for the Members of Federal Administrative Tribunals* (Ottawa: The Law Reform Commission of Canada, 1978), p. 171.

26. Gordon Robertson, "Official responsibility, private conscience and public information," *Optimum*, Vol. 3, No. 3, 1972, p. 10.

27. See G. Kitson Clark, "Statesmen in Disguise: Reflexions on the History of Neutrality of the Civil Service," *The Historical Journal*, II, No. 1, 1959, pp. 19-39.

28. See "Report on the Organisation of the Permanent Civil Service," reprinted from U.K. Parliamentary Paper (1854, No. 1713), XXVII, pp. 367-387. Reprinted in *Public Administration* (London), XXXII, (Spring 1954), p. 1.

29. See Kitson Clark, "Statesmen in Disguise: Reflexions on the History of Neutrality of the Civil Service," p. 24. Also S.E. Finer, "Patronage and the Public Service," *PA* (London) XXX, 4, (1952), pp. 329-360; F.M.G. Willson, "Ministries and Boards: Some Aspects of Administrative Development since 1832," *Public Administration*

(London) XXXIII, 1 (1955), pp. 43-58; Henry Parris, *Constitutional Bureaucracy: The Development of British Central Administration Since the Eighteenth Century* (London: George Allen and Unwin, 1969).

30. Kitson Clark points out that in the formative years of ministerial responsibility, between 1830 and 1880, there were in Britain "some of the most formidable divergencies in the behaviour of eminent officials from anything that could be called neutral or anonymous." Many of these senior men had spent a lifetime in the public service before the doctrine of ministerial responsibility had a chance to congeal. Hence, as these veterans retired, the all-encompassing norms of the doctrine slowly but surely became effective in the socialization processes of bureaucrats. See Kitson Clark, "Statesmen in Disguise," p. 30.

31. For an excellent treatment of this theme, see John A. Armstrong, *The European Administrative Elite* (New Jersey: Princeton University Press, 1973). See also by the same author, "Old Regime Administrative Elites: Prelude to Modernisation in France, Prussia and Russia," *International Review of Administrative Sciences*, XXXVIII, No. 1, 1972, pp. 21-40.

32. For the initial development of this concept see J. Donald Kingsley, *Representative Bureaucracy: An Interpretation of the British Civil Service* (Yellow Springs, Ohio: Antioch Press, 1944).

33. See John A. Armstrong, *The European Administrative Elite*, especially Chapters 10 and 11.

34. See Kenneth John Meier and Lloyd C. Nigro, "Representative Bureaucracy and Policy Preferences: A Study in the Attitudes of Federal Executives," *Public Administration Review*, 36 (July-August 1976), pp. 458-469. For a similar Canadian point of view see John Porter, "A Reply to Professor Rowat," *Canadian Journal of Economics and Political Science*, 25, No. 2 (May 1959), p. 208.

35. For an analysis of representative bureaucracy in a Canadian context read the following articles (and footnotes) in *Canadian Public Administration* (Winter 1978):
    (i) W. Kenneth Kernaghan, "Representative Bureaucracy: The Canadian Perspective."
    (ii) V. Seymour Wilson and W.A. Mullins, "Representative Bureaucracy: Linguistic/Ethnic Aspects in Canadian Public Policy."

36. In writing about the professionalism of the public service D.V. Smiley makes essentially the same point when he argues that "In terms of policy, neutrality means that civil servants will execute government measures as effectively and efficiently as they can despite their private doubts about such measures and even their opposition to them prior to such policies being adopted." D.V. Smiley, *The Freedom of Information Issue: A Political Analysis*. Research Publication No. 1 (Toronto: The Commission on Freedom of Information and Individual Privacy), September 1978, p. 51.

37. Herbert A. Simon, "The Changing Theory and Changing Practice of Public Administration," in Ithiel de Sola Pool (ed.), *Contemporary Political Science: Toward Empirical Theory* (New York: McGraw-Hill, 1967), p. 98.

38. H. Simon, *ibid.*, p. 108.

39. Kenneth Kernaghan, *Ethical Conduct: Guidelines for Government Employees* (Toronto: Institute of Public Administration of Canada, 1975), p. 13.

40. *Ibid.*, pp. 13-16.

41. W.D.K. Kernaghan, "The Political Rights and Activities of Canadian Public Servants," in W.D.K. Kernaghan and A.M. Willms (eds.), *Public Administration in Canada: Selected Readings* (2nd edition) (Toronto: Methuen, 1971), pp. 382-390; O.P. Dwivedi and J.P. Kyba, "Political Rights of Canada's Public Servants," Frederick Vaughan et al., (eds.), *Contemporary Issues in Canadian Politics* (Scarborough: Prentice-Hall, 1970), pp. 230-239; P. Garant, "L'ethique dans la fonction publique: Un essai de theorie generale," *CPA*, Vol. 18, (Spring 1975) pp. 69-90.

42. C. Lloyd Brown-John, "Party Politics and the Canadian Federal Public Service," *Public Administration* (London), Vol. 52, Spring 1974, pp. 79-93.

43. Hugh Lawford, "Privacy versus Freedom of Information," *Queen's Quarterly*, LXXXVIII, No. 3, Autumn 1971, pp. 365-371 at p. 365; Frank G. DeBalogh, "Public Administrators and 'The Privacy Thing': A Time to Speak Out," *PAR*, XXXII, No. 5, September/October 1972, pp. 526-530.

44. D.C. Rowat, "The Problem of Administrative Secrecy," *International Review of Administrative Science*, XXII, 1966, pp. 99-100.

45. Gordon Robertson, "Access to Government Documents," unpublished address given to the Institute of Public Administration of Canada, Twenty-Eight Annual Conference, September 7-10, 1976, p. 7.

46. Carl J. Friedrich, *The Pathology of Politics* (New York: Harper and Row, 1972).

47. For an example of this "book ends" debate see Donald C. Rowat, "We need a Freedom of Information Act," unpublished address given to the Institute of Public Administration of Canada, Twenty-Eight Annual Conference, September 7-10, 1976. See also D.C. Rowat (ed.), *Administrative Secrecy in Developed Countries* (London: The MacMillan Press Ltd., 1978) Apart from the very knowledgeable comparative survey and excellent discussion on Canada by Rowat, the preface remarks by Andre Heilbronner are particularly noteworthy for their clarity and balance.

48. See, as an example, D.C. Rowat, "How Much Administrative Secrecy?" *CJEPS*, XXXI, No. 4 (November 1965), pp. 479-498. In reply to this article see K.W. Knight, "Administrative Secrecy and Ministerial Responsibility" and D.C. Rowat, "Administrative Secrecy and Ministerial Responsibility: A Reply," *CJEPS*, XXXII, No. 1 (February 1966), pp. 77087.

49. John Swift, "Ministerial Responsibility, ministerial control of government documentary information and Freedom of Information Legislation—Are they related?" *The Advocate*, Vol. 37, Part 2, February/March 1979, pp. 121-125; T. Murray Rankin, *Freedom of Information in Canada: Will the Doors Stay Shut?* The Canadian Bar Association, 1977.

50. Kenneth Kernaghan, "Power, Parliament and Public Servants in Canada: Ministerial Responsibility Reexamined," *Canadian Public Policy*, Vol. 3, Summer 1979, pp. 383-396.

51. Report of the Tribunal . . . (on) the Vehicle and General Insurance Co. Ltd., H.L. 80, H.C. 133, (London: Her Majesty's Stationery Office) 15 February 1972.

52. Great Britain. House of Commons Debates, Vol. 835 (1 May 1972), column 62; Richard A. Chapman, "The Vehicle and General Insurance Affair: Some Reflections on Public Administration in Britain," *Public Administration*, Vol. 5, (Autumn 1973), pp. 273-290.

53. It is therefore no wonder that in the aftermath of this affair the senior officials' union (called the First Division Association) made some rather ominous remarks that the time may be fast approaching when public servants will prefer to take their chances in answering to Parliament directly rather than relying on the now "dubious" doctrine of ministerial responsibility. See Lewis A. Gunn, "Politicians and Officials: Who is Answerable?" *Political Quarterly*, Vol. 43, No. 3, July/September 1972), pp. 254-255.

54. Maxwell Cohen, "Secrecy in Law and Policy: The Canadian Experience and International Relations," in Thomas M. Franck and Edward Weisband (eds.), *Secrecy and Foreign Policy* (New York: Oxford University Press, 1974), p. 357.

55. G. Bruce Doern, "Canada," in I. Galnoor (ed.), *Government Secrecy in Democracies* (New York: Harper Colophon Books, 1977), pp. 143-156.

56. Royal Commission on Security, Report (Abridged) (Ottawa: Queen's Printer, June 1969).

57. D.F. Wall, *The Provision of Government Information* (Ottawa: Privy Council Office, 1974). Also available as an appendix in Parliament, First Session, Thirtieth Parliament, 1974-75, Standing Joint Committee on Regulations and Other Statutory Instruments, Minutes of Proceedings and Evidence, Issue No. 32, Wednesday, June 25, 1975 (Ottawa: Queen's Printer, 1974), pp. 30-71.

58. *Report: To Know and Be Known*, Vol. II: *Research Papers* (Ottawa: Queen's Printer, 1969), p. 26.

59. Statistics Canada 1970-71-72, c.1, especially section 41. For a comprehensive review and analysis of Canadian law on the matter of Crown privilege see Linstead, "The Law of Crown Privilege in Canada and Elsewhere," 3, *Ottawa Law Review*, 79, 449 (1968-69).

60. Issued by the Secretary of State (Ottawa: Supply and Services Canada, 1977).

61. *Minutes of Proceedings and Evidence*, Issue No. 34, Third Session of the Thirtieth Parliament, 1977-78 (June 27, 1978), pp. 3-12 at p. 9. The report of the Joint Committee was referring to T. Murray Rankin, *Freedom of Information in Canada: Will the Doors Stay Shut?* (Ottawa: Canadian Bar Association, August 1977).

62. Kittey McKinsey, "New information law promised for session," *Ottawa Citizen* (October 11, 1978), Section 4, p. 45.

63. Walter Gellhorn, *Ombudsmen and Others: Citizens' Protectors in Nine Countries* (Mass.: Harvard University Press, 1967), p. 93.

64. Perhaps one of the first articles to popularize the concept in North America was Henry J. Abraham, "A People's Watchdog Against Abuse of Power," *PAR*, 20:3 (Summer 1960), pp. 152-157. In Canada, Donald C. Rowat has been *the* individual identified with popularizing the ombudsman concept. His contribution on this topic has been prolific, but two publications are illustrative, *The Ombudsman: Citizen's Defender* (Toronto: University of Toronto Press, 1965) has been an important document in the ombudsman movement. See also his "Recent Developments in Ombudsmanship," *CPA*, Vol. 10, No. 1 Spring 1967, p. 35ff.

65. Sir Guy Powles, "Aspects of the Search for Administrative Justice with Particular Reference to the New Zealand Ombudsman," *CPA*, Vol. IX, No. 2 (June 1966), p. 146.

66. Albert S. Abel, "Constitutional Commonwealth Complications," in D.C. Rowat (ed.), *The Ombudsman*, p. 285.

67. Ontario Royal Commission Inquiry into Civil Rights (McRuer), *Report*, No. 2, Vol. 4, p. 1383.

68. Roy Gregory and Alan Alexander, " 'Our Parliamentary Ombudsman,' Part II: Integration and Metamorphosis," *Public Administration* (London) Vol. 50, Autumn 1972, pp. 313-331 at p. 331.

69. For a review of provincial developments see D.C. Rowat, *The Ombudsman Plan* (Toronto: McClelland and Stewart, 1973), pp. 97-105.

70. Academic studies continue to call for integration of these offices. See G.B. Sharma, "A Proposal to Integrate the Offices of the Privacy and Information Commissioners, in D.C. Rowat (ed.), *The Right to Know: Essays on Governmental Publicity and Access to Information* (Ottawa: Carleton University Bookstore, 1980), pp. 285-305.

71. Daniel Mayo, "Privacy and Social Control," Unpublished M.A. essay (Ottawa: Carleton University, 1974), pp. 61-65.

72. Donald C. Rowat, *Public Access to Government Documents: A Comparative Perspective.* A Research Report prepared for the Ontario Commission on Freedom of Information and Individual Privacy, October 1978, p. 69.

73. Gerald Baldwin, "Freedom of Information: Another Personal View," *Canadian Political Science Bulletin*, Vol. 7, January 1978, p. 63.

74. Robert D. Putnam, "The Political Attitudes of Senior Civil Servants in Britain, Germany and Italy," in Mattei Dogan (ed.), *The Mandarins of Western Europe: The Political Role of Top Civil Servants* (New York: John Wiley and Sons, 1975), pp. 122-123 by permission of the Publisher, Sage Publications Inc. (Beverly Hills/London). This

article originally appeared in the *British Journal of Political Science* 3 (July 1973): 257-290.

Notes

The notes for Chapter Seven would again suffice for Chapter Eight. Just a few additional pieces are cited:

1. D.C. Corbett. "The Politics of Bureaucracy in Canada," *Public Administration* (Sydney), Vol. XXXII, No. 1, March 1973, pp. 42-55.

2. J.R. Mallory, "The Two Clerks: Parliamentary Discussion of the Role of the Privy Council Office," *CJPS*, X:1, March 1977, pp. 3-19.

3. D.C. Rowat, "How Much Administrative Secrecy?" *CJEPS*, XXXI, No. 4, (November 1965), pp. 479-498. See footnote 45, this chapter.

4. D.C. Rowat, *Public Access to Government Documents: A Comparative Perspective*, Research Publication 3, (Toronto: Commission on Freedom of Information and Individual Privacy, November 1978).

5. V. Seymour Wilson and W.A. Mullins, "Representative Bureaucracy: Linguistic/Ethnic Aspects in Canadian Public Policy," *Canadian Public Administration*, 21:4 (Winter 1978), pp. 513-538.

CHAPTER NINE

THE POLITICS-ADMINISTRATION ARCH: THE CONVERGENCE OF POLITICAL AND BUREAUCRATIC ACTORS

Hankey's Doggerel:
And so while the great ones depart to their dinner
The Secret'ry stays, growing thinner and thinner
Racking his brains to record and report
What he thinks that they think that they ought to have thought.

> Lines by (Lord) Maurice Hankey,
> Secretary to the British Cabinet,
> 1916-1938.

The conjunction of the concept of "responsibility" with that of an administrative staff is inherent . . . in the empirical data on bureaucracy afforded by Western historical experience. This is true to the extent that a history of Western bureaucracy is inconceivable without this conjunction being assigned a central place.

> Carl J. Friedrich.

Introduction

The complex and somewhat fluid nature of the pragmatic paradigm outlined in Chapter Seven becomes, in part, more concrete when applied to the points of convergence between the political and senior bureaucratic actors in the political system. In the Canadian literature this major point of convergence is usually referred to as "the executive-bureaucratic arena," to highlight the central importance of the interaction between and among the chief actors in the process.[1]

However, while we have no serious quarrel with the use of this term, we intend to describe this "meeting place" of the political and senior bureaucratic actors as the "politics-administration arch," a term which has several excellent features to it. First of all, in keeping with our pragmatic paradigm, it helps us to emphasize the "interactive and adversarial" process of this "meeting place" of politicians and bureaucrats. One arch serves to represent the political arm of government while the other arch symbolizes the administrative arm.[2] The point of convergence or the fulcrum of the structure represents "the critical point" at which a series of bureaucratic and political structures intertwine to ensure the working physiology of the system.

Secondly, the term is well suited to describe the apex of interaction both *at the departmental and at the system-wide levels of government (the latter commonly known as central agencies)*. Each department duplicates the arch arrangement, culminating of course in the over-arching meeting place at the cabinet and cabinet-committees level. Thirdly, "the politics-administration arch" reminds the reader that it is at this locus of the organization that doctrines of responsibility (either the policy/administration dichotomy or ministerial responsibility and its derivatives) come into full play and are concretized by the interactions of the various senior actors involved. However, as one moves away from the fulcrum of power, the interaction between administration and politics lessens, with politicians deeply concerned with the political character of policy, and administrators "sticking to their last" by being engrossed more with administrative detail and matters of an instrumental nature. Political concerns of public policy and administrative detail are, however, never entirely removed from each other in public administration. As we have maintained in previous chapters, they are inextricably interrelated. However, it is usually true that on an ongoing basis, "the great bulk of administrative operations continues in political obscurity, and the main interactions between politics and administration occur at the top levels of government."[3]

In conventional organizational theory (that is scientific management), theorists of the past attempted to grapple with this interaction of the organizational "head" and its various component parts by adapting and developing theories around the concepts of (i) "staff" and "line" and (ii) span of control. Today's students, looking back at the adaptation of these theories to modern day bureaucracies sometimes tend to forget what these apparently inadequate conceptualizations did for organizations at the time. These precepts introduced some sharper thinking concerning authority, responsibility and delegation, and placed an emphasis on clearer lines of command and the subdivision of organizational functions.* Although these theories are now believed to be somewhat naive and lacking appropriate sophistication about twentieth century, non-military organizational life, it is claimed that they have fulfilled a vital function: "simple and boring in cold print," they nevertheless made "the essential difference between an organization that works and chaos."[4]

Notwithstanding their usefulness it is true that theories of scientific management are only partial theories. As we have maintained in Chapter Five we must add the insights of the behavioralists to better understand the dynamics of bureaucracy. Herbert Simon maintains in *Administrative Behavior* that the best way to analyse a bureaucracy is to find out where the decisions are made and by whom.[5] Normally most people would assume that in the bureaucracy the decision pattern follows the structure of the formal hierarchy. However as Simon has shown this is certainly not a valid assumption or generalization: the power and authority network may cut across the hierarchical channels. In other words, what we normally have is an overlay of the pragmatic paradigm on the hierarchical responsibilities paradigm. Thus power and authority as *relational* concepts do not necessarily undermine the *structural* concept of hierarchy: structure affects behavior just as behavior affects structure. Behavioral patterns of interaction modify the harsh overtones of hierarchy by depicting how actual organizations allow, need and are profoundly affected by a flow of cross contacts within and beyond its boundaries. These patterns force us to think in terms of a decision *process* rather than a decision *point*. Mary Parker Follett's argument about order-giving mirrors this perspective when she contends that "an order, (or a) command is a step in a process, a moment in the movement of interweaving experience. We should guard against thinking this step a larger part of the whole process than it really is."[6]

These behavioral insights help us to realistically examine the policy/administration arch and to posit a working definition of central agencies. The hierarchical paradigm does not supply us with sufficient information on which a realistic definition can be based. We will therefore examine important aspects of the arch in the following manner. First, we will discuss the conventional theory which attempts to

---

* *The "principles" of "staff and line," "unity of command", "span of control" and so on were essentially borrowed from the military, and also found a receptive climate in the type of hierarchical, authoritarian structures found in the great Western religions. These borrowings are not as farfetched as they at first appear: the historical development of European bureaucracy reveals that two key evolutionary features were (i) the cooption of clerics into its ranks (hence the English word "clerk"), and (ii) the transformation of military controllers into civilian officials.*

explain and regularize the interaction between manager, organizational head and advisers in the organizational context. We will limit our theoretical discussions to cabinet and cabinet committees/central agencies/departmental and agency relationships, although much of what we write about and evaluate could be meaningfully applied, at a micro scale, to the minister-deputy minister/departmental manager/department adviser level as well. Second, we will assess the distinctive characteristics of the federal "staff" agencies (defined here as central agencies of the government). Third, we will project an analysis, drawn from some of the insights of contemporary organization theory, which conceive central agencies as influential but not all-omnipotent actors in the politics-administration arch.

The picture which emerges from this essentially behavioral analysis is one of a multiplicity of bureaucratic forces and a formidable complex of situational limitations on the activities of each of these forces. It is not too farfetched to conclude from all this that power relationships among the constituent elements of the policy/administration arch tend to be in an equilibrium which reflects an optimum adjustment for all concerned. Who therefore has the ultimate power? Where does the *focus* and *locus* of responsibility lie in such a complex system of relationships? These are not easy questions to answer, but in the final section of this chapter we will posit some views on the matter, in light of recently published behavioral analyses on accountability in the higher ranks of the Canadian public service.

I. "Staff" and "Line" Theory and a Definition of Central Agencies

The concept of "central agencies," or "central machinery of government," or "centralized bureaucratic institutions" has been shrouded in ambiguity because of a lack of definitional clarity in the literature on Canadian public policy and administration. Some writers, like Humpty Dumpty, use the concept to mean exactly what they choose it to mean, nothing more nor less. In a word, no definition is given.[6] Others discard the term entirely using such descriptions as "single purpose centralized departments" in its place.[7] Yet others utilize the concept but then proceed to exclude organizational units generally presumed by many to be "central agencies."[8]

While it is not our intention to get the reader embroiled in this semantic confusion, it is, nevertheless, important to realize that this ambiguity is not intentionally created. The organizational design and purpose embodied in the concept of "central agencies" lies at the heart of such notions as "staff" and "line" and "span of control"—notions whose theoretical inadequacies became the major catalyst leading to the critical reassessment of the whole corpus of early organization theory. To this date the dust from this debate has not entirely settled.

It is therefore important that we should give some consideration to the theory of "staff" and "line" and "span of control" in our discussion of the role of central agencies in the Canadian federal bureaucracy. In defining the principles of sound scientific management, students of organization theory in the 1920s and 30s were very much preoccupied with logical and precise modes of organizing. It is instructive to follow the logical procedures involved. The first step in the process of organizing involves a definition of the objectives of the proposed organization, and having thus defined the objectives, the next task is to isolate the functions to be performed to achieve them. These functions are then divided into their component activities, which are then grouped into operational units according to a classification emphasizing the following categories of allocation: (1) a common purpose, (2) clientele, (3) location, (4) skill or profession, or (5) the use of common facilities or matériel. [9] The choice of which allocation to use depends on the nature of the organization and its objectives, but it should be such so as to promote efficiency and better coordination. The reader should note that this general classification is still considered to be useful by organization theorists, and is frequently used today for taxonomic purposes in organizational study. [10]

The next task is a definition of duties to be performed and by whom. In scientific management theory this is known as position classification and job description, and is a complex specialty in organization. [11] Finally, the grouping of activities are tied together horizontally and vertically through authority relationships. Sitting astride this whole logical edifice are the so-called elements of administration: *planning, organization, command, coordination* and *control.* As already mentioned in Chapter Five, it was the French industrialist, Henri Fayol, who first outlined and developed these elements in the theoretical literature. Luther Gulick's famous elaboration of Fayol's five elements became known in the literature as PODSCORB, a verbal artifact made up of the initial letters of the elements:

1 Planning, that is working out in broad outline the things that need to be done and the methods for doing them to accomplish the purpose set for the enterprise;

2 Organizing, namely the establishment of the formal structure of

authority through which work subdivisions are arranged, defined
and coordinated for the defined objective;

3 Directing, that is the continuous task of making decisions and em-
bodying them in specific and general orders and instructions and
serving as the leader of the enterprise;

4 Staffing, which covers the whole personnel function of bringing in
and training the staff and maintaining favorable conditions of
work;

5 Coordinating, which encompasses the all-important duty of inter-
relating the various parts of the work;

6 Reporting, which involves keeping those to whom the executive is
responsible informed as to what is going on, which thus includes
being informed and keeping subordinates informed through records, research and inspection;

7 Budgeting, with all that goes with budgeting in the form of fiscal
planning, accounting and control.[12]

There is a subdivision of work in these administrative elements.
Conceptually, all of the above functions represent the scope of the
manager's day-to-day activities: budgeting, directing, coordinating
and so on are all concerns of the job. Nevertheless, the deputy minister or chief executive officer cannot perform all these functions
alone: help is needed in the form of staff and line organizations. Line
places emphasis on ranks in the organization, and is considered to be
in the front line of duty, so to speak, having full authority over the
production processes of the organization. Staff directs attention to
specialization, and personnel engaged in this type of activity usually
function in a research or advisory capacity, furnishing specialized and
technical advice to the appropriate line officials in the organizational
hierarchy. In other words, staff activities are auxiliary in that they are
supportive or advisory in nature. Gulick himself contributed to this
functional conception of staff and line expertise when he argued that
the task of staff experts is to "devote their time exclusively to the
knowing, thinking and planning functions." They must achieve results only by persuasion, by the "authority of ideas" and must not be
given administrative authority or responsibility.[13]

The fluid nature of social relationships defy water-tight definitions,
and even the formulators of these scientific management principles
could not brush aside the obvious variations and exceptions in reality
to these laws. Some writers argued that line and staff are distinguished not by *function*, as Gulick posited, but by their *authority relationships* to the central executive. Positions concerned with the main
operations of the organization and within the direct chain of com-

mand are part of the line hierarchy. Those concerned with auxiliary services and outside the direct chain of command are part of the staff hierarchy. Line authority is the direct relationship between superior and subordinate while staff is auxiliary. As one exponent puts it, "staff assists, counsel and advises the line executive but has no direct authority over any portions of the organization except the immediate subordinate within the staff department."[14]

Gulick's later writings made concessions to this point of view when he wrote of "general staff" as opposed to "special staff." General staff is distinguished by their *authority* to assume such functions of the executive as control, command and coordination. The semantic confusion and ersatz complexity of a "simple" division of organizational labor became more and more glaring. For example, consider the complexity of this discussion of "staff" and "line" functions:

> Just as there can be line within staff, so there can be staff within line. And to further indicate the elaborate requirements to which the line-staff concept is sometimes subject, a line function within a staff group may in turn be supported by its own staff services.[15]

Considerations for the shape of the hierarchical pyramid to effect better control of organizational activities also received attention by the theorists. Originally the notion of "span of control" was developed as a practical principle to guide line managers as to how many subordinates they can effectively control. In their search for "scientific principles" however, the exponents of "span of control" soon elevated it to a mathematical principle. The French management consultant V. A. Graicunas produced a formula which purported to show that the maximum number of an efficient span is "possibly five or most probably four" individuals. This formula assumed that the manager's difficulty in ensuring control arises from the need to maintain contact not only with all his or her subordinates, but also all their subordinates, and with the mutual relationships of all these people.[16]

We have come a long way from these earlier assertions. Subjected to empirical testings over the years, the concepts of "line" and "staff" and "span of control" were at first ridiculed, then rejected, subsequently resurrected, and in today's literature it is fair to say that they are used as good rule-of-thumb indices for organizational structuring.[17] It is instructive to note one aspect of the debate which has direct relevance for us in this chapter. The reader will recall that the contribution of March and Simon to organization theory had revolved around the concepts of *power* and *control*. Power is expressed quite simply as a manifest or latent ability to control the organizational set-ting, aspects of uncertainty which are forever present in the environ-ment. Organizations are therefore one form of a system of power whose major components are really vectors of power that contribute to or inhibit tasks performance.

If this conception is accepted, the whole notion of organizational dynamics takes on a complex fluid nature: *the relative contributions of various activities are too variable over time and over different situations to accord an organizational inferiority or superiority to any activity.* This is a central point which we will emphasize and illustrate throughout this chapter and in other chapters of this book. Thus, the architectonics of organizations are much more than simply technical in character. It is, as one student puts it, "a network of power" in which all units of an organization are represented.[18] Under such conditions, another stu-dent concluded, "no organization structure can ever be considered as final."[19] The basic skeleton might remain the same, but the organs are all subject to change in a dynamic environment. H. A. Simon, one of the leaders in criticizing the old "scientific" notions, argued that such principles which attempt to describe "the one best way" of organiz-ing are, in reality, proverbs which "attempt to prove too much."[20]

But the heady analytical concepts of power, influence, authority and so on also contain some inherent dangers. A preoccupation with these concepts to the exclusion of other important considerations can easily lead to the ignoring of structural or organizational constraints, so vital in attempting to understand *how, under what circumstances* and *when* power is exercised within an organization. When the flood of literature critical of the orthodox line/staff relationships became a tidal wave,[21] Simon felt constrained to warn his intellectual protégés that "an overreaction from the excessive emphasis on formal organi-zation in the work on organization theory has led, in the last two decades, to an equally serious neglect of the importance of attitudes toward legitimacy." Formal structures, Simon continued, oftentimes significantly influence the nature of informal structures. Implicit in his warning is the assumption that proper formal structure can ac-commodate healthy, adaptive behavior of people within organiza-tions.[22] In other words, such concepts as "line" and "staff" may in-deed have some redemptive value, so please do not "throw out the baby with the bath water."

For the most part, much of the critical analysis and reevaluation of "line" and "staff" and "span of control" was buttressed by some rather keen observations at the practical level. More specifically, the American theorists had an actual "living laboratory" in "the institu-tionalized Presidency" since it was the Brownlow Committee, created by the President at that time, Franklin Delano Roosevelt, which popularized PODSCORB, "staff" and "line," and "span of control" concepts in American public administration.[23] *The establishment of the Executive Office of the President was a direct result of the recommendations of this Committee, instituting the concept of "staff agencies" at the highest level of governmental authority.* "The President needs help," was the cryptic conclusion of the Brownlow Committee after surveying the awesome administrative responsibilities heaped on the shoulders of the chief executive of the United States.

However, it was not too long before the staff agencies obtained their "baptism in fire" in the political arena. Congress and agencies of the federal government soon realized that the "staff" functions of the Executive Office were highly political, and the President's staff agencies, while providing administrative support for many presidential functions, had the excellent capacity to be used as a control lever on the other arms of government, particularly the administrative and the legislative. Even Committee Chairman Brownlow had to subsequently admit that his Committee's value lay in strengthening the President's will and not in the putting into place of rationalized administrative procedures.[24]

Thus the growth of the institutionalized Presidency has come to be viewed as one manifestation of the continuing and interminable struggle to achieve political dominance between Congress and the President, and the concept of staff played an important role in this evolution.[25] A distinguishing characteristic of all central agencies is this ultimate control function. The growth of "staff" agencies around the Canadian Prime Minister has been viewed by some in analogous fashion, and there has been considerable debate both in the popular and academic literature as to the nature of this growth. There is, however, no doubt that the 1968-69 restructuring of the Prime Minister/ Privy Council Offices was an exercise aimed at achieving more effective executive control. Whether this control can be so easily achieved by executive fiat in a complex, dynamic bureaucratic environment is another matter, a question to which we will return in the last section of this chapter.

Theory, according to scientific management, had dictated one set of principles, but practice, in a very political environment, had markedly qualified the rationalized administrative arrangements derived from these principles. How then can central agencies be characterized? *It is quite evident that these bureaucratic bodies perform very essential, auxiliary or supportive functions for the executive.* Furthermore most central agencies are distinguished by the fact that they are not burdened by functional responsibilities in the form of government programs to be administered.[26] But we remain essentially Weberian by not forgetting a central insight given to us by him, namely that bureaucracy's essential function is to achieve control over its environment. Thus we maintain that another major distinguishing characteristic of central agencies is, *their service-wide control functions.*[27]

But a basic distinction (or qualification) about control should be made. One should not infer that the control function of central agencies means a continuous dictating, in Kafka-like style, to the departments, regulatory boards and other agencies of government. The argument about central agencies/departmental relationships put forward in this chapter rejects this "ride saddle" argument. There is a need to differentiate between different concepts of command hierarchy to make our point clear.[28] There are times when a "positive hierarchy" is in operation: goals are clearly and successfully articulated from the cabinet or cabinet committees' deliberations, and firm instructions move down the hierarchy. In other instances articulation of goals is not that clear or they are formulated at the departmental level (because of the department's statutory responsibilities for this formulation). In such instances central agencies may not actively dictate policy. But when called upon to synchronize overall governmental policy central agencies perform a "negative hierarchical function" by colliding on occasions with departmental points of view leaving the final resolution of the conflict to cabinet. On other occasions central control agencies may be called upon to mitigate intradepartmental conflict by "coordinating" overlapping functional responsibilities. Thus it is helpful to view these control functions along a continuum, with the function of "coordination" at one end (the task of mitigating real or potential conflict among units of the bureaucracy), to the utilization of naked coercion at the other (mandatory budget cutting or the strict enforcement of executive directives). In between, of course, one can find a whole series of combinations to fit the situation of the moment.

Finally, it should be noted that *service-wide control functions are necessary but not sufficient conditions* to make organizational units into central agencies. *The powers of central agencies must be continuously reinforced by the legitimate executive power in the system.* The executive must clearly and continuously signal that named central agencies do in fact have coercive clout if and when such clout must be swung into use. In Canada we have seen central agencies armed with impressive statutory powers being slowly deprived of such despite their clearly mandated control and service-wide allocative functions. This has been the position of the Public Service Commission, certainly between 1918 and 1968, and recent analyses point to the same phenomenon in regard to the Department of Finance. In recent times we have also been treated to the interesting spectacle of the Department of External Affairs laying public claim to central agency status. This "power jostling" for agency status is made clear from the following quote from a speech made by the Department's Under-Secretary.

Within the government there are a few departments and agencies which have traditionally been regarded as central agencies . . . Perhaps less appreciated is the fact that External Affairs falls into this category. It is part of my purpose to ensure that this is understood and that the Department acts accordingly . . . *Central agencies not only coordinate and consult, they lead on key issues of national policy* . . . The Government considers the Department of External Affairs to be a central agency because *it has a responsibility to provide other departments with coherent policy and priority guidance* covering the full range of Canada's international relations . . . To do this effectively the Department must exercise both day-to-day and long term influence over the balance and direction of other departments' international activities.[29]

These words speak for themselves. "Coordinate", "consult" but "lead", and having "responsibility for . . . coherent policy and priority guidance" are diplomatic euphemisms for the concepts of "power and control" within the bureaucratic environment. What then is our working definition of central agencies? Central agencies are organizations which provide *service-wide facilitative and control roles* in government. However these roles are necessary but not sufficient conditions for these agencies to perform their central functions. They must also be forearmed with *continuous sustaining power and influence derived from the political executive, the cabinet.**

II. Central Agencies and the Canadian Cabinet System

The first feature of notable importance of Canadian central agencies is that almost all of them were initially created as, what Gulick calls, "special staff" agencies: they have all performed for lengthy periods

---

* *It is fascinating to watch the dynamics of bureaucratic power being displayed in the creation, during 1980-81, of two second generation ministries of state. (See Chapter Eleven for a more detailed look at the ministry of state concept). Both the Ministry of State for Social Development and the Ministry of State for Economic Development have been created to provide "service wide facilitative and control roles"* in these two areas of public policy. But it is their growing legitimacy which is interesting to watch: both are headed by powerful Ottawa mandarins; both are staffed by a small, carefully selected group of experts; and both have been designated as secretariats of important sub-committees of the federal cabinet. Are we in the process of witnessing the creation of two new central agencies? This is a process which only time will resolve.*

of their history, instrumental auxiliary roles in the service of the cabinet, departments and agencies of the government.[29] Why has this been the case?

In Canada the long struggle to control the power of the purse was effectively won by the political executive during the nineteenth century, but remnants of that battle still remained as the executive, in turn, sought to ensure that its financial prerogatives were safely secured. A good example of this continuing zealous guarding of prerogatives is the resistance of any government in our system to the introduction of money bills in Parliament that were not initiated by itself.

The continuing fray between Parliament and the executive should not mask the fact, however, that the executive was also engaged in consolidating its power over the bureaucracy. Hence the Civil Service Commission, the forerunner to the present Public Service Commission, was essentially a service agency to departments between 1880 and 1918. In 1918 it was reconstituted, with extensive service-wide control functions, to ensure executive control of staffing in the federal bureaucracy.[30] Next on the agenda was the "remodelling and refurbishing" of the Treasury Board and the Department of Finance during the Depression of the 1930s to enable both to effectively apply financial controls to growing governmental expenditures.[31] And finally, we have witnessed in the last decade the substantial remodelling of the cabinet committee system and the PMO/PCO complex, ostensibly to give the Prime Minister and the cabinet more effective control of the decision-making processes of the federal government.[32]

In all three examples (Finance, Treasury Board, and the PMO/PCO complex) the initial service functions were heavily supplemented by control powers to be exercised on the bureaucracy. Thus, a hall-mark of Canadian public administration has been the turning of specialized service units into service-wide control devices, or central agencies. And in each case these institutions were initially introduced in the Canadian environment, patterned after what the modellers thought were British models of "staff services" in administration.

But to argue that this control was fashioned for the aggrandizement of Prime Ministerial power alone would be to grossly misrepresent the style of administrative control which is the hallmark of a cabinet system as compared with a presidential system of government. In all cases control has been exercised in the name of the *collective responsibility of the cabinet,* and not as the instrument of a supreme political authority figure. In other words, the lines of control have been horizontal rather than vertical, ensuring the imposition of a collective discipline upon a group of parallel departments. This collegial principle is a crucial distinction in Canadian government, for it enables ministers to collectively have responsibility for public policy. Though it seems farfetched to blame, say, the Minister of Veterans Affairs for bad policy-making in agriculture, this convention provides for the continuation of the notion of legitimate collective responsibility to the electorate. As part of the government of the day the Minister of Veterans Affairs must take responsibility for the policies of Government whether it be in fisheries, health, communications or any public policy field. This is a central theoretical pillar of our system of government.

But even the collegiality principle which seeks to center power in the collective hands of the cabinet has some limitations. A government cannot effect reforms by pleading the collegiality principle and then *appearing to flagrantly violate* those principles when the reforms are put into practice. Thus the Trudeau government was forced to practically abandon the concept of regional desks in the PMO, because many within the Liberal party viewed them as undermining "the traditional representative role of Parliament, party and Cabinet."[33] Both politicians and bureaucrats in central agencies have been particularly sensitive to the criticisms of aggrandizement of power: the image of being identified as "Kafka's castle incarnate" does not appeal to them. As a consequence, growth of central agencies is usually restricted, and any evolution of their bureaucratic structures is accomplished with a minimum of fanfare.[34]

Moreover, personnel growth in many of these central agencies is usually instrumental in character, that is, growth usually takes place in the support services categories.[35] Irvine and Simeon have pointed out that much of the growth of the PMO since 1968 has occurred in those areas providing logistical support services to the Prime Minister. As an example the Correspondence Section of the office accounts for more than half of the growth: public servants such as file clerks, messengers and correspondence analysts have been hired to service the heavy volume of mail addressed to the Prime Minister. On the average the volume of this mail is about 120,000 letters per year. Irvine and Simeon present an image of an efficient machine-like organization for this section of the PMO which accounts for most of its growth. When one compares this highly efficient organization with the same office during the Pearson years "it seems clear the volume of mail was less, the staff much smaller, and both the analysis and the answering of mail much more haphazard: 'a shambles,' one staffer put it."[36]

It also seems clear that at the cabinet and cabinet committee levels the "new" techniques of cybernetics and systems analysis have done much to introduce certain structural and procedural adaptations to technological progress. It is almost a truism to state that government has become more complex and this complexity has been, in part, due to the demands of the welfare state. But the concrete nature of this growth can only be gauged by assessing the volume of work large government has placed on the shoulders of the political executive who, in the final analysis, bears the full responsibility for it all. In 1969 Donald S. Macdonald, government house leader at the time, revealed in the House of Commons the volume of work covered by the cabinet and cabinet committee system in a one-year period: between July 1, 1968 and June 30, 1969, for example, the full cabinet met 70 times, cabinet committees had met 378 times, and 1,315 cabinet documents had been considered in all.

Now we need not stress here that no amount of cybernetics or other new-fangled techniques can eliminate the serious problems of reconciling this large, almost impossible, volume of work with the capacities and other limitations of the ordinary human being. Cabinet ministers and their colleagues are not super humans: apart from attending cabinet meetings they are additionally responsible in law and in political reality for large complex departments, attending to the needs of their constituency, daily attendance in the House of Commons when in session, general "fence mending" for their government (speeches to luncheon clubs etc. throughout the country), and last, but by no means least, taking care of their families.

Structural changes at the apex or fulcrum of power have sought to give more order to the decision processes so as to give Ministers more time for their other duties and preoccupations and, as well, to ensure meaningful participation when they do meet in cabinet or in cabinet committees. The literature we have cited here points to some significant substantive and procedural changes which may be in the process of revolutionizing the cabinet decision-making process. From accounts that we have, cabinet meetings in the era of Mackenzie King,[37] St. Laurent and Pearson,[38] were more or less informal gatherings, sometimes without a fixed agenda, and, particularly in the eras of King and St. Laurent, dictated almost wholly by the whims of the prime minister.

With the advent of Pierre Elliott Trudeau, substantive changes have occurred in cabinet procedures which indicate that full cabinet, or even the Prime Minister acting alone on behalf of the cabinet, must share power with other principal decision-making structures in Ottawa. This situation might undoubtedly change in a crisis when the Prime Minister may or may not have to act alone, but on a day-to-day ongoing basis power is much more dispersed at the apex.[39] We briefly summarize these significant developments which have so widely been described in the academic literature:

1 The shortlived Clark administration created a formal inner cabinet structure of five major subcommittees of cabinet, each having the responsibility for establishing overall expenditure limits and allocating resources among policy sectors in accordance with the overall policy objectives of the government. The cabinet system is therefore composed of a series of functional committees which are in turn grouped in an "envelope" system of five policy sectors. Each cabinet committee has the power to discuss and make appropriate recommendations on its policy responsibilities, but this must be done within the financial and resource limits set by the inner cabinet.[40]

2 Cabinet leadership has been divided and has become more specialized by the appointment of regular committee chairmen (members of the cabinet), who exercise, within their terms of reference, powers similar to the prime minister.[41]

3 These committees have formal agendas, documents issued beforehand for study and perusal, and regularized procedures. Senior civil servants are required to attend, including senior members of Treasury Board, Finance, PMO/PCO/FPRO or any of the central agencies or departments summoned to do so. There senior government officials express their views freely in verbal exchanges with ministers and other civil service mandarins. As Gordon Robertson puts it, "It is *a blending of roles* that requires mutual confidence and an awareness of their differences. The seasoned public servant will recognize that what are at issue are the policies of the government, to be decided by the judgment of the ministers, even though this means accepting gracefully decisions that may be personally distasteful."[42] And D. R. Yeomans concurs when he points out that the division of authority between the minister and his senior departmental officials "cannot be precisely defined since it depends in large measure, on a working arrangement forged out of good faith and mutual confidence."[43]

4 Many aspects of functional specialization have been moved upwards from interdepartmental committees of officials and even from cabinet committees to reside in committee structures designed to fashion overall policy. For example, aspects of broad policy direction in financial and economic matters have been removed from Treasury Board and even from the jurisdiction of the Department of Finance and placed under the aegis of the Committee of Priorities and Planning which is chaired by the Prime Minister. What is now recognized

is that in times of crisis or other emergency situations, this committee, or even the Prime Minister himself as *primus inter pares* or chairman of the board can assume the full reins of power and responsibility in the system, aided and abetted by his staff in both the PMO and PCO. As the *Financial Post* of August 19, 1978 noted somewhat dryly, this realization "raises the bizarre prospect that tax changes will be pinpointed, proposed and designed not by Department of Finance but by the political advisers" (in the PMO and PCO).[44]

Though somewhat exaggerated, the *Post* makes a significant point in indicating how fluid the structural processes of decision-making could be. Cabinet and its reformed committee structures have not solved the information-processing dilemma entirely. There are still serious limitations in expediting policy recommendations and proposals. The cabinet system can act deliberately on only some of the matters which come before it each year, and much must be left to the bureaucracies in central agencies and departments. But there is no matter, however large or small, to which Cabinet cannot direct its attention if that matter comes to the "top of the agenda," so to speak. Hence there is no public policy subject that is "in principle" exempt from political or for that matter prime ministerial control. Normally, the Prime Minister would leave detailed economic matters to the Department of Finance and the Treasury Board Secretariat to propose and dispose. In a period when decisive economic decision-making is imperative he may single-handedly change the machinery of government to reflect an image of government which is both decisive and reasoned in strategy.

5 In this "rationalizing process" there are some definite "flies in the ointment," so to speak. Greater decisional effectiveness cannot be realized without paying a price. As Szablowski has argued, "ministerial relationships characterized by collegiality and transactional ties are likely to change into a pattern resembling bureaucracy."[45] If ministers and their bureaucratic officials are now required to emphasize the interconnectedness of policies and programs, this inevitably enhances the potential for achieving the objectives of one agency through the policies and programs administered by another agency. This free flow of information and awareness of interconnectedness means that an agency can "devise ways of influencing other agencies so that they will add, subtract or modify activities in a way they would not do if they were left to pursue none other than their own sectoral goals."[46] Usually a healthy skeptic of bureaucratic processes, Herb Laframboise recognizes, however, that because of the fundamental structural reforms which inaugurated this process *"program*

bending," although "changing in form perhaps, and varying in intensity is certainly here to stay."[47]

But there is another fundamental point. The euphoria of "discovering" the practical consequences of these recondite theoretical tools may have been too premature. Perhaps too much was expected, in 1968-69, of cybernetics and systems engineering. The experts made much ado about hierarchical controls flowing from political executive to bureaucracy and beyond.[48] What we may have in effect realized is a system which has been further bureaucratized (in the formalized "rational" Weberian sense), and which in turn emphasizes collegiality, efficiency in decision-making, and a dispersal of powers which heretofore resided solely in the person of the Prime Minister. We have thus sketched, in broad brush outlines, a picture of the very top of government, but what does the average public servant make of all this? How, for example, is the relationship between "we" (the particular department or agency) and "they" (the central agency, be it Treasury Board or the PCO or any other) perceived? First of all, very few public servants, if indeed any, would subscribe to the pristine theoretical notion that central agencies are "staff" and departments can be categorized as "line." Indeed they can point, with some justification, to the concrete reality that Treasury Board is management by legislative fiat,[49] and, as such, the staff/line conception simply does not stand up to the realities of bureaucratic life. Moreover, in times of crisis management, it is widely reported that the Privy Council Office assumes the "reins of command" with the Secretary to the Cabinet, the most important civil servant in the land, taking the helm.[50] Central agencies are therefore collectively portrayed as "Kafka's Castle":

. . . the apparent if unknown source of authority which governs the village (the Public Service)—remote, mysterious, all-powerful, beyond comprehension in terms both of reason and judgment, and above all beyond the reach let alone the influence, of the ordinary mortals governed by [them]. The public servants in turn have been the citizens of the village: performing their daily task in the shadow of the Castle . . . —obeying [their] rules without reason or recourse, abiding by [their] decisions with resignation, and above all accepting [their] authority without question.[51]

How valid is this portrayal of bureaucratic life along the arch? Do we indeed have a situation of bureaucratic hegemony which the Chinese so graphically call "mountain-top stronghold mentality"? Are there any variations on this theme which might give a more realistic portrayal of central agencies-departmental relationships?

III. Central Agencies/Departmental Relationships: An Interactive Process[52]

(i) A Conception of the Process

"The lifeblood of administration is power. Its attainment, maintenance, increase, dissipation and loss are subjects the practitioner and student can ill-afford to neglect."[53] This opinion about the way bureaucracy interacts with its component parts was written over three decades ago. Students of public policy and administration over that time have done much to reaffirm this view of bureaucracy as more than mere instrument and Caliban.

What has not been emphasized in the literature until recently is that this fourth branch of government is no monolith, and that to "understand" bureaucracy one needs to conceptualize over time the *political* and *organizational* system from which policy emerges, and the fluid environment in which the system operates. As one author recently reminded us:

A public service system contains a large number of institutions which can be analysed according to the underlying values which colour their work, the client groups to whom they relate, and the institutional artifacts which sustain them.[54]

Let us pause for a moment and elaborate on the meaning of this quotation. The various components of the bureaucratic phenomenon (departments, regulatory bodies, commissions, boards and agencies), are not just passive pawns in the game of politics which swirl around them and affect their daily organizational lives. The bureaucracy's personnel are active participants in the power-sharing in their environments, interacting among themselves and others (politicians and interest groups) to preserve the integrity and enhance the smooth running of the bureaucratic component to which they belong.

Experienced bureaucrats are also very adept at applying various techniques to ensure their own preservation. At stake can be such considerations as job preservation, reputation and professional status which may be tied to programs or departments, commitment and even organizational loyalty. Bureaucrats cultivate their allies within the larger bureaucracy, leak selected bits of information to the mass media, and even strike bargains with those organizational foes they cannot hope to whip into submission.

It should therefore come as no surprise to find that central agencies/departmental relationships bear much, if not all, the characteristics enumerated above. To quote a former deputy minister of Finance, Mr. Simon Reisman, about his experience in the last ten years:

> For a while new programs were coming in so fast we felt like a pair of goalies trying to bat them away. Sure a lot went by. But we won on the big one—the social welfare legislation that Marc Lalonde and his deputy [Al Johnson,] were pushing. That was a multi-million dollar program and we really went to the trenches on that one.[55]

A glimpse of relationships such as this forces us to place emphasis on the fact that for those who participate in government at this level, the terms of daily employment cannot be ignored: as was pointed out in Chapter Seven political and bureaucratic leaders have competitive, not homogeneous, interests; priorities and perceptions are largely shaped by positions; problems are much more varied than straightforward, strategic issues; the management of piecemeal streams of decisions is more important than steady state choices; making sure that the government does what is decided—and does not do what has not been directed—is more difficult than selecting the preferred solution.

Therefore, while it would be false to depict all actors (cabinet and senior public servants, for instance) as equal, because this would misrepresent both constitutional and political reality, it nevertheless remains true that power is always *relational* and *relative*. Thus, an actor by himself is not powerful or weak; he may be powerful in relation to some actors in regard to some matters, and weak in relation to others on other matters. Thus Reisman's view of winning some and losing others becomes quickly evident in the political and bureaucratic relationships among departments and agencies, and between levels of government.

Because there is a plurality of political and bureaucratic goals, and a scarcity of instruments, it follows that actors will tend to resist other actors in the sense of hampering each other's actions. However, this hampering should not be construed as a constant prevailing mode of relationship. Day-to-day life in the bureaucracy is not total warfare: if this were so absolutely everything would be immobilized. The legitimacy of the environment is not open to question: actors therefore share many goals in common and attempt to work out a set of priorities and establish a pattern of allocation of scarce instruments. Cooperation is therefore institutionalized and encouraged. Power and cooperation are thus not a mutually exclusive pair of concepts: cooperation often has a power base, and power is exercised through cooperation. Power to make decisions is therefore visualized as a series of concentric circles: diffused among the legitimate institutions, each acting on and reacting to one another. The result is that although we have powerful loci of decision-making within the institutions of government, this power can, from time to time, be constrained by societal values: actors restrain the use of power under certain circumstances because elites as well as followers *believe* they ought not to use whatever power they command in every situation.[56]

Put another way, political power in the bureaucracy is not a zero-sum game. Power, as Carl Friedrich reminded us many years ago, is like the two faces of Janus: while the Prime Minister and his political and administrative advisers do exercise power and influence, they do so in relationship to others who exert considerable influence on them in return. Consequently, even the Prime Minister cannot hope to be effective if he fails to anticipate the reaction of his closest colleagues. On substantive issues he and his advisers must guide the cabinet and cabinet subcommittees towards a policy path which avoids a coalition of hostile interests capable of blocking government initiatives. No prime minister or policy adviser can embark on a new policy direction without securing the loyalty of his followers and anticipating obstacles in the legislative system. As A. W. Johnson puts it, the act of governing after all ". . . is a process of reconciling, of harmonizing, of choosing between conflicting social values and goals and objectives. This, perhaps, is its ineluctable attraction, both to politicians and to public servants!"[57]

Another example of this relational aspect of power is in order. It is almost trite to say that the political resources at the fingertips of the Prime Minister, or the executive acting as a collectivity, are potentially extensive: the constitutional prerogatives to introduce legislation, spend money, and make order-in-council appointments are among the most important of these assets. But the importance of this collegial body is not derived from the exercise of these assets in isolation. The executive's greatest trump card, for instance, stems from its ability to command at will *the maximum possible amount of intelligence about the political environment,* and to use this resource in persuading or commanding political and administrative actors to follow policy initiatives.

But to show how relational this process is, it must be readily apparent that even that "maximum" amount of intelligence can proscribe ministerial power. To the extent that certain types of intelligence are gathered and proffered and others are not, implies that there is power in the hands of the intelligence gatherer (that is, the administrators down the line). As E. E. Schattschneider puts it:

All forms of political organization have a bias in favor of the exploitation of some kinds of conflict and the suppression of others because *organization is the mobilization of bias*. Some issues are organized into politics while others are organized out.[58]

And in a somewhat exaggerated illustration the Hon. R. H. S. Crossman of Great Britain sums up his ministerial predicament:

My minister's room is like a padded cell and in certain ways I am like a lunatic, cut off from real life and surrounded by male and female trained nurses and attendants . . . they make sure I behave right and the other person behaves right, and they know how to handle me.[59]

In short, an understanding of decision-making at the politico-administrative levels must take into full consideration the actors involved, and the *organizational* and *political* constraints within which they perform.

Finally, the interactive paradigm recognizes some of the major difficulties which exist in the interaction process among the members of the bureaucracy, politicians and the general public. Because of shortcomings in their interests and information, all individuals in a liberal democratic system require some organized intermediary between themselves and those who formulate and influence the making of public policy. *This concept of the intermediary acting as a buffer between government and individual citizen is the cornerstone of liberal democracy.* On occasion, the mass media have added significantly to the public's information about a social problem or a public policy, and have generated strong pressures on policymakers in their role as intermediaries between citizen and government.

However, the media suffers from some of the same problems as individuals. They have other functions that distract them from the role of political intermediary. Commercial and recreational functions consume many resources which might otherwise be employed in politics. Also citizens "protect" themselves from mass media just as they protect themselves from other involvements in politics. Many people do not consume the political news and editorials which the media provide.

Interaction between interest groups and the bureaucracy is nebulous and is extremely difficult to define and document precisely. First of all, the status of lobbying is ambiguous, and many bureaucrats take a guarded position both in their dealings with interest groups and in talking about their interaction with them. This aspect of confidentiality is crucial. As A. Paul Pross observes: "It is this capacity of the executive-administrative arm of government to define the terms of its relationships with pressure groups and other segments of the political communications system that constitutes the critical element in the policy equation. . . ."[60] We will return to the interaction of pressure groups and the bureaucracy in Chapter Thirteen.

(ii) Some Illustrations of the Process in Operation

When this interactive process is applied to central agencies/ departmental relationships, some observations become readily apparent. From what we have already written it should come as no surprise to the reader that departmental officials cannot be that easily excluded or dominated by actors from the central agencies of the federal government. In fact central agencies may be in a far weaker position than is usually purported.

In the first place, while much has been made about the growth in the size of the central agencies, the disproportionate distribution of manpower resources between central agencies and the operating departments must be recognized. As an illustration let us take the current concern about financial administration and control in the federal government. Lamenting the lack of sufficient central control on governmental expenditures, the Auditor General has argued that while there has been a more than five-fold increase in the level of federal government budgetary expenditures, there has been a relatively small proportion of resources and man-years devoted specifically to financial administration policy and evaluation in the Treasury Board (8 man-years in 1972; 10 in 1973; 10 in 1974; 15 in 1975; and 35 in 1976.[61]

More often than not, in the majority of central agencies staff are "overburdened and overextended with responsibilities." As an illustration of this consider the activities of the Federal-Provincial Relations Office (FPRO), the latest in the federal government's central agencies. This example is not atypical, because some evidence exists to indicate that the lack of adequate staff has been a recurrent problem due to a deliberate policy to keep such agencies as small as possible.[62] An officer in charge of an "operating desk" in FPRO is responsible for monitoring not only three or four departments, but also several provinces.[63] The result is that the officer is not only very busy in simply trying to fulfill daily responsibilities, but his or her knowledge is extremely general because of constant "brush fire" activity or day-to-day routine. It is no accident that most junior and middle-level officers transferring from the central agencies usually opt for a functional area of expertise where in time they can become specialists. Much the same situation applies in the case of the Privy Council Office. Thus, while these officers may be appreciated for their show of versatility and working "hard not to be encumbered by program responsibility," and while it is correct that they leave the central agencies "with an intimate appreciation of the central decision-making process and the working of the total system,"[64] it is nevertheless true that they depart from the central agencies with a strong appreciation of the staying power of functional expertise.

In government, the complexity of most issues requires reliance on specialists. Such specialists are primarily found in the operating departments where they are of course actively engaged in both the inter- and intra-governmental policy formation processes. "Versatility" and a "general appreciation of the total system" are more often than not acknowledged to be no match for functional expertise when specific policy issues are involved.

It is in the interactions between central agencies and operating departments that such assets as manpower resources, functional responsibility for statutory programs, and expertise become extremely important. As Schultz has pointed out, functional responsibility for statutory programs ensures that

departments are normally the initiators of the policy process, and because such tasks are initially and principally departmental responsibilities, the departments gain enormous leverage over the process. Departments are also the primary sources of policy alternatives, and because they ultimately must implement any program that emerges, these functions further ensure that departmental preferences will be accorded due respect.[65]

Indeed, the Auditor General suggests that in matters financial, the departments operate in an almost total politically controlled vacuum because of a lack of challenge to their authority from the central agencies.[66]

As mentioned earlier, the timing aspects of policy initiation can also be very crucial. Departments, while they must admit that at some point in the policy process central agencies will be involved, may work to ensure that at that point their position is given favored consideration. This can be done through the mobilization of certain strategic support before the central agencies are involved in the process or the imaginative exploitation of information, a flood of which central agencies may have neither the time nor the expertise to digest.[67]

Strategies adopted by departments to counter the attacks of central agencies and other departments are varied and ingenious. It involves, among others, the marshalling of public opinion, lobbies of allies, interdepartmental committees to influence and inform, staying close to the letter of the cabinet decision rather than the spirit in which it was made, and a host of other influential "levers." As H. L. Laframboise describes it:

Once it was recognized that interconnectedness and multiple objectives were becoming the order of the day, and that collegial, as opposed to sectoral decision-making was the dominant style of the federal Cabinet, the search for levers began. . . . These levers needed to serve two purposes. The first was to protect one's own turf from the program-benders of the other [departments]. The second was to provide the ammunition needed to bend the programs of those other [departments].[68]

In this strategic flow of information and influence central agencies are, of course, not without their own assets as well. Being located near to the Prime Minister, or his chief ministers, surrounded by the aura of his office, and the ability to "obtain his ear" when it is a question of vital stakes, are assets not to be dismissed lightly. Also specialists can at times become so bogged down in the mire of their specialties that there is a failure to see the forest for the trees. Being in the vantage point of recognizing the interconnectedness of much policy, and having the power to inform and to withhold information from other actors gives central agencies tremendous leverage as well.

IV. The Ultimate Issue of Administrative Responsibility

In an address to the annual meeting of the Institute of Public Administration of Canada in 1975 Michael Pitfield declared that:

In matters of the administrative process [a technical problem] of enormous practical impact upon government occurs to me [namely], the question of the lines and standards of accountability that should apply to senior officials in a system which also requires the interplay of ministerial and collective responsibilities in a parliamentary forum . . .[69]

Given the multiplicity of bureaucratic and political forces which we have just described, how can a complex system of actors such as this be held to account? Given also the position of this interplay on the arch (at the fulcrum of the structure) there is no doubt that the *focus* of responsibility is at the ministerial level. A policy worked out for inflation and announced to the nation, or a constitutional proposal made to the provincial premiers are all policies of the government and the cabinet must therefore take full political responsibility for such. But, to return to our themes of Chapter Seven, where is the *locus* of responsibility? How is the answerability component of responsibility taken care of?

In the day-to-day administration of the government, answerability is composed of four elements present in varying degrees under different circumstances: resources, knowledge, purpose and choice.[70] As we have stated previously, answerability places a direct spotlight on behavioral realities. The senior officials at the fulcrum of the arch who act on behest of the cabinet or a minister in the daily running of the government have at their disposal human, institutional and material resources with which to get the job accomplished. They also have an explicit responsibility to a minister or cabinet committee to garner the best knowledge available for the policy proposals and options to be presented to the government. These officials have the capacity to muster purpose, commitment or resolution in the pursuit of the ends agreed upon at the bureaucratic level. Finally, they must choose and argue persuasively as policy advisors, why choices advocated are in the best interests of the government and of the nation. Almost every policy decision must run this gauntlet of both factual and normative considerations. Rowland Egger succinctly describes the position in which the senior official is placed:

. . . in performing one of his most important functions—that of rendering advice to constitutionallly responsible instrumentalities of government—the public official is directly involved in the formulation of legislative and executive policy itself. Eventually, the administrator finds his back to the wall, where he must consult his conscience and consider the gods he worships.[71]

What, to use the metaphor of Egger, are some of these gods? We have emphasized all along that liberal democratic societies have placed emphasis upon a *variety* of avenues of accountability—the prime minister, the collective executive, the courts and so on—and we have formalized many of the procedures and circumstances of accountability. But not every measure of accountability can be formalized. Liberal democracies have also placed emphasis on informal methods such as conscience or professionalism to supplement formal methods of accountability.

It should therefore come as no surprise that senior officials responsible for policy formulation and implementation would point to this multi-dimensionality of control methods when asked to whom they felt accountable. In interviews conducted for their analysis of the structure and behavior of central agencies Campbell and Szablowski found that respondents viewed their accountability in several different ways: staff, line, democratic and personal. Furthermore, many of these respondents named more than one type of responsibility. Thus, approximately fifty-three percent of their respondents view accountability partially in terms of staff responsibilities (they must provide best possible information and policy advice); another forty-four percent view it in terms of "classic line bureaucratic obligations to their immediate superior"; another twenty-six percent maintained that accountability meant that public servants must also hold themselves ultimately accountable to the Canadian public; and finally almost ten percent based their accountability on the personal qualities of a specific leader, usually the Prime Minister.[72]

The degree of multidimensionality becomes even clearer when a close examination of the various objects of accountability is made. Campbell and Szablowski report that thirty-three percent felt directly accountable to the Prime Minister, twenty-nine percent to the minister of their department, and thirty percent to the cabinet in a general collective responsibility sense. While thirty-five percent expressed some responsibility to the public, only ten percent felt directly responsible to the Canadian Parliament. Significantly Campbell and Szablowski add that ". . . the low proportion mentioning conscience [a mere one percent] probably indicates that bureaucrats prefer not to act on their own authority."[73]

Similarly the Royal Commission on Financial Management and Accountability uncovered much the same response to accountability amongst the senior officials in line departments. *Thus we have a classic example of behavior conditioned or affected by structure.* Liberal democracies have created and encouraged this behavioral response by instituting a variety of accountability measures over time. Moreover many commentators claim that this is the best way to handle the situation, that the bureaucrat must derive his/her responsibility from a multiplicity of sources—for differing purposes, to differing degrees, and in terms of differing though mutually complementary standards.[74]

But this is not satisfactory to everyone. Hodgetts finds that this multiplicity leads to a "fuzziness in, or even an absence of, a sense of accountability" and that we do have a real "problem of establishing appropriate accountability regimes for central agencies."[75] Essentially this is the same conclusion of Campbell and Szablowski. These principals therefore make structural recommendation which in their opinion would bring about a better synchronization of the locus and focus of responsibility in the administrative state.

Other commentators however argue that these recommendations

exhibit an excessive concern for measures to restrain bureaucrats. The emphasis is too much on restraining structure and not enough on creating situations to maintain and improve responsibility. Herbert J. Spiro, for example, argues that to create situations to maintain responsibility "is the imperative that should guide friends of constitutional and democratic government. For this purpose, and not just to restrain bureaucrats, they should be accountable." Spiro is particularly perceptive when he addresses himself to the questions: How should the senior official resolve conflicting claims of accountability? Which should take precedence? His categorical reply to these questions is worth quoting in full:

When conflicting claims of accountability arise, the person who exercises delegated responsibility should heed each of the different claimants only to the extent that he derives his resources, knowledge, choice and purpose from them (that is, specific answerability criteria), or to the extent of their special accountability for his decisions. Ultimately, however, all conflicts of this kind must be resolved in terms of answers and processes provided by the constitution, written or unwritten, and by its proper interpreters. The constitution *is* the structure of responsibility. It expresses the aims and purposes of the people organized as the constituent group. Accountability to it should override all other claims. Conflicts should therefore be decided on the basis of two criteria: First, the maintenance, improvement, or creation of situations of responsibility; and second, the preservation of the constitutional order itself.[76]

In the arguments of Hodgetts, Campbell, Szablowski, Spiro and others we still see shades of the Friedrich-Finer debate of the 1930s and 40s. There is still a tendency in the literature to emphasize either subjective or objective standards of responsibility. Obviously we have not heard the last word on this crucial subject for democratic governance. Spiro however emphasizes a point of view which those of us who are too preoccupied with rational machinery to achieve accountability should heed:

As soon as we admit the possibility that nonresponsible government *may be* more successful in the struggles of world politics, or *may be* more efficient or more rational in its operations, we admit also that constitutional democracy aims less at achieving success, or efficiency, or rationality, than at affording men the opportunity to take a hand in shaping their own individual and collective future.[77]

Conclusions

The approach used here highlights three fundamental factors in central agencies/departmental relationships: (i) the roles of power and influence, stressing the fluid nature of such assets, (ii) the role of ideological values held by the actors (the conception of the process as being legitimate, the mobilization of bias in information gathering), and (iii) the *political and organizational context* of public policy making.

If then our interactive-adversarial approach is to be believed, central agencies should be viewed more as providing one set of actors among many in the system of government who, rather than being in a position to constantly dictate to others, must "influence, bargain and persuade" their fellow bureaucrats. The dynamics of the public policy process call for a series of shifting roles and strategies which will change as the circumstances and issues change. Central agencies might therefore find themselves "going to the trenches," or they may be cast in the role of neutral coordinators smoothing over potential conflicts on ongoing policy areas, or they might find themselves openly taking positions in bureaucratic disputes. Indeed, central agencies may be called upon to play a multiplicity of roles ranging all the way from practising the fine arts of diplomacy to being cast in the image of ruthless enforcers or "bulls in a china shop."

We have reviewed rather briefly management theory which attempts to explain the interaction of political and bureaucratic actors at the fulcrum of power in the bureaucracy. Using as an illustration the experience of the United States government, we have attempted to show the inadequacy of this theory, particularly when it purports to deal with the *organizational, political* and *human* relationships at the top of the arch. In positing this interactive-adversarial approach we have liberally utilized the many insights provided for us by the behavioral or pragmatist writings mentioned in Chapters Five and Seven.

Finally we addressed ourselves to the question of accountability in such a fluid interactive environment. The reality of the heavy involvement of senior bureaucrats in the making of public policy has continued to keep the debate on administrative responsibility alive. Friedrich considers this conjunction of responsibility with an administrative staff as an enduring question in the history of Western bureaucracy. Constitutional government would be impossible without responsibility measures being in place. In the memorable words of Herman Finer, "The first commandment is, Subservience."[78] Thus most commentators agree on this criteria. Opinions however vary widely when the answerability question is posed: subservience exactly to whom, when and for what? This remains a compelling question for democratic government as we continue to confront the reality of the administrative state.

Will Rogers on Policy and Administration

[During World War I Will Rogers] put forward a suggestion for getting rid of the German submarine menace. "All we have to do is to heat up the Atlantic to two hundred and twelve degrees fahrenheit. Then the submarines will have to surface and we can pick them off one by one. Now some damn fool is going to want to know how to warm up that ocean. Well, I am not going to worry about that. It is a mere matter of detail, and I am a policymaker."

Footnotes

1. G. Bruce Doern and Peter C. Aucoin, eds., *The Structure of Policy-Making in Canada* (Toronto: Macmillan Company of Canada, 1971).

2. The concept of the arch is borrowed from Peter Self, *Administrative Theories and Politics* (Toronto: University of Toronto Press, 1973), pp. 150-151. We have, however, developed it further for our purposes.

3. *Ibid.*, p. 151.

4. R.J.S. Baker, *Administrative Theory and Public Administration* (London: Hutchinson & Co., 1972), p. 31.

5. Herbert A. Simon, *Administrative Behavior* (New York: The Free Press, 1966) Introduction pp. ix-xxxvii.

6. Henry C. Metcalf and L. Urwick (eds.), *Dynamic Administration: The Collected Papers of Mary Parker Follett* (New York: Harper and Brothers, 1940), p. 49.

7. J.E. Hodgetts, *The Canadian Public Service: A Physiology of Government, 1867-1970* (Toronto: University of Toronto Press, 1973), pp. 164-168.

8. For a wide definition of central agencies which include even the Department of Supply and Services, see H.L. Laframboise, "Portfolio Structure and a Ministry System: A Model for the Canadian Federal Service," *Optimum* especially pp. 34-35. Laframboise's effort is partly speculative but in our view he captures the essential characteristic of central agencies: a definition which emphasizes the *horizontal links of control* to all governmental departments.

9. Luther Gulick, "Notes on the Theory of Organization," in Institute of Public Administration, *Papers on the Science of Administration*, ed. Luther Gulick and L. Urwick (New York: Columbia University Press, 1937). This work was initiated by Gulick as a result of his service on the Committee on Administrative Management (commonly known in the literature as the Brownlow Commission), set up by President Franklin Delano Roosevelt during the 1930s. Apart from Brownlow who was chairman, the third member of the committee was Professor Charles Merriam, an outstanding political scientist, and a strong advocate of the application of Taylorism to government operations.

10. See Hodgetts, *Physiology of Government*, especially Chapter Six.

11. V. Seymour Wilson, "The Relationship Between Scientific Management and Personnel Policy in North American Administrative Systems," *Public Administration* (London), Summer 1973, pp. 193-205.   .

12. Adapted from Gulick, "Notes," p. 13.

13. Ibid., pp. 30-31.

14. J.A. Litterer, *The Analysis of Organizations* (New York: John Wiley and Sons, 1965), p. 174.

15. *Line-Staff Relations in Production* (New York: American Management Association, 1957), pp. 7-8.

16. V.A. Graicunas, "Relationship in Organization," in L. Gulick and L. Urwick, eds., *Papers on the Science of Administration* (New York: Columbia University, 1947), pp. 181-187.

17. Robert T. Golembiewski, "Civil Service and Managing Work," *American Political Science Review* 56 (December 1962): 961-974; also reprinted in Robert T. Golembiewski et al., eds., *Public Administration: Readings in Institutions, Processes, Behavior* (Chicago: Rand McNally & Co., 1966), pp. 164-189.

18. O. Glenn Stahl, "The Network of Authority," *Public Administration Review* XVIII (Winter 1958): ii-iv; and O. Glenn Stahl, "More on the Network of Authority," *Public Administration Review* XX (Winter 1960): 35-37.

19. Raymond Villers, *Dynamic Management in Industry* (Englewood Cliffs, N.J.: Prentice Hall, 1960), p. 159.

20. H.A. Simon, "The Proverbs of Administration," *Public Administration Review* 6 (Winter 1946):pp. 53-67; also H.A. Simon, *Administrative Behavior: A Study of Decision-Making Processes in Administrative Organization,* 2nd ed. (New York: Free Press, 1957), pp. 20-44.

21. We do not intend to submerge the student with too much material on this topic, but in addition to those already cited a few of the better articles would suffice to illustrate the point. See Herbert A. Simon, Donald V. Smithburg and Victor Thompson, *Public Administration* (New York: Knopf, 1950), especially pp. 280-291; William Hogan, "A Dangerous Tendency in Government," *Public Administration Review* VI (Autumn, 1946): 362-367; Gerald C. Fisch, "Line-Staff Is Obsolete," *Harvard Business Review* XXXIX (September-October 1961): 67-69; and Peter F. Drucker, *The Practice of Management* (New York: Harper, 1954), pp. 241ff.

22. H.A. Simon, "Comments on the Theory of Organizations," *American Political Science Review* XLVI (December 1952): 1130-1139 at 1133.

23. In 1939, after the Brownlow Committee had reported the need for Presidential staff help, the Executive Office of the President came formally into existence. These "staff" facilities, popularly known as "the institutionalized Presidency" are an odd assortment of personal and institutional staffs and of interagency committees. Chief among them are the personal White House staff, the Office of Management

and Budget (formerly known as the Bureau of the Budget), the National Security Council (first established in 1947) and the Council of Economic Advisers (created in 1946).

24. See the *Report of the President's Committee on Administrative Management* (Washington: Government Printing Office, 1937). For background material, see the second volume of reminiscences by the Committee's chairman, Louis Brownlow, *A Passion for Anonymity* (Chicago: University of Chicago Press, 1958), Chapters 28, 30, 31 and 33. For some detail into the power intrigues and struggles at the time, see Gerald E. Caiden, *The Dynamics of Public Administration: Guidelines to Current Transformations in Theory and Practice* (New York: Holt, Rinehart and Winston, Inc., 1971), pp. 118-123.

25. Richard E. Neustadt, "Approaches to Staffing the Presidency: Notes on F.D.R. and J.F.K.," *American Political Science Review* (December 1963), pp. 855-864 (including letter from Brown to Neustadt); James W. Fesler, "Administrative Literature and the Second Hoover Commission Reports," *A.P.S.R.* (March 1957).

26. There are exceptions to this, for example, the Public Service Commission of Canada which was given functional responsibilities for service-wide language training in the late 1960s.

27. For a perceptive machinery of government study which makes this identical point see Peter Aucoin and Richard French, "The Ministry of State for Science and Technology", *CPA* (Fall, 1974), Vol. 17, No. 3, pp. 461-481 especially p. 477.

28. Peter Self, *Administrative theories and politics* (Toronto: University of Toronto Press, 1973) p. 69. For an article which argues strongly that a clear delineation should be made between *the control function* and *the service function* in government see H.R. Balls, "Common Services in government", *Canadian Public Administration* Vol. 17, No. 2, Summer 1974, pp. 226-241.

29. Allan Gotlieb, "Canadian Diplomacy in the 1980s: Leadership and Service." A public lecture given in Toronto, February 15, 1979, pp. 7-8. Given our working definition of central agencies we identify the following organizational units as central agencies of the federal government: The Prime Minister's Office (PMO), the Privy Council Office (PCO), Treasury Board, the Public Service Commission (PSC), the Department of Finance and the Federal-Provincial Relations Office (FPRO). Our definition is also flexible in that it provides for any future unit of government to become a central agency or to lose its status as such if so dictated by the executive and by environmental conditions.

30. Hodgetts et. al., *The Biography of an Institution*, Chapters 1, 2.

31. Ibid., ch. 7, pp. 137-142. Norman Ward also points out that in the Canadian experience Finance was continually hampered by having to exercise supervision, in name only, over the affairs of departments of equal rank with itself. This came to an end during the crisis period of World War I when the department was finally given some control teeth. See Norman Ward, *The Public Purse* (Toronto: University of Toronto Press, 1964), p. 233. In contrast the British Treasury has always possessed a higher status than its fellow departments as a consequence of its power to control.

32. It is interesting to note that Mackenzie King, who initiated the development of the PMO/PCO office, initially visualized its function as a supportive auxiliary role and not much more. See J.R. Mallory, "Mackenzie King and the origins of the cabinet secretariat," *CPA* 19:2 (Summer 1976):254-266; A.D.P. Heeney, *The Things that are Caesar's: Memoirs of a Canadian public servant* (Toronto: University of Toronto Press, 1972), especially Chapter 6, "Secretary to the Cabinet," pp. 73-81.

33. D'Aquino, p. 63.

34. See the low-key parliamentary discussion when the "hiving off" of the Federal Provincial Relations Office from the Privy Council Office was announced, along with the establishment of two secretaries to the federal cabinet. House of Commons Debates, December 18, 1974.

35. The major exception to this is the growth of Treasury Board after the basic changes in public service legislation in 1967. See Hubert L. Laframboise, "Counter-managers: the abandonment of unity of command," *Optimum* 8:4 (1977):18-28.

36. W.P. Irvine and R.E.B. Simeon, "The Prime Minister's mailbag," *Canadian Public Administration* 19:2 (Summer 1976):292.

37. Heeney, *The Things that are Caesar's,* Chapter 6.

38. A former executive assistant to a minister in the Pearson and Trudeau governments has claimed that "Under Pearson, the cabinet behaved in the fashion of a mollified Confederation of Chinese warlords. There were several strong Cabinet ministers who vied for attention and power, and competed quite openly for the implementation of their own individual programmes." N. Lloyd Axworthy, "The Task Force on Housing and Urban Development: A Study of Democratic Decision-Making in Canada," (Doctoral dissertation, Princeton University, May 1972), p. 83.

39. To argue that effective power in Canada (like in Britain) has passed " . . . from Parliament to Cabinet; from Cabinet to public service; and now, from public service to Prime Minister," is simply not congruent with the facts. See Fred Schindeler, "The Prime Minister and the Cabinet: History and Development," in Thomas A. Hockin, ed. *Apex of Power,* p. 22. Indeed, one could argue that to a great extent the opposite has happened and that the Prime Minister must share a large measure of his powers with his fellow cabinet ministers and even some of the senior members of the bureaucracy.

40. The Clark administration created the following committees:
    (1) The inner cabinet dealing with fiscal transfers and the public debt.
    (2) Social and native affairs committee.
    (3) Economic development committee.
    (4) Economy in government committee.
    (5) Foreign policy and defence committee.
    These policy committees allocated the resources within each policy area. The Trudeau administration discarded the formal structuring of the previous administration but the envelope system has however been retained. This aspect of cabinet structure is best pursued in a discussion linking structure to the processes of allocating and controlling expenditures in the government.

41. George J. Szablowski, "The Optimal Policy-Making System: Implications for the Canadian Political Process," in Thomas A. Hockin, ed., *Apex of Power*, pp. 197-208.

42. Robertson, "The Changing Role," p. 500.

43. D.R. Yeomans, "Decentralization of Authority," *Canadian Public Administration* 12:1 (Spring 1969):10.

44. "Tax cuts to be extra-deep?" *Financial Post*, August 19, 1978, p. 1.

45. George J. Szablowski, "Policy-Making and Cabinet: Recent Organizational Engineering at Queen's Park," in Donald C. Macdonald, ed., *Government and Politics of Ontario* (Toronto: Macmillan of Canada, 1975), p. 129.

46. Hubert L. Laframboise, "Here come the program-benders," *Optimum* 7:1 (1976):40-48 at 41.

47. Ibid., p. 47.

48. The initial speeches of Prime Minister Trudeau on the PMO/PCO changes are rather revealing in their communications and cybernetics biases: "We are like pilots of a supersonic airplane"; "genetic and physiological engineering"; the questions we face on "techniques to be applied to human beings" are not science fiction fantasy and so on.

49. Johnson, "The Treasury Board of Canada and the Machinery of Government of the 1970s," pp. 346-348.

50. *Financial Post*, February 19, 1978, p. 1.

51. Johnson, "The Treasury Board of Canada and the Machinery of Government of the 1970s," p. 346.

52. The arguments presented in this section of the Chapter owe an intellectual debt to the following:
    (i) Donald Gow, unpublished *Rebuilding Canada's Bureaucracy*, edited by Edwin R. Black and Michael Prince, School of Public Administration, Queen's University, 1976; (ii) the scattered and extremely insightful essays of Norton Long; (iii) Mancur Olsen, Jr., *The Logic of Collective Action* (Harvard University Press, 1965); (iv) Phillip A. Selznick, *TVA and the Grass Roots* (Harper, 1966); (v) Graham T. Allison and Morton H. Halperin, "Bureaucratic Politics: A Paradigm and Some Policy Implications," *World Politics*, Vol. XXIV, Spring 1972, pp. 40-79.

53. Norton Long, "Power and Administration," *Public Administration Review* 19:4 (1949):257.

54. Quoted by M. Kogan in " 'The Politics of Public Expenditure' by Rudolf Klein: A Comment," *British Journal of Political Science* 6 (1976):507-508.

55. See the editorial of *The Ottawa Journal*, Saturday, January 24, 1976. "Simon Reisman speaks out: A View from the Inside." For a revealing account of Treasury Board-departmental relations which mirrors this perspective as well see the un-

published doctoral dissertation of the late Walter LeRoy White, *The Treasury Board in Canada*, University of Michigan, 1965, especially Chapter IV "The Dimensions of the Modern Treasury Board", pp. 97-131.

56. Richard Schultz, "Prime Ministerial Government, Central Agencies, and Operating Departments: Towards a More Realistic Analysis" in Thomas A. Hockin (ed.) *Apex of Power: The Prime Minister and Political Leadership in Canada* (2nd edition), Toronto: Prentice Hall of Canada Ltd., 1977, pp. 229-36.

57. For an excellent analysis of some of the Byzantine complexities of this process see A.W. Johnson "Management theory and cabinet government," *Canadian Public Administration*, Vol. 14, No. 1, Spring 1971, pp. 73-81.

58. E.E. Schattschneider, *The Semi-Sovereign People*, (New York: 1960), p. 71.

59. R.H.S. Crossman, *The Sunday Times*, 26 January 1975, quoted in W.I. Jenkins, *Policy Analyses* (London: Martin Robertson, 1978), p. 65.

60. A. Paul Pross, "Canadian Pressure groups in the 1970s: their role and their relations with the public service" *CPA*, Vol. 18, No. 1 (1975), p. 131.

61. Canada, House of Commons, *Report of the Auditor General of Canada*, Fiscal Year ended March 31, 1976, p. 13.

62. Before his death, A.D.P. Heeney frankly admitted to me in personal interviews that it was his objective to keep the then fused PMO/PCO offices as small as possible. Similar sentiments were held by previous Secretaries to the Treasury Board for instance. The central agencies' high visibility plus their sensitive tasks of ensuring austerity in the whole public service when commanded by cabinet to do so, meant that they of all agencies "must keep their skirts clean."

63. Richard Schultz, *op. cit.*, p. 231. When Michael Pitfield was approved Clerk of the Privy Council and Secretary to the Cabinet, the Federal-Provincial Relations Office was simultaneously created with R.G. Robertson, the former Clerk to Cabinet, appointed Secretary to the Cabinet for Federal-Provincial Relations. The new office was created by statute, Bill C-38 in December, 1974. See the House of Commons debates, December 18, 1974.

64. Gordon Robertson, "The Changing Role of the Privy Council Office." Address to the Institute of Public Administration of Canada, September 8, 1971, p. 34 (mimeo).

65. R. Schultz, *op. cit.*, p. 232.

66. Auditor General, *Report, op. cit.*, p. 29.

67. R. Schultz, *op. cit.*, p. 231.

68. H.L. Laframboise, "Here Come the Program-Benders," *Optimum*, vol. 7, no. 1, 1976, p. 43.

69. Michael Pitfield, "The Shape of government in the 1980s: techniques and instruments for policy formulation at the federal level," *CPA* (Spring 1976), Vol. 19, No. 1, p. 19.

70. Herbert J. Spiro, *Responsibility in Government* (New York: Van Nostrand Reinhold Co., 1969), p. 16.

71. Rowland Egger, "Responsibility in Administration: An Exploratory Essay," in Roscoe C. Martin (ed.), *Public Administration and Democracy* (Syracuse: Syracuse University Press, 1965), p. 304.

72. Colin Campbell and George Szablowski, *The Super-Bureaucrats: Structure and Behaviour in Central Agencies* (Toronto: Macmillan of Canada, 1979), pp. 192-194.

73. *Ibid.*, p. 194.

74. Arthur Maass, *Muddy Waters: The Army Engineers and the Nation's Rivers* (Cambridge: Harvard University Press, 1951).

75. J.E. Hodgetts, "On Tap or On Top?," *The Canadian Forum*, Vol. LIX, February 1980, p. 33.

76. H.J. Spiro, *Responsibility in Administration*, p. 170.

77. *Ibid.*, p. 174.

78. Herman Finer, "Better Government Personnel," *Political Science Quarterly*, vol. 51 (1936), p. 569.

Notes

The literature on central agencies is not plentiful. We have tried to give as full a series of footnotes to help sort out the chaff from the wheat on this issue. The reader is asked to consult the specific footnotes for particular information required. One book however comes highly recommended for its analytical treatment of the concept of responsibility.

1. Herbert J. Spiro, *Responsibility in Government*. It is a slender volume, but a must for any serious student of the subject. We have simplified Spiro's subtle distinctions for purposes of this book, but generally speaking our analysis synchronizes with his. We assume that the reader is conversant with the literature which describes the central machinery of government in Canada. For review we recommend the following readings:
    (i) Thomas D'Aquino, "The Prime Minister's Office: Catalyst or Cabal?" *Canadian Public Administration* XVII:1 (1974):55-79; Dennis Smith, "Comments on the Prime Minister's Office: Catalyst or Cabal?" ibid, 80-84.
    (ii) Michael Hicks, "The Treasury Board of Canada and its clients: five years of change and administrative reform, 1966-71," *CPA* 16:2 (1973): 182-205.
    (iii) Thomas A. Hockin, ed., *Apex of Power: The Prime Minister and Political Leadership in Canada*, 2nd ed. (Toronto: Prentice Hall, 1977), especially articles by Schin-

deler, Sharp, Hockin, Lenoski, Doern, Szablowski, Dobuzinskis, Schultz, Smith and Wearing.

(iv) J.E. Hodgetts et. al., *The Biography of an Institution* (Montreal: McGill-Queen's University Press, 1972), especially chapters 1, 2, 3, 4 and 7.

(v) A.W. Johnson, "Management Theory and Cabinet Government," *CPA* XIV:1 (1971):73-81; A.W. Johnson, "The Treasury Board of Canada and the Machinery of Government of the 1970's," *Canadian Journal of Political Science* IV:3 (September 1971)

(vi) Marc Lalonde, "The Changing Role of the Prime Minister's Office," *CPA* XIV:4 (1971)

(vii) Gordon Robertson, "The Changing Role of the Privy Council Office, *CPA* 14:4 (Winter 1971)

CHAPTER TEN

THE ORIGINS OF THE MINISTERIAL PORTFOLIO

In the view of Graham Wallas, foundation professor of political science at the London School of Economics, "the one great political invention of the nineteenth century was the drawing of a clear distinction between the appointed non-political officials and the elected political executive . . . [this reform] demonstrated how an expert bureaucracy could be constructed out of elements quite apart from Parliament and Ministers, and how it could be both subordinate to them and yet one of their most valuable resources in government."

R. L. Wettenhall

I. Introduction

The previous chapter discussed the role of the cabinet as the pinnacle or "apex" of a machinery of interdepartmental relations. We emphasized that the cabinet is not unitary, but is a complex differentiated institution. For all intents and purposes the cabinet is now a series of committees taking on the characteristics of a pyramid. While it is too early in the development of the Canadian cabinet to form a definite conclusion, it may be that positions in the hierarchies of various subcommittees are becoming as important as formal membership in the cabinet. More and more the types of committees and the classification of ministers are taking on added significance.

Our definition of central agencies emphasized the concepts of *power* and *control*. Whoever controls the reins of political power at a particular time can remould almost at will the central machinery of government. But there is much more to this complexity at the apex of power. As the cabinet has become increasingly complex, and as the official apex of our government is now a group of units, so too must the contemporary ministerial portfolio be viewed as a nucleus for a variety of complex tasks and assignments which often seem to bear no functional or necessary relations to each other when grouped together under one ministerial "roof."

The machinery of government is in part dictated by the responsibilities of the individual minister in the government. Therefore this chapter will attempt to do two things. First, we will analyse the package of relationships which surround the individual minister of the Crown: the legal relationships to Parliament, the conventional relations to the political cabinet to which the minister belongs, and finally the relationships with the chief departmental administrative officer answerable to the minister, namely, the deputy head of the department or ministry for which the minister is responsible. This description will provide a composite picture of the politics/administration arch at the individual ministerial level.

Secondly, we will attempt to show that the series of complex roles and relationships which now prevail, and the institutions which enshrine them, have their roots in a soil which is rarely mentioned, namely the philosophical prescriptions of such celebrated liberal thinkers as Jeremy Bentham, John Stuart Mill and Walter Bagehot. We will discuss these theoretical contributions to show how relevant they were to both Britain and Canada during the period of administrative reform experienced in both countries in the nineteenth century.

A few words of clarification are also in order. The terminology "ministry" and "ministerial portfolio" could be confusing, especially in the comparative literature of political science and public administration. In Canada the term "ministry" is used in two ways. First, it most commonly refers to the tenure of a Prime Minister. A ministry begins on the date the oath of office is administered to a Prime Minister, and ends on the date the Prime Minister either dies in office or the Governor General accepts his resignation (for example, the Diefenbaker Ministry 1957-63; the Pearson Ministry, 1963-68). Secondly, the term describes the total jurisdiction of a few ministers in the cabinet. These jurisdictions contain several bureaucratic units arranged in a particular configuration (for example, *Ministry of State* for Science and Technology or the *Ministry* of Transport). These latter uses of the term will be elaborated upon in the succeeding chapter.

The term "ministerial portfolio" refers to the total pattern of role relationships comprising the minister's responsibilities including the structural administrative arrangements which give expression to these roles. Thus, for example, the deputy minister's relationship to the minister or the particular administrative configuration of a department or ministry are included in our discussion of the ministerial portfolio.

II. The Canadian Ministerial Portfolio in Contemporary Times

Most Canadians take as given the legal foundations of our political system.[1] A few of these legal underpinnings should be mentioned here, for they serve to reveal the complex dimensions built into the position of Minister of the Crown. First is the concept of ministerial headship. The Minister *in law* is individually responsible both to the Crown and to Parliament. This responsibility is symbolized whenever members of Parliament become ministers, in that as advisors in the Queen's Privy Council, they must swear a *personal legal obligation* regarding the fulfillment of ministerial duties. Power is therefore inherent in ministerial positions, and with power comes the notion of individual ministerial responsibility. Thus just about every statute pertaining to the functions of government machinery begins by naming the specific organization (department, ministry or ministry of state), after which it is stated that: "The Minister of _____ holds office during pleasure and has the management and direction of the Department/Ministry of _____." The minister's responsibility therefore remains a personal one, giving rise to a number of parliamentary conventions emphasizing this fact. The House of Commons when in session reserves the right to question almost every day ministers of the Crown on specific details of their administrative charges. Another legal provision is that a minister cannot be held responsible for the acts of predecessor(s) in office.

But, as we have shown in previous chapters, individual ministerial responsibility is very much circumscribed by the assumptions and conventions of *collective* ministerial responsibility.[2] Here we find that a series of collective responsibilities, geared to meeting the needs of an increasingly complex government environment, have grown up over the decades. This fact causes many students and observers of government to ignore our legal foundations as irrelevancies and concentrate on the collective conventional reality of today.[3] But one ignores this foundation at one's own peril, for study will reveal the vital connections and deeper understandings embodied in "our living consitution"[4]—a document which is the product of continuous selection, rejection, reformulation and addition of ideas of government. A constitution and its conventions can be likened to a coral reef: what one finally "sees" and "enjoys" is the product of a continuous building, rebuilding and adaptation to a changing environment without losing or discarding the essential substructure. K. N. Llewellyn is worth quoting on this point:

The discrepancy between theory and fact found in private law is exaggerated in the constitutional field, because under a code of rigid words no easy and gradual rewording of outmoded rules in such a manner as to hide the changes made in their content, is possible. The consequence is that with growing age all force in the actual words of a code withers and dies. What is left, and living, is not a code, but an institution. Many of the institution's roots trace back through time into the code. Many do not. But the living institution is neither the dead code nor its "interpretation." It is not even by any parthenogenesis descended from its great-grandmother code alone. It is new, it is different, it is growing; and in its blood run so many other streams that resemblance to the code is seldom strong and always confined to single traits.[5]

Thus the legal foundations of our system which emphasize individual ministerial responsibility to the Crown are joined by a constellation of assumptions and conventions on collective ministerial responsibility which are, to push our analogy a little further, like barnacles on the coral reef substructure. Mentioned previously is the Parliamentary practice of delegation of powers for various legislative acts to the governor-in-council (that is, the collective cabinet), rather than to the individual minister. Others are the Prime Minister's prerogative of appointment to the cabinet, reinforcing the concept of a team to act collectively, and also the government's collective responsibility for presenting all spending proposals to Parliament. The collective nature of the cabinet creates a number of other collective conventional practices which have been explored elsewhere.[6] The complex system of individual and collective ministerial responsibilities operating together have added a series of overlapping dimensions to some ministerial portfolios.

For example, there are a series of cabinet positions which are collective in nature, that is, they have coordinative functions which cut across the ministerial jurisdictions of many other cabinet colleagues. An example is the coordinative role in economic matters assigned to the Committee of Economic Ministers, a cabinet subcommittee created by the Trudeau administration in the autumn of 1978. Similarly, the relationships among the ministerial portfolios of Finance, the Treasury Board and a number of "economic departments" further illustrate this overlapping of ministerial portfolios. R. M. Burns describes this overlapping as it relates to fiscal and economic policy:

Departments of finance have commonly been accepted as the arm of government responsible for the budget and hence for fiscal policy. While finance has retained an important influence over economic policy, the responsibility has been more widely distributed through the various operating departments, such as trade and commerce, agriculture, natural resources, etc., and the various crown corporations and other agencies. While the finance minister still retains the responsibility for the revenue budget in large degree, in many jurisdictions he must now share the responsibility on the expenditure side with a treasury board or some similar committee of cabinet. The sort of budget he prepares, and particularly the direction of the policies he recommends, are increasingly influenced by the overall direction of public policy and more particularly by demands of his colleagues and the advice they give as to the way in which these demands should be met.

In the Government of Canada it was the custom, until quite recent times, for the budget to be discussed by the Minister of Finance with the Prime Minister only. Except for specific proposals, the other members of the cabinet were not made familiar with the details until shortly before presentation. Policy formulation has been extensively reorganized and the cabinet collectively has assumed a much greater part. The budgetary process has thus become much more involved and is now related less to the function of control than to the total scope of government policy.[7]

This intricate and complex overlapping of ministerial jurisdictions and portfolios is an efficiency and economy expert's nightmare, for utilitarian rationality is constantly preoccupied with attempting to reallocate the machinery of government to eradicate "sprawling tendencies" or "chaos in establishments." This efficiency and economy drive is, as we shall now show, a vital part of the story on the evolution of the ministerial department.

As we examine the interaction between the cabinet minister and the administrative charge, that is, the department or ministry for which, under law, the minister is "responsible," the web of relationships becomes further complicated. The most important aspect of this interaction is the minister's relations with the chief departmental administrative officer, the deputy head. Faced with time demands for cabinet and subcommittees of cabinet meetings, political fence mending in the constituency, appearances in the House of Commons almost daily when it is in session, and various political appearances at home and abroad in the capacity as minister, it is really not surprising that the busy politician must leave the day-to-day administrative duties of the department or ministry to deputy and senior departmental officials.[8] Edmund Burke's observations about "ministers of state" have become equally applicable to these senior officials:

Constitute government how you please, infinitely the greater part of it must depend upon the exercise of the powers which are left at large to the prudence and uprightness of ministers of state. Even all the use and potency of the law is dependent upon them. Without them your commonwealth is no better than a scheme upon paper; and not a living, acting effective constitution . . .[9]

This statement becomes even more relevant when one considers that within two or three years the chances are extremely high that the minister will be either transferred to another ministerial portfolio, or dismissed as a member of the cabinet: a political "bird of passage."

Undoubtedly because of the relatively transient nature of these ministerial-public servant relationships we find that there is a web of other relationships to ensure continuity, stability and both political and administrative responsibility. For example, let us examine how the roles themselves are filled. It is the Prime Minister and not the minister who appoints the deputy minster, although the minister is often consulted on the choice. Insofar as other senior appointments in the department are concerned, the minister has no formal say in the final selection, but would be consulted in the early stages of screening. It is the Public Service Commission's statutory mandate to staff the public service on the basis of merit, and free from as much political or personal biases as possible. Over the last decade or so a few senior ministers have expressed the desire to make changes in this requirement of the law, allowing political considerations to determine senior appointments other than at the deputy ministerial level. This desire has, however, been vigorously countered publicly by the chief executive officers of the Public Service Commission.[10] As the law presently stands the minister must largely rely on personnel chosen by others to help carry out individual responsibilities as a Minister of the Crown.

The interface of relationships between the deputy minister and the minister is also complex and ambiguous. There are no neat divisions of responsibility and authority between the two.[11] Ostensibly, the deputy chief's role is to be adviser to the minister, particularly in relation to financial and personnel administration. Included also in the responsibilities is the preparation of departmental expenditure budgets and new policy proposals, all the while ensuring that these are done in conformity with the legislation agreed to by Parliament. Accomplishments in these tasks are judged by the minister who provides an annual appraisal of the deputy's performance to the Prime Minister.[12] However, the deputy's lines of responsibility do not end with advisory/managerial roles to the minister. There is also, since 1967, the responsibility for specifically delegated managerial roles of various kinds to the Public Service Commission (personnel administration) and the Treasury Board of Canada (financial administration).[13]

Our deputy, then, is an individual of many parts, "[an] efficient closet statesman [providing] a wise and constant instrumentality at work upon administrative measures (distinguished as they might be from the measures of political parties)."[14] Various complicated roles must be played within the public service, each requiring diplomatic and managerial skills of a high order if success as senior management is to be achieved. We could outline these complex roles as follows: while having special responsibilities to the minister of the department the deputy is also responsible to the Prime Minister who made the appointment to the position and, in an indirect way, to the mandarins in the Privy Council Office and the Public Service Commission who monitor and record job performance. The deputy is also responsible to the central managerial agencies, in particular the Treasury Board and the Public Service Commission, and in the final analysis to the department which she/he heads. Furthermore, Parliament has decreed other restraints on the deputy's managerial freedom. For example, some decisions to "make or buy," or generally to partake of the common services of government, do not allow wide discretionary options to the deputy,[15] who is further hemmed in by the legislation which allows investigatory and other powers to the Human Rights Commissioner or to the Language Commissioner, two officers of Parliament. The result is a chief administrative officer very much unlike any other in a comparable large and complex organization. As A. W. Johnson puts it:

The deputy minister has many loyalties. His first is to His minister, of course. But he also has a loyalty to the institution of parliament. . . . He has a loyalty to the programs he administers, a loyalty which opposition members sometimes construe to be a political loyalty. He has a loyalty to his own profession and to his own conscience, a loyalty which causes him to speak out against certain policies. . . . This is the context within which one must evaluate the role of the deputy minister—indeed in some ways the context has already defined the role.[16]

In summary, the context of decision-making, both for the minister and deputy, is comprised of a series of complicated role relationships. Both individuals find themselves "responsible" to a number of superiors or peers. For the minister it is the Prime Minister, cabinet colleagues, and ultimately Parliament. Both must spend much time looking up or sideways to their superiors or peers. Secondly, both individuals find themselves hemmed in and pressured from all sides. The minister is constrained in what can be done as a minister by the collective responsibilities of the cabinet. Thus, the minister simply cannot make departmental policies then sit back and wait for all sorts of things to happen. Even if the minister and deputy are strongly predisposed to prompt action and the cutting of all "red tape," they will be immediately faced with a labyrinth of adminstrative procedures in their attempt to secure administrative and financial resources.[17]

Thirdly, the minister, and particularly the deputy, are faced with the immediate responsibilities of managing their organizations. This role has increasingly become one of awesome pressures, as governments become increasingly larger and more complicated. Fourthly, in addition to policy advisory roles and general managerial roles, the deputy minister has had the direct responsibility of introducing a flood of civil service reforms in recent years: first came the Glassco reforms in the latter 1960s, followed by collective bargaining, bilingualism, and new budgetary systems. As one senior public servant observed:

Taken one at a time the merits of these decisions are defensible or at least arguable. Taken in their totality, and considering the changes consequent upon them, they have resulted in such an increase in the internal administrative work-load that only huge increases in staff numbers and unprecedented demands on available managerial work-time have made their imperfect implementation possible. . . . The symptoms of conflict are strong. They must be heeded if we are to avoid either of two unacceptable consequences: (a) the psychological immobilization of our managers in the face of insistent and conflicting demands, (withdrawal and apathy); (b) a revolt by the managers against innovators leading to an outright hostility to change, whatever its real or apparent merit (aggression).[18]

These are strong words, words of despair. Thus our managers "at the top" find themselves being "the people in the middle": they are not at the apex of a triangle, but at the center of a confused and whirling vortex of centripetal forces.[19]

How did this all come about? The roles we have been describing here in a preliminary way illustrate graphically the subtle blend of responsibility for policy formation and managerial accountability. These roles have evolved over the last one hundred years and will continue to evolve in an incremental fashion as the needs and pressures of Canadian society continue to make specific demands on government organization. These roles which comprise the Canadian ministerial portfolio have their roots in a historical soil rich with interesting theoretical and practical implications. It is to an explanation of these "roots" that we now turn.

III. British Theoretical Origins of the Ministerial Department

In studying the theories of organization, most contemporary students tend to assume that this preoccupation began with the study of scientific management. However, Dwight Waldo has given us a reminder "that anyone who thinks theory of organization began with Fayol or Taylor owes himself a look at the frontspiece of Hobbes' *Leviathan*. Now *there's* an organization chart!"[20] (See Figure I). Similarly, a reading of most Canadian writings on the organization of the federal government gives the distinct impression that at least the early ministerial portfolios are orthodox forms of central administration transported *holus bolus* from Great Britain and firmly planted in the new and hopefully fertile soil of British North America during the early part of the nineteenth century.[21] This distinct impression is further buttressed by a prevailing tendency to dub all non-departmental forms of administration as "structural heretics," implying, of course, that the departmental form is, and continues to be, the norm in public administration.[22] This historical evolution cannot be entirely denied. However, recent historical evidence also points to the fact that both the ministerial department and portfolio, as it is conventionally assumed today, were nineteenth century innovations, one of the many outcomes of the thorough-going processes of administrative reform worked out *simultaneously both in Great Britain and the more important segments of her Empire* (India, Canada, Australia).

Indeed, in the case of Canada, the evidence points to the fact that the evolution of Canadian self-government, and the shaping of some governmental machinery to give expression to this evolution, *actually predated in some unique ways the refining in the British political system of techniques to ensure administrative accountability to the British Parliament*. This is a significant point to which we will return in the next chapter. What is clear, however, as Dwight Waldo's words illustrate, is that the theoretical foundations for such practical reforms came from philosophical sources which in contemporary times we are not generally inclined to look to as the originators of such practical reforms. Thus, a brief look at the political and social realities of early nineteenth century England would provide an instructive backdrop to the practical reforms fashioned in Britain, and her other dependencies at that time.

English Social and Political Realities by Mid-Nineteenth Century

England, at the beginning of the nineteenth century, was not a nice place to live unless you were "management" or a member of the landed aristocracy. The industrial revolution, which was to transform western European society, was in full swing, bringing widespread technological innovations in communications, transportation and a host of other fields. But the English masses who fled the countryside

FIGURE I

THE FRONTISPIECE FROM HOBBES' *LEVIATHAN*

Source: *Michael Oakeshott (ed.) Thomas Hobbes' Leviathan or, the matter, forme and power of a commonwealth, ecclesiasticall and civil. (London: Oxford University Press, 1946)*

for the congested cesspools called workers' tenements paid a heavy price in selling their labor to the industrial tycoons of the day. Karl Marx and many other social critics at the time correctly pinpointed this social horror by painting a sombre and powerful vision of a world of loneliness and abandonment, misdirected aims, perverse zeal and troubled consciences. Various pressures were inevitably brought to bear for government action to regulate child labor, to protect public health, to provide minimum care for society's indigents and to ensure that the rudiments of education were supplied to the young, but all these measures met with varying degrees of success. A little knowledge of these realities places our concern about political and organizational change in perspective. The author Charles Dickens, perhaps the most brilliant satirist and novelist the English language has ever produced, provides us with a panoramic view, reminiscent of Dante's Hell, of early nineteenth century London on a Sunday evening that is:

Melancholy streets, in a penitential garb of soot, steeped the souls of the people who were condemned to look at them out of windows, in dire despondency . . . Nothing to see but streets, streets, streets. . . . Miles of close wells and pits of houses where the inhabitants gasped for air stretched far away towards every point of the compass. Through the heart of the town a deadly sewer ebbed and flowed in place of a fine fresh river. . . . Nothing for the spent toiler to do but to compare the monotony of his seventh day with the monotony of his six days, think what a weary life he led, and made the best of it—or the worst, according to the probabilities.[23]

Changes in Political and Administrative Realities

The picture we have of early nineteenth century English administration is also one of widespread patronage, graft, inefficiency, disorganization and a lack of bureaucratic controls. In the first half of his important book on English administrative history, J. Donald Kingsley documents a bizarre administrative world of patronage appointments given to the illegitimate children, indigent relatives and daft relations of the nobility; men who held civil service office and sat in Parliament at the same time; the selling of administrative positions and the regarding of such positions as personal property; the performance of work by proxy; a proliferation of sinecure offices; remuneration by fee rather than by fixed salary; unbelievably archaic accounting and administrative methods; small ministerial offices comprised of a few inept and patronage-appointed officials personally beholden to the minister; and a proliferation of multimember independent and usually amateur boards and commissions which did most of whatever administration there was to be done by the government.[25] The administrative scene is one of chaos, a state of affairs satirized most brilliantly by Dickens as he describes that Byzantine labyrinth called the Circumlocution Office:

Numbers of people were lost in the Circumlocution Office. Unfortunates with wrongs, or with projects for the general welfare (and they had better have wrongs at first than have taken that bitter English recipe for certainly getting them), who in slow lapse of time and agony had passed safely through other public departments; who, according to rule, had been bullied in this, over-reached by that, and evaded by the other; got referred at last to the Circumlocution Office, and never reappeared in the light of day. Boards sat upon them, secretaries minuted upon them, commissioners gabbled about them, clerks registered, entered, checked, and ticked them off, and they melted away. In short, all the business of the country went through the Circumlocution Office except the business that never came out of it; and *its* name was Legion.[26]

Dickens' description of English bureaucracy is certainly an accurate one. The machinery of government landscape during the early nineteenth century was an appallingly untidy one in Britain. *Administration was characterized by a proliferation of administrative boards, virtually independent of Parliament, as well as by a small group of "ministries," some of which were served by very distinguished, powerful and controversial "public servants."*[27] The general administrative scene was marked, however, by "the old British spirit of hugger-mugger" in doing things, that is, the creation of a "confused pile of administrative bric-a-brac, each piece fashioned separately for some particular purpose, known or forgotten, and with no connecting links."[28] The more Parliament attempted to exercise authority over the confusion, the less satisfactory were the results.

Times were changing, however. Two developments in the political system are of significance. Britain was still feeling the severe shock of her losses and national calamities: the loss of the American colonies, the maladministration, nepotism and absolute callousness of a government that sent men to needless death in the frozen mud of the Crimea, and the enormous expenditures caused by the Napoleonic War—all lent credence to the belief that the national government was incompetent and incapable of even the rudimentary services required of it.[29] Secondly, constitutional reform was inexorably curtailing the power of the Crown. The cabinet system of government was slowly evolving, changing the relationship between the monarch and his ministers. The notions of collective and individual ministerial responsibilities were gradually gaining ground, and Parliament, for one brief period in its history, was on the threshold of enjoying absolute supremacy. The Great Reform Acts which democratized government were in the offing: the Act of 1832, for instance, transformed the relationship between the executive and legislature in such a way that ". . . it was only a matter of time before Parliament took a close interest in, and devised means of, keeping the administrative machinery under continuous and detailed control."[30]

A series of other reforms were to follow: the enfranchisement of adult male citizens; the establishment of the supremacy of the House of Commons over the Lords; further curtailment of the monarch's absolute powers; votes for women; equal electoral districts; the abolition of plural voting by business proprietors and university graduates and so on. Of chief concern to us here is what these vast social reforms meant to the administrative structure of government, and what "blueprints" existed or were being advocated to accommodate the politico-administrative changes needed for the new era of liberal-democratic government.

During the second half of the nineteenth century experimentation with administrative forms finally settled upon the "right" solution to the problem of administrative control—the notion of ministerial responsibility. Willson argues:

The political and constitutional climate of the second half of the 19th century ensured that administration by a Minister was orthodox and the use of a board suspect. Once the idea of the individual responsibility of Ministers was thoroughly grasped it was rigidly applied to the central administration. . . . The ministries, fashioned into an acceptable constitutional shape, were made capable of expansion by the reform of the Civil Service. There was therefore no need to have recourse to new boards whenever new tasks were created: the opposite happened in that boards were superseded when the work was judged to be too big for them. The system of vesting all administrative powers in Ministers was sealed, as it were, by procedural changes in the House of Commons.[31]

What is of extreme significance is that these changes did not occur overnight. Willson documents a clear trend away from administration by boards after the early 1850s.[32] The ideological debate surrounding these changes and the incrementalism which characterized these innovations in the machinery of government are perhaps the two most important issues to be derived from this historical narration. The English philosopher and patriarch of modern parliamentary reform, Jeremy Bentham, combined a philisophical concern for administrative responsibility with an intellectual and political advocacy of practical administrative changes to ensure this responsibility.[33] As B. B.

Schaffer puts it, "The gravamen of his case was that answerability for results was weakened by the aggregation of positions constituting a board."[34] His main concern was the abolition of boards and commissions and the adoption of the American invention of "single-seated functionaries" to rectify the problem:

A Board, my Lord, is a screen. The lustre of good dessert is obscured by it—ill dessert, shrinking behind, eludes the eye of censure—wrong is covered by it with a presumption of right, stronger, and stronger in proportion to the number of folds: and each member having his own circle of friends, wrong in proportion again to the number, multiplies its protectors.[35]

Some three or four decades later Bentham's Utilitarian successor, John Stuart Mill, carried this attack one step further. While advocating that boards and commissions should be abolished, he was further preoccupied with *how a chain of responsibility could be fashioned which would connect the public official to the legislature through the Minister of the Crown.* Mill's chief claim was to create both representative and responsible government: "This required a distinction between the legislature and the Minister and between the Minister and the official. . . . Mill's opening paragraph on this topic in *Representative Government* states a belief very similar to what was to be stated in the Haldane Report nearly eighty years later: that responsibility is best provided and the work best done if all functions of similar subject be allocated to single departments."[36] Some aspects of what we now call "scientific management" were very much in evidence in the philosophical and political literature of the early nineteenth century.

The advocacy of reforms and actual changes to both the parliamentary and administrative systems continued apace as these theoretical arguments were aired. There was first the abolition of sinecures and other "undesirable practices" mentioned earlier. The Northcote-Trevelyan personnel reform proposal of 1853 became a historical bellwether in its call for a non-political, merit-recruited career Civil Service.[37] The incremental nature of its acceptance is evidenced by the fact that it took close to two decades before the Report's principal recommendations were implemented. When the Report was first released, the *London Economist* said icily of its principal proposals: "They have all the air of having been borrowed, cut and dried, from Berlin or Pekin."[38] Although a Civil Service Commission was created in 1855 to take care of recruitment procedures to the bureaucracy, it was not until 1870 that the Gladstone Ministry issued an Order-in-Council which introduced the concept of competitive examinations to fill vacancies in the civil service.

On the constitutional front, the 1832 Reform Act served to transform the House of Commons from that of an opponent of executive government to that of being the principal source from which the executive derived its legitimacy and authority. In other words, the linkage between parliamentary democracy and the public interest was finally established when the people's elected representatives were accepted as the legitimizing source of political authority. It was during this period that the Commons established its hegemony over the financial control of administration: the Consolidated Revenue Fund was introduced; the annual budgetary cycle culminating in parliamentary approval was established; and the principle that only Parliament can legally appropriate public moneys became a central tenet of the Parliamentary system. By the late 1860s the financial control structures to ensure the smooth running of the new reforms were being put into place: the Auditor General, a Comptroller of the Treasury and a Public Accounts Committee of the Commons. Augmenting these controls was a new and direct system of accountability: "The old system of petitions calling attention to injustice in administrative practice gave way to the Parliamentary Question—certainly the most direct and popular method of controlling the Executive. The procedural changes all helped to shape and emphasize the position of Ministers, who were regarded as the only proper administrative authorities in a parliamentary system of government."[39]

The final theoretical contribution to these reforms we could note here is that of the English editorialist Walter Bagehot. *Bagehot's contribution was specifically in the area of departmental design to accommodate the doctrine of ministerial responsibility.* This English essayist is famous for his description of the "dignified" and the "efficient" parts of the Constitution, and his exposure of the "secrets" of the functioning of cabinet government. The monarch reigns, but it is the cabinet which really rules. Less well-known, but equally important, particularly to students of public policy and administration, are his detailed and profound insights into the new relationships between civil servant and minister brought on by the complex web of innovative changes introduced to the Parliamentary system.[40] In a derisive, tongue-in-cheek editorial style aimed at the daily goings-on in Parliament, he nevertheless enunciates a profound basic premise which had been slowly coming into focus in British parliamentary government; the doctrine of ministerial responsibility had now been established, a point which is echoed by Earl Grey in 1858:

It is no arbitrary rule, which requires that all holders of permanent offices must be subordinate to some minister responsible to parliament, since it is obvious that, without it, the first principles of our system of government—the control of all branches of the administration by parliament—would be abandoned.[41]

From this premise flows what Wettenhall describes as the "delicate but wonderful arrangement that developed in British public administration."[42] First, the acceptance of the principle of subordination meant that other aspects of the ministerial/civil servant relationship could then unfold. As discussed in previous chapters, R. MacGregor Dawson subsumed these other aspects under the term, "the principle of official independence." Official independence, he argued, meant that officials who were professionally trained, can now be relied upon to make decisions with probity and integrity, for the responsible minister or ministers. For this diligence the professional public servant receives an assurance that he will not be subjected to undue political interference.[43]

Secondly, the minister cannot conceivably hope or be expected to master all the expert knowledge needed to run the complex machinery under his jurisdiction. Nevertheless, expertise cannot be allowed to operate solely on its own initiative either. If left to itself it "will become technical, self-absorbed, self-multiplying. It will be likely to overlook the end in the means; it will fail from narrowness of mind; it will be eager in seeming to do; it will be idle in real doing." Hence, in order to effect new relationships of minister and civil servant and to ensure that these servants of the state are all held accountable, there is a need for an "extrinsic chief" at the head, "a fit corrector of such errors." Thus, "it is he, and he only, that brings the rubbish of office to the burning glass of sense."[44]

Thirdly, this combination of "sense" and "expertise," this admixture "of minds which attend to the means, and of minds which attend to the end," requires a hierarchical organization structure to function properly, with a permanent chief at the helm, for "in all great administrative departments there ought to be some one permanent responsible head through whom the changing Parliamentary chief always acts, from whom he learns everything, and to whom he communicates everything."[45] Fourthly, although Bagehot does not express it explicitly, the sentiment is obviously there that the ministerial form of organization with all its trappings is obviously the best form for Parliamentary democracy: "Why should not the rest of our administration be as good if we did but apply the same method to it?"[46]

Thus the departmental design was complete. Not all organizational structures conformed to this design, however: there were a few stragglers which remained beyond the pale, the later Victorians conveniently ignoring them by classifying them as "outlying departments of the Treasury."[47] But as both Willson and Wettenhall have confirmed, the ministerial department by the late 1860s was in its apogee.[48] Willson documents this by his detailed survey of the many boards and commissions existing in nineteenth century England. As he puts it, "Boards of all shades of independence flourished between 1832 and 1855. . . . In the middle period [that is, between 1855 and 1906] the use of boards declined and many of those which survived were clearly subordinated to Ministers. The later Victorian era was the Golden Age of ministerial administration."[49] Wettenhall is even more explicit about the completion of this ministerial design:

It was equally the high-water mark in the movement for a fully integrated Civil Service, recognized as a constitutional entity in its own right, and made up of a group of administrative agencies similarly organized, similarly related to Cabinet and Parliament, and similarly assimilated into the new but now standard patterns of public personnel and public financial management. In its concern for the orderly arranging of hierarchy, division of functions and the quality of personnel, British public administration was now also a leading example of the system of bureaucratic organization about to be immortalized conceptually in the scholarship of the social sciences by the great German scholar Max Weber. *In other words, what we have been considering is a concurrent development of the processes of ministerialization and bureaucratization.*[50]

Figure II is a chronological chart depicting the interplay of political and bureaucratic reforms of the nineteenth century. What we have been describing here is a highly complex series of *social, political, economic* and *legal* changes which occurred in Britain and, give or take a few years, *in all societies which followed the path of Western technological development. These societies were rationalized in a variety of ways.*[51] First, a process of social rationality began which sought to change societal relations in the direction of greater fundamental harmony and stability. Concomitantly, a process of *technical and economic rationality* called for society to adapt means to ends in a more efficient manner. In other words, technological rationality has been reinforced by the mechanisms and associated values of Western economic progress. These are the two forms of rationality with which scientific management has been concerned.

Thirdly, *a political rationality* or what some would view as democratization was also occurring aimed at the preservation and improvement of society's decision structures. The slow devolution of powers from monarch to the people's representatives, and the complex parliamentary changes which "peaked" in the nineteenth century—a

FIGURE II

CHRONOLOGICAL CHART SHOWING INTERPLAY BETWEEN POLITICAL AND
BUREAUCRATIC REFORMS IN GREAT BRITAIN

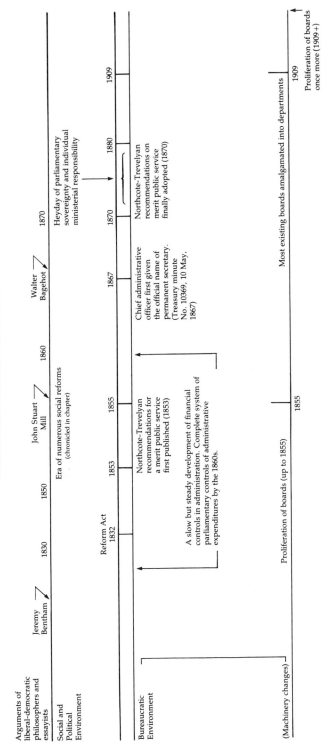

process which Leon Blum calls "a long and happy series of ursurpa-tions"—are examples of this rationalizing of the political process. Fourthly, a concomitant process of *legal rationality* was also taking place. In the quote above, Wettenhall draws our attention to both the *political* and *legal* rationality. Legal rationality—or what Max Weber called bureaucratization—is the rationality of fundamental rules. So-cieties develop rules in order to regulate and structure conflicts among the normative elements of social life. Rules thus serve the pur-pose of ensuring predictability and formal order. Therefore, notwith-standing the skepticism of Carlyle, Spencer, Palmerston and so many others, "Bureaucracy" finally held sway in England. There were, it is true, many "skeptics in the pantheon" who feared this new bureau-cratic phenomenon. For example, Lord Hewart, the Chief Justice of England during the 1920s made a particularly virulent outburst about the "new despotism" which he defined as a pernicious outgrowth of bureaucracy and "administrative discretion." But the die was cast for England as it has been for all the countries in Europe which had fol-lowed the path of technological advancement and industrialization: "Bureaucracy is the result of a long, incremental, evolutionary process. [It legitimizes social action] so that techniques may be ap-plied methodically and results may be recorded and accumulated. In this way mankind has climbed out of the primeval slime. . . . This process will continue."[52] Whether one agrees or disagrees with this viewpoint about the inexorable nature of bureaucracy in Western technological societies is another subject in itself. But we too in Can-ada have followed this pattern of industrialization and have experi-enced the same rationalizing processes with some unique Canadian differences. Our next chapter is devoted to describing and analysing this evolution of the processes of "bureaucratization and ministeriali-zation" in Canada.

Political Rationality and Metaphysical Madness: a Burkean comment

A statesman differs from a professor in a university; the latter has only the general view of society; the former, the statesman, has a number of circum-stances to combine with those general ideas, and to take into his consider-ation. Circumstances are infinite, are infinitely combined, are variable and transient; he who does not take them into consideration is not erroneous, but stark mad—*dat operam ut cum ratione insaniat*—he is metaphysically mad.

Edmund Burke,
Speech on the Petition of the Unitarians.

Footnotes

1. For an excellent detailed account of these foundations, the reader is directed to Chapter 4, "The Legal Foundations" in J.E. Hodgetts, *The Canadian Public Service: A Physiology of Government, 1867-1970*, pp. 55-83.

2. See Chapter Seven for this theoretical discussion.

3. For an illustration of this trend of argument, see Brian Chapman, *The Profession of Government* (London: Unwin University Books, 1959), p. 44.

4. For a competent treatment of this theme, see Alan C. Cairns, "The Living Canadian Constitution," *Queen's Quarterly*, LXXVII:4 (Winter 1970), 483-498.

5. K.N. Llewellyn, "The Constitution as an Institution," *Columbia Law Review*, 34 (1934), 6, and cited in Alan C. Cairns, *ibid.*, p. 487.

6. See for example W.A. Matheson, *The Prime Minister and the Cabinet* (Agincourt: Methuen, 1976).

7. R.M. Burns, "The Operation of Fiscal and Economic Policy," in G. Bruce Doern and V. Seymour Wilson, eds., *Issues in Canadian Public Policy* (Toronto: The Macmillan Co., 1974), pp. 294-295.

8. As Michael Hicks reports:
   > Ministers are, as ever, overworked, but the situation is worse than usual and is partly due to the demands of "collective decision-making" in Cabinet Committees. One deputy reported that he saw his minister for one hour a week on average. He reckoned that the Minister did about seven hours a week of departmental business. The rest of his seventy hour week was spent in Cabinet, Committees, House and political obligations.

   Michael Hicks, "The Treasury Board in Canada and Its Clients: Five Years of Change and Administrative Reform, 1966-71," *Canadian Public Administration*, 16:2 (Summer 1973), 182-205, at p. 192.

9. Edmund Burke, "Reform of Representation in the House of Commons" (1782), *Works* Vol. VI, p. 145.

10. There are about a dozen Governor-in-Council appointments at the senior executive level [specifically at the SX3 level] just below the deputy minister category. These appointments go to some length to meet the criticisms and demands of the politicians for such appointments.

11. There are a good many articles on the role of the deputy minister in our bureaucratic system. Four of the most helpful are:
    (1) A.W. Johnson, "The Role of the Deputy Minister," *Canadian Public Administration*, 4:4 (December 1961), pp. 363-373.
    (2) Herbert R. Balls, "Decision-Making: The Role of the Deputy Minister," *CPA*, 19:3 (Fall 1976), pp. 417-431.
    (3) J.S. Hodgson, "The Impact of Minority Government in the Senior Civil Servant," *CPA*, 19:2 (Summer 1976), pp. 227-237.

(4) J.W. Pickersgill, "Bureaucrats and Politicians," *CPA*, 15:3 (Fall 1972), pp. 418-427.

12. The Cabinet Committee on the Public Service is one of the subcommittees of the Canadian Federal Cabinet. This subcommittee has three main functions:
(a) to recommend senior appointments and other personnel changes to the prime minister;
(b) to coordinate all changes in the structures of the public service under the framework of regular government organization acts;
(c) to oversee the implementation of any reorganization in the public service.
The secretariat and advisory body to this subcommittee is the Ad Hoc Steering Committee of Senior Officials on the Public Service, comprising the "two clerks" (Secretary to the Cabinet and Secretary to the Cabinet for Federal-Provincial Relations) and a selected group of senior mandarins. The same group of individuals who make up this Ad Hoc Steering Committee also form the membership of the Ad Hoc Steering Committee of Senior Officials on Government Organization. For a brief, sensitive discussion of these two extremely influential screening agencies, see Gordon S. Smith, "Relationship to the Privy Council Office and the Cabinet" in *Speaker's Remarks: Seminar for Members of Federal Administrative Tribunals*, April 5-7, 1978 (Ottawa: Law Reform Commission of Canada, 1978), pp. 165-179.

13. Section 6, "Delegation of Authority" of the Public Service Employment Act, Stats. Can. 1966-7, c.71 states:
> [The Public Service Commission] . . . may authorize a deputy head to exercise and perform, in such manner and subject to such terms and conditions as the Commission directs, any of the powers, functions and duties of the Commission under this Act, other than the powers, functions and duties of the Commission in relation to appeals under sections 21 and 31 and inquiries under section 32.
Section 7(2) of the Financial Administration Act, Stats. Can., 1966-7, c.74 states:
> The Treasury Board may authorize the deputy head of a department or the chief executive officer of any portion of the public service to exercise and perform . . . any of the powers and functions of the Treasury Board in relation to personnel management in the public service and may, from time to time as it sees fit, revise or rescind, and reinstate the authority so granted.

14. The picturesque phraseology is from Sir Henry Taylor, an English poet and senior civil servant of the nineteenth century. H. Taylor, *The Statesman* (Cambridge: W. Heffer and Sons, 1957), pp. 82-83 (first published in 1836).

15. Herbert R. Balls, "Common Services in Government," *Canadian Public Administration*, 17:2 (Summer 1974), pp. 226-241.

16. A.W. Johnson, "The Role of the Deputy Minister," reproduced in W.D.K. Kernaghan, ed., *Public Administration in Canada: Selected Readings*, 2nd ed. (Toronto: Methuen, 1971), pp. 348-357 at pp. 350-351.

17. H.V. Kroeker, *Accountability and Control: The Government Expenditure Process* (Montreal: C.D. Howe Research Institute, 1978), p. 16.

18. H.L. Laframboise, "Administrative reform in the federal public service: signs of saturation psychosis," *CPA*, 14:3 (Fall 1971), pp. 303-325. Quoted from *CPA's* Twentieth Anniversary issue, pp. 113, 109-110.

19. Bertram M. Gross, *The Managing of Organizations: The Administrative Struggle*, Vol. I (New York: The Free Press of Glencoe, 1964), pp. 280-216.

20. Dwight Waldo, "Organization Theory: An Elephantine Problem," *Public Administration Review*, 11 (Autumn 1961), p. 225.

21. Usually described in graphic efficiency terms as the "machinery of government." Very few definitions abound as to what this actually means; B.B. Schaffer defines the term as:
    In simple, it is the organization of those branches of government, and generally national as against local government, other than the primarily legislative and judicial sections: the structure of executive government.
    B.B. Schaffer, "Brownlow or Brookings: Approaches to the Improvement of the Machinery of Government," in B.B. Schaffer, *The Administrative Factors: Papers in Organization, Politics and Development* (London: Frank Cass, 1973), p. 77.

22. J.E. Hodgetts, *The Canadian Public Service*, pp. 138-156. Hodgetts augments this impression by asserting that all the "control agencies," are "single purpose centralized departments," a categorization with which we have some difficulty with. See his pages 163-168.

23. Charles Dickens, *Little Dorrit*.

24. H. Spencer, *The Study of Sociology* (1st ed. 1837), 1961, p. 111.

25. J. Donald Kingsley, *Representative Bureaucracy: An Interpretation of the British Civil Service* (Yellow Springs, Ohio: Antioch Press, 1944).

26. Charles Dickens, *Little Dorrit*, p. 96. For the actual case study which interested Charles Dickens and influenced his book *Little Dorrit*, see Victor J. Alexander, "A Nineteenth Century Scandal," *Public Administration* (London) XXVIII (Winter 1950), pp. 295-300.

27. The contributions of such illustrious public servants as Sir James Stephen, Henry Taylor, Stafford Northcote, Charles Trevelyan, and the unsurpassed brilliance of Edwin Chadwick, are all well known and publicized in British administrative history. For an excellent article on this topic, see G. Kitson Clark, " 'Statesmen in Disguise': Reflexions on the History of the Neutrality of the Civil Service," *Historical Journal* II;1 (1959), pp. 19-39.

28. G. Kitson Clark, *ibid.*, p. 28.

29. R.L. Wettenhall, "The Ministerial Department," *Public Administration* (Sydney), XXXII:3 (September 1973), p. 235. Courtesy, Australian Journal of Public Administration.

30. F.M.G. Willson, "Ministries and Boards: Some Aspects of Administrative Development Since 1832," *Public Administration*, journal of the Royal Institute of Public Administration, (London) 33 (Spring 1955), p. 45.

31. F.M.G. Willson, *ibid.*, p. 53.

32. *Ibid.*, p. 52ff. Interest in boards was again revived by 1905, a point which we will follow up in our analysis of the Canadian situation.

33. B.B. Schaffer, "The Idea of the Ministerial Department," *Australian Journal of Politics and History*, 3:1 (Queensland: University of Queensland Press: November 1957), pp. 60-69. Jeremy Bentham devoted much of his philosophical energies to elaborating on the utilitarian conceptions of tidiness and efficiency. The basic root of utilitarianism has always been a passion for order and the elaboration of a set of incentives which would encourage the individual to the correct degree of rectitude and work. It is therefore no coincidence that public administration, like economics, has always been branded with the label of "efficiency and effectiveness" studies— despite profound evolutionary developments in the field over the last fifty years.

34. *Ibid.*, p. 62.

35. *Ibid.*, pp. 62-63. Part of *Works of Bentham* as quoted in Schaffer.

36. *Ibid.*, p. 72.

37. For the best historical treatment of these reforms, see Edward Hughes, "Civil Service Reform, 1853-5," *Public Administration* (London) XXXII (Spring 1954), pp. 17-51. The Americans learnt and were later to copy a great deal from these reforms, inculcating them in the Pendleton Act of 1883. See Paul P. Van Riper, "Adapting a British Political Invention to American Needs," *Public Administration* (London) XXXI:4 (Winter 1953), pp. 317-330.

38. Quoted from Fritz Morstein Marx, *The Administrative State: An Introduction to Bureaucracy* (Chicago: University of Chicago Press, 1957), p. 55. Many of the English political leaders looked somewhat askance at the powerful Prussian bureaucracy, an experience they were dedicated to prevent in England. For example, Lord Palmerston, adviser to the Queen during the early part of Victoria's reign, was the first to inform the monarch what the word "bureaucracy" meant, and he regarded a permanent civil service "as a danger to, not a condition of, ministerial responsibility." B.B. Schaffer, "The Idea of the Ministerial Department," p. 61.

39. F.M.G. Willson, "Ministries and Boards," p. 54.

40. See particularly his Chapter V, "On Changes of Ministry," pp. 183-213, undoubtedly a classic in the study of public administration in a parliamentary system. Walter Bagehot, *The English Constitution* (London: Fontana Library, March 1963).

41. Quoted in Henry Parris, *Constitutional Bureaucracy: The Development of British Central Administration Since the Eighteenth Century* (London: George Allen and Unwin Ltd., 1969), p. 80.

42. R.L. Wettenhall, "The Ministerial Department," p. 239.

43. R. MacGregor Dawson, *The Principle of Official Independence* (London: P.S. King and Son Ltd., 1922), pp. 6-7.

44. Walter Bagehot, *The English Constitution*, p. 199. Later on, Bagehot adds: "The use

of a fresh mind applied to the official mind is not only a corrective use, it is also an animating use" (p. 200).

45. *Ibid.*, pp. 198, 213.

46. *Ibid.*, p. 212.

47. Schaffer, "The Idea of a Ministerial Department," p. 77.

48. Willson, "Ministries and Boards," p. 48.

49. *Ibid.*

50. Wettenhall, "The Ministerial Department," pp. 239-240.

51. I have greatly simplified the analysis of "rationality" given by the political philosopher Paul Diesing. It is an analysis which I believe to be enlightening. For further exploration of these themes, the interested reader should find the following sources particularly helpful: Paul Diesing, "Noneconomic Decision-Making," *Ethics*, Vol. LXVI, No. 1, Part I, (October 1955), pp. 18-35; "Socioeconomic Decisions," *Ethics*, LXIX, No. 1 (October 1958), pp. 1-18. Also see his *Reason in Society* (Urbana: University of Illinois Press, 1962), for a comprehensive treatment of this subject.

52. Victor A. Thompson, *Bureaucracy and the Modern World* (Morristown, N.J.: General Learning Press, 1976), pp. 133, 129.

Recommended Readings

Readings for Chapters Ten and Eleven are found at the end of Chapter Eleven.

CHANGES IN MINISTERIALIZATION, 1841-1980

. . .*responsible government is foreign neither to our habits nor our traditions. In fact, the term is a Canadian invention,* and our cabinet system was developed here at about the same time that the modern cabinet was emerging in Britain. We built it out of our own experience—as much in French Canada as in English Canada. Whatever the trouble with the system, it stems from our own political culture.

J. R. Mallory

. . . the concept of "responsible government" appears not to have been introduced into British political debates until as late as 1829, and then in relation to Canada rather than Britain.

A. H. Birch

I. Introduction

The study of government organization or, more appropriately, the machinery of government, is conceived by many to mean a study of organization charts to discover how administrative work might be allocated in "rational" fashion. Rationality used in this sense conjures up the most recent meaning bestowed on the term by utilitarianism, that is, not the rule of reason, but the rule of measurement and efficiency.[1] Structural change and functional reallocation in the name of economy and efficiency are not subjects liable to excite the imaginations of most social scientists interested in public policy. Generally then, the subject matter is stereotyped as being banal and largely inconsequential. This dismissive viewpoint recently provoked one student of public policy and administration to make the following defence of his machinery of government study:

There is a simple, straightforward defence that can be mustered in favour of the procedures used for analysing the allocation of programmes to departments and agencies and for exploring the internal division of labour: it has not yet been done and it should be done before we fly off to the esoteric realms inhabited by modern-day organizational theorists and administrative behaviouralists. The failure to adopt these exciting contemporary tools of analysis is not a mark of disapproval or disagreement: the preference for more pedestrian modes of inquiry is simply based on an old-fashioned notion that we must first learn to walk before we can fly.[2]

"Learning to walk" in public administration means that the student should have a firm grasp on public administration's "historical roots," that is, some understanding of the stages of the evolution of contemporary governmental machinery and the main factors which have guided this evolution.

A study of the machinery of government should encompass much more than mere "bureau shuffling." Above all, it is concerned with the *political implications* of the following factors: (a) the grouping and delegation of administrative functions in government, (b) the arrangements about the distribution of entirely new functions or existing functions which must be considered afresh or are not functioning as anticipated, and (c) the creation of ministerial positions under whose political jurisdiction (a) or (b) will rest.[3]

In this chapter our concerns will be narrowed as we examine how the growing complexity of the ministerial portfolio has created "new," "different" and "growing" conceptions of governmental machinery in Canada. We do not give a detailed analytical critique of the machinery of government. Our mission was conceived as one which would present a "bare-bones" description of the various ministerial forms. Therefore we will briefly describe the modes of ministerialization which we now possess. As we will later show these modes are composed of liberal borrowings from British and other Western European politico-administrative experiences, fashioned to the needs of the Canadian political and administrative environments.

II. Canadian Practical Adaptations: Going Our Own Way, 1841-1912

Fifteen years before *Little Dorrit* was to be published (1857) and British society and its public administration so brilliantly lampooned, Charles Dickens set foot in Canada for a visit. He was not impressed:

Of course there is no place like old England. There never was, and never will be. What has a rational man to do with Canada? Nothing at all. Nobody who "calls himself a gentleman" . . . has anything in common with such outlandish parts.[4]

But it was precisely in these "outlandish parts" that an early experiment in administrative reform, *which the British were still at least two decades away from adopting, was being conducted.* That was in fact the ministerial department, introduced in the "hothouse experiment" called Canada by a leading Whig politician, friend of Jeremy Bentham and utilitarian reformer of sorts, Lord Sydenham, the Governor-General of Canada between 1839 and 1841.[5] Parenthetically, it should be mentioned that the introduction of this innovation is reminiscent of the manner in which personnel reforms were also introduced in the British environment. English utilitarian reformers first experimented with recruitment of personnel by merit for the East India Company, and as these reforms proved successful in India they were copied by Northcote and Trevelyan in 1853 and introduced in England as the reform model to be followed. As indicated in the previous chapter, it took close to two decades *after* 1853 before these innovations became administrative reality in Britain.

As Adam Shortt, J. E. Hodgetts and J. R. Mallory have all indicated, Sydenham was responsible for introducing two important reforms.[6] First, he singlehandedly created cabinet government in Canada, "by conferring inititative and power on the Canadian elite operating through the Canadian party system"[7] Thus, the party system in the legislature was born due to his initiatives. However it was to the Governor-General that the party was ultimately responsible and not the legislature. Still a few decades away was the notion of responsible government as we conceive it today.[8]

More germane to our purposes is Sydenham's second reform. Before coming to Canada, Sydenham had acquired an impeccable administrative background as President of the Board of Trade, efficient businessman, a proponent of administrative reform and a former member of Parliament. Upon becoming Governor-General in Canada, he instituted Lord Durham's recommendations for the improvement of the organization of the executive by creating ministerial departments and making the executive Council a body of ministers responsible to him rather than to the legislature. It is worth quoting Hodgetts at length on these reforms because at least two significant facts about Canadian administration flow from Sydenham's innovations:

The principle of unified command and co-ordination was carried down from the Governor to the head of each department. Syndenham, following Durham's advice, created a separate political head for each major department. This measure necessitated a reshuffling of duties amongst existing departments and the creation of several new agencies. This process of administrative "rationalization" was responsible for the reforms in the Executive Council, Civil and Provincial Secretary's Offices, and the Offices of the Inspector General and Receiver General. At the same time new departments like Crown lands and the Board of Works were created. Sydenham's insistence upon the adoption of the British practice of having all money bills introduced by members of the executive further tightened the reins of control held at the top. Since each departmental head was made individually responsible to the Governor rather than jointly responsible to the popular assembly, Sydenham's plan obviously fell far short of the modern cabinet system.[9]

The fact, however, remains that the innovation of having all money bills introduced by members of the executive was not established in British practice, but at that very same period it was being introduced in the British Parliament. As Norman Ward has indicated, Sydenham, on the eve of the union of the two Canadas, "had written cheerfully that 'one of the greatest advantages of the Union will be, that it will be possible to introduce a new system of legislation, and above all, a restriction upon the initiation of money votes.' "[10] Financial control of administration had been tightened somewhat before 1832 in England but it was not until the 1860s that the complete system of financial control, as we have come to know it, was established in that country.[11]

This process of tandem introduction of reforms has created some other interesting Canadian variations in the ministerial portfolio and in the practices of responsible government. In Canada, responsible government meant that in law ministers responsible to Parliament, and not civil servants, are assigned the powers and duties exercised by their departments. This is a unique Canadian practice. Another Canadian variation is that governments have always obtained parliamentary approval before departments and/or agencies could be created. This is distinctly at variance with the United Kingdom practice where the creation of departments is historically the Crown's prerogative, and no parliamentary approval is therefore needed for such creation.

Since the 1850s we have always had a civil service act for Parliament "to regulate" the public service. This has not been the case in the United Kingdom because the British public servant is not hired under a general civil service act and the public service is regulated by executive decrees (except for pensions and prohibitions on holding political office).

Other significant variations abound. One of the most interesting is the naming of the chief administrative officer of each department. In England the position of "secretary" existed on an informal basis in a few departments during the eighteenth century, but it was not until May 1867 that the title of Permanent Secretary was formally established in British administration.[12] In contrast, Canadians using both their own colonial experience and ingenuity coined, sometime in the 1840s or early '50s, the term *deputy minister* to refer to the administrative heads of Canadian departments.[13] J. R. Mallory notes that the term deputy minister "is confusing to outsiders because it implies that the deputy head has the power to act in place of the minister. . . . This difficulty is not only in the misleading sound of the title but also in the fact that the permanent heads of departments elsewhere in the Commonwealth generally go by the title of 'secretary' or 'permanent secretary' while the term 'deputy minister' is used for what in Canada is called parliamentary secretary."[14]

As a matter of fact, apart from the use of the term prime minister to identify the leader of the government, the British have never used the term "minister" to refer to political departmental heads until during World War I when the Minister of Munitions was so designated, and his department became the first "Ministry" ever in British government.[15] By 1935, Britain had five ministers (the Ministries of Agriculture and Fisheries, Health, Labour, Pensions and Transport), and by 1956, twelve. Gradually, the cabinet titles such as President of the Board of Education, First Commissioner of Works, Chief Secretary to the Lord Lieutenant of Ireland, Secretary for Scotland and President of the Local Government Board have all been replaced by new or renamed "ministerial" designations (Minister of Education, Works, Housing and Local Government, etc.).[16] As with the concept of responsible government the evidence points to the fact that both terms, minister and deputy minister have been popularized and officially used in the Canadian federal government long before they were adopted in other jurisdictions.[17]

Another significant Canadian variation from the English administrative experience is the strikingly noticeable absence of boards and commission in this country during the nineteenth century. Indeed, Sydenham had a marked success in his administrative reforms, perhaps more than is generally realized. Canadian Confederation was started with an administrative apparatus of ten major departments of government with individual ministers; three other agencies generally classified as departments with separate deputy heads, but forming joint ministries with one of the major departments; and the North West Mounted Police which reported to the President of the Privy Council.[18] Few boards and commissions existed on the Canadian administrative landscape. In 1841, Sydenham established a Board of Works with corporate status to construct a canal system, but even this board quickly lost its independence when it was integrated into the Department of Public Works in 1846.[19] Between 1852 and 1917 a few public corporations were established but these were all restricted to administering harbour facilities across Canada.[20]

During the early twentieth century, almost simultaneously as in Britain, this administrative picture began to change drastically.[21] By the start of World War I Des Roches reports that there were some thirty departments and agencies and ". . . an increasing use of the commission or board of commissioners as an instrument of administration. Another new phenomenon was the creation of agencies to control more effectively the growing internal administrative activity or to provide central services."[22]

By 1911, this proliferation of departments and independent boards and commissions was considered untidy, *a far cry from the neat administrative arrangement of ministerial departments, responsible ministers and Treasury control.* With the perspicacity of admiring colonials, Canadian advisers to the Prime Minister thought they saw this neat arrangement in Britain (where, by this time, reality was quite the reverse): "In Britain alone do we find a system which is at once sufficiently effective and entirely suited to our system of government, as framed on the British model. The British system of 'Treasury Control' is worthy of most serious consideration in view of the present and prospective needs of the Canadian Executive Government."[23] As a result of this advice, Sir George Murray, a former permanent secretary of the British Treasury, was commissioned to report on the organization of the public service of Canada.[24] Not surprisingly, the Murray Report called for sweeping reforms along the lines of the ideal "British model": the devolution of more legal and administrative powers to individual ministers, thereby circumscribing the Canadian practice of collective cabinet responsibility; the grouping of administrative tasks under departments rather than the proliferating boards and commissions slowly but steadily being created by government;[25] the adoption of an "inner" and "outer" cabinet; the creation of "political deputy ministers" to relieve the ministers from many administrative tasks; and the abolition of the Treasury Board and the assignment of all duties pertaining to "Treasury control" to the Department of Finance. The overwhelming bias of the Report is in the utilitarian tradition: the streamlining of the machinery of government, the reaffirmation of the "orthodoxy" of individual ministerial responsibility, the recommendation for centralized financial and administrative controls, and the introduction of personnel reforms along the lines of the Northcote Trevelyan recommendations. Although personnel reforms in the public service were yet to be realized, already the ministerial department was being dated, ostensibly because of the needs of an increasing welfare state and the desire for administrative flexibility.[26] Summing up the English experience, Willson wistfully remarks:

In contemplating the arrangements of that era [between the late 1850s and 1905] from amidst the sprawling administrative empires [of the present time] it is not difficult to be convinced that we are unlikely to see again a constitutional system at once so simple, so comprehensive and so satisfying.[27]

The reader would by now have realized that *it is no accident that the heyday of Parliamentary supremacy and power coincided with the orthodoxy of individual ministerial responsibility which in turn both coincided with the "best" form of ministerial administration, namely, the departmental form.* This is one of the central themes of this chapter, namely, *that the ideal norm of both responsible government and the doctrine of ministerial responsibility is the departmental form of administration.* However, this perfect synchronization of institutions and political philosophy was short-lived. Why was this so? Social scientists tell us that as societies continue to evolve, as technology continues to advance and as tasks become increasingly complex, "these simple and satisfying" arrangements are also subject to various rates of change.[28] What is indeed interesting is that well over eighty years ago in Canada the machinery of government began to manifest certain changes in response to these societal dynamics, and our social science "institutionalists," steeped in the tradition of Parliamentary government, were able to recognize this central fact. As already pointed out, both Graham Wallas and R. MacGregor Dawson have argued that the belief of the "all-sufficiency of representative government" is really ephemeral in nature, and suggested that more complex forms of relationships must be adopted if liberal democracy is to survive and function properly.[29]

Sir George Murray's report failed to gain political acceptance in Canada because its error was in its inability to see this evolution clearly. Its assumptions and biases, particularly as regards the machinery of government, prevented it from making recommendations which would be suited to a changing administrative landscape.[30] In a three to four months' visit Sir George made some of the most sweeping administrative and political recommendations which would have wrought profound political changes in the machinery of government for that time: his "inner" and "outer" cabinet concept, as well as his abolition of the Treasury Board, not to mention his views on the need to return to the principles and pristine form of ministerial departmentalization, were all too idealistic. Sir Robert Borden's comments therefore seem much more politically realistic when he argued that the Report was ". . . very sweeping in character [with a] mixture of practical and impractical suggestions . . . In fact Sir George Murray has probably an imperfect conception of the difficulties that would confront any administration in the attempt to put in force some of his recommendations however valuable they appeared to him."[31] After this adventure Canadians had to wait another half a century before the advent of another administrative "Samurai" who would, by pure reason, introduce the benefits of economy, efficiency logic and order into the processes of government.[32]

III. Housekeeping Changes: 1912-1950s

J. A. Corry is reported to have once said that a tidy mind was a liability in dealing with Canadian federalism, a remark which in our view is borne out by any "rational" attempt to deal with the logical growth of ministerial portfolios between 1912 and 1939. All four of our prime ministers during that period (Borden, Meighen, Bennett and King) refused to engage in any wholesale reform similar to the proposals of Sir George Murray. What we did have, however, were a series of incremental changes in portfolio structures, changes which now seem to be permanent innovations in cabinet government.

By the turn of this century, Canadian ministries began the use of Ministers without Portfolio. Before 1926, however, incumbents were sworn as Privy Councillors, but attended cabinet meetings only at the invitation of the Prime Minister. This was changed by 1926, and all Ministers without Portfolio since then have been recognized as full-fledged members of a ministry.[33] Also considered part of a ministry but not of the cabinet were the various appointments of Parliamentary Secretaries and Parliamentary Under Secretaries, made from amongst the members of the House of Commons, to assist various ministers or to act in their absence. This practice began in 1916. Parliamentary Assistants, first appointed during the King Ministry in the 1930s, also had the responsibilities of assisting various designated ministers, until the positions were abolished by the Government Organization Act of 1970-71.[34]

Administrative relief for ministerial portfolios was therefore centered on a series of important incremental reforms on the parliamentary front to relieve ministers of the pressures emanating from the House of Commons.[35] One major reform which took place in the 1930s should be mentioned. The Bennett government at the beginning of the Depression revitalized the Treasury Board from a position of relative insignificance to a central piece of machinery having the *de facto* status of being the chief governmental control agency. The extension of Treasury Board's control over departmental expenditures and personnel matters is a complex development, which cannot be adequately dealt with here.[36] Generally speaking, however, we can state that the seeds for the basic machinery of government changes which took place in the 1960s were sewn slowly but inexorably some three and a half decades before they were finally enshrined in legislation.[37]

The advent of hostilities in both Europe and the Pacific, and Canada's entry into the war meant that cabinet's business simply proliferated. The government was forced to introduce three basic changes which further relieved both the Prime Minister and his cabinet of the awesome volume of work with which they were now faced. First, the cabinet was subdivided into a system of functional subcommittees which enabled ministers to participate more meaningfully in the collective decisions of the cabinet. Cabinet as a whole could only meet for so many hours weekly, and it was therefore impossible for the whole cabinet to review all policy recommendations and proposals for legislation and orders-in-council. The committee structure thus reduced the work load considerably on individual ministers, particularly on those who had responsibilities directly related to the Canadian war effort.[38] Although this system of committees fell into disuse following World War II (as also happened after World War I), the precedent was thus established, and the committee structure was again revived in the 1960s.

Secondly, the result of these changes meant that the administrative structure around the cabinet had to be rationalized both politically and legally. Thus the office of the Secretary to the Cabinet was created, fusing it with the more historic position of Clerk to the Privy Council. Cabinet meetings were then scheduled for and administrative procedures instituted to record cabinet decisions and to issue orders-in-council.[39] For the first time in Canadian history cabinet ministers began to be briefed *before* cabinet meetings, and were kept much more informed of the ongoing policy developments of their government.[40] Thirdly, by the Financial Administration Act, 1951, and a number of other statutes, a vast quantity of the delegated legislation which flowed from the growth of cabinet activities was rerouted to other parts of the machinery of Canadian government.[41] J. R. Mallory summarizes these changes by observing that:

. . . the central executive machinery of the government of Canada has undergone considerable change and adaptation to meet the needs imposed on contemporary government. Functioning under the 1939 procedure the central executive would have broken down in a few weeks under the burden of ordinary government operation today. This change and improvement has taken place rapidly and quietly on ministerial (and, no doubt, official) initiative. It demonstrates again the remarkable flexibility of Cabinet government.[42]

However, many problems still surfaced. A restructuring of responsibilities remained to be accomplished between the revitalized Treasury Board and another central agency, the Public Service Commission. Problems dealing with departmental financial responsibility awaited solution, and the strident calls from public servants for the rights of collective bargaining signalled that fundamental changes in government machinery had to be effected if these demands were going to be met. Thus a basic but complex sortation of the machinery of government was required before the introduction of these reforms in the public service. At the ministerial portfolio level it meant a restructuring of one of the central subcommittees of cabinet, the Treasury Board of Canada.

IV. The Sixties

By the mid-1960s, certain other housekeeping functions were attended to, notably by the Pearson government. The Diefenbaker ad-

DR. JAMES R. MALLORY
Professor, Department of Political Science, McGill University. From his pen flows a breadth of legal and historical knowledge and a subtlety of constitutional interpretation matched by few Canadian political scientists. Mallory has made a distinct contribution to the understanding of Canadian public policy and administration through his writings on the political environment.

ministration (1957-1963) had, however, earlier sewn the seeds for basic changes in the machinery of government by creating the Royal Commission on Government Organization (Glassco) in 1960. In 1963, when the Liberals were returned to power as a minority government under Lester Pearson, it was left to that administration to implement the Glassco recommendations. Prior to dealing with these problems, however, the Prime Minister, Mr. Pearson, took the unusual step of placing the Presidency of the Privy Council in hands other than his own.[43] This change seemed to be aimed at shifting the burden of house leadership onto the shoulders of another minister other than the Prime Minister.[44] The Government Reorganization Act, 1966 finally created the Department of the Solicitor General, a portfolio which is comprised of the Royal Canadian Mounted Police, the Penitentiaries Service and the National Parole Board.[45] Two new ministerial positions were also created: The Registrar General, who assumed the responsibilities for bankruptcy, combines investigations, patents, copyrights, etc., and the President of the Treasury Board, giving to this cabinet subcommittee and its secretariat its own minister for the first time in its long history.[46] This change in the Board's status was in anticipation of the 1967 legislation which would give to the Treasury Board new powers as the *Cabinet's Committee on the Expenditure Budget* and the *Cabinet's Committee on Management.*[47]

Actually, this cosmetic narration of changes in the machinery of government fails to reveal the deeper forces which brought about this juggling of portfolios. Most Canadians have a general perception that governmental activity has for some time been growing both in complexity and extent. As the functions of government are extended its nature changes in response, and for our limited purposes here this means a growth in expenditures, employees and organizational units. A cursory view of some random growth figures for that period of time gives us some dimensions of growth. As approximate figures they verify the simple generalization that with the growth of the positive state in Canada, both the number of governmental employees and our system of organizational units have correspondingly increased.

Hodgetts presents a concise handy summary of organizational considerations accompanying this growth:

In the early years after Confederation there were more departments than the limited public agenda of the period required; accordingly, for a time as the agenda grew, existing departments could easily absorb the added duties. When "spill-overs" began to develop, new portfolios were added but only to the extent of a modest doubling of their original number. Since the notion of a British ministry with a selected group making up a smaller cabinet was rejected a practical limit to the number of ministerial portfolios was soon established. There then remained no other option but to move outside the departmental form to establish "quasi-departments," statutory executives, public corporations, crown companies, and numerous commissions. The resultant organizational mix may be a testimony to our inventive (and imitative) genius but it is also a reflection of our *ad hoc* response to the increasingly crowded public agenda.[48]

Whether machinery of government questions can be anything other than *ad hoc* decisions, responding to a complex and ever-changing public agenda is a debatable question which we shall not pursue here. Hodgetts' remarks, however, do point to the stark changes in organizational machinery by the late 1960s. Figures I and II present these facts graphically. In Figure I we attempt to show how significant Canadian developments of ministerialization predated and differed from the British developments. As our epigrams demonstrate, both J. R. Mallory and A. H. Birch point to the significant, early development of responsible government in Canada. We have attempted to show what this political development meant for Canada in terms of administrative reform.

In 1867, the new Confederation started out with no more than a few thousand employees, ten major departments and three agencies. It is no wonder that this period was the heyday of individual ministerial responsibility. Hodgetts records that it was entirely feasible for an energetic minister to both know most of his staff personally and to attend to much of the day-to-day business of departmental administration. Furthermore, ". . . evidence of this direct personal concern of ministers in the detailed management of their departments is provided in the records of the privy Council in which we find lengthy memoranda dealing with proposed reorganization, right down to the last low-grade clerk."[49] By the turn of the century government was too big for ministers to engage in this detailed administrative interference, and thus machinery of government questions as well as personnel reform loomed as significant problems in governmental administration. By 1975 we had twenty-five ministerial portfolios, approximately a quarter of a million public servants and, supposedly, fifty-two Crown corporations and agencies. The reader should note that the emphasized areas in Figure II* are our traditional departments, the departments of Mill, Bagehot, Sir George Murray and others. By 1975, these organizational units appear to be almost swallowed up by the other units in the complex amalgam that makes up a ministerial portfolio.

* *See end of book for figure II.*

FIGURE I

CHRONOLOGICAL CHART DEPICTING IMPORTANT CANADIAN AND BRITISH
DEVELOPMENTS OF MINISTERIALIZATION

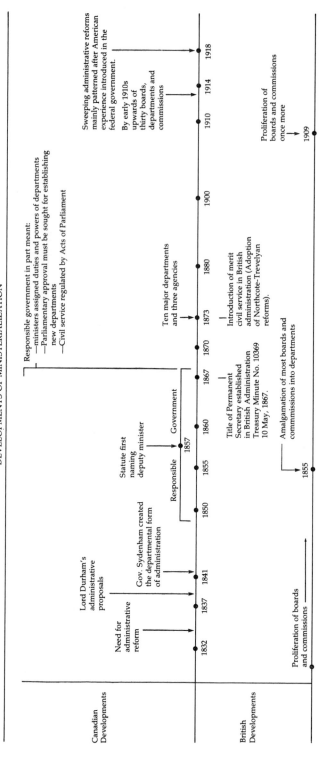

TABLE I
APPROXIMATE NUMBERS OF FEDERAL GOVERNMENT EMPLOYEES AND MAJOR DEPARTMENTS AND AGENCIES IN CANADA, SELECTED YEARS

Selected Years	No. of Employees	No. of Major Depts. and Agencies
1900	12,000	28
1920	42,000	43
1930	44,000	43
1939 (pre war)	46,000	57
1945	116,000	114
1950	127,000	78
1960	200,000	92
1966	228,000	97

Adapted from: Jacques M. DesRoches, "The Evolution of the Organization of Federal Government in Canada," CPA 5 (1962); 408-427; J.E. Hodgetts and O.P. Dwivedi, "The Growth of Government Employment in Canada," CPA 12 (1969): 224-238.

V. Ministerial Portfolios in the 1970s

The advent of Pierre Elliot Trudeau in 1968 saw some major changes in ministerial portfolios being effected. Behind these reforms was a philosophy which has been well-publicized. One quote from the works of Trudeau, written in 1964, illustrates:

In the world of tomorrow, the expression "banana republic" will not refer to independent fruit-growing nations but to countries where formal independence has been given priority over the cybernetic revolution. In such a world, the state—if it is not to be outdistanced by its rivals—will need political instruments which are sharper, stronger, and more finely controlled than anything based on mere emotionalism: such tools will be made up of advanced technology and scientific investigation, as applied to the fields of law, economics, social psychology, international affairs, and other areas of human relations; in short, if not a pure product of reason, the political tools of the future will be designed and appraised by more rational standards than anything we are currently using in Canada today.[50]

To the Trudeau administration, "rational standards" in part meant rational machinery to achieve results. In the previous chapter we have already discussed what this has meant to the cabinet and its committee structure. In early 1971, the Government Organization Bill was passed in the House of Commons, and among other things it identified two new kinds of ministers in addition to the existing departmental ministers and ministers without portfolio. These were "Ministers of State" and "Ministers of State for designated purposes." The Hon. C. M. Drury, then President of the Treasury Board, described the spectrum of ministerial portfolios then in existence:

Departmental ministers would occupy an office created by statute to which are attached powers, duties and functions defined by statute; have supervision and control over a portion of the public service known as a department; be limited in number by the number of statutory ministerial offices; have salaries provided for by title in the Salaries Act; and seek appropriations on their own from Parliament to cover the cost of the activities for which they are responsible.

Ministers of State for designated purposes would occupy an office created by proclamation on the advice of the prime minister; be limited in number by statute to five; be charged with responsibilities for developing new and comprehensive policies in areas where the development of such policies is of particular urgency and importance; have a mandate effectively determined by the prime minister which would be of such duration as to enable them to come to grips with the policy problems assigned to them; receive powers, duties and functions and exercise supervision and control of relevant elements of the public service; and seek parliamentary appropriations independently of any minister to cover the cost of their staff and operations. They would have a "secretary" who would have the status and authority of a deputy head for the purpose of the Financial Administration Act and the Public Service Employment Act, *and would preside over ministries which would eventually either become parts of new or existing departments or whose existence would be terminated.*

Ministers of State would be appointed to assist a departmental minister in the discharge of his responsibilities; receive powers, duties and functions; be limited in number by the appropriations that Parliament is willing to pass to cover their salaries and expenses, and receive the same salary as a minister without portfolio provided for them in the estimates of the minister with whom they were to be associated. Finally, *ministers without portfolio* would have responsibilities assigned by the prime minister and would not normally exercise statutory powers, duties and functions.[51]

The historical background, including the rationale for the creation of the ministry of state concept, has been comprehensively developed elsewhere.[52] A few other observations, coming from our perspective, should be made here about these ministerial portfolios. While there are a whole host of other policy intentions implicit in government reorganization, one which came out most clearly was the government's intention of rearranging ministerial portfolios into recogniz-

ably *horizontal coordinative, administrative coordinate,* and *vertical constituency* portfolios. What is the distinction here? Canadian ministries
have never adopted the Murray/Haldane recommendation, from earlier this century, to legally create an "inner" and "outer" cabinet and
neither had they thought too much of the "rational idea" that machinery of government can only be structured according to *allocation
by service* and not *allocation according to the persons or classes to be dealt
with.*[53] No government has ever been that impolitic to accept the idea
that allocation by service is the *only* rational criterion for structuring
the machinery of government. However, sixty years after the recommendation was first made the increasingly crowded public agenda
has forced an "inner functional cabinet" in the sense that certain cabinet roles have evolved to be inherently more important than others.[54]
This has come about primarily because of the need to have more and
more control of a complex machinery. Thus certain portfolios inherently cross-cut, in a horizontal manner, the whole public agenda.
Such portfolios are concerned with the "overall political leadership
and strategy, foreign policy, and the foreign implications of domestic
policy fields, aggregate economic and fiscal policy, the basic legal and
judicial concepts and values of the state and the overall management
of government spending programmes."[55] Doern classifies the portfolios of External Affairs, Finance, Justice, the Treasury Board, the
Prime Minister and the President of the Privy Council as falling into
the above category.

Among other portfolios of government there are a number, which
by providing common services to all government departments, also
crosscut horizontally all other ministerial portfolios. However, as we
have already pointed out in the previous chapter, *service-wide functions are necessary but not sufficient conditions* to make organizations into
instruments of power and high policy influence. Such portfolios as
National Revenue, Public Works, and Supply and Services are categorized as *administrative coordinative portfolios* dealing with the administrative "nuts and bolts" aspects needed to keep the whole of government in operation.

The third category is *vertical constituency portfolios,* a classification
which Doern calls "the vertical dimension of government" in that
they tend to extend outward to deal not so much with service-wide
functions but with clearly delineated constituencies characterized by
allocation of services and/or persons or classes. Such portfolios as
Agriculture, Energy, Mines and Resources, Indian Affairs and Northern Development, Labour, and Veterans Affairs, are included in this
category.

The fourth category covered under the 1970-71 reorganization is the ministry of state, a portfolio which, as the Hon. C. M. Drury noted earlier, was conceived as a *flexible coordinative arrangement* which could be dissolved or inflated as the government so wished. In the years since the designation was created, we have seen ministers of state appointed in Urban Affairs (since abolished), Science and Technology, Social Development and Economic Development, and ministers of state for such designated purposes as multiculturalism, small business, fitness and amateur sport, fisheries and federal-provincial relations. In the latter case the minister assisted was the Prime Minister, who held the responsibilities for coordinating federal-provincial relations. A further indication of the flexibility of the minister of state portfolio was indicated when one of the most senior ministers of the Trudeau ministry 1974-79, the Hon. Robert Andras, was appointed both a Minister of State and President of the Board of Economic Development Ministers, a coordinating cabinet committee which some commentators view as a strong rival to the "traditional" horizontal coordinative portfolios of Finance and the Treasury Board.*

This classification of *horizontal coordinative, administrative coordinative* and *vertical constituency* portfolios is suggestive rather than definitive. This classification, however, makes the central point: *the subtle interplay of individual ministerial and collective responsibilities is the essence of our system of government.* Moreover, this subtlety places the question of political influence as central to the whole process: as emphasized in our introductory remarks to this chapter, the machinery of government cannot be realistically studied apart from the politics of government, as some antiseptic exercise somehow immune from politics. Aucoin and French express this point superbly when they point out that the study of government machinery:

> . . . represents not only the objective of better formulated and co-ordinated policy in specific fields, but also the attempt to alter in the most fundamental way the scope and nature of Cabinet decision-making. [It provides us with an insight into the efforts of government] both to increase the flexibility and prerogative of the government in dealing with "priority problems" (policy issues which are not being effectively dealt with by existing government departments or agencies), and to enshrine rational analysis and planning in place of the interplay of traditional sources of power in Cabinet.[56]

Figure III is an attempt to pictorialize this "stream" of influences and interconnections. This presentation cannot grasp all the subtleties of

* *Note the comment on this point in Chapter Nine.*

FIGURE III

PROJECTION OF THE MACHINERY OF CANADIAN GOVERNMENT

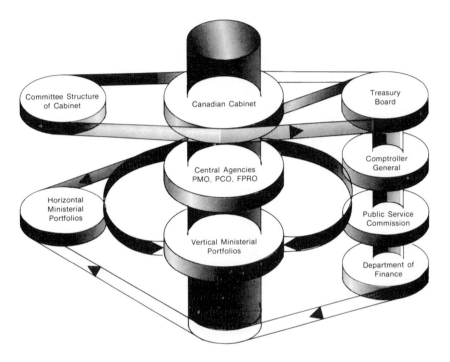

Diagram adapted from: André Gélinas, *Les Organismes autonomes et
centraux de l'Administration Québécoise*
(Montréal: Les Presses de l'université du Québec, 1975)

classification amongst central control agencies, cabinet committees, and ministerial portfolios, but it does present the overall conception of the machinery of government in such a manner as to emphasize *the aggregate political and organizational relationships* which we first introduced in the simplified notion of the politics-administration arch.

We come now to the latest form of experimentation with the ministerial portfolio. At about the same period when the minister of state portfolio was being devised (or even before it was conceptualized), yet another ministry form, patterned somewhat after the Swedish military experience, was being fashioned to reorganize the Secretary of State portfolio. As Figure II shows, this ministerial portfolio is a compilation of boards, commissions and crown corporations of varying degrees of independence, as well as the traditional departmental form (that is, the department of Secretary of State proper). This "congeries portfolio" as H. L. Laframboise called it, presented a challenge to effective policy planning and coordination, posing three essential questions which, if satisfactorily answered, could lead to better ministerial coordination.

1 How can a Minister of the Crown learn about, and manage within, a web of relationships which varies from one agency to another in his portfolio?

2 What is the role of the Deputy Minister who, while he is the administrative head of a "regular" government department, is in an ambiguous position in respect of the operations of the other agencies in his Minister's portfolio?

3 Are there advantages in the "independent" agency arrangement which could usefully be incorporated into the structure of a "regular department" or of its elements?[57]

The organizational solution sought was one which would fulfill two functions. First, part of the solution must be to centralize policy planning and coordination under the direct jurisdiction of the minister and a secretariat. This secretariat would have an adroit mix of a deputy minister, senior staff and such senior advisory bodies required for administrative and technical support. Second, the structure must at the same time preserve the treasured "independence" of the boards, commissions and crown corporations attached to the ministerial portfolio, while simultaneously serving to encourage closer cooperation and synchronization of policy planning between the minister's support staff and the independent agencies.

The solution devised was the Ministry system patterned partly after the Swedish ministry model. As H. L. Laframboise explained.:

A Ministry System, in its essence, consists of: a "general staff" headed by an appointed Deputy Minister and responsible to the Minister for advisory, coordinative and monitoring responsibilities over all of the agencies in the Minister's portfolio, whether these be regular departments or Crown corporations; a staff responsible to the Ministry for party and constituency matters; and, a number of agencies, each self-contained in respect of operating and administrative resources, and each headed by an administrator responsible directly to the Minister. . . . From the Minister's point of view, Ministry staff would operate as his own comprehensive central control agency, combining for him the attributes of a Treasury Board (evaluating priorities, alternatives and costs on a program basis), a Privy Council Office (preparing briefs and purveying advice on matters of Ministry policy and legislation), a Public Service Commission (advising on very senior appointments and monitoring delegated staffing authority), a Department of Supply and Services (providing management consulting at the highest level and monitoring delegated procurement authority), and so on.[58]

In Figure IV we have presented a very simple design which should serve to emphasize the basic changes in ministerialization experienced in the Canadian federal government. The original ministerial form depicted by mode 1 has very few, if any, examples extant. Perhaps the Departments of Public Works, the Post Office, National Revenue and Communications serve as the closest approximates to this mode. Much more common, of course, are variants characterized by modes 2 and 3, with the ministry of state and the ministry system being the latest models. Mode 4 depicts the Ministry of State without any reporting lines of authority from the departments (each with its own statutory minister and responsible for its own programs) to the Secretariat. This design emphasizes the purely coordinative role of ministries of state. As pointed out earlier, however, this role has the

FIGURE IV

MODES OF MINISTERIALIZATION: THE CANADIAN EXPERIENCE, 1867-1979

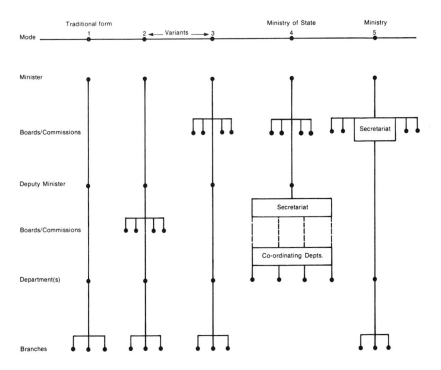

potential of changing from a merely passive one to that of control and high policy influence.

Mode 5, the Ministry system, was not introduced to the Secretary of State portfolio for various political and bureaucratic reasons. Initial attempts to create the same or an approximate design for the Department of Energy, Mines and Resources have also proved fruitless. The only modestly successful application to date has been the ministerial portfolio of Transport, and as John Langford's comprehensive study indicates, the success was to a great extent due to a skillful combination of timing, personalities, and political circumstances.[59] The simplified design attempts to show how the boards and commissions, though independent of the secretariat, are nevertheless part of the team and reporting through the minister to Parliament. (For a generalized depiction of these modes on a governmental organization chart, see Appendix A.)

VI. Conclusions

So much for the concept of the ministerial department and its present-day derivatives. In giving this account we have attempted to weave together some political philosophy from Jeremy Bentham and John Stuart Mill, British and Canadian administrative history, a little from the popular writings of novelist Charles Dickens and political commentator Walter Bagehot, and a broad-brush account of the development of our machinery of government to the present day. This, to be sure, is a kaleidoscope of topics, each of which could be a subject for investigation in its own right. Be that as it may, it is our belief that all these issues are really tangential to the larger issues involved in the machinery of government, issues which we have attempted to keep central throughout our account: *the political coherence of the cabinet, the distribution of functions and responsibilities among ministers of the Crown, and the linkages between them and the public bureaucracy.* The political dimensions have been emphasized as paramount in this seemingly dry, dull "nuts and bolts" aspect of public policy and administration. On re-reading the Haldane Report some years ago, Professor W. J. M. MacKenzie emphasized this point superbly in his critique of the report:

What? No reference *at all* to the fact that these men are first and foremost party leaders? that the Cabinet is historically a cabal of politicians who must hang together, lest they hang separately? that in constitutional theory its primary role is to keep the vessel on some steady course amid the high seas of public clamour and political intrigue? The committee's assumption here is that the machinery of Government can in the twentieth century be studied apart from the politics of Government; that such a study will suggest improvement of the highest order of importance; and that these improvements can in some sense be carried through "outside politics." Did they seriously believe that there can be anything of first-rate importance in Government which is not politically important?[60]

Like MacKenzie, we do not believe that the subject of governmental machinery can be divorced from the political dimensions of its environment. The story of government machinery is, however, far from told as the next chapter will show. Some of the independent boards, commissions, and crown corporations—those supposed "structural heretics" or "barnacles" on the ministerial department— have in turn spawned organizational forms few students of public policy and administration realize exist. It is to an examination of this phenomenon that we now turn.

Three major calamities: fire, flood and officials.

A Burmese proverb

Footnotes

1. For an excellent exposition on the various meanings of rationality, see the award-winning essay by John M. Pfiffner, "Administrative Rationality," *Public Administration Review* 20:3 (1960), 125-132.

2. J.E. Hodgetts, *The Canadian Public Service: A Physiology of Government, 1867-1970* (Toronto: University of Toronto Press, 1973), p. xii.

3. D.N. Chester and F.M.G. Willson, *The Organisation of British Central Government, 1914-1956* (London: Allen and Unwin, 1957), pp. 333-338.

4. Charles Dickens to Captain Frederick Granville, 20 October 1842, in Madeline House, Gragam Storey and Kathleen Tillotson, eds., *The Letters of Charles Dickens* (Vol. III) 1842-1984 (Oxford: Clarendon Press, 1974), p. 354.

5. It was Sydenham who united the two Canadas in 1840. In Canadian history books much ado is made about his introduction of cabinet government but very little is said about the basic administrative reforms he undertook in the three brief years before his untimely death. Moreover, Canadian scholars who mention these administrative reforms erroneously assume that these changes had already been *fait accompli* in England before they were introduced in Canada. As we now know this was not so. This erroneous assumption has been partly fostered by the language of the Durham Report of 1837 which made the advocacy for Canadian reform sound as if the recommended changes on cabinet government and responsible administration were already accomplished feats in British government. One scholar who has been particularly perceptive of this discrepancy is J.R. Mallory. See his discussion of parliamentary government in his *The Structure of Canadian Government* (Toronto: Macmillan, 1971), pp. 7-11.

6. Adam Shortt, "The Relations between the Legislative and Executive Branches of the Canadian Government," *American Political Science Review* VII:2 (May 1913), 181-

196; Mallory, *ibid.*, pp. 10-11; J.E. Hodgetts, *Pioneer Public Service: An Administrative History of the United Canadas, 1841-1867* (Toronto: University of Toronto Press, 1955), especially Chapter III.

7. Mallory, *The Structure of Canadian Government*, p. 11.

8. J.R. Mallory, "Responsive and Responsible Government," *Transactions* of the Royal Society of Canada, Series IV, Vol. XII, 1974, pp. 207-225, at p. 209.

9. Hodgetts, *Pioneer Public Service*, p. 34.

10. Norman Ward, *The Public Purse: A Study in Canadian Democracy* (Toronto: University of Toronto Press, 1951), p. 22. Ward was in turn quoting from G. Poulett Scrope, *Memoir of the Life of the Right Hon. Charles Lord Sydenham, G.C.B.* (London, 1843), p. 172.

11. F.M.G. Willson, "Ministries and Boards: Some Aspects of Administrative Development Since 1832," *Public Administration* (London) 33 (Spring 1953): p. 54.

12. Maurice Wright, *Treasury Control of the Civil Service* (Oxford: Clarendon Press, 1969), especially his Appendix I (Treasury Minute No. 10369, dated 10 May, 1867).

13. Hodgetts writes that the title was first given statutory recognition in the Civil Service Act of the United Canadas in 1857. For further exploration of this theme, see Hodgetts, *Pioneer Public Service*, p. 92ff.

14. Mallory, *The Structure of Canadian Government*, pp. 120-121.

15. D.N. Chester and F.M.G. Willson, Eds., *The Organization of the British Central Government, 1914-1964* (London: George Allen & Unwin Ltd., 1957), p. 24.

16. *Ibid.*, see their Table 4.

17. Indeed, to this present day the term "deputy minister" is unknown to other countries *in the context in which it is used* in the federal government and our various provincial governments.

18. Jacques M. DesRoches, "The Evolution of the Organization of Federal Government in Canada," *CPA* 5:4 (1962), 408-427 at p. 411.

19. See Hodgetts, *Pioneer Public Service* (appendix entitled "Chronological Perspective of Public Departments, 1841-1867,"); Canada, Privy Council Office, *Crown Corporations: Direction, Control, Accountability* (Ottawa: Minister of Supply and Services, Canada, 1977), p. 11.

20. *Crown Corporations: Direction, Control, Accountability*, p. 11.

21. Willson, "Ministries and Boards," p. 55. Willson puts the date of revival of the board concept as 1909.

22. DesRoches, "The Evolution of the Organization of Federal Government in Canada," p. 414.

23. "Memorandum on Improvements Required in the Dominion Civil Service," prepared by Adam Shortt and D. Malcolm, n.d., Borden Papers, Vol. 229, 128577-93 at p. 128581.

24. It is this same Sir George Murray who, along with Hankey, Haldane, Morant, Webb and Montagu, was one of the influential persons behind the Haldane Report on the Machinery of Government in the United Kingdom.

25. "The branches of administration which come within the purview of the Dominion Government are so numerous and so varied in their nature that it is clearly necessary to adopt some system of grouping; and it is certainly desirable not only that the branches to be dealt with by each Minister should be as nearly cognate as possible, but that all work of the same character should be concentrated into one department. In the system under which the present distribution has been arranged it is not easy to recognize any underlying principle."
    Sir George Murray, *Report on the Public Service of Canada*, November 30, 1912. Quoted in J.M. DesRoches, "The Evolution of the Organization of Federal Government in Canada." p. 419.

26. Willson, "Ministries and Boards," pp. 55-56.

27. *Ibid.*, p. 56.

28. Peter M. Blau, *Bureaucracy in Modern Society* (New York: Random House, 1956), pp. 36-43.

29. Graham Wallas, "Introduction," in R.M. Dawson, *The Principle of Official Independence* (London: P.S. King and Son, 1922), p. xiv.

30. Our criticisms of Murray are of the same genre as Mackenzie's and Schaffer's criticisms of Haldane. (See W.J.M. Mackenzie, "The Structure of Central Administration," in Sir Gilbert Campion *et al.*, *British Government Since 1918* (London: George Allen and Unwin Ltd., 1950); B.B. Schaffer, *The Administrative Factor* (London: Frank Cass, 1973), pp. 57-76.) As mentioned earlier, Murray was very influential in the framing of the Haldane Report. For a Senate Report sympathetic to both Murray and Haldane, see Senate of Canada, *Report of the Special Committee of the Senate on the Machinery of Government, 1919* (J.S. McLennan, Chairman).

31. Sir Robert Borden, "Problem of an Efficient Civil Service," Canadian Historical Association, *Report of the Annual Meeting*, 1931 (reprint), p. 15.

32. I have paraphrased W.J.M. Mackenzie's mild satire of the Haldane Report. See his "The Structure of Central Administration," p. 82.

33. Since the Government Organization Act, 1970-71, Ministers without Portfolio have been replaced by Ministers of State who may be assigned to assist any Minister having responsibility for a department or portion of the public service.

34. See Privy Council Office, *Guide to Canadian Ministries Since Confederation*, July 1, 1967-April 1, 1973. (Ottawa: Information Canada, 1974).

35. For an excellent review of those ministerial changes, the student should consult J.R. Mallory, *The Structure of Canadian Government*, pp. 69-121.

36. J.E. Hodgetts et al., *The Biography of an Institution: The Civil Service Commission of Canada, 1908-1967* (Montreal: McGill-Queen's University Press, 1972), Chapter 7.

37. For a comprehensive description of these machinery changes, see Hodgetts, *The Canadian Public Service, 1867-1970*, pp. 241-257.

38. A.D.P. Heeney, "Cabinet Government in Canada: Some Recent Developments in the Machinery of the Central Executive," *Canadian Journal of Economics and Political Science* XII:3 (August 1946): 282-301; "Mackenzie King and the Cabinet Secretariat," *Canadian Public Administration*, X:3 (September 1967), pp. 366-375.

39. Heeney, "Mackenzie King and the Cabinet Secretariat," pp. 369-370.

40. A.D.P. Heeney, *The Things that are Caesar's: Memoirs of a Canadian Public Servant* (Toronto: University of Toronto Press, 1972), pp. 37-81.

41. J.R. Mallory, "Delegated Legislation in Canada: Recent Changes in Machinery," in J.E. Hodgetts and D.C. Corbett, eds., *Canadian Public Administration* (Toronto: University of Toronto Press, 1960), pp. 504-514.

42. *Ibid.*, p. 514.

43. Hodgetts, *The Canadian Public Service*, p. 260.

44. J.R. Mallory, "The Two Clerks: Parliamentary Discussion of the Role of the Privy Council Office," *Canadian Journal of Political Science* X:1 (March 1977), p. 16.

45. Actually various ministries have played musical chairs with the Solicitor General's office for years. The Solicitor General of Canada, the Controller of Customs, and the Controller of Inland Revenue—all cabinet positions at various times of our history, have been considered of the Ministry but not of the Cabinet. These ministers were not appointed to the Privy Council and did not attend Cabinet meetings.

46. Actually between 1963 and 1966 the Secretary to the Treasury Board reported to the President of the Privy Council in anticipation of the legislated changes in machinery. See G.V. Tunnoch, "The Bureau of Government Organization: Improvement by Order-in-Council, Committee and Anomaly," *Canadian Public Administration* 8:4 (December 1965), pp. 558-568.

47. A.W. Johnson, "The Treasury Board of Canada and the Machinery of Government of the 1970s," *CJPS* IV:3 (September 1971) pp. 346-366.

48. Hodgetts, *The Canadian Public Service*, pp. 346-347.

49. Hodgetts, *The Canadian Public Service*, p. 49.

50. P.E. Trudeau, *Federalism and the French Canadians* (Toronto: Macmillan of Canada, 1968), p. 203. A good description of the Trudeau philosophy can be found in G. Bruce Doern, "Recent Changes in the Philosophy of Policy Making in Canada," *CJPS* 4:2 (June 1971), pp. 243-264.

51. House of Commons Debates, January 26, 1971, p. 2772.

52. See Peter Aucoin and Richard French, *Knowledge, Power and Public Policy* Science Council of Canada Background Study No. 31 (Ottawa: Information Canada, 1974), pp. 12-38.

53. Ministry of Reconstruction, *Report of the Machinery of Government* Committee, Cd. 9230, 1918, Part I, para. 18-19.

54. G. Bruce Doern, "Horizontal and Vertical Portfolios in Government," in G. Bruce Doern and V. Seymour Wilson (eds.), *Issues in Canadian Public Policy* (Toronto: Macmillan of Canada, 1974), p. 316.

55. Ibid., pp. 316-317.

56. Aucoin and French, *Knowledge, Power and Public Policy*, p. 13.

57. H.L. Laframboise, "Portfolio Structure and a Ministry System: A Model for the Canadian Federal Service," *Optimum* 1:1 (Winter 1970), p. 30. Reproduced by permission of the Minister of Supply and Services Canada.

58. *Ibid.*, pp. 37-44.

59. Since 1972 the Department of the Solicitor General has called itself a ministry after the Canada Consulting Group made recommendations to this effect. However, by 1980 there has been no statutory change to give this recommendation parliamentary sanction.

60. W.J.M. Mackenzie, "The Structure of Central Administration," in Sir Gilbert Campion, et al., *British Government Since 1918*, p. 59.

Notes For Chapters 10 and 11

Both chapters were written in a historical, comparative and descriptive vein, to illustrate to the reader how deep-rooted in our societal ethos this subject of the structure or anatomy of our institutions can be. Accordingly, the references given are scattered in various journals in Canada, Australia, and England in particular. The reader should have no problem in gaining access to most of this material for further in-depth reading and analysis.

Books and Monographs

1. Peter Aucoin and Richard French, *Knowledge, Power and Public Policy*, Science Council of Canada Background Study No. 31 (Ottawa: Information Canada, 1974).

This is the best critique of the Ministry of State concept in the literature. The mono-graph is readable, and its treatment of the subject is concise. It is highly recom-mended for background reading to this chapter.

2. Walter Bagehot, *The English Constitution,* Introduction by R.H.S. Crossman (London: Fontana Library, 1963).
Most beginning students of political science are usually familiar with this edition, particularly the introduction about cabinet government by R.H.S. Crossman. For students of administrative history, public administration and public policy, Chapter V, "On Changes of Ministry," is a classic. We have already summarized some salient parts in Chapter 10, but for those who wish to return to the original source it is highly recommended reading.

3. Charles Dickens, *Little Dorrit.*
Dickens is simply brilliant on bureaucracy. Though a long novel, with some maud-lin characteristics, the book is highly recommended.

4. Arnold Heeney, *The Things that are Caesar's: Memoirs of a Canadian Public Servant.* (Toronto: University of Toronto Press, 1972).
As one of the most distinguished public servants Canada has ever produced, "A.D.P.H." was also discreet to a fault. His memoirs say very little to the general reader, unlike the entertaining and revealing memoirs of his earlier British counter-part Lord Hankey. Heeney's account of his sojourn as principal secretary to Prime Minister King and his days as Secretary to the cabinet is good background reading for anyone interested in the origins of the contemporary PCO/PMO complex.

5. J.E. Hodgetts, William McCloskey, Reginald Whitaker, and V. Seymour Wilson, *The Biography of an Institution: The Civil Service Commission of Canada, 1908-1967* (Montreal: McGill-Queen's University Press, 1972).
Chapter Seven provides a good historical background on the evolution of the Trea-sury Board. Chapter Three covers the 1918 administrative reforms.

6. J.E. Hodgetts, *Pioneer Public Service: An Administrative History of the United Canadas, 1841-1867* (Toronto: University of Toronto Press, 1955).
This is a superb reference book on Canada's early administrative history. For a good introduction to the beginning student, we recommend the first thirty-four pages.

7. John W. Langford, *Transport in Transition: The Reorganization of the Federal Transport Portfolio* (Montreal: McGill-Queen's University Press, 1976).
Langford's study is a comprehensive one on the introduction of the ministry con-cept in Canada. It is, however, detailed reading to the uninitiated. We recommend Chapters 1, 2 and 3 for a good historical backdrop and Chapters 7 and 8 for an anal-ysis of the ministry system as applied to the transport portfolio.

8. J.R. Mallory, *The Structure of Canadian Government* (Toronto: Macmillan of Canada, 1971).
Mallory is one of the leading constitutional experts in Canada, and his treatment of the constitution and the executive of Canadian government is perhaps the best that we have in writing at the moment. We highly recommend Chapters 1 to 3 of his book.

9. Henry Parris, *Constitutional Bureaucracy: The Development of British Central Administration Since the Eighteenth Century* (London: George Allen and Unwin Ltd., 1969). This book is considered the authority on "recent" administrative history in Great Britain. The book is heavy going, but there are portions which are very helpful. Chapters 3 (Ministerial responsibility), 4 (Ministers in their departments), and 10 (Our present discontents), are particularly useful.

10. Canada, Royal Commission on Financial Management and Accountability, *Final Report,* March 1969.
Chapters 9 and 10 of the Report are highly recommended as detailed background reading to this chapter of the text.

Articles

Articles from widespread sources are all listed together. Those marked with double asterisks (**) are highly recommended, while those with one asterisk (*) can be read lightly for introductory purposes.

** Peter Aucoin and Richard French, "The Ministry of State for Science and Technology," *CPA* 17:3 (Fall 1974), 461-481.

** Alan C. Cairns, "The Living Canadian Constitution," *Queen's Quarterly* LXXVII:4 (Winter 1970), 483-498.

* Hans Daalder, "The Haldane Committee and the Cabinet," *Public Administration* (London) 41:2 (Summer 1963), 117-135.

* S. Kitson Clark, " 'Statesmen in Disguise': Reflexions on the History of the Neutrality of the Civil Service," *Historical Journal* II:1 (1959), 19-39.

* Jacques M. DesRoches, "The Evolution of the Organization of Federal Government in Canada," *CPA,* 5:4 (Winter 1962), 408-427.

* S.E. Finer, "The Individual Responsibility of Ministers," *Public Administration* (London) 34:4 (Winter 1956), 377-396.

* Edward Hughes, "Civil Service Reform, 1853-5," *Public Administration* (London) XXXLL:1 (Spring 1954), 17-51.

** Hubert L. Laframboise, "Portfolio Structure and a Ministry System: A Model for the Canadian Federal Service," *Optimum* 1:1 (1970), 29-46.

* Oliver MacDonagh, "The Nineteenth Century Revolution in Government: A Reappraisal," *Historical Journal* 1:1 (1958), 52-67.

** James R. Mallory, "The Two Clerks: Parliamentary Discussion of the Role of the Privy Council Office," *CJPS* X:1 (March 1977), 3-19.

** James R. Mallory, "Responsive and Responsible Government," *Transactions* of the Royal Society of Canada, Series IV, Vol. XII, 1974, pp. 207-225.

** W.J.M. Mackenzie, "The Structure of Central Administration," in Sir Gilbert Campion, et al., *British Government Since 1918* (London: George Allen and Unwin Ltd., 1950), pp. 56-84.

** B.B. Schaffer, "The Idea of the Ministerial Department: Bentham, Mill and Bagehot," *Australian Journal of Politics and History* 3:1 (November 1957), 60-78.

** G.V. Tunnoch, "The Bureau of Government Organization: Improvement by Order-in-Council, Committee and Anomaly," *CPA* VIII:4 (December 1965), 558-568.

** F.M.G. Willson, "Ministries and Boards: Some Aspects of Administrative Development Since 1832," *Public Administration* (London) XXXIII (Spring 1955), 43-58.

* Paul P. Van Riper, "Adapting a British Political Invention to American Needs," *Public Administration* (London) XXXI:4 (Winter 1953), 317-330.

** R.L. Wettenhall, "The Ministerial Department," *Public Administration* (Sydney) XXXII:3 (September 1973), 233-250.

CHAPTER TWELVE

BEYOND THE MINISTERIAL DEPARTMENTS: THE BEHEMOTH OF PUBLIC ENTERPRISE

Government as Porcupine Hunter
[In its relations with public enterprises] the government must often find itself in the same position as that of a porcupine hunter. [The porcupine] has quills that protect it, and you catch it most effectively with a wash-tub. You drop the wash-tub on it and sit on top and say 'Now what do I do?'

Anonymous in Andre Gélinas (ed.)
Public Enterprise and the Public Interest

"The dogs may bark, but the caravan passes on."

An ancient Arab proverb

I. Introduction

In giving a definition of public administration in Chapter One, we indicated that there was some difficulty with the notion of "public" primarily because of the increasing interpenetration of the public and private sectors, thus blurring the distinction between the two. We also noted this phenomenon of interpenetration has occurred and continues to occur not only in Canada but throughout the Western world.

Why has the state found it necessary to intervene in areas of economic and social activity traditionally considered to be the preserve of the private sector? Explanations abound attempting to shed light on the reasons why this process has taken place, and to give the reader any insights into this question would get us into the wider questions of the relations between the Canadian state system and the economy, specifically placing emphasis on the role of the bureaucracy in these relations. Our intention in this chapter is far more modest in that we will confine ourselves to much narrower concerns. We will accept the fact that government has intervened in the economy, and we will explore some dimensions of that intervention.[1]

What is the extent of this intervention? What institutional forms does this intervention presently take? And what are some of the political implications of "active government"?

Since World War II the Canadian federal government has increasingly spawned these institutions thereby creating some profound concerns for all students of public administration. The first concern is the usefulness of the traditional narrow definition of the "public service" which is generally understood to include only central agencies and the departmental form of organization, conveniently excluding public enterprises.[2] Second is the notable fact that an increasing number of these enterprises, originally created to be *ostensibly instrumental* in character, have become "regularly involved in a direct or indirect sense in the spawning and development of public policy initiatives."[3] Third, as far back as 1971 Canadian federal politicians were becoming uneasy about their relationships with crown corporations. First came some revealing information about Polymer Corporation: its participation in a South African firm (Sentrachem Limited) and the acquisition of Polymer (now Polysar) by the Canada Development Corporation. Then in 1976 came the so-called "horror stories" associated with Atomic Energy Canada Ltd., which paid some $15 million to an exclusive agent allegedly as "a commission" for arranging the $500 million sale of a nuclear reactor to South Korea, and an additional $2.4 million "commission" to another agent for services in a similar deal with Argentina. By this time Ministers of the Crown were openly expressing their concern over the formal relationships which they had with specific Crown corporations within their jurisdiction; about the process of approval of capital budgets of Crown corporations before tabling in the House of Commons; and the type and extent of control and direction which ministers might exert over Crown corporations through that process. Economist Andrew Schonfield goes to the heart of the matter when he asserts that:

The central question is how far an active government wielding great and varied economic power, intervening in the detailed conduct of private business affairs, discriminating between one citizen and another on the basis of subtle and complex judgments of the community's needs ten or twenty years ahead, driving bargains with particular interest groups as administrative convenience dictates, can be subjected to effective democratic control.[4]

For our introductory purposes, governmental intervention in the economy can be classified under three headings: *subsidization, regulation,* and *management or direction*. It is almost trite to observe that governments wield extensive powers over economic policies and programs that have a vital bearing on the performance of the economy in relation to the societal goals of full employment, a qualitatively satisfactory pattern of growth, price stability and a viable balance of payments. In addition, governments are also very much involved with the attainment of rising standards of education, better health care services, efforts to minimize pollution and so on. In order to effect these policies and programs governments use certain fiscal tools: financial resources and reserves are used to generate the goods and services conferred. In other words, governments use their powers to redistribute wealth in society: the deployment of a variety of redistributive tools to affect the choice of goods and services in such a way as to make such choice more attractive than it otherwise would be.

The term redistribution is used advisedly here: this form of decision-making is characterized by its workings "through large groups or classes within which individual behaviour takes place. Normally redistribution effects a transfer of resources within a society and is characterized by centralized and hierarchical decision making."[5] Another name for this transfer is *subsidization*. Subsidization takes a variety of forms, but a good example is the manner in which governments affect the timing and quantity of such agricultural staples as eggs, wheat and milk by directly granting financial subventions or other tax benefits to encourage or discourage production. This subsidization policy is the commonly known, and highly disputed concept of supply management.

Another form of governmental intervention is *regulation*. To regulate is merely to choose one instrument of governing from a range of other instruments. Its interventionist characteristics are revealed, however, in that regulation normally involves direct choices regarding the indulgence and deprivation of individuals, resulting in direct confrontations between the indulged and the deprived on any particular issue. At any rate, regulatory policy is specific, individualistic in impact, encourages a multiplicity of participants, and has a tendency to be characterized by a decentralized process of decision-making.[6] A common regulatory form is licensing. In Canada, licensing regulation is a governing device used in the area of food and drugs, broadcasting, transportation, the production and distribution of a variety of agricultural products (wheat, tobacco, potatoes, eggs, etc.), professional certification (doctors, lawyers, engineers, plumbers, etc.), and a whole host of other areas of social and economic activity.

The third form of intervention by government is that of *management or direction of private production*. By this we mean that government has found itself in the business of supplanting or supplementing private production. Thus we find governmental management, in the majority of instances, seeking to make up for certain inadequacies in the normal distribution of economic rewards by going outside the "free enterprise" market to furnish goods and services directly to consumers. This aspect of intervention, namely that of government as business, is basically the subject matter of this chapter. Gracey sums up the complexity, variety, and range of these activities:

[Government intervention is now evident in] marketing boards, . . . an export insurance and guarantee company, an oil company, and companies in the fields of telecommunications, administration of the St. Lawrence Seaway, coal mining, industrial development, electric power production, heavy water and nuclear reactor production and construction, uranium processing, sale and stockpiling, unemployment insurance, and science, medical and economic research and advice. [7]

It should be made clear that the three modes of governmental intervention categorized above are not mutually exclusive: very often one form of government enterprise might find itself performing two or more interventionist activities. It is not unusual to find, say a government agency as a regulatory body, at the same time competing with and supplementing private production. As a matter of fact such a situation did exist at one time in the communications field in Canada, when the Canadian Broadcasting Corporation, one of our Crown corporations, had the double role of being the regulator of broadcasting while supplementing and competing with private enterprise in the broadcasting business. [8] However, normally these functions are distinct, and governments tend to keep them that way, but it does not necessarily follow that conceptual neatness is always attained or desired.

We will first give a short historical description of public enterprise in Canada, highlighting the very pragmatic nature of this form of governmental intervention in the economy. Since the end of World War II, however, government has used the public enterprise form in a motley collection of ways, calling into question the older explanations given in the literature for this intervention. Our second task therefore will be to give the reader some conception of the diversity of institutional forms now existing and to describe and analyse the many reasons given in the political economy literature for the growth of these institutions in the Canadian environment. Third, we will revert to the "porcupine" problem posed in the epigram of this chapter by giving consideration to the democratic notions of accountability and control to which these organizational forms must be subjected in a liberal democratic society.

II. A Brief Historical Background

The earliest form of public enterprises were chiefly concerned with public works: throughout the nineteenth century and the early part of the twentieth, there were a few Crown corporations engaged in the building of canals, the administration of harbour facilities and the restoration of Canadian historic sites. However, the first significant public enterprise venture in the provision of goods and services was the creation of the Canadian National Railways in 1919. Canadian economic history shows that by 1916, following a period of a prematurely optimistic railway expansion in the country, the Canadian Northern, Grand Trunk, and Grand Trunk Pacific Railways found themselves in serious financial difficulties. Thus, following on the recommendations of the 1917 Royal Commission on Railway Transportation, these railway lines were taken over, amalgamated and renamed the Canadian National Railways. This action by the federal government was aimed at protecting Canada's credit in the foreign capital markets and rescuing the large investments in the railway lines held by both federal and provincial governments. For well over a decade after the takeover, the CNR with its subsidiary CN (West Indies) Steamship Ltd., occupied "the position of sole representative of the strictly business-type government enterprise."[10]

By the end of the second decade of this century, both Liberal and Conservative governments were turning to other ventures, and finding the corporation structure useful in this regard. First came, in 1927, the Federal Farm Loan Board (reconstituted in 1959 as the Farm Credit Corporation), then in 1932 the Canadian Radio Broadcasting Commission (the forerunner of the present Canadian Broadcasting Corporation), the Canadian Wheat Board in 1935, and the Bank of Canada in 1938. By the outbreak of hostilities in 1939 there were in existence some fifteen government corporations in shipping, rail, air transportation, banking and credit, harbour administration, and commodity marketing fields.[11]

It was the decade of the forties which witnessed a veritable explosion of corporate forms in Canada. Again, pragmatic considerations seemed to be in the forefront: the immediate emergencies of the war meant that organizational forms that were flexible, not under the normal budgetary and personnel constraints of departmental administration, were needed to pursue Canada's war effort with vigor and imagination. Some thirty-three Crown companies, most of them known as the "C. D. Howe corporations" after the then energetic Minister of Munitions and Supply, Clarence Decatur Howe, were established. Of these, four were created by letters patent under the Canada Companies Act pursuant to the authority vested with the government by the War Measures Act, and twenty-eight by the Minister of Munitions and Supply under the Canada Companies Act, pursuant to the Department of Munitions and Supply Act.

By the end of World War II, although the majority of these wartime Crown companies were disbanded, many continued operations and were subsequently augmented by other corporations established during the reconstruction period between 1946 and 1950. By 1951, there were thirty-three public enterprises in operation at the federal level of government. The variety of these organizational forms also seem to follow no fixed logical pattern of organizational sequence: corporations engaged in lending and guaranteeing transactions, commodity trading and procurement functions, price support functions for agricultural and fishery products, and industrial and commercial enterprises to name a few. To borrow a phrase from Mackenzie and Grove, this organizational landscape looked very much like a jungle in which the theoretical student was lost for clues.[12]

DR. JOHN EDWIN HODGETTS

Professor of Political Economy, University of Toronto. Canadian public policy and administration owe a heavy intellectual debt to the contributions of this scholar. Hodgetts' prolific writings, running the gamut from administrative history to the problems of financial management and accountability in Canada, have been elegant in style and prose, timely in their prognostications and above all, intellectually stimulating.

III. The Dimensions of Canadian Public Enterprise

Diversity in Organizational Forms

Even the government which had spawned these organizational behemoths seemed to be deluged by the jungle's underbrush. Parliamentary and ministerial controls of these public enterprises were weak, and Crown corporations could successfully avoid any detailed financial scrutiny so long as they did not approach Parliament for financial appropriations to expedite their mandates. Through Part VIII of the Financial Administration Act of 1951 (FAA) the government therefore sought to establish some financial accountability and control of these organizations.[13] Section 66(1) of the amended FAA (1970) defines a Crown corporation as:

a corporation that is ultimately accountable, through a minister, to Parliament for the conduct of its affairs and includes the corporations named in Schedule B, Schedule C and Schedule D (of this Act).

The Act goes on to group Crown corporations into three classes or schedules: B, C and D. The first group (Schedule B) is known as "departmental corporations" which, according to the legislation, conduct "administrative, supervisory or regulatory services of a governmental nature." The second grouping (Schedule C) is classified as "agency corporations," namely those corporations engaged in the "management of trading or service operations on a quasi-commercial basis on the government's behalf." Finally there is Schedule D, known as "proprietary corporations," which includes those organizations managing "lending or financial institutions or commerical and industrial operations" dealing with such activities as the supplying of specific devices to the public and production of a variety of goods done in the name of the public interest. Schedule D corporations were given a wide range of autonomy in that they were to be self-sustaining, financing themselves not through the regular Parliamentary appropriations but by retained earnings, repayable loans and government-held-equity.[14] The Act also provides for regulating the reserves, banking accounts and surplus moneys, the form in which annual budgets are to be presented and the requirement of an annual and other reports to the minister. Annual reports include audited financial statements the form of which must be subject to prescription by the appropriate minister responsible for the corporation and the Minister of Finance. Finally, the minimum content requirements of the annual financial statements and the reporting requirements for the auditor of a Crown corporation are stipulated in a fairly extensive way in Part VIII of the FAA.[15] Appendix B presents the classification scheme of the corporations along with specific corporations involved. As the reader can see, there are now 12 "departmental" corporations, 19 "agency" corporations, and 22 "proprietary" Crown corporations.

It does not take much analytical ability to discern that the definition which was given above for a Crown corporation is no definition at all: it says precious very little about the essential distinguishing characteristics of a corporation as opposed to a department of government. Furthermore, it is tautological (a Crown corporation is a corporation accountable through a Minister to Parliament), lacks definitional clarity and is basically taxonomic in orientation. It is therefore not surprising to find that by 1976 the Auditor General also found this state of affairs far from satisfactory:

. . . no central agency recognizes the need to identify all corporations owned or controlled by the Government of Canada.

and,

If the Financial Administration Act is to continue to serve as the basis for parliamentary and governmental control of Crown corporations it must embrace all government-owned and controlled corporations. This will ensure that the government's ability to monitor their performance is clearly defined and recognized by all parties concerned.[16]

Largely as a result of these complaints by the Auditor General the Treasury Board undertook the required survey, and in May 1977, published a list of 366 public corporations owned (on a majority or minority basis) or controlled by the Government of Canada. A subsequently revised list was published in January 1978, showing an increased number of corporations, some 384 in all!

However the confusion continues. In August 1979 the Office of the Comptroller General released a list containing 401 corporations: 79 of these are listed as corporations "owned or controlled solely by the Government of Canada"; another 25 are labelled "mixed enterprises—corporations owned or controlled jointly with other governments and/or organizations"; another category catalogued as "subsidiary corporations and their subsidiaries" (165) and "associated corporations" (109) of previously listed Crown corporations; and finally a list of 23 corporations which it is obvious that the Office of the Comptroller General is unable to classify. Thus if one excludes the fifty-four crown corporations enumerated in the FAA, there are close to three hundred and fifty corporations which the government either partially or wholly owns or controls that are not designated as corporate bodies under the FAA and therefore not subject to its financial management and accountability provisions.[17] There have been very few attempts in the Canadian literature to classify and label the various forms of corporations financially connected in one way or the other with the federal government.[18] Indeed, this vacuum of knowledge is understandable because, until recently, the Government of Canada itself lacked this knowledge. What follows is an analysis of the classification presented in the Treasury Board's two surveys of 1977 and 1978. This classification is already outdated as the government continues to discover and categorize corporations it either owns or with which it is affiliated. Despite this state of flux the Treasury Board's two surveys serve as good bases for illustrating some of the major questions and problems involved in dealing with these corporate forms.

The corporation universe can be identified under the following headings: (i) Crown corporations and other government controlled corporations (or "scheduled" and "unscheduled" corporations), (ii) Mixed enterprises and their subsidiaries, and (iii) the Quasi non-governmental organization or what the British call, "the Quango."[19]

(i) Crown Corporations and Other Government Controlled Corporations

The Privy Council Office is rather frank in admitting the ambiguity and lack of definitional clarity caused by subsection 66(1) of the Financial Administration Act:

For some time much confusion has surrounded the term "Crown Corporation," owing to the definition established by subsection 66(1) of the FAA. . . . Confusion stems from the fact that this definition is not exhaustive, since one must always look beyond the FAA to determine what are Crown corporations. The fact that the present definition only "includes" the corporations listed in Schedules B, C and D indicates that the Schedules themselves may not be comprehensive. One is always left with the question as to whether a corporation not included in the Schedules is or is not a Crown corporation.

The Government proposes that any ambiguity associated with the term Crown corporation be removed. It is proposed, therefore, that the term "Crown corporation" be applied correctly only to those corporations listed in the Schedules of the FAA. Further, a corporation could be added to the Schedules and thereby become a Crown corporation *only if it were wholly owned by the Government of Canada, either directly or indirectly.* Such a criterion would potentially cover all corporations now listed in the Schedules of the

FAA, plus subsidiaries of Crown corporations and their subsidiaries and all situations where a minister holds the shares of a corporation in trust for Her Majesty.[20]

The PCO document, including its proposed amendments to the FAA, does not attempt to give a text-book definition of a Crown corporation, but a perusal of its proposals indicates that the following definition may not be too far off the mark:

A Crown corporation is an agency, wholly owned either directly or indirectly by the Government of Canada, and ultimately accountable, through a Minister, to Parliament for the conduct of its affairs. These agencies, listed in Schedules B, C or D of the FAA are created with the purpose of performing objectives dictated to be in the national interest, and are purposely given a wide degree of policy and administrative flexibility to expedite these objectives.

It is noteworthy that the definition recognizes that there may be government-owned corporations which, for certain political reasons, are not included in the Schedules. These therefore do not entirely fulfill the definitional characteristics of Crown corporations, but are without doubt "government controlled corporations," perhaps candidates for "Crown status" as political circumstances dictate. As such, we have simply skirted the problem of second guessing the politicians as to why a certain corporation should or should not be a "Crown" corporation.

According to the Treasury Board, there are two classifications of corporate bodies containing 45 agencies (of which 30 are wholly owned by the Government of Canada), which could be legitimately defined as Crown corporations. These groupings include such well-known agencies as the National Arts Centre Corporation, the Canada Council, the Social Sciences Research Council, the Bank of Canada, and de Havilland Aircraft of Canada Ltd. Also listed are some 85 majority owned subsidiaries of wholly owned government corporations. If the proposed amendments to the FAA are put into legislation in the near future, most of these "unscheduled Crown corporations" might soon be listed as Crown corporations coming under the Schedules B, C or D. Failing this categorization, it is being proposed that some other classification, such as "government controlled corporations" will have to be the designation for them.[21]

(ii) Mixed Enterprises and their Subsidiaries

The academic literature on public enterprises provides no fully comprehensive definition of the concept of mixed enterprises. Lloyd A.

Musolf, one of the few scholars who over the last decade has written extensively on public enterprises both in Canada and elsewhere, gives the following definition: "Mixed enterprise . . . has the participation—in the form of capital, or appointments to its board of directors or both—of a nation's government and its private enterprise."[22] However, over the past decade Canadian governments have established a number of these organizations, reflecting a diversity both in the extent of government ownership and the nature of the partnership between the public and private sectors. In some instances the federal government shares ownership with other provincial governments and private investors (for example, Syncrude Canada Ltd., which is a partnership between the federal government, the provincial governments of Ontario, Alberta, and certain private oil companies).[23] In other instances, the partnership is only between the federal government and private firms (for example, Pan Arctic Oils, Canada Ltd., or Telesat Canada) or with Canadian citizens (the Canada Development Corporation).[24] In all, the federal government has a controlling interest in 24 companies or "mixed enterprises." The January 1978 list published by the Treasury Board shows that there are some 155 subsidiaries and subsidiaries of subsidiaries connected to these mixed enterprises.[25] A general characteristic of these mixed enterprises to note is that in all cases the Canadian government has retained more than 50 percent ownership or has the power to appoint a majority of the directors. There are, however, a group of some 24 subsidiaries of the above majority owned subsidiaries in which the federal government has only a minority ownership position.

(iii) Quasi Non-Governmental Organizations

Contracting out government projects is to some extent an alternative to internal administrative operations. For the last two decades in Canada we have seen the increasing use of organizations not directly administered by government employees in the execution of federal government programs. In Canada, we had a good deal of contracting out of social programs: as examples we have had the Opportunities for Youth Program (OFY) and the Local Initiatives Program (LIP).[26] The objective of these programs was to ensure that certain disadvantaged constituent groups had direct and adequate access to public funding, thereby allowing the use of public funds for the institution of programs which generated goods and services of the groups' choosing. Politicians did not of course lose the opportunity of gaining some political mileage from these projects.

This concept of using private organizations in the public interest is not a phenomenon characteristic of Canada only. There has been a very rich crop of what has been called "interstitial organizations" in Italy, Japan, Australia, the United Kingdom, and indeed in all the advanced industrial countries of the Western world.[27] The pressures of rapid technological advances in the West have forced governments to heavily subsidize the costly research and development projects of continuing industrialization and, as Dupré and Gustafson remind us, such innovations require

. . . systematic research and development, which in turn call for sophisticated technical capacity, refined managerial skills, and flexible financial arrangements. Accordingly, the government has had to devise new standards in its contractual relationships with business firms. Essentially, the government now assumes the financial risk involved in innovation. Free competition no longer characterizes the process of bidding for government contracts. While private firms have thus been freed from restraints of the open market, they have acquired new public responsibilities. They are no longer merely suppliers to the government, but participants in the administration of public functions. The capacity of private firms to promote the public interest in the absence of market forces poses serious conceptual and administrative problems.[28]

Here in Canada the federal government has been heavily involved in the development of an aircraft industry, to the extent that this industry has become a virtual ward of the Canadian state. The nature of governmental involvement with private industry has been varied: special tax provisions; subsidy programs; loan guarantees; tariffs; procurement programs with offset requirements and preferential "Canadian content" provisions; marketing assistance; and several experiments in public ownership.[29] If government were to remove its patronage this whole structure of "private enterprises" will fold like a pack of cards. Where then does government involvement end and private enterprise begin? As one recently critical analysis of the Canadian aircraft industry puts it: "The new result of substantial federal intervention, both direct and indirect, is a relationship which is characterized by a high degree of industry dependence on government policies. Indeed, in many respects, it could be argued that the aircraft industry *is* a state industry."[30]

While much analysis and critical commentary have been done in Western European countries and the United States on this aspect of government sponsored "private" enterprises, in Canada we have barely begun to examine the dimensions of the topic.[31] All we can therefore do at this stage is to briefly mention this important aspect of public policy and administration, thus giving another example of the vastness and complexity of state intervention in the economy of our society. However, by now the reader may have received a rude shock from all this variety and complexity in organizational forms. If one is accustomed to think of governmental organizations in terms of 28 ministerial portfolios in charge of the conventional departments, a few ministries and some boards and commissions, it would therefore be natural to view deviations from these more familiar structures as barnacles or "structural heretics." It is now clear that this conception of government needs serious reconsideration in light of the classification of behemoths we have barely outlined in this chapter. What explanations then are given for this diversity in organizational forms?

Diversity in Organizational Forms: Some Widely Accepted Explanations[32]

In any course on Canadian economic history, one learns that one of the most distinguishing features of the Canadian economy is the vital role which the Canadian state has played, and continues to play, in the development of Canadian society. Writers who depend heavily on this explanation of the interplay of economy, state and society develop it even further by contending that Canadian economic development, and indeed Canadian political unity, could only have been accomplished by a national government which acted aggressively to establish and maintain national economic unity. Alexander Brady's statement on this theme is unequivocal: "the role of the state in the economic life of Canada is really the modern history of Canada. . . ." Furthermore, he contends, the positive, pragmatic state was an absolute necessity due to the following distinguishing characteristics of Canada: "the pioneer nature of the country, the physical structure of the half continent, the imperial sweep of settlement after 1867, the influence of the interacting ideas and institutions of Britain and the United States, and the quick response of the whole society to the advance of western industrialism."[33] And, one of Canada's most distinguished economic historians, the late W. A. Mackintosh, echoed this pragmatic outlook when he argued that:

What is distinctive in this field is not the effectiveness of the policies nor their originality but the lack of any doctrinal limitations. In a period where laissez-faire policies were at their peak of respectability, the Canadian attitude to the question of public versus private enterprise was purely pragmatic. In the vital field of railway transportation there was not generally any clear view on the merits of public versus private action so long as the railways were actually built.[34]

Three main types of "managerial explanations" usually flow from this concept of positive pragmatic government: (i) public enterprises of a "business" nature are best performed by independent corporations; (ii) the corporation form of organization is much more flexible, innovative and possesses much wider discretionary powers than the departmental form; (iii) the corporate form is well suited to making economic decisions and should be relieved of political and uneconomic activities. These latter activities are more efficiently and effectively handled by the departmental form of organization.

The argument that public enterprises of a business nature are best performed by independent corporations is not new. During the 1930s and 40s English Labour M.P. Herbert Morrison (later Lord Morrison of Lambeth) was one of the leading exponents of this form of organization specifically for this reason.[35] Dealing with the business world and recruiting business people to join government meant that government itself had to adopt many of the ways of the business community. Hence the recruitment of staff compensation packages, and other general conditions of employment, had to conform as closely as possible to what were the accepted practices in the business community.[36] To Clarence Decatur Howe, the minister most responsible for the creation of Crown corporations in the 1940s, this organizational form was necessary as an inducement to "men with business responsibilities of their own to give a good deal of their time to the government, in executive positions associated with a form of administration with which they were wholly familiar." Furthermore, it permitted "the head office [to] be established in a location most convenient to those men whom we wished to attract to the business."[37] Advocates of the corporate "business" form of organization also argued that there was nothing sacrosanct about the departmental form. To quote Lord Bridges on this point:

One is apt to think of Government Departments organized on orthodox lines as being the normal, and to regard every other way of doing Government business as a deviation—probably a fairly recent deviation from the normal.

This is misleading. [In England] until 100 or 150 years ago we governed through a very large number of small, separate offices, usually taking the form of Boards or Commissions, each charged with a very narrow range of duties. . . . But as Parliament became more democratic, Ministers more busy, and businesslike, most of the little Boards were absorbed into Government Departments to make a more compact Administration.[38]

Hence if the "right" personnel outside the public service were required to serve these organizational forms, then governments must create the "right" atmosphere by adopting the corporate form.

A corollary to this argument is that flexibility, creativeness, innovativeness and speed are not, at any rate, the hallmarks of the public bureaucracy, so the pragmatism of a positive government must be accommodated through other organizational forms. J. A. Corry was one of the earliest advocates of this point of view:

> when governments begin to operate public utilities, they turn the dynamics of trade into the statics of routine administration. The illogical situation forced into the logical category, the impersonal touch in personal contacts, the curious operation of prestige incentives, the sad procession of files to the last pigeon hole, and the budgetary system of accounting, audit and finance all tend to make government operation of commercial undertakings cumbrous and expensive.[39]

And C. D. Howe agrees with Corry's viewpont by arguing in the House of Commons that: ". . . for a commission to operate and do business it seems to be necessary that it be formed into a corporation. All of the commissions I know of that are operated around Ottawa are formed into corporations."[40]

Flexibility, speed and innovativeness are not usually the hallmarks of any bureaucracy be it public or private. Bureaucracy's language, hierarchy and pursuit of rationality, all serve the ultimate ends of predictability and control. In contrast, innovation and the creative process is irregular, often seemingly aimless and unpredictable. Hence in many ways Howe and his cohorts were correct in pointing to the difficulties inherent in government bureaucracy, but dead wrong in believing that some of these difficulties are not hallmarks of modern business organizations also. However, in the 1940s one could have argued that the attributes of flexibility, speed and innovativeness were best met by organizations which approximated "the ideal structure" for the private sector: clear objectives (no efforts to be wasted in achieving victory in war), free from the encumbrances of control legislation (no civil service acts of financial and personnel control designed to ensure probity in administration), and possessing the distinctive characteristics of proper size, hierarchy of command and so on.

Finally there is the belief that the corporate form should be used in government to make mostly economic decisions, leaving non-economic and political decision-making to the departmental form of organization. In this way the special appropriateness of corporations for highly discretionary, innovative and speedy expedition of tasks will be enhanced.[41] This third position is the logical inference of the two previous positions enumerated above. However, all these arguments advocating the managerial theories of flexibility, innovativeness, and businesslike methods are open to some serious questioning when it is realized that other "business oriented" approaches to public management have advocated theories which argue almost the exact opposite. As an example, the 1968 Fulton Committee Report on the British Civil Service, known for its admiration and advocacy of businesslike methods for British public administration, is associated with the notion that "one might expect non-Departmental bodies to exist where there are relatively *routine* operations which permit of accountable management (i.e., by clear-cut performance indicators) with civil service Departments as the 'brain' but not the 'muscle' of the government machine." Instead of flexibility and innovativeness one gets the argument that routine bureaucratic tasks should be "hived off" to the corporate form of organization. Hood concludes:

This is not, of course, to deny that "managerial" considerations can help to explain agency type; only to point out that there is no single managerial explanation and that a combination of all managerial explanations is so all-encompassing as to be of little value as a predictor. Such a combination merely turns the question the other way round to ask why any agency should be constituted as a "Department" (an equally difficult explanatory task).[43]

In maintaining the primacy of politics in the determination of organizational form, one leading student of Canadian public administration flatly declared: "Politics involves policy, and if the cabinet is to remain responsible for policy, an important sector of the economy run by a government corporation cannot be taken out of politics."[44] Thus, quite a few theories of the political variety have been suggested to explain the differences in non-departmental forms. Three of the more prominent ones are presented here, and each will be briefly discussed in turn.

The first is the use of patronage to ensure the mobilization of political support. The word "patronage" is customarily used to refer to all forms of material benefits which politicians may distribute to party workers and supporters. Here it is used to refer to jobs and favors in bureaucratic appointments: patronage is the act of filling all those governmental positions which remain within the full prerogative of political leaders. No observer of the Canadian political scene would deny that government uses this discretion at its pleasure. It is important to note, however, that most of the political encumbents to these positions are well qualified for them.[45] Most patronage positions nowadays are not used by the government in an overt spoils sense, as was the common practice before the civil service reforms of 1918.[46]

It would, therefore, be farfetched to argue that the purpose of non-departmental forms of organizations is to accommodate the patronage proclivities of governments. Patronage is certainly not the be-all and end-all of government's policies regarding the evolution of governmental machinery. Other reasons, just as political, also suggest themselves as equally plausible explanations.

Another explanation put forward suggests that the determination of agency type is made by allocating the more politically sensitive work to the departments (where it is under the direct control of a minister of the Crown), while the "less politically sensitive" or "highly technical" is relegated to the "independent" agencies or corporations. Certainly anyone familiar with the Canadian machinery of government can point to examples of this: the creation of the National Energy Board in 1959 was one such instance. In retrospect, a present-day observer can point to the fact that the Board's mandate was potentially political in very profound ways. Yet in the 1950s it was generally felt that the problems which the National Energy Board had to deal with were "inherently technical [and] best resolved between industry and regulatory experts"[49] without any political interference.

But another observer can point to examples which suggest the exact opposite. In the case of transportation policy the Canadian government has "hived off" politically sensitive areas giving these to a regulatory body (the Canadian Transport Commission), and leaving the so-called routine activities of transportation administration to the department (the Department of Transportation, before the Ministry system came into being).[50] In both illustrations, the end results turned out to be quite different from the original intentions of creating the machinery. The point, however, is made: the theory of political sensitivity is so flexible that it ends up proving too much.

A variant of the theory of political sensitivity attempts to explain the variations in governmental machinery by reference to the clientele of the agency or department involved. As Christopher Hood points out ". . . it might plausibly be argued that the more powerful [an agency's] clientele, the more powerful [it] will be vis-à-vis the rest of the government machine and the more likely it is to be a full-blown government Department. On this theory the state bureaucracy is seen as a type of mirror and map of political power in the society."[51] This approach to clientelism of course assumes that bureaucrats are dominated or are the cohorts of the dominant economic and social interests of the society they purport to serve.[52]

Finally, we come to the argument that over time governmental machinery has become so "over-institutionalized" that "conflicting demands for policy space arise between agencies and that unorthodox constitutional machinery is used for flanking movements in the struggle."[53] While this argument makes a very valid point that bureaucracy should never be construed as a monolith, it seems nevertheless true that political conservatism in the Canadian instance always moves to methods seeking to preserve political control and accountability. Hence a proliferation of "unorthodox constitutional machinery" does not seem to lend itself to the Canadian political environment. As Michael Pitfield expressed it:

In dealing with the growth, the magnitude, and the complexity and pressures of government, many important options have been taken that would seem to discourage experimentation with more drastic organizational changes tried in other countries. I have in mind such measures as the creation of tiered departments, of super departments, or of the hierarchical structuring of central agencies to control departments. Recent changes in the techniques and instruments for policy formulation at the federal level have been at pains not only to preserve but also to reinforce the subtle interplay of individual ministerial and collective ministerial responsibilities that are the essence of our system of government. Ours is a confederacy of institutions co-ordinated by various techniques for common objectives, not rigidly commanded but enriched by a certain degree of built-in countervailance.[54]

That "built-in countervailance" was supposed to have been enhanced by a ministry system for policy co-ordination rather than the creation of a series of "independent" agencies. If indeed we are over-institutionalized in a formal departmental sense, what we have in effect witnessed during the last two decades is the growth not only of "independent" agencies but traditional departments and ministries that are subject to control in the traditional formal way. Posited as an explanation then, "over-institutionalization" seems less than satisfactory. Christopher Hood, therefore, appears to be correct when he argues that: . . . it does seem fairly clear that there is no single determinate explanation of why twentieth century government . . . should have taken place to a large extent through non-Departmental bodies, and of why government agencies should be constituted in one form rather than another . . . if it is a mistake to search for a single explanation of the problem, it is clearly necessary to move from deterministic to probabilistic and from single-factor to multi-factor explanations. [At the present, our explanations] can only be fairly rough and intuitive."[55]

The "Porcupine" Problem: Consideration of Democratic Notions of Accountability and Control

"The great increase in the number of state-owned-and-operated business enterprises during the last decade has confronted almost every nation with a basic dilemma: how can the operating and financial flexibility required for the successful conduct of a business enterprise be reconciled with the need for controls to assure public accountability and consistency in public policy?"[56] Those lines were written by Harold Seidman almost three decades ago, and if anything, the problem he alluded to has intensified because of the proliferating growth of public enterprises, and governments' inability to put forward satisfactory solutions to the dilemmas posed by this growth.

In theory there are at least three ways by which the Canadian federal government can control Crown corporations. Those three ways are: financial controls as specified in the FAA; appointment to the board of directors; and the issuance of occasional directives to certain specified Crown corporations.

Given the above specified controls, what is the crux of the problem? The key to this whole issue is the expressed objectives of government in creating these organizational forms.[57] For whatever reason, be it ideological, political or economic, governments have been attempting, as Lord Morrison of Lambeth puts it, to "combine progressive modern business management with a proper degree of public accountability."[58] In other words, the public corporation is an administrative device which attempts to deflect political direction and interference in its day-to-day management functions while simultaneously permitting a measure of political control and legislative surveillance over its corporate policies. This is no easy task for any government to accomplish.

Many Canadian scholars argue that at the federal level, these quasi-public, quasi-private hybrids have operated in almost a policy vacuum: government policy as it applies to Crown corporations in general have seldom been clearly enunciated.[59] In some cases this vagueness may have been the justifiable outgrowth of a deliberate government intent that its policy relationship to a Crown corporation or specific Crown corporations should be one of subtle interplays and nuances of informal relationships.

But, as R. H. Hall has indicated, "the techniques that are effective and efficient within a simple structure just may not be effective or efficient in a more complex case."[60] The establishment of most of our government corporations has taken place over the last five decades, and the environment in which they were established and in which they still operate has fluctuated rather significantly over this period of time. C. D. Howe operated a control system which was somewhat informal; after all, he had specific objectives in mind (winning the war at all costs)—objectives shared by his appointees to the boards, so a telephone call, a luncheon or dinner date, or some other informal means, created the atmosphere for effective government direction and monitoring of the corporations' activities. But since the 1940s in Canada the administrative state has evolved, and the machinery of government has mirrored that complex growth. It follows then that the control devices of yesteryear had to be scrutinized to ascertain their adequacy for public accountability and control in the 1980s and beyond.

First the financial controls of corporations were found to be inadequate. Capital and operating budgets of the corporations have not fulfilled their potential as instruments for policy direction and accountability.[61] Government critics, including the Auditor General, point out that there is generally a lack of specific information on operation performance and corporate goals, and the usual one year time framework of budgetary projections provides very little meaningful explanation on long term corporation planning. Furthermore, strenuous efforts to obtain this type of information have invariably led to delays in the present cycle of the budgetary process, creating frustrations, disappointments and a breakdown of the administrative process.

Second, the board of directors has indeed provided and continues to provide an informal means of public control. If, for example, corporations proved to be particularly difficult in heeding political direction, then the rather blunt instruments of "packing" the board of directors or outright dismissal of the recalcitrants can be resorted to. However, as the corporations and their subsidiaries multiplied, a series of problems with this type of control presented themselves. Simple informal controls could no longer meet the difficulties posed by interlocking directorates, particularly when the government was unaware of the dimensions of this practice. Having interlocking directorates in the public and private sector simultaneously could present serious problems of conflict of interests to directors. Thus by 1973 the federal government prohibited full time senior officials of Crown corporations from retaining or accepting directorships in private sector corporations that are not affiliated with their Crown corporations or the Crown itself.

Additionally, no federal statute gave any firm guidance to cabinet on the selection criteria for directors, aside from a few constituent acts which stipulated representation criteria from geographic areas of the country.[62] What exactly were the responsibilities of these boards of directors or chairman of these proliferating corporations, remained imprecise and too informal for conditions of the 1980s.

Third, the use of the directive power has increasingly become a reserve power of the government. True, a number of Crown corporations such as Petro-Canada, Teleglobe Canada, the Agricultural Stabilization Board and the Canadian Commercial Corporation are still subjected to specific directive powers, but as a whole the authority by which directives may be issued remains largely restricted by government.

The Blue Paper on Crown Corporations issued by the Privy Council Office seeks to, as the document proclaims,

. . . clarify and to increase the consistency in the relationships between the government and Crown corporations on one hand and Crown corporations and Parliament on the other. Integral to the clarification of these relationships are the following: the role of Crown corporations in the pursuit of policy objectives and government priorities; the role and functions of boards of directors of Crown corporations; the use which Crown corporations make of subsidiaries and the government's control over their creation. The Government's proposals also seek to clarify the role of the minister designated as the appropriate minister for a Crown corporation by establishing that minister as the focal point in the government's policy direction, control and accountability of a particular corporation. [63]

Briefly stated here, the government's proposals would attempt to clarify the role of Crown corporations by definitely placing *more control functions and a significant amount of policy direction power in the hands of the collective cabinet, the Treasury Board and the Department of Finance.* This should not be too surprising given our description and analysis of the role of central agencies in Chapter Nine. Central agencies exist primarily as important instruments of control, and to miss this crucial function of these bodies is to lose sight of their main *raison d'être.* The Blue Paper's proposals are therefore as follows:

1 The corporate plans of these bodies would henceforth be more influenced in their form and content by the requirement that corporations must have Treasury Board's scrutiny of these plans and approval for them by the government.

2 The policy directive would become a more effective instrument of executive control. It is to be actively used as a binding directive of unlimited scope to departmental and agency corporations while proprietary corporations would receive directives "of a general nature." All directives would be tabled in the House of Commons for scrutiny and debate, and could be the subject of consultation with the board of directors before its issuance.

3 Interlocking directorates remain forbidden, and approval for the establishment of subsidiary corporations must be specifically ap-

proved by the Governor-in-Council. Performance evaluation of Crown corporations will henceforth be carried out by the department of the designated minister. Exactly how this evaluation is to be accomplished remains somewhat vague and imprecise thus far.

These proposals in the Blue Paper were concretized in legislation designed to bring 178 *wholly owned* Crown corporations into an effective reporting relationship and introduced in the House of Commons by the Hon. Perrin Beatty, Minister of State for the Treasury Board, on November 26, 1979. Langford points out that "the most obvious policy carry-over from the Blue Paper [in the legislation] is the continuing intention to deal, at this time, only with Crown corporations—defined in precisely the same terms as in the Blue Paper."[65] The omnibus bill required Crown corporations to submit their capital and operating budgets to government for approval and continuing scrutiny. The bill was also designed to arrest unrestricted proliferation of Crown corporations and their subsidiaries by requiring both statutory authority and Cabinet approval of any future acquisitions or corporations.[66] The bill, however, died on the order paper when the Clark government was defeated in December 1979. But the legislation (known as Bill C-27) did reflect the fact that the Conservative government had largely accepted the approach to Crown corporations taken by the Trudeau government before its defeat in early 1979. It is therefore to be expected that this legislation on Crown corporations would be reappearing almost intact sometime during 1980-81.

Thus the debate continues, but it still remains uninformed on a number of issues pertaining to public enterprises. In Canada we are learning a little about the extent of the use of this corporate form of government. Indeed, given the classification list of 1977 which was amended in January 1978, and according to informed sources will be amended again, the government is also just learning how extensive is the use of the public corporation in Canada. Furthermore, where "public" ends and "private" begins still remains shrouded in mystery. We do have some inkling as to the roles some of these corporations play in the development of our provinces, but the extent of these roles remains unclear and very imprecise.[67]

The rather explosive growth and the extent of this corporate form has alarmed and would continue to alarm students of public policy and administration in Canada.[68] Part of that alarm is due to the fact that we are now learning how extensive is the use of public corporations in our economy, but it is partly due as well to the traditional liberal democratic concern to ensure control of all instruments of government.

"The dogs may bark, but the caravan passes on" is an old Arab proverb which we quoted in our epigram. The barks of politicians and students of public policy and administration become a little more nervous as it is realized how extensive the caravan really is. These barks may even be reduced to desperate whimpers as we increasingly learn how gargantuan and complex a load these caravans are really carrying. Written in the 1950s, the words of John Edwin Hodgetts therefore still remain very pertinent to our times:

Lord Macaulay long ago admonished the British electors that in selecting their representatives they should choose wisely and confide liberally. His admonition would appear today to apply with particular relevance to the Crown corporation. Parliament and even the responsible minister must show confidence in the corporation by refraining from breathing down the neck of management. On the other hand, the Canadian system of parliamentary government can impose responsibility only on the ministers of the Crown. Hence the public corporation cannot be used as a means of evading ultimate responsibility. Where to draw the line between the claims of managerial autonomy and the claims of parliamentary responsibility remains for Canada a problem that has been seriously posed rather than solved by contemporary use of the public corporation. [69]

A First-Class Rejection

If you write, chances are you have had a rejected manuscript. What do you think of this rejection letter? Is the manuscript that good, or is it that bad?
The English publisher, Sir Charles Petrie, got his hands on the following rejection slip from a Chinese publisher: "we have read your manuscript with boundless delight. If we were to publish the book it would be impossible in the future to publish any book of a lower standard. As it is unthinkable that within the next 10,000 years we shall find its equal, we are, to our great regret, compelled to return this divine work, and to beg you a thousand times to forgive us."

Footnotes

1. Students of Canadian public administration are just beginning to explore the vast dimensions of "the contract state," namely government policies in contracting our research and development contracts to "business" organizations. Comments on this dimension will therefore be barely mentioned in this chapter. For a good British study on the topic see D.C. Hague, W.J.M. Mackenzie and A. Barker, *Public Policy and Private Interests* (London: MacMillan, 1975). For Canada, see Peter Meyboom, "In House vs. Contractual Research," *CPA*, Vol. 17, No. 4, pp. 563-585; Melvern B. Skinner, *The Federal Make or Buy Research and Development Policy: A Pre-*

liminary Evaluation of Policy and Implementation, M.A. Thesis, School of Public Administration, Carleton University, Ottawa, 1978.

2. John W. Langford, "Crown corporations as instruments of policy," in G. Bruce Doern and P.C. Aucoin (eds.), *Public Policy in Canada: Organization, Process and Management* (Toronto: Macmillan of Canada, 1979), p. 239.

3. J.W. Langford, "Crown corporations as instruments of policy," p. 239. For the purposes of this text we have adapted the definition given by Allan Tupper: Public enterprise refers to organizations, owned wholly or partially by the state, engaged in either the production of goods, or the marketing of natural products, or the provision of services. See Allan Tupper, "The Nation's Business: Canadian Concepts of Public Enterprise," unpublished Ph.D. Thesis, Queen's University, 1977, p. 12.

4. Andrew Shonfield, *Modern Capitalism: The Changing Balance of Public and Private Power* (London: Oxford University Press, 1965), p. 385, by permission of Oxford University Press.

5. G. Bruce Doern, "The Concept of Regulation and Regulatory Reform," in G. Bruce Doern and V. Seymour Wilson (eds.), *Issues in Canadian Public Policy* (Toronto: Macmillan of Canada, 1974), p. 13.

6. G. Bruce Doern, "The Concept of Regulation and Regulatory Reform," p. 13.

7. Don Gracey, "Public Enterprise in Canada," in Andre Gélinas (ed.) *Public Enterprise and the Public Interest* (Toronto: The Institute of Public Administration of Canada, 1978), p. 27.

8. For an engaging account of this part of our history see E. Austin Weir, *The Struggle for National Broadcasting in Canada* (Toronto: McClelland and Stewart Ltd., 1965), especially Chapter 18. Further examples include such public corporations as the Sydney Steel Corporation or Polymer competing with private industry or what is called "metaphytic" competition, namely public enterprise competing with private enterprise with both enterprises being regulated by government. See D.C. Corbett, *Politics and the Airlines* (Toronto: University of Toronto Press, 1965), Metaphytic competition is defined as competition between privately owned and publicly owned agencies within a regulated industry (p. 117.)

9. This historical account is derived from J.E. Hodgetts, *The Canadian Public Service: A Physiology of Government 1867-1970* (Toronto: University of Toronto Press, 1973), especially Chapter 7, and Canada, Privy Council Office, *Crown Corporations: Direction, Control, Accountability* (Ottawa: Supply and Services Canada, 1977), pp. 11-13.

10. J.E. Hodgetts, *The Canadian Public Service*, p. 150.

11. Canada Privy Council Office, *Crown Corporations*, p. 12.

12. W.J.M. Mackenzie, and J. Grove, *Central Administration in Britain* (London: Longmans, 1957).

13. For a more comprehensive examination of the financial controls put into place at the time, see H.R. Balls, "The Financial Control and Accountability of Canadian Crown Corporations," *Public Administration*, Vol. 31, (Summer 1953), pp. 127-143; Lloyd D. Musolf, *Public Ownership and Accountability: The Canadian Experience* (Cambridge, Mass.: Harvard University Press, 1959).

14. All these definitions of the various schedules are taken from S. 66(3) of the Financial Administration Act (FAA).

15. See. H.R. Balls, "The Financial Control and Accountability of Canadian Crown Corporations" for the best description; also for a comprehensive taxonomic study of Crown corporations in general see C.A. Ashley and R.G.H. Smails, *Canadian Crown Corporations: Some Aspects of their Administration and Control* (Toronto: The Macmillan Company of Canada Ltd., 1965), especially Chapters 1-11.

16. Canada. House of Commons. *Report* of the Auditor General of Canada to the House of Commons, Fiscal Year ended March 31, 1976 (Ottawa: The Queen's Printer, 1976), pp. 49, 51.

17. Don Gracey, "Public Enterprise in Canada," p. 26. Space precludes listing these 384 organizations. For a full listing see Canada. House of Commons. *Minutes* of Proceedings and Evidence of the Standing Committee on Public Accounts. January 24, 1978, especially Appendix PA-20; John W. Langford, "The identification and classification of federal public corporations: a preface to regime building." *CPA*, Vol. 23, No. 1, Spring 1980, pp. 76-104.

18. For a recent attempt of classification with which we disagree, see A.G. Irvine, "The delegation of authority to Crown corporations," *CPA*, Vol. 14, No. 4, Winter 1971, pp. 556-579. As a traditional economist, Irvine is primarily interested in the maximization of efficiency performance. Hence he ends up with the somewhat curious definition that Crown corporations should not be undertaking *political* or *judicial* functions, but should be heavily judged on the basis of the maximization of the use of their resources in achieving certain *specific* objectives.

19. See C.C. Hood, "The Rise and Rise of the British Quango," *New Society*, 18, August 1973, pp. 386-388; C.C. Hood, "Government by other means," in Brian Chapman and A. Potter (eds.), *W.J.M. Mackenzie: Political Questions* (Manchester: Manchester University Press, 1975), pp. 147-161.

20. Privy Council Office. *Crown Corporations*, p. 37.

21. The conclusion of the PCO document advances the following statement:
    Although the Government intends to have as many wholly-owned corporations as possible listed in the Schedules of the FAA, several will undoubtedly remain unscheduled. For those corporations that are not listed as Crown corporations in the FAA, including all mixed enterprises, the Government has begun a study and will make proposals as soon as possible respecting the appropriate schemes of Parliamentary and government control, direction and accountability that might be applied. (p. 45)

22. Lloyd D. Musolf, *Mixed Enterprise: A Developmental Perspective* (Lexington, Mass.: D.C. Heath and Co., 1972), p. 3. For another brief treatment of the "mixed enterprise" theme see Hugh J. Mullington, "The Federal Government as an Entrepreneur," unpublished M.A. Thesis, School of Public Administration, Carleton University, 1969, especially Chapter 5.

23. For a most elucidating analysis of this partnership see Larry Pratt "The State and Province Building: Alberta's Development Strategy," in Leo Panitch (ed.) *The Canadian State: Political Economy and Political Power* (Toronto: University of Toronto Press, 1977), pp. 133-162; also by the same author, *The Tar Sands* (Edmonton: Hurtig Publishers, 1976).

24. Karen Zavitz, *The Canada Development Corporation: The Relationship to Government.* M.A. Thesis, Carleton University, School of Public Administration, 1977.

25. For an overview of Canadian mixed enterprise see Frank Swedlove, "Business-Government Joint Ventures in Canada," *Foreign Investment Review*, Vol. 1, No. 3 (Spring 1978), pp. 13-17. The complications of interlocking subsidiaries have the potential of boggling the mind of any reader. To illustrate and partly clarify the complications we have reproduced Don Gracey's footnote #2 from his above mentioned article:

> The government of Canada participates in a number of "mixed enterprises." Of these the government has a controlling interest in twenty-four companies. These companies in turn have often established a number of subsidiaries. The Canada Development Corporation, for example, is a mixed enterprise that has established or acquired five subsidiaries. One of these subsidiaries (Polysar Ltd.) has established some forty-six subsidiary companies located around the world. The federal government has also assumed a partial ownership of companies through programs such as those under the Department of Regional and Economic Expansion Act whereby the government may assume equity in a company for a short term for the purposes of regional development. Mixed enterprises have also been established for joint administration with the United States (e.g., the Blue Water Bridge Authority) or provinces. Only two mixed enterprises (Telesat and the Canada Development Corporation) have been established by an act of Parliament. There is no general legislation for the creation or control and direction of federal mixed enterprises. The prerogatives and powers of the government in such situations are by and large those of shareholders under federal or provincial corporation law.

Don Gracey, "Public Enterprise in Canada," p. 26, footnote #2. See also Herschel Hardin's description of the diverse holdings of a provincial agency, the Manitoba Development Corporation. Herschel Hardin, *A Nation Unaware: The Canadian Economic Culture* (Vancouver: J.J. Douglas Ltd., 1974), pp. 89-90.

26. The best analysis so far of these programs has been done by Robert Best in his "Distributive Constituent Policy and its Impact on Federal-Provincial Relations: The Case of OFY and LIP," unpublished M.A. Research Essay, Carleton University, 1973. An abridgement of his analysis of the OFY program appears in G. Bruce Doern and V. Seymour Wilson (eds.), *Issues in Canadian Public Policy* (Toronto: Macmillan, 1974), Chapter 6. For a further analysis testing proposition about partisanship in the allocation process of LIP, see Donald E. Blake, "LIP and Partisanship: An Analysis of the Local Initiatives Program," *Canadian Public Policy*, II, No. 1 (Winter 1976), pp. 17-32.

27. Andre Gélinas (ed.), *Public Enterprise and Public Interest*, especially the articles by Musolf, Orrenius, France and Marsan.

28. J. Stefan Dupre and W. Eric Gustafson, "Contracting for Defense: Private Firms and the Public Interest," *Political Science Quarterly*, Vol. 77, No. 2 (June 1962), pp. 161-177, at p. 161.

29. Dan Middlemiss, "The Political Economy of Defence: Dimensions of Government Involvement in the Canadian Aircraft Industry." A paper presented to the 50th Annual Meeting of the Canadian Political Science Association, London, Ontario, May 1978.

30. *Ibid.*, p. 2.

31. For a spirited beginning in asking questions covering these wider dimensions, see Allan Tupper's review article, "The State in Business," *Canadian Public Administration*. Vol. 22, No. 1 (Spring, 1979), pp. 124-150.

32. This section of the chapter is particularly indebted to Christopher Hood, "Keeping the Centre Small: Explanations of Agency Type," *Political Studies*, Vol. XXVI, No. 1, pp. 30-46.

33. Alexander Brady, "The State and Economic Life," in George W. Brown (ed.) *Canada* (Berkeley: University of California Press, 1950), p. 353.

34. W.A. Mackintosh, "Canadian Economic Policy: Scope and Principles," *Canadian Journal of Economics and Political Science* 16:3 (August 1950), p. 317.

35. Herbert Morrison, *Socialisation and Transport* (London: Constable and Co., 1933). A strong advocate of the London Passenger Transport Board, Morrison argued: "The Board must have autonomy and freedom in business management. It must not only be allowed to enjoy responsibility; it must even have responsibility thrust down its throat." (p. 170).

36. See the comments of J. Harvey Perry in *Proceedings* of the Eighth Annual Conference of the Institute of Public Administration of Canada, pp. 146-147.

37. Canada. House of Commons Debates. Vol. II; Second Session, Twentieth Parliament, May 14, 1946, p. 1512.

38. The Rt. Hon. Lord Bridges, "The Relationship between Government and Government-controlled Corporations," *CPA*, Vol. VII, September 1964, pp. 295-296.

39. J.A. Corry, "The Fusion of Government and Business," *Canadian Journal of Economics and Political Science*, Vol. II, No. 3 (August 1936), p. 304.

40. Canada. House of Commons Debates, Vol. V, Third Session. Twentieth Parliament, June 17, 1947, p. 4249.

41. For a Canadian illustration of this argument see A.G. Irvine, "The delegation of authority of Crown corporations," *CPA*, Vol. 14, No. 4 (Winter 1971), pp. 556-579.

42. Christopher Hood, "Keeping the Centre Small: Explanations of Agency Type," *Political Studies*, Vol. XXVI, No. 1, p. 38.

43. *Ibid.*, p. 38.

44. John Edwin Hodgetts, *Proceedings* of the Fifth Annual Conference of the Institute of Public Administration of Canada, p. 305.

45. While some senior public servants insist that the needs for innovation and political sensitivity in the bureaucracy are fulfilled by purposely recruiting "senior outside talent," others have stressed that the process does harbour inherent dangers for a "career" public service, and that the practice has gone too far in its attempts to rectify a recruiting problem. See J.J. Deutsch, "Some Thoughts on the Public Service," *Canadian Journal of Economics and Political Science*, Vol. XXIII, No. 1 (February 1957), p. 85.

46. J.E. Hodgetts, W. McCloskey, Reginald Whittaker and V. Seymour Wilson, *The Biography of an Institution: The Civil Service Commission of Canada* (Montreal: McGill-Queen's University Press, 1972), Chapters 1-3.

47. Most senior level public service appointments at the level of Assistant Deputy Minister and above, including executive positions to boards and commissions, are Orders-in-Council appointments.

48. Volker Ronge, "The Politicization of Administration in Advanced Capitalist Societies," *Political Studies*, 22 (1974), pp. 89-93.

49. Ian MacDougall, "The Canadian National Energy Board: Economic "Jurisprudence" in the National Interest or Symbolic Reassurance?" *The Alberta Law Review*, Vol. XI, No. 2, 1973, pp. 327-382 at p. 346.

50. John W. Langford, *Transport in Transition: The Reorganization of the Federal Transport Portfolio* (Montreal: McGill-Queen's University Press, 1976), especially Chapter 2.

51. C.C. Hood, "Keeping the Centre Small." p. 44.

52. A good illustration of this clientele argument can be found in Riane Mahon's "Canadian public policy: the unequal structure of representation," Leo Panitch (ed.), *The Canadian State: Political Economy and Political Power* (Toronto: University of Toronto Press, 1977), pp. 165-198.

53. Christopher Hood, "Keeping the Centre Small," p. 38.

54. Michael Pitfield, "The Shape of Government in the 1980s: Techniques and instruments for policy formulation at the federal level," *CPA* Vol. 19, No. 1 (Spring 1976), p. 17.

55. C. Hood, "Keeping the Centre Small," p. 45.

56. Harold Seidman, "The Government Corporation: Organization and Controls," *Public Administration Review*, Vol. 14, No. 3 (Summer 1954), pp. 183-192.

57. Even knowing the objectives of the corporate form is no help in solving "problems" according to some students of organizations. Where objectives are multiple, conflicting and/or unacknowledgeable only compound the problem. As Boyle has remarked, to say, "First define your objectives, then you can solve your problems" is really no more than to say, "First solve your problems, then you can solve your problems."

L. Boyle, "Politics and the Royal Commission on Local Government," *Local Government Finance*, Vol. 73, No. 10 (October 1969).

58. *First Report of the Select Committee on Nationalised Industries*, Vol. 1, (H.M.S.O., London, July 1968), para. 53, p. 13.

59. For an excellent illustration of this genre of criticism see the article by J.E. Hodgetts, "The Public Corporation in Canada," in W. Friedmann (ed.), *The Public Corporation: A Comparative Symposium* (Toronto: The Carswell Co. Ltd., 1954), pp. 51-86; John W. Langford's "Crown Corporations as Instruments of Policy," provides the best criticisms to date of the Blue Paper on Crown Corporations.

60. R.H. Hall, *Organizations: Structures and Process* (N.J.: Prentice-Hall, 1972), p. 167.

61. It has been possible for some Crown corporations to use their corporate powers to establish subsidiaries, and through these bodies avoid Parliamentary scrutiny and control. Although this has not occurred to any great extent so far, evidence before the Estey Commission on Air Canada indicated that a subsidiary of the CNR (Venturex Ltd.) was used as a corporate instrument of Air Canada, thereby achieving significant freedom from scrutiny from the CNR, Air Canada, and most importantly, Parliamentary scrutiny and control. See Air Canada Inquiry Report, October 1975, pp. 161-185, 248-252, 284-285.

62. Don Gracey, "Public Enterprise in Canada," p. 33.

63. Canada. Privy Council Office. *Crown Corporations*, p. 21.

64. For a very good critique of the government's proposals in the Blue Paper, see John W. Langford, "Crown Corporations as Instruments of Policy."

65. John W. Langford, "The identification and classification of federal public corporations: a preface to regime building," p. 102.

66. For a brief but good review of Bill C-27, see John Langford, *ibid.*, pp. 102-104.

67. See the study of the development of natural resources in Ontario by H.V. Nelles, *The Politics of Development* (Toronto: Macmillan of Canada, 1974); Peter Silcox, "The ABC's of Ontario: Provincial Agencies, Boards and Commissions," in Donald C. Macdonald (ed.), *Government and Politics of Ontario* (Toronto: Macmillan), pp. 135-152.

68. W. Friedmann writes very skeptically of mixed enterprises and contends that this experimentation between public and private sectors is fraught with danger for government controls and adequate scrutiny. See W. Friedmann, "Public and Private Enterprises in Mixed Economies: Some Comparative Observations," in W. Fried-

mann (ed.), *Public and Private Enterprises in Mixed Economies* (New York: Columbia University Press, 1974), pp. 359-394.

69. J.E. Hodgetts, "The Public Corporation in Canada: Background and Development," in W. Friedmann (ed.), *The Public Corporation*, pp. 51-86, at p. 86.

TABLE I
PUBLIC EMPLOYMENT BY COMPONENT CATEGORY,
TOTAL TAX RETURNS, 1947, 1961 AND 1975

Component	Number			Per Cent		
	1947	1961	1975	1947	1961	1975
Federal[1]	129936	231136	356997	31.0	22.8	15.5
Provincial	69431	200343	475414	16.6	19.8	20.6
Municipal	69770	181521	450920	16.7	17.9	19.6
Educational	79830	160771	322272	19.1	15.8	14.0
Institutional	69551	239921	697494	16.6	23.7	30.3
Total Public[1]	418518	1013692	2303097	100.0	100.0	100.0
Total Canada[1]	3502766	5964383	11926199	11.9[2]	17.0[2]	19.3[2]

1. *Excludes Armed Forces.*

2. *Total Public as a percent of Total Canada (excluding Armed Forces).*

Source: Adapted from David K. Foot and Percy Thadaney, The Growth of Public Employment in Canada: The Evidence from Taxation Statistics. *Technical Report, No. 1,* Growth of the Public Service in Canada. *Issued by the Institute for Research on Public Policy, 1977.*

CHAPTER THIRTEEN

THE BUREAUCRACY AND ITS PUBLICS*

Government is simply not just a reflection of a variety of interest groups either contending for greater access to resources, as the pluralists might describe, or reflecting the dominance of particular interest groups, as class analysts allege. It may be this, it is true, but it is also much more . . . government as an institutional area, once in existence, continues largely in response to its own imperatives. . . . Interest groups may have an impact on them, but governmental activities are still independent of interest groups in the most essential ways. Not to recognize this explicitly and not to take this into account in the study of interest groups results is an apolitical if not mindless analysis.

Mildred A. Schwartz

We know virtually nothing about the process of "exchange" that enters into the transactions between the bureaucracy, its clients, and the general environment.

John Edwin Hodgetts

I. Introduction

The first epigram quoted above and taken from the writings of the noted sociologist Mildred A. Schwartz, sums up one of the central perspectives of this chapter: government officials in the ongoing performance of their duties seek to attract support, stabilize, or even dominate, if possible, their relationships with their constituencies. Bureaucrats are acutely aware that lack of support from the constituencies they serve can severely circumscribe their ability to achieve agreed-upon goals, and may even cause the demise of their organiza-

---

* This chapter owes a heavy intellectual debt to various social scientists many of whom are quoted and footnoted throughout. However the most important insights on the nature of interest group activity were derived from the theoretical writings of E. E. Schattschneider. His 1957 presidential address to the American Political Science Association is used extensively here, as well as his book, The Semi-Sovereign People, a classic in the annals of political science.

tions. In a world of "blooming, buzzing confusion," the urgency of ordering and stabilizing one's relationship with one's publics is therefore always present. The intensity, direction and scope of these relationships is the subject matter of this chapter.

The thesis that bureaucracy acts in its own self-interest by attempting to maximize its "own private utility functions," as the economists put it, is not a new one entirely. Public choice economists, particularly spurred by the theoretical works of Mancur Olson Jr. and Anthony Downs, have been theorizing and suggesting several hypotheses which, in sum, suggest that bureaucratic organizations, when administering public policy, attempt to maximize their own "private utility functions" rather than the "social utility functions" expressed in the legislation they have been given to administer.[1] However, thus far, these hypotheses can be described at best as crude, based as they are on narrow empirical formulations from specific case studies.[2] Furthermore they make no attempt to explain *why* bureaucratic self interest becomes such a *crucial independent variable* for the survival of bureaucratic organizations.[3]

Our task in this chapter will be to put forward some perspectives of the political strategy of the bureaucracy in its interaction with its publics, and to roughly classify these various publics.

First, we assume that the political system is a dynamic one in the sense that there is a constant tendency within the system to change or to evolve. Change is endemic because our system faces basic problems to which no overall continuous solutions exist. The dynamic of politics therefore finds its origins in this strife of constant change. But in order to make the system viable or work smoothly a society must be able *to effectively manage its conflicts.*[4] Political strategy therefore deals with the way conflict is exploited, used or suppressed. Thus we visualize conflict not as a clash of wills necessarily leading to bodily coercion, but rather an inevitable human propensity to see reality in different ways, and to have different perspectives or opinions on matters of public concern. To quote Schattschneider, "pressure politics is an instrument for the socialization of conflict."[5]

Second, these conflicts can be differentiated into "public interests" and "special interests." Although it may seem trite it is worth emphasizing that *there are* some interests which transcend the special interests of groups or individuals. Without some common interests no democracy can survive very long. We can safely assume, for example, that among the vast majority of Canadians there is a common consensus that medical research to better the health of our citizenry is vital, or that government should encourage scientific and technological achievements by our scientists, or that the economy should be carefully analysed and monitored to ensure the viability and prosperity of the Canadian economy. Such broad consensus is manifested in the creation of structures like the Medical Research Council, the National Research Council and the Economic Council of Canada.

This is not to deny the fact that professionals who staff these structures do not, from time to time, become embroiled in specific controversies, and are then viewed as special interest groups by the bureaucracy or the government. However, their common mandate on the specific "public interest" for which they were created remains intact, and as such both the bureaucracy and government have devised special procedures for dealing with these structures and the various interests sectors they represent.

Third, insofar as special interests are concerned, their general characteristics are that they are usually exclusive issue groups, identifiable and readily recognizable. Such special interests may or may not be well organized. Special interest groups prefer to privatize their interests, that is they work to "restrict the scope of conflict or to keep it entirely out of the public domain. Ideas concerning individualism, free private enterprise, localism, privacy and economy are designed to privatize conflict ǫr to restrict its scope."[6] However, privatization does not always work, and when conflict is aired in public it is never restricted to the groups most immediately involved. For, by going public, these groups now appeal for support from the vast number of people who are sufficiently remote from the conflict to have a more detached and hopefully sympathetic perspective (e.g., save our small businesses, pollution probe, decriminalizing the use of marijuana, save the seals, gay rights, right to life, and so on).

Bureaucrats come to know these groups and are able to work and have a mutually exploitative relationship with some of them. Thus organizational procedures are devised by the bureaucracy to mobilize some interests "in," while those issues considered "on the fringes" or marginal are mobilized "out." In a word, bureaucratic organization is the mobilization of bias. However, this mobilization is not exactly a "cosy affair" in favor of the "in-groups." For, *and this is extremely significant, bureaucracy seeks to modify private power relationships to ensure the public interest by enlarging the scope of conflict.* Thus we see the bureaucracy encouraging the formation of special interest groups, funding these organizations from the public purse, creating governmental structures (i.e., regulatory boards) to ensure such interests are given hearings, and putting forward at times policy positions consistently and diametrically opposed to the views of some of the most powerful special interests in the political system.[7]

Fourth, it is common knowledge that those who are mobilized

"out" of the system appeal to the ultimate arbiter of public opinion for relief. Schattschneider puts this very well:

> It is the weak who want to socialize conflict, i.e., to involve more and more people in the conflict until the balance of forces is changed. In the school yard it is not the bully, but the defenseless smaller boys who "tell the teacher." When the teacher intervenes the balance of power in the school yard is apt to change drastically. [8]

Thus the "weak" appeal to our courts, to the press, television and other media for redress and may even go to the extreme by using outlandish methods to achieve publicity for their cause, and to keep the conflict before the public. As an example, the Canadian Greenpeace Foundation has performed some of the most hair-raising acts of bravado on the high seas by maneuvering their small crafts between hunted whales and the powerful harpoons of the massive Soviet or Japanese fishing trawlers. Some of these groups perform acts to ensure continuous publicity, hoping that eventually public opinion will force the corridors of power to be opened to them, and "their interests" taken into full consideration in the making of public policy. We will develop this theme of "unorganized" private interest groups later in the chapter.

Finally, we assume that in some sense the interactions among politicians, bureaucracy and pressure groups are important in the determination of public policy. [9] What we do not assume is what particular or specific weight these interactions have in the final determination of public policy issues, both in the short and long term. Schattschneider's counsel is again instructive on this score:

> . . . The notion of "pressure" distorts the image of the power relations involved. *Private conflicts are taken into the public arena precisely because someone wants to make certain that the power ratio among the private interests most immediately involved shall not prevail.* To treat a conflict as a mere test of the strength of the private interests is to leave out the most significant factors. This is so true that it might indeed be said that the only way to preserve private power ratios is to keep conflicts out of the public arena.
>
> The assumption that it is only the "interested" who count ought to be reexamined in view of the foregoing discussion. The tendency of the literature of pressure politics has been to neglect the low-tension force of large numbers because *it assumes that the equation of forces is fixed at the outset.* [10]

Indeed, despite the growing knowledge of pressure groups/ governmental interactions and the positing of various theories attempting to explain the interaction among *economy, state* and *society,* [11] we are still very much ignorant of the specific qualities of these interactions, or "equation of forces."

Following A. Paul Pross, we define pressure groups as "organisations whose members act together to influence public policy in order to promote their common interest."[12] As the reader has already surmised, our overall general subject deals with the role of pressure groups in the policy process, *but* with a special emphasis on the much more narrow sub-theme of pressure groups/bureaucratic interactions. The chapter has therefore been entitled "Bureaucracy and Its Publics" for a specific reason, for it connotes a much more dynamic interaction of bureaucracy and its environment than if it were entitled "Bureaucracy and Interest Groups." We also wish to reiterate an additional factor of this interaction: bureaucracy seeks to influence interest groups in turn, and employ various devices to ensure that this influence is a two-way street. One method used seeks to foster favorable attitudes and opinions in the public at large, but this is usually disastrous because bureaucracy, as both Karl Marx and Max Weber have indicated, is inevitably plagued with an image which alienates, an image without sympathy or compassion.[13]

The second method of fostering influence is amply demonstrated by bureaucracy's much more successful achievements in building support among its "attentive publics." Mark Nadel and Francis Rourke define "publics" as:

. . . groups that have a salient interest in the [bureaucracy]—because it has either the capacity to provide them with some significant benefit or the power to exercise regulatory authority in ways that have a critical impact on their welfare as they perceive it.[14]

Nadel and Rourke add that both methods of seeking to achieve popular support and compliance are not mutually exclusive: "A [bureaucracy] can seek to create general public support while building alliances with interest groups that have a special stake in its work."[15]

This perspective, while mirroring the many unique and dynamic characteristics of the American environment, contains comparative features common to the Canadian political system as well. *In seeking to create more general support of public policies, the Canadian bureaucracy, with the full acquiescence of the government, has enlarged the scope of conflict by fostering and encouraging interest groups, particularly over the last three or four decades.* This encouragement has taken a variety of structural forms: from outright financial support of selected interest groups, to the revitalization, creation and funding of many functional and central advisory councils, and to the spawning of more broadly positional policy structures for collecting and transmitting knowledge for policy purposes.[16] (Such as "new style" royal commissions, task forces, advisory committees of various sorts, and planning bodies for the co-ordination of regional growth policies, to name only a few examples.)

However, the larger Canadian environment has witnessed a momentum of societal change to which both politicians and bureaucrats have had to respond. During the last decade Canadians have witnessed the proliferation of various kinds of interest groups, the majority of them unorganized in the conventional ways encouraged by the government and the bureaucracy. Indeed, many of these groups are disorganized, but they have survived and have even flourished despite their spontaneous and disorganized beginnings, a fact not entirely lost on both the government and the bureaucracy. In the idiom of Schattschneider, we have in effect witnessed some breakdown in the usual socialization procedures devised for societal conflict. Both the political executive and the bureaucracy have responded by making structural changes in the machinery of government to accommodate many of these new demands on the political system, but they have met with mixed results. The attempt to accommodate has led to the publication of white papers on policy areas, the drafting of legislation and its presentation in Parliament *without prior group consultation* (thus allowing group pressures to be more fully felt at the political than at the bureaucratic levels), letting it be known that the bureaucracy will be open to "consultation" in the drafting of regulations once policy legislation has been passed by Parliament, the use of the judicial system as the final arbiter in group disputes when other attempts at "consensus-making" have failed, and finally the recent attempts by the government to encourage the concept of corporatism and the building of corporate structures, with the government, the private sector and the unions as chief participants, to ensure more adequate social and economic legislation for a modern Canada.[17]

Thus to the message: the catholicity of our perspective for this chapter will be demonstrated in a variety of ways. First we will analyse the traditional and more contemporary ways in which the bureaucracy has succeeded in institutionalizing and regularizing its relationships with its organized publics (that is, with organized special interest groups and public interest groups). In attempting to give the reader a perspective of these relationships we will discuss a few of the structural forms described above, although comprehensive descriptions of each must be left to the more specialized articles and books in the academic literature to which we will refer.

The increasing complexity of the interaction between bureaucracy and its publics was first identified by Pross and further commented upon by Aucoin.[18] Relevant aspects of the analyses made by these two students of Canadian public policy and administration will be summarized as we discuss the factors responsible for this complexity and describe the newer structural forms spawned by the ever changing and dynamic Canadian environment.

II. Some Conventional Structural Forms of Participation in Public Policy Formation

(i) Organized Special Interest Groups

In recent years a number of Canadian studies of organized special interest groups have identified the bureaucracy as the main focus of pressure group activity in Canada.[19] As Robert Presthus puts it, "the civil service is the lodestar of the political system. As a result, we may safely assume that the most common pattern of elite interaction is between high-level bureaucrats and interest group representatives."[20]

Groups, of course, also move in the larger political environment—the world of the elected official, the political executive, the legislature and the courts. However, pressure groups must lay a heavy emphasis on parrying with the bureaucrats who perform many of the same roles as elected officials or judges. There are trade-offs between officials and groups: bureaucracy trying to effect an alliance while groups try to influence policy outputs. In such a context, the bureaucracy operates with discretion, often exercising judicial, legislative and executive powers in a seamless web. The important point is that groups recognize this relatively autonomous power and seek to channel its exercise on their own behalf.

Yet it must not be forgotten that the activities of bureaucrats take place largely in the context and surveillance of the larger political environment. The bureaucrat in the Canadian political system may exercise considerable independent and autonomous authority, but, as we have argued in previous chapters, it is the elected official, the minister who is held politically and ultimately responsible for the public bureaucracy. If, for example, influential pressure groups are unable to obtain favorable rulings from the public service, the channel of redress is clear for the group to appeal directly to the minister, who then has the option of directing the behavior of public servants within the hierarchy. Helen Jones Dawson reports, for example, that the Canadian Federation of Agriculture, the major Canadian form of organization, ". . . . is capable of going to the minister when it meets what it considers to be unwarranted obstacles at the administrative level; it does not make public announcements about these appeals."[21] This influence is not lost on those groups considered to be on the periphery of the interactive process. "What counts for Mr. Bulloch," one report on a lobbyist reads, "is being able to get his foot in the heavy brass-furnished doors of the inner sanctums and have the minister answer his telephone calls. He does and they do."[22] As Pross observes, to get to these inner sanctums of "heavy brass-furnished doors" and "oak panelled offices":

. . . the lobbyist must have resources of information, financial or economic power and political weight, but he must also be prepared to observe the confidentiality of the relationship. It is this capacity of the executive administrative arm of government to define the terms of its relationships with pressure groups and other segments of the political communications system that constitutes the critical element in the policy equation . . .[23]

This emphasis on direct access and a low profile is manifested in several ways.[24] First, if an interest group wishes to gain access it must be properly organized. H. H. Hannam, first president and managing director of the Canadian Federation of Agriculture told the 1953 annual meeting of the Institute of Public Administration of Canada how agricultural representation on the original board of directors of the Bank of Canada was omitted because of this lack of organization:

In the course of our early remarks, Dr. Clark [former Deputy Minister of Finance] said to me, "We want to get one representative of agriculture. . . . We want to do that, the government wants to do that, and we are soliciting your help." He went on to say, "You have not a national organization representing agriculture, have you, which is a national interest group?" I said, "No, we have not." He said, "It is too bad, isn't it?" That was a remark I will never forget. I used it quite often in the days when we were organizing the Federation.[25]

Once organized there are a series of ground rules to be followed. From the perspective of the bureaucracy, "the group and its officials must have a reputation for expertise, reliability and political non-partisanship."[26] Groups also must ". . . be able to provide accurate information quickly [and] they must be reliable about confidences."[27] Helen Dawson also notes that a crucial requirement is that groups must not have a penchant for publicity. If all these criteria are satisfactory Dawson notes that there will then be a constant "two-way flow of information."[28]

When the relationship is institutionalized and there is a predisposition to exchange confidences with one another with a fair degree of frequency, the term "clientele" relationship has been coined to describe the pattern of interaction. Dawson has outlined the relationship in the following terms: "after years of exchange of information and getting together over general policy problems, the relationship becomes so intimate that each one will be able to make a very good estimate of the other's likely reaction to a given development."[29] But a clientele relationship, while it means that influence can be exerted by the group in question, does not mean that the government department has become a "captive" to the interest of that particular group. It is common for a department of government to have a clientele relationship with several client groups which are basically different in their respective philosophies. As an example, the federal Department of Agriculture has close relationships with two clientele groups with basically different agricultural philosophies, namely, the Canadian Federation of Agriculture and the Canadian Farmers' Union.

Therefore what exists at the bureaucratic level in relation to one department is mirrored with variation throughout the federal public service. There are a series of clientele relationships: for example, the small business groups with the Ministry of State for Small Business, the Canadian Association of Consumers with the Department of Consumer and Corporate Affairs, the Canadian Legion with the Department of Veterans Affairs, and various interest groups in the manufacturing sector with the Department of Industry.

While groups foster the creation of departmental "homes" it is equally true that the bureaucracy has fostered and encouraged the creation of specific interest groups from time to time. For example, in the nineteenth century the Canadian Manufacturers' Association was instrumental in obtaining the creation of the Department of Trade and Commerce.[30] During the First World War the Department of Trade and Commerce in turn fostered commodity based export associations.[31] The Consumers' Association of Canada "traces its origin to a plea made in 1941 to Canadian women by the Minister of Finance and the chairman of the Wartime Prices and Trade Board for help in maintaining wartime price ceilings."[32] In recent years the creation of Ministries of State have also facilitated the accommodation of various interest groups which have been proliferating in the 1960s and 70s. Today groups benefitting from privileged relationships arising from contact with Ministries of State include a multitude of ethnic organizations consorting with the Ministry of State for Multiculturalism, and various athletic associations with the Ministry of State for Physical Fitness and Amateur Sports.

Once a clientele relationship is established it can never be taken for granted that it will be a permanent feature of privileged access. An example is the Fisheries Council of Canada, the national representative of the Canadian fishing industry. For many years the Council enjoyed a clientele relationship with the federal Department of Fisheries. The potency of this arrangement seems to have been reduced in the late 1960s with the creation of the Department of Fisheries and Forestry,. and a further reduction of status occurred with the assumption of fisheries responsibilities by the Department of the Environment, a composite department of many representational functions. Fisheries interests have been particularly unhappy about these trends of events over the years. The trend, however, may be reversing if a proposed Department of Fisheries and Oceans is created.

Another example of this fluctuation in clientele relationship is reflected in the 1977 brief of the Canadian Federation of Agriculture which expressed concern about the threat ". . . of pressure real or imagined, to further split and diversify the responsibility of matters related to food and agriculture policy within the structure of government."[33] The gist of the Federation's brief is that it views with alarm the possibility of its clientele liaison with the Department of Agriculture being reduced in significance, and its representational basis as a spokesman for the farm community in the bureaucratic structure being minimized. Yet, with the rise of the consumer movement the pressures are present to regard agricultural policy in the context of food policy. If this is accomplished consumer groups will increasingly have more say in agriculture with a commensurate loss to the Federation's privileged position of influence in the determination of agricultural policy.

Pressure groups serve many useful roles for bureaucracy in the prosaic but nonetheless exacting work of administering to society's needs. First, they assist in the monitoring of on-going government programs. In many instances trade associations, labor unions, fraternal and service groups have a valuable linkage with the hinterland of Canadian society. Bureaucrats also know that one of the most potentially disastrous aspects of their jobs is communicating public policy effectively.[34] Therefore a two-way communication with these groups enable the bureaucracy to adjust its programs and to fine tune the mechanisms of administration so that the goals of a particular policy and program can be fulfilled. This process is quite important to a bureaucracy which has in the last decade come to be increasingly aware of the necessity for thinking in terms of program goals and monitoring the social impact of programs.

Bureaucrats also employ pressure groups to "sell" programs to their communities. At worst this may take the form of a more blatant species of propaganda, but at best it is usually an effort to make the clientele of a government department aware of the full implications of a new policy or a departmentally administered program. Much of the successes of such utilization of a group by the bureaucracy is predicated on the strength and viability of the pressure groups in question. Governmental elite are constantly checking whether group leaders' opinions "truly represent" the composite views of their respective associations.[35] If a group is viable and effective and is generally regarded as the legitimate representative of a community's interest, then it possesses strong potential as a vehicle of communication for a government agency.

Pressure groups are also the recipients of government funding. Many groups in the early 1970s were amply funded by special programs such as Opportunities for Youth (OFY) and the Local Initiatives Programmes (LIP).[36] The Public Accounts is an excellent source of information in gauging how much support is going to whom. M. L. Friedland reports that the 1975 Public Accounts indicated substantial grants to organizations actively engaged in lobbying on the issue of gun control: Environment Canada gave $10,000 to the Canadian Wildlife Federation; the Department of Justice allocated $10,000 for the Law Amendments Committee of the Canadian Association of Chiefs of Police, and the Department of the Solicitor-General appropriated $50,000 for the same Association; the Department of Indian Affairs and Northern Development distributed over $14 million to band councils and Indian associations; and the Department of National Defence appropriated $90,000 for rifle associations. And these are only approximate figures for a few of the more prominent interest groups.

Friedland's short assessment of the variety and the scope of this funding is instructive. To quote:

A comparison of grants (in terms of numbers and amounts) in the two earlier periods of 1927 and 1952 (the dates of the Revised Statutes of Canada) shows, not surprisingly, that direct grants to pressure groups have increased substantially in the last 50 years. There were only a few dozen grants in each year in the mid-1920s and the majority of these were to such established service agencies as the St. John Ambulance Association, the C.N.I.B. [The Canadian National Institute for the Blind], and the Victorian Order of Nurses.

Government funds are now used to assist groups involved in preparing submissions on matters such as the Berger Inquiry into the Mackenzie Valley Pipeline and the Hartt Inquiry into Development in Northern Ontario. The

Consumers' Association of Canada receives increasingly large sums of money, some of it specifically for advocacy before courts and tribunals. The Association's annual government grant has grown from $150,000 in 1972-73 to $440,000 in 1976-77. The Canadian Labour Congress recently agreed to accept $10 million over five years from the Federal government for union leadership training.[37]

No doubt this training is critical for ". . . few groups in Ottawa have sufficiently specialist staff to be able to face the departmental experts on an equal basis."[38] Many groups feel constrained by the size and complexity of the federal technocratic infrastructure. In one particular sense, the "knowledge explosion" has greatly increased the dependency of some groups on the government, but it has also made government's responsibilities more arduous and complex, with resulting consequences for bureaucratic/pressure groups relationships. We will deal with this aspect of the topic later in the chapter.

For many pressure groups the environment can be a harsh and uncertain one, and many indices point to some measure of dependence on the bureaucracy. The need for year-by-year governmental funding, the superior technical abilities of the vast technocratic structure of the Canadian bureaucracy, the inability of any pressure groups to cement for all times a position of clientele relationship—these are some of the critical factors which determine the bureaucracy's abilities to dominate many aspects of its relationships with pressure groups. For other groups outside the pale of bureaucratic recognition or struggling to obtain a "place in the sun," so to speak, the situation may even be much worse.[39] Nevertheless, this relationship remains a symbiotic one, for the bureaucracy also depends in several ways on an environment populated with interest groups.

(ii) Public Interest Groups: The Role of Functional and Central Advisory Councils

Canadian scholars have long recognized the advisory roles which many councils, committees, boards, and commissions perform in the Ottawa environment.[40] These public pressure groups sometimes can bypass the bureaucracy, that is, they may be given direct access to cabinet and cabinet committees, providing information which has not been screened by traversing the regular departmental route. One of the major reasons why this is so is the general public interest mandate enjoyed by these groups. However, as Aucoin observes, it is also true that "the independence such advisory bodies have from the bureaucracy depends both on the collective expertise of the advisory body's personnel and its need for information from the bureaucracy. The position of such councils of committees thus varies considerably from one policy area to another."[41]

There are a number of characteristics of these advisory bodies which indicate a different relationship to government compared to the organized special interest groups we have discussed previously. First, these advisory bodies receive all or a substantial portion of their financial backing from the public treasury. They are therefore heavily dependent on the public trough, analogous in a financial way to the more conventional departmental structures. Second, for some advisory bodies this similarity to departmental structures becomes even closer because, like departments, they are responsible for their own on-going programs. Thus, for example, the National Research Council is responsible for funded programs in science and technology, and the Medical Research Council conducts its own research in many of the subject areas important to medical science. Those bodies vested with both advisory and functional program responsibilities are known as *functional advisory councils* while those with advisory functions only (for example the Science Council or the Economic Council of Canada) are known as *central advisory councils.*[42]

In their statutes, advisory bodies are all vested with the ultimate responsibility to advise the executive on specific subject areas because they are conceived to be representative of particular communities of interests in our society. This leads us to the third important characteristic of these bodies, namely that their personnel are chiefly non-governmental. These advisory councils are usually dominated by part-time lay people and experts drawn from the private sector or from the nation's university communities. Thus these bodies derive additional legitimacy and influence because of their established links to non-governmental constituencies in our society. As such their "outside advice" is construed as much more important than that tendered by an ordinary interest group in the sense that it is openly solicited and institutionalized by government; paid for on an on-going basis by public funds; and portrayed as both objective and expert and removed from the narrow parochialism of pressure tactics aimed at "getting something" from government. In fact, as Peter Aucoin has demonstrated, these bodies do aim at affecting the structure of influence at the point where policies are formulated. As he notes: "A good deal of policy activity by individuals and groups is related not so much to securing (at least in the short run) an allocation of desired values but rather the attainment of desired positions vis-à-vis other individuals or groups. What is sought is a share of the coercive abilities of the government."[48] This type of policy activity is identified as "positional."

These unique features of advisory bodies have led some commentators to refer to them as "policy ombudsmen," namely that governments have purposely "created their own critics."[44] Case studies of various advisory bodies however seem to point to the fact that they are much more successful as functional entities than as central advisors to government.[45] This is due in part to the political scenario of having an advisory body, no matter how distinguished, facing the almost impregnable rivalry and staying power of various parts of the bureaucracy. The ongoing day-to-day expertise in formulating policy and managing the programs of government are bureaucracy's most formidable trump cards. Therefore, to the politicians and senior bureaucrats, advice *must be shown to have practical payoffs*, and the more immediate the better. It is no accident that during both World Wars, the National Research Council, one of the earliest advisory bodies to government, enjoyed tremendous prestige and influence in governmental circles. It is also no accident that one of the National Research Council's most prestigious and successful presidents, Dr. Henry Marshall Tory, understood the urgent need for practical payoffs, and always utilized, for other longer term benefits, the Council's abilities to deliver "the immediate practical payoffs." As Mel Thistle has indicated, Dr. Tory favored the practical short term problems "that would make a noise" and emphasized the long-term projects "with a staggering pay-off, preferably in the tens of millions of dollars." While not ignoring the vital importance of theoretical science he "invariably selected the highly practical applied work for special mention, relegating the theoretical achievements to a bare list, by title, in an appendix."[46]

(iii) The Receiving, Transmitting and Absorbing of Knowledge: The Role of Royal Commissions and Task Forces

Whether the clientele for a government service has to be organized by the public authority makes use of already existing organized interest groups, the fact remains that communications links supplementary to or substituting for our traditional representative and political organs have had to be brought into play by the bureaucracy. Without these newer direct channels, knowledge and information vital to decisions taken by public power centres would be less effectively transmitted, and the agents working in such centres would lack the assurance that there were not developing programs in a vacuum.[47]

As the above quote from John Edwin Hodgetts notes, the *receiving, transmitting* and *absorbing* of knowledge is of crucial significance to the

Canadian bureaucracy. Perhaps the most commonly and traditionally known way to accomplish all three of these functions is to create royal commissions of inquiry. Between July 1867 and January 1967, for the first one hundred years of Confederation, the Federal government appointed 352 royal commissions[48] (or an average of three-and-a-half a year), but most of these bodies had very restricted scope as instruments for new policy initiatives.[49] As an example, transportation policy, particularly regarding railways, was but one aspect of a clear national policy to develop the wheat economy of Western Canada. According to economist V. C. Fowke, royal commissions were appointed again and again to transmit this essential information to the Canadian public, especially the inhabitants of the West:

> To suggest that the numerous investigative commissions appointed after 1900 played any significant part in the formulation of agricultural policy is therefore, to place the cart before the horse. The policy was there and the only information needed concerned its detailed application and the removal of impediments to its ultimate success. More important than any information which the agricultural commissions assembled was their service in educating electors and legislators to the need for particular enactments, and in performing the safety valve function for the explosive agrarian mentality which characterized the period.[50]

Political scandals and rumours of scandals were also part of our early historical past and government very often used royal commissions to investigate or to lay such charges to rest. The frenzied activity of opening up Canada's frontiers by roads, canals, and railroads often afforded opportunities for graft to politicians, public servants, party "bagmen" and sleazy entrepreneurs. Between 1870 and 1879, for example, twelve of the fifteen royal commissions appointed by the federal government were charged with investigating problems of this nature.[51] As a matter of fact between 1867 and 1969, fifty-five royal commissions (or one-sixth of all the royal commissions appointed in that time) were concerned with scandal and charges of bureaucratic corruption.[52]

During the 1930s as Canada faced serious economic dislocations caused by the Great Depression, royal commissions increasingly assumed a new policy advisory role. V. C. Fowke observed, for example, that in agriculture "governments were genuinely at a loss to know what to do. . . . Governments were uncertain: they appointed many Royal Commissions."[53] In the late 1960s G. Bruce Doern also echoed this sentiment:

> The fact that Canadian public policy-makers have found themselves con-

fronted with technological complexities in many social and economic fields probably accounts for a basically investigative motivation for recent commissions such as those on transportation, energy, taxation, and banking.[54]

Actually this trend of using royal commissions for gathering infor-, mation for input into the public policy process could be clearly discerned from the creation of the Royal Commission on Dominion-Provincial Relations (commonly known as the Rowell-Sirois Commission) in 1937. If one views the process of policy making not in terms of goal-seeking but in terms of a continuous interaction between systems and environment, namely between those who are generally understood to be actively thinking and deciding and those who are affected by the policy making as implementers and beneficiaries, then one can begin to understand the many ways devised by policy makers to utilize "inquests" such as royal commissions.

According to Sir Geoffrey Vickers a real policy decision always involves the clashing of several competing values, and in order to arrive at some decision on the matter several alternative options are open to the decision-maker: by compromising (giving up a little on a whole series of values); giving up a large number of values temporarily; integrating them all; rejecting them for new values; and even giving up one's values temporarily only to pursue them more methodically on a long-term basis.[55] If one accepts these theoretical formulations on the nature of policy making then one can begin to understand the various other functions which the policy makers have increasingly allotted to royal commissions during the last three or four decades: (1) to secure information on a basis for policy decisions, (2) to educate the public in order to generate pressure for intended legislation, (3) to permit the airing of conflicting values and to sample public opinion before decisions are taken, and (4) to enable the government to postpone decision-making on policy issues which have the potential to embarrass the government.

Space precludes a lengthy discussion of these aspects of royal commissions, but a few examples are noteworthy. The wide ranging recommendations of the Rowell-Sirois Commission advocating fiscal centralization were at first blocked by the provinces, then partly implemented in wartime and are now scarcely visible characteristics of our federal state.[56] Some recommendations however, remain central, as, for example, the federal government eventually assuming the responsibility for unemployment. The Hall Commission on health services met a similar fate in that some recommendations were acceptable while others were rejected outright by the Pearson government.[57] The O'Leary Commission's controversial recommendations on Canadian publications and periodicals created an extensive storm of protest and lobbying by the multinationals in the publication business, but the federal government said very little, waited for four years, and then implemented the Commission's recommendations. The 1946 Gordon Commission on Administrative Classification in the Public Service was effectively blocked by an impasse of bureaucratic institutions which created such a situational complexity that it would take a full chapter of this book to unravel the dimensions to the reader.[58] In 1946 the Gordon Commission had shown the way to innovative reforms. Within the bureaucracy its advocates had to wait another twenty years before they could see badly needed machinery of government changes implemented. In effect, the Royal Commission on Government Organization (the 1965 Glassco Commission) was a high-powered replay of the 1946 Gordon Report, this time more thorough, more formidable, and more devastating.[59]

The Royal Commission on Bilingualism and Biculturalism illustrates another dimension of these bodies, namely their viability as instruments to demonstrate to Canadians the government's concern for improved policy making. The Commissioners traversed the length and breadth of Canada holding extensive public hearings, and served the two-fold purpose of listening to the views of average Canadians on bilingual and bicultural issues, while educating them that the time had come in Canada for all the governments to act decisively on these serious matters affecting national unity. This experimentation in public consultation and education was also adopted by other commissions such as the Federal Commission of Inquiry into the Non-Medical Use of Drugs (LeDain), the Royal Commission on the Status of Women (the Byrd Commission), the Mackenzie Valley Pipeline Inquiry (the Berger Commission), and the permanent Law Reform Commission, to name a few of the more recent important commissions. As Mr. Justice Thomas Berger himself indicated, ". . . in recent years, Commissions of Inquiry have begun to take on a new function; that of opening up issues to public discussion, of providing a forum for the exchange of ideas."[60]

Another interesting feature of royal commissions is the manner in which successful and innovative researchers have been co-opted by the bureaucracy into actual managerial and decision-making roles, and asked to apply their findings. A preliminary check of royal commissions within the ten year span of 1961 to 1971 showed that about thirty-five out of a possible one hundred and sixty persons who were in charge of special studies for various commissions have been recruited to important senior positions within the federal public service.[61] One can choose to interpret this fact in several ways. Some choose to see cooptation as a loss in the researcher's objectivity[62] and even a "sell-out" to the bureaucracy, others view it as only incremental and inadequate, while yet others conceive it as a novel method of infusing in the senior hierarchy of the bureaucracy new blood and new ideas certainly advantageous for the ongoing policy process.[63]

Thus, viewing royal commissions as simply geared to choice making and problem solving is much too simplistic a conception of the processes of policy formulation. Making such disparaging remarks that royal commissions are Canada's "biggest industry,"[64] or calling Ottawa "the graveyard of royal commissions,"[65] and keeping a score card as to how many recommendations are implemented forthwith after disbanding these bodies, simply obscure the many other dimensions of this viable form of investigatory machinery. V. C. Fowkes' incisive remarks are therefore worth remembering. "Such comments and criticism," he opined, "fall far short of careful analysis of the part which Royal Commissions play in political life."[66]

It would, however, be an unbalanced analysis if some of the more cogent criticisms of royal commissions are not mentioned and discussed here as well. One of the most important is the view that such devices are too *ad hoc* and particularistic and therefore have no ongoing interest in the implementation of its recommendations.[67] J. E. Hodgetts considers this perhaps "the most serious defect" of all defects, because of its "stop and start" characteristic and he poses the rhetorical question: If it is logical to assume that the repeated re-assignment to successive royal commissions of topics like transportation, resources, taxation, and like matters indicated that these are permanent and continuing issues, should we not be thinking of more permanent research devices than royal commissions? And if, by the same token, royal commissions tend to become *ad hoc* devices for assembling even larger teams of social scientists for a series of "crash" investigations into these continuing problems, does not this suggest a possible answer?"[68] The answer is of course more permanent structures of public policy supported and financed, and independent of all governments, so that they can be both critical and advisory in nature. This type of advice has contributed to the creation of such non-governmental structures as the Institute for Research on Public Policy and the C. D. Howe Research Institute.[69]

Some critics have contended that certain topics should be "off limits" to researchers outside the public service. T. H. McLeod, in commenting on the Glassco Report, has been highly critical of this aspect of "outsiders research" pointing to the difficulties posed in implementation: "The Royal Commission approach to administrative reorganization creates an irreparable breach in the course of a process which to be fully effective must be continuous and single."[70] The real facts, however, are somewhat different for the Glassco Report. It is precisely because of its heavy financial costs, high visibility of its recommendations, and its clarion call for wide-ranging administrative changes that the Glassco Report materialized as being so effective a weapon in achieving administrative reform in the federal public service. Certain key senior civil servants, aided by an impressive coterie of former Glassco researchers coopted for the assignment, actually *made the process continuous and single.* This is a crucial point which cannot be overemphasized, for it illustrates that if the time is propitious and the recommendations meet with the general favor of the bureaucratic elite, then the transformation of recommendations into legislation can be highly successful.[71] This, however, should not detract from McLeod's argument, for there are many "commissionable" problems of a recurring social and economic nature which need continuous and single machinery to ensure effective implementation.

Critics have also been particularly unhappy about the high cost of royal commissions. G. V. Tunnoch estimated that the Glassco Commission involved some 40,000 man-days of work, resulting in almost 2,000 pages of final reports at a direct cost of over $1400 per page, and an indirect cost of about as much again.[72] J. E. Hodgetts has estimated that between 1958 and 1968 seven major royal commissions cost the Canadian taxpayer close to $20 million, and again he is reflective on this point: "Could some better way be found by allocating sums of this size to the task of bringing knowledge to the service of power?"[73]

Part of the remedy to curtail the spiralling costs of formal commissions and to obtain information and new ideas in the shortest period of time at minimum expense has been the increasing use of task forces in governmental circles. Developed during the Kennedy administration in the United States the task force concept was initially used by the American president to introduce what has been termed "broadly innovative" ideas into his administration.[74] Kennedy's "task forcing" was aimed at fostering frequent and innovative interactions between the American bureaucracy and informed members of its public. After his election in November 1960 the then President-elect commissioned twenty-nine task forces of leading Democrats and experts in various areas of foreign and domestic policy: of these twenty-four reported back to the president before his inauguration in January 1961. The device therefore had attractive features: informal executive appointment of its members, reliance to a greater or lesser degree on outside expertise, inexpensively funded, and speediness in its deliberations.

Task forcing, however, has been somewhat different in Canada. The experience we have had so far with task forces indicates that the device cannot be foisted on to the Canadian bureaucracy without its acquiescence. Two examples will serve to illustrate this point. When the Hon. Walter Gordon, the Minister of Finance in the early Pearson Liberal administration, attempted to appoint outside advisers to "advise" him on his first budget, he met with implaccable opposition from the senior public servants in his department which led to the early dismissal of these outsiders. In the late 1960s another minister, the Hon. Paul Hellyer, then Minister of Transport, and the political head responsible for housing and urban policy, attempted to use the task force device to introduce "new ideas" on land banking and other aspects of housing and urban development.[75] According to Hellyer, "the idea of a task force had been born without official bureaucratic 'blessing' and Central Mortgage and Housing Corporation, in particular, was reluctant, almost hostile."[76] The end result was a task force report which was virtually ignored by the bureaucracy and the cabinet, contributing, in part, to the eventual demise of Hellyer as a member of the Trudeau cabinet.

On the other hand, where the senior bureaucracy has agreed to work and consult with outside experts on task forces, the results of this interaction have increasingly proven to be productive ventures. The best example we have of this in the public record is John Langford's study of the reorganization of the federal transport portfolio during the 1970s.[77] The Deputy Minister's Task Force on Departmental Objectives, as it was commonly known, exhibited characteristics which became typical of the task force format. It conducted its investigations chiefly within the confines of the bureaucracy and relevant constituency arenas; it was essentially a fact-finding and innovative vehicle through which new ideas were funnelled and tested for administrative feasibility; and it employed a number of experts already involved both in the formulation and execution of public policies. Furthermore, this mode of inquiry was definitely cheaper than any comparable royal commission created to study the same subject matter, and its terms of reference were determined in a specific way by the political executive to ensure prompt reporting and predictable results within a restricted time frame. An excellent glimpse of the sheer size of one department's publics is given by Langford in explaining why the task force on transportation decided to confine its fact-finding investigations, during its initial stages, within the federal government:

Some consideration was given . . . to the question of consulting outside groups from the general public and industry. It was estimated by the task force that there were probably a few hundred such groups ranging from organizations like the UN's International Civil Aviation Organization, which was closely associated with the attainment of some of the Air Services objectives, down to pressure groups or users of D.O.T. services such as the Air Cadet League or the Canadian Airline Engineers. It was argued that if the task force saw any of these groups, it might be necessary to see them all. Also, it was the view of the task force members that if any of these groups put forward recommendations then they would expect to be dealt with on an individual basis and have their suggestions adopted by the department unless good reasons were provided. [78]

The earliest example of a successful task force along the lines enumerated above is the Preparatory Committee on Collective Bargaining, a body which was composed in the early 1960s of senior public servants, businessmen, and union leaders which deliberated on how collective bargaining should be first introduced into the Canadian public service. [79] Over the past decade the use of task forces has proliferated in Canada, particularly at the federal government level, but without official statistics it is extremely difficult to give an accurate picture of the use of this instrument of policy advice. The more visible of these bodies have been allotted such topics as national unity, information, computer communications, transportation, privacy and computers, electronic data processing, and bilingualism policy in the public service. They run the gamut from high visibility, openness and the publication of reports like the task forces on computer/communications and Canadian unity, to the highly secretive deliberations of the task force of senior officials dealing with the bilingual issue in the federal government.

The reasons why it is so difficult to assess the full extent of the use of task forces is that these devices are informal administrative aids to the executive, and, unlike royal commissions, are not required by statute or convention to publish their reports or to make accessible, within a specified time, the research studies on which their recommendations are based. Schindeler and Lanphier admit that task force reports "may not even reach the eyes of persons beyond the Cabinet and a few senior civil servant cadres."[80] Furthermore, they contend that the task force device avoids the "shortcomings" of the two-way communication practices of some royal commissions by being geared only to collect information.

Whatever its advantages or deficiencies, it is clear that the task force device has proved to be a flexible and less costly method of obtaining the latest information on specific topics. Assessment of the device is perhaps premature at this stage, but the general impression received from researching this topic suggests that "task-forcing" is particularly successful in the gathering of up-to-date knowledge on specific technical subjects. Immediate disclosure of these reports seems to serve no useful purpose unless such technical information has tremendous social significance, such as the Canadian Computer Communications Task Force,[81] the task force advocating further development of community health services,[82] or in the case of broader social questions, the task force on national unity.[83]

III. Environmental Changes and the Consequent Adjustments in Pressure Groups/Executive-Bureaucracy Interactions

A. Paul Pross has articulated what we consider to be two central theses about pressure groups/executive-bureaucratic interactions.[84] Pross first pointed to a growth trend in the activity of pressure groups in Canada, although he admitted that it was extremely difficult and cost-prohibitive to give a comprehensive empirical picture of the magnitude of this growth. His first thesis is that there are a number of environmental factors chiefly responsible for this growth. There is, he contends, a growing complexity in the social and economic systems of modern states, exemplified by the increasing regulatory activities of governments, the growth of the corporate form of organization, and the specialization and geographic dispersal of manufacturing and commerce, attended by a parallel division of labor amongst business and labor groups.

This complexity of large-scale societal development is further complicated by the growth of information technology in society. Television, computerized communications, radio investigative reporting and telecommunications have made our population acutely aware of societal problems, and have generally aided increased public demands for accountability in our governing system. Potential groupings of people become more informed, threatened or even confused by and through information technology. These groups may then coalesce to make demands on the political system for change, encouraged by the media news they receive of similar efforts elsewhere in the country and even in other parts of the world.[85]

Pross however goes further than simply noting the growth of groups and accounting in a general way for their proliferation. Drawing on the work of Peter Aucoin he argues that the complex social and technical problems of today's society require technical competence from those who must confront these issues.[86] *Hence the behavioral patterns of groups become a much more crucial factor than their proliferation.*

Groups must now formulate their proposals with more competence and with due consideration for other competing groups; groups must interact to an even greater extent with technical bureaucratic experts rather than relying solely on political contacts; and groups must conduct their activity under more intense political scrutiny and media publicity.[84] However, all of this in turn complicates matters for the bureaucracy by reducing the ability of government agencies to dictate the nature of their relationship to pressure groups. Why is this so? Pross argues that:

In multiplying the number of actors participating in policy-making, it increases the complexity of the system and considerably heightens the degree of uncertainty in the public servants' decision environment. Both effects make working with pressure groups in the seventies vastly more difficult than it was in the past. Appeals to the public are more frequent; the likelihood of confrontation is greater; public scrutiny of administrative action and of policy advice seems to occur more often; criticism of individual administrators, rather than their political superiors, and attacks on the bureaucracy appear to be more prevalent.[88]

Another commentator reinforces this crucial perspective by asserting that "special interest groups are becoming more specialized, more vocal and more insistent. Public opinion is fractured beyond recognition and everyone claims to represent it."[89]

Governments have responded in various ways to this new reality. At the federal level there have been some interesting new developments in the past decade. A response to the need for "participatory democracy" has meant that *all* the known methods of accommodating interest group demands have been utilized by the political executive and the bureaucracy to cope with this new situation. We have therefore witnessed an interesting resurgence of the older methods of pressure group activity, such as pressures on private members of Parliament and on parliamentary committees, and the use of the courts to obtain judicial remedies when the legislative/executive/bureaucratic channels prove fruitless. It is at this stage somewhat premature to dismiss as insignificant the effects of pressure groups to influence the individual private member of Parliament,[90] to use the court for judicial redress,[91] and even to engineer blocs of voting power as a tactic of political pressure.[92]

To comment in detail on most of these new developments is beyond our immediate purview. We will however make a few parenthetical observations on some of these efforts, for they exemplify the ways in which the political system has attempted to cope with the new reality of interest group behavior. First, legislators are receiving "a little more heat" than is usually the case. Studies of legislative behavior, notably those of Thomas A. Hockin and Robert Presthus, point to the increased activity of pressure groups before standing committees of the House of Commons.[93] This increased activity has placed new demands *both* on the House of Commons and on the groups themselves. Over the long run Parliament must attempt to influence policy even more than it does at the present time or face increased resentment and frustration from groups appearing before it.[94] Groups, on the other hand, have had to respond to the new parliamentary access accorded them by taxing even further their personnel and financial resources, in the gathering, assembling and presentation of briefs to the various parliamentary committees.

The policy process is simply too complicated to resolve all problems at the legislative stage, and both pressure groups and politicians know this all too well. A development which is extremely interesting is the increasing tendency to shift the focal point of pressure to the public service *after* the legislation has been passed, by ensuring that the drafting of regulations and the monitoring of both the legislation and the regulations are done in concert with pressure groups.[95] Friedland points out one example of this but there are a host of others:

The Government released a document in June 1977 entitled "Policy Directives for Preparation of the Regulations in the Gun Control Provisions of Bill C-51." Not only was it prepared in consultation with a number of interest groups such as the Retail Council of Canada and the Trucking Associations, but it envisaged continuing widespread consultation. "As soon as possible after the bill is passed," it stated, "further consultation will be held with manufacturers, wholesalers, retailers and transporters before the regulations are finalized." Moreover, "A commitment has also been made to the Canadian Wildlife Federation and other interest groups that they would be consulted on the regulations. Finally, the National Advisory Council on Firearms Use will be established to monitor the effectiveness of firearms control laws and regulations, with a view to eliminating unwarranted action." This Council will be made up of licensing officials and persons "interested in gun sports."[96]

David Kwavnick's study on organized labor in Canada was the first article, of which we are aware, which noted the positional influence of an established interest group, but apparently this is now becoming increasingly common. Friedland further reports that a cursory examination he conducted of the 1970 Revised Statutes of Canada turned up over 30 such pressure group involvement in a consultative or advisory capacity. Moreover, a check with earlier sets of Revised Statutes showed that only about one-third of those found in the 1970 Revision were in the 1952 Revision, and less than one-tenth were in the 1927 Revision. The variety of consultative mechanisms was also an interesting phenomenon:

In some cases the group has the right to nominate a person to a government board or advisory body; in others it is involved in a consultative role in selecting members of a board or advisory body; more frequently the legislation simply provides that the government board or advisory body should be composed of representatives of various groups. There are also examples where the legislation provides that the Minister or government body may consult with pressure groups. . . . The Canadian Criminal Code incorporates references to non-governmental bodies which are involved in regulating some of the activities covered by the Criminal Code. . . . One sees this with racing associations in connection with horse racing, charitable or religious organizations with lotteries, agricultural fairs and exhibitions with games of chance, accredited or approved hospitals with abortions, and shooting clubs with gun control.[97]

Increasingly we are witnessing instances where the resolution of conflict cannot be achieved even after consultation with the bureaucracy has taken place. In some cases the bureaucracy does not even attempt a resolution, leaving the matter up to the courts to achieve a final decision. The courts on the other hand, and particularly the Supreme Court of Canada since the appointment of Mr. Justice Bora Laskin as Chief Justice, has responded with a more activist role in public policy formulation, indicating a new departure from past inclinations. The Supreme Court has increasingly been allowing pressure groups to appear before it in both civil and criminal cases. Chief Justice Laskin has stated extra-judicially that such appearances would be permitted "where it appeared to the Court that it would be helpful to have as wide a canvas as possible of the public law issues raised by the immediate parties but limiting the intervenors to those issues and not inviting them otherwise to speak to the merits."[98] At this stage it may be perhaps somewhat premature to assess the significance of this development but according to Friedland:

The new approach by the Supreme Court of Canada in allowing *amici curiae* to appear in non-reference cases no doubt reflects Chief Justice Laskin's view of the proper role of the Supreme Court . . . . the Court's attitude, practices, and rules regarding the granting of permission to file *amicus* briefs may indicate the extent to which it desires to engage in quasi-legislative activities and to depart from a role of narrowly resolving adversary disputes.[99]

Amici curiae appearances for a variety of pressure groups have been permitted in such examples as the *Lavell* case (1973),[100] the Morgentaler abortion prosecution,[101] and the Anti-Inflation reference case,[102] to name the most prominent in recent years. A. Alan Borovoy, the general counsel of the Canadian Civil Liberties Association, once wrote that "pressure without reason may be irresponsible, but reason without pressure is ineffectual."[103] Pressure groups seemed to have recognized that in an environment increasing in complexity "reason," accompanied by any kind of legitimate pressure, is perhaps the most effective weapon at their disposal.

We have seen how environmental changes have revitalized some traditional ways of dealing with pressure group activity at the legislative and post-legislative stages of policy formulation. In the last decade or so, governments of the industrialized countries have realized that the process of participation must be even wider in scope if the problems posed by environmental complexity and change are to be solved or at least stabilized. For example, governments have found it increasingly difficult to attain such macro-economic goals as steady economic growth, low unemployment and price stability. Moreover, the traditional tools of fiscal and monetary policy have been judged to be inadequate to deal with galloping inflation, unemployment and the other economic difficulties associated with modern liberal capitalist economies. In a word, the market is seen as a poor goal-setting mechanism. The goals it establishes reflect the buying power of the rich far more than that of the poor, are distorted by powerful aggregates of massed corporate wealth, and are without recognition of any end-result of economic activity that bears no price tag.[104] Planning at the *pre-legislative* stage is espoused as a remedy to rectify this distorted or missing goal-setting ability of our economy.

Planning is not advocated as the perfect panacea which will replace the market entirely, for it is generally acknowledged by all economists that the market is a remarkable administrative mechanism of allocation: it provides factories and stores with opportunities to deal with efficient suppliers; it oversees the quick adaptation of new techniques; and it offers customers the ultimate weapon of choice.[105] Planning is therefore an intervening mechanism only in non-market ways, such as control over prices and wages or by direct materials allocation. And if it is to succeed in such ways groups from all sectors of society must cooperate. The Government of Canada is unequivocal about this:

Governments can encourage an open discussion of the real dimensions of our economic situation and help to provide the information needed by the participants in the economy if they are to understand the impact of their actions. Governments must also be prepared to address specific situations where it is clear that in making price and income decisions, some of the wider social and economic implications are being ignored. But if we are to avoid much more direct government intervention on a regular basis in all spheres of economic activity, individuals and groups must share the wider responsibility for their actions. The government, in proposing the consultation process . . . is endeavouring to assist the development of this sharing of responsibility.[106]

We will not discuss in any detail here this commitment to *discuss* and to *share responsibility* with societal groups which the government of Canada is espousing. Suffice to state here that this consultative process is known as *tripartism*, a system of formal collaboration involving the private sector, government and labor, the aim of which is to ensure economic stability by substituting joint agreement with society's major economic pressure groups for market power.

It is interesting to view this consultative process along with another pre-legislative device of policy formulation, namely the white paper. Originating in the United Kingdom, and first used in Canada as a method of *informing* the public about new policy proposals being put forward by the federal government, the device was redesigned by the Liberal administrations of the late 1960s. White papers were then employed with an avowed intention of asking for the advice of expert and interested bodies *before* and *not after* the Government had made up its mind what to do.[107]

Audrey Doerr's case study of the white paper on taxation provides some interesting insights into the way pressure groups were affected by the device. First she notes that the increase in "participatory democracy" was marked when the government released its white paper on the subject. The House of Commons Standing Committee which heard the various interest groups affected concluded that "The degree of public participation in the formulation of tax policy, as far as your Committee is aware is unparalleled."[108] Secondly, this participation in our pluralist society was very selective in that the groups reacting to the white paper were "the articulate and financially well-endowed sectors of the community."[109] One is reminded of E. E. Schattschneider's oft-quoted remark that "The flaw in the pluralist heaven is that the heavenly chorus sings with a strong upper-class accent. Probably about 90 per cent of the people cannot get into the pressure system."[110]

Given these facts about "participatory democracy" it seems to us that another scenario suggests itself. The political executive and the bureaucracy are both well aware of the biases of the pressure group system. On the one hand, the public interest cannot be subservient to the powerful private interests of the various groups in society making up the ten per cent of the population. Nevertheless, these groups are vital to the stability and integrity of the economy. Could devices such as white papers and tripartite consultation not be construed as an attempt to "take the heat" off the political executive and the bureaucracy by, to use a term popularized by Richard Nixon, "letting it all hang out?" All the issues handled by both devices have been politically explosive ones: for white papers it has been such policy areas as taxation, Indian policy, pensions for all Canadians, and for tripartism it has been that fundamental issue of all times, the economy and what to do about it in difficult and complexing times. The number of differing views and the depths of emotional feelings about these issues are enough to scare all but the lion-hearted. When an issue is known to be excessively "loaded'" is it not a wise policy to put forward tentative proposals, allow the multifarious points of view to be expressed, and then reconsider before putting forward legislation on the subject? Legislative fiat in such instances would definitely be political suicide and bureaucratic bungling of the first magnitude.

H. G. Wells once said that you must have bureaucracy because you cannot settle a railway time table or make a bridge by public acclamation. However, it is equally true that to run empty trains on time or build a bridge in the middle of nowhere are equally nonsensical acts. Both the white paper and tripartite devices are mechanisms *par excellence* for building some measure of consensus. In both instances there is an aura of *government consulting in the open* and not in the secret conclaves of Ottawa behind "the heavy brass-furnished doors" of the mighty: there is a public perception that the government is taking *all the expressed views into consideration;* and finally there is a strong impression that the government *is particularly deliberative in its actions* on the sensitive issues with which it must deal and finally make decisions. Moreover those not immediately involved with the issues could sympathize with Parliament, the political executive and the bureaucracy while the process is working itself out to some conclusion. One has to be hard-hearted indeed not to be sympathetic to public officials who must finally make choices, but are faced with situations analogous to this one described by an embattled public servant not too long ago:

The tenor of [the public interest groups'] briefs ran from advisory to exhortatory to demanding to vituperative, and at times the council chambers, where the briefs were presented, looked like the stage of the Royal Alexandra Theatre during a performance of *Hair.* [111]

When the process is finally completed public officials can claim that the final result is an honest attempt at compromise, the best of all possible worlds. Government officials claim that in the case of taxation, their white paper or "trial balloon" proposals were definitely influenced by the public comments and interest group representations made to effect changes. In other instances, like Indian policy, most of the proposals have had to be shelved and the process begun in earnest all over again because of the vituperative criticisms the proposals aroused from Canada's native population. Having stated this particular perspective about white papers and tripartism devices, we however should point out that proof of this perception is non-existent at the moment. A considered evaluation of the effect of consultation in advance of the formulation of policy can only be made in the light of a good number of final decisions reached by government. Tripartism is presently only a suggestion, and our universe of policy matters emanating from white papers is still too limited for any firm conclusions to be made here.

The picture drawn in this chapter portrays a complicated and complex scene. Public officials must feel at times that they live in an environment with an Alice-in-Wonderland touch of logic to it, where croquet is played with flamingoes, publics are analogous to the mallets, balls and wickets of the fairy tale, operating with a high degree of independence and consequent bedlam, and words mean whatever the Humpty Dumptys of parochial interests want them to mean. Paul Appleby once wrote that "Government is different." In part what Appleby meant is that making choices for others is at the very heart of public policy making, but it fits uneasily with the search for strict personal meaning and non-authoritative behavior in a frustrating and complex environment. In the final analysis H. G. Wells is right, for choices must be made *for all* by public authorities in the political system. That choice must however be tempered at all times by values which must rise above the turmoil of the immediate political environment. This is what Stephen K. Bailey's eloquent homiletics, expressed some years ago, is all about:

. . . if history teaches anything, it is that neither Plato's philosopher-kings nor Jackson's untutored citizenry can safely manage a free society. Something besides national or divine law must contain the propensities of the powerful; something beyond the transient prejudices and groupings of the demos must determine the end and means of society.*

The role that bureaucrats play in the processes of policy formation is a complex one, not amenable to easy or oversimplistic generalizations. Hedged in by a complex accoutrement of values and institu-

* *The quote is Bailey's, but I have misplaced the exact reference.*

tions, some of which are of its own making, the bureaucracy must manoeuvre among these trappings in order to sew that seamless web of policy formation. The bureaucracy is therefore far from being the slave of the politicians' policy lamp.[112] It is indeed, as Neo-Marxists have recently conceded, an institution of "relative autonomy,"[113] but we contend that this "relative autonomy" is circumscribed by the legal and ethical foundations of our political system.

In concluding we revert to the epigram taken from the writings of John Edwin Hodgetts. It is, as he contends, still true that a profound understanding of the process of "exchange" between the Canadian federal bureaucracy, its clients, and the general environment eludes us. But in viewing the bureaucracy as "an institutional area," operating "largely in response to its own imperatives," we have presented a perspective which emphasizes the multifarious roles which the "various barnacles" (or publics) attempt to play in the political system. To borrow another analogy from a famous source, these various publics we have described in this chapter are like the barns, shacks and silos that attach themselves to the original farmstead."[114] Precisely what influence they do possess in ongoing policy formation is still a matter of conjecture, for the evidence in the public domain is very conflicting. We have however presented a perspective which we feel merits the attention of the student of public policy and administration.

Problem Solving at a Problem Price

When Mitchell F. Hepburn became the Premier of Ontario during the Great Depression in the 30s, some charlatan obtained a meeting with him and offered to be "the balm of Gilead" by "unloading" all the Premier's personal problems from his troubled shoulders, and solving all the problems of his newly elected administration. Mr. Hepburn asked how much he would require to take on this problem-solving job. "Twenty-five thousand dollars," was the reply. "Well," said Mitch, "you're hired." "But when do I get my twenty-five thousand dollars?" "That," said Mitch, in a slow emphatic tone, "is your first problem."

Footnotes

1. Mancur Olson Jr., *The Logic of Collective Action: Public Goods and the Theory of Groups* (Cambridge, Mass.: Harvard University Press, 1967); Anthony Downs, *Inside Bureaucracy* (Boston: Little, Brown and Co., 1967).

2. For Canadian examples of this see K. Acheson and J.F. Chant, "The choice of monetary instruments and the theory of bureaucracy" *Public Choice*, Spring 1972, and "Bureaucratic theory and the choice of central bank goals: the case of the Bank of Canada" *Journal of Money, Credit and Banking*, 5, May 1973, pp. 637-655; J.C.H. Jones "The bureaucracy and public policy: Canadian merger policy and the Combines Branch, 1960-71" *Canadian Public Administration*, Summer 1975, Vol. 18, No. 2, pp. 269-296.

3. The most penetrating critique of this genre of academic effort is Brian Barry's, *Sociologists, Economists and Democracy* (London: Collier-Macmillan, 1970). As Barry notes more generally, "The powerful attraction which economics holds for the other social sciences is not hard to understand . . . since it has for so long possessed a theoretical structure much more impressive than theirs." (pp. 10-11).

4. Ithiel de Sola Pool, "The Public and the Polity" in I. de Sola Pool (ed) *Contemporary Political Science: Toward Empirical Theory*. (New York: McGraw-Hill Co., 1967) pp. 22-52.

5. E.E. Schattschneider, "Intensity, Visibility, Direction and Scope," *The American Political Science Review*, Vol. LI, No. 4, December 1957, pp. 933-942. at p. 942.

6. E.E. Schattschneider, p. 941.

7. For two case studies indicating these facts see (i) W.T. Stanbury, *Business Interests and the Reform of Canadian Competition Policy, 1971-1975* (Toronto: Carswell/ Methuen, 1977), (ii) R.W. Lang, *The Politics of Drugs* (Lexington, Mass.: Saxon House/Lexington Books, 1974). In the Stanbury study one of the most interesting aspects of the case study is the manner in which the bureaucracy kept putting forward proposals for competition policy revision which were implacably opposed by the business interests. Ronald Lang's study of the powerful lobbying activities of the Canadian Pharmaceutical Association documented the tenacity of the bureaucracy to frustrate pressure group activity considered not in the general public interest. For a newspaper report of this case study see *The Globe and Mail*, October 28, 1975.

8. E.E. Schattschneider, *The Semi-Sovereign People* (New York: Holt, Rinehart and Winston, 1960), p. 40.

9. Canadian social scientists were recently warned not to assume this, but a reading of the whole article in which this warning occurs gives no clear indication as to how this assumption should be displaced. See Richard Simeon, "Studying Public Policy," *C.J.P.S.*, Vol. IX, No. 4 (December 1976), pp. 548-580, al p. 552. In an excellent critique R.F.I. Smith suggests that theoretical studies like Simeon's "are all concerned with questions of theory but they do not, either on their own or together, suggest a single compelling theory of institutions and policy processes." R.F.I. Smith, "Public Policy and Political Choice: A Review Article," *Australian Journal of Public Administration*, Vol. XXXVI, No. 3, September 1977, pp. 258-273, at p. 259.

10. E.E. Schattschneider, *The Semi-Sovereign People*, p. 38.

11. We shall give descriptions of these theories and the role bureaucracy is assigned in them in Chapter 12.

12. A. Paul Pross (ed.), *Pressure Group Behaviour in Canadian Politics* (Toronto: McGraw-Hill Ryerson, 1975), p. 2.

13. Victor A. Thompson, *Without Sympathy or Enthusiasm* (Alabama: U. of Alabama Press, 1975).

14. Mark V. Nadel and Francis E. Rourke, "Bureaucracies" in Fred I. Greenstein and Nelson W. Polsky (eds.), *Government Institutions and Processes* (Reading, Mass.: Addison-Wesley Publishing Co., 1975) pp. 373-429, at p. 391.

15. *Ibid.*, p. 391.

16. Following Aucoin we define *positional policies* as "those outputs which affect the structuring of influence in the conversion system. A good deal of policy activity by individuals and groups is related not so much to securing (at least in the short run) an allocation of desired values but rather the attainment of desired positions vis-à-vis other individuals or groups. What is sought is a share of the coercive abilities of the government." See Peter Aucoin, "Theory and Research in the Study of Policy-Making" in G. Bruce Doern and Peter Aucoin (ed.), *The Structures of Policy-Making in Canada* (Toronto: Macmillan Co., 1971) p. 25. An excellent case study illustrating a pressure group's concern with positional policy is David Kwavnick's "Pressure Group Demands and the Struggle for Organizational Status: The Case of Organized Labour in Canada," *C.J.P.S.*, III, No. 1, pp. 56-72.

17. Robert Presthus describes "corporatism" as "a conception of society in which government delegates many of its functions to private groups, which in turn provide guidance regarding the social and economic legislation required in the modern nation state." R. Presthus, *Elite Accommodation in Canadian Politics* (Toronto: Cambridge University Press, 1973), p. 25.

18. A. Paul Pross, "Canadian Pressure Groups in the 1970s: their role and their relations with the public service," *Canadian Public Administration*, Vol. 18, No. 1, Spring 1975, pp. 121-135; Peter Aucoin, "Pressure Groups and Recent Changes in the Policy-Making Process" in A. Paul Pross (ed.), *Pressure Group Behaviour in Canadian Politics* (Toronto: McGraw-Hill Ryerson Ltd., 1975), pp. 174-192.

19. We refer to the writings of Hugh Thorburn, Helen Jones Dawson, A. Paul Pross, J.E. Andersen, Robert Presthus, R. Van Loon and M.S. Whittington in particular. We will have occasion to refer to some of these writings in this chapter. Some others we will highly recommend for further reading and close study.

20. Robert Presthus, *Elite Accommodation in Canadian Politics*, p. 211.

21. Helen Jones Dawson, "An Interest Group: The Canadian Federation of Agriculture," *Canadian Public Administration* III, No. 2, (June 1960), pp. 134-149 at p. 145.

22. Jonathan Manthorpe, "Lobbyist who wins with any party," *Globe and Mail*, 14 June 1974 quoted in A. Paul Pross, "Canadian pressure groups in the 1970s: their role and their relations with the public service," p. 131.

23. *Ibid.*, p. 131. "Lobbying," "interest group" and "pressure group" are terms used synonymously in this chapter. For a theoretical treatment of these terms, see Leon Dion, *Societe et politique: La vie des groupes* (Quebec: Les Presses de l'université Laval, 1971), Vol. 1, pp. 98-108.

24. Pross elaborates on this theme in A. Paul Pross, "Pressure Groups: Adaptive Instruments of Political Communication" in A. Paul Pross (ed.) *Pressure Group Behaviour in Canadian Politics*, pp. 9-12.

25. H.H. Hannam, "The Interest Group and Its Activities," *I.P.A.C., Proceedings of the Fifth Annual Conference, 1953*, p. 173.

26. Helen Jones Dawson, "National Pressure Groups and the Federal Government," in A. Paul Pross (ed.), *Pressure Group Behaviour in Canadian Politics*, p. 46.

27. *Ibid.*

28. *Ibid.*

29. *Ibid.*

30. O. Mary Hill, *Canada's Salesman to the World* (Montreal: McGill-Queen's 1977), p. 2.

31. *Ibid.*, pp. 172-173.

32. Helen Jones Dawson, "The Consumers' Association of Canada," *Canadian Public Administration*, 6, March 1963, p. 92.

33. *Presentation to the Prime Minister and the Cabinet by the Canadian Federation of Agriculture, May 1977.*

34. M. Dale Beckman, "The Problem of Communicating Public Policy Effectively: Bill C-256 and Winnipeg Business." *C.J.P.S.*, Vol. VIII, No. 1, March 1975, pp. 138-143.

35. Robert Presthus writes that:
    In some cases governmental elites require that directors appear armed with a resolution from their members. Such action not only commits members to the collective group position and tactics, it also assures governmental elites that the director really has the green light from his group . . .
    Robert Presthus, *Elite Accommodation in Canadian Politics*, p. 198.

36. For an excellent analysis of this funding see Robert Best, "Distributive-Constituent Policy and Its Impact on Federal-Provincial Relations: The Case of OFY and LIP" (unpublished M.A. Research Essay, Carleton University, 1973). An abridgement of his analysis appears in G. Bruce Doern and V. Seymour Wilson (eds.) *Issues in Canadian Public Policy* (Toronto: Macmillan, 1974), Chapter 6, "Youth Policy." For a further analysis testing propositions about partisanship in the allocation process of LIP see Donald E. Blake, "LIP and Partisanship: An Analysis of Local Initiatives Program," *Canadian Public Policy* II, No. 1, (Winter 1976), pp. 17-32.

37. M.L. Friedland, "Pressure Groups and the Development of the Criminal Law" in P.R. Glazebrook (ed.) *Reshaping the Criminal Law: Essays in Honour of Glanville Williams* (London: Stevens and Sons, 1978), p. 237.

38. Helen Jones Dawson, "An Interest Group: The Canadian Federation of Agriculture," p. 144.

39. For example Pross reports that non-institutionalized groups:
    . . . have limited organizational continuity and cohesion; most are very basically organized. Their knowledge of government is minimal and often naive. Their membership is extremely fluid. They encounter considerable difficulty in formulating and adhering to short-range objectives, and they usually have a low regard for the organizational mechanisms they have developed for carrying out their goals.
    A. Paul Pross, "Pressure Groups: Adaptive Instruments of Political Communication" in A. Paul Pross (ed.) *Pressure Group Behaviour in Canadian Politics*, p. 11.

40. See, for example, the general piece by Peter Silcox, "The Proliferation of Boards and Commissions" in Trevor Lloyd and Jack McLeod (eds.), *Agenda 1970: proposals for creative politics* (Toronto: University of Toronto Press, 1968) pp. 115-134. Silcox notes "The semi-independent public agency . . . has the advantage of making it easier to give interested groups a partnership role in the government's work." (p. 118).

41. Peter Aucoin, "The Role of Functional Advisory Councils" in G. Bruce Doern and Peter Aucoin (eds.) *The Structures of Policy-Making in Canada* (Toronto: Macmillan, 1971), p. 155.

42. For some detailed commentary on select central advisory and functional councils see the articles by Aucoin, Phidd and Doern in G. Bruce Doern and Peter Aucoin (eds.) *The Structures of Policy-Making in Canada*.

43. Peter Aucoin, "Theory and Research in the Study of Policy-Making" in G. Bruce Doern and Peter Aucoin (eds.), *ibid.*, p. 25.

44. G. Bruce Doern, "The Role of Central Advisory Councils: The Science Council of Canada," *ibid.*, p. 263.

45. Case studies of advisory bodies tend, on the whole, to be much more critical of their advisory roles than of their functional responsibilities (if they have any). As examples of this point see the following literature:
    1 Gilles Paquet, "The Economic Council as Phoenix" in Lloyd and McLeod (eds.), *Agenda 1970*, pp. 135-158.
    2 G. Bruce Doern, *Science and Politics in Canada* (Montreal: McGill-Queen's University Press, 1972).
    3 In addition there are the articles on advisory councils by Aucoin, Doern and Phidd, already mentioned and footnoted.

46. M.W. Thistle, *The Inner Ring* (Toronto: University of Toronto Press, 1966), p. 131.

47. J.E. Hodgetts, "Public Power and Ivory Power," in Lloyd and McLeod (eds.) *Agenda 1970*, p. 265

48. A.M. Willms, "The Administration of Research on Administration in the Government of Canada," *CPA*, Vol. X, No. 4, December 1967, pp. 405-416 at p. 408.

49. In Canada, royal commissions both at the federal and provincial levels are appointed under Public Inquiries Acts. This power of appointment allows the various Canadian political executives to determine the terms of reference of royal commissions. In Britain no such general act exists and royal commissions are therefore not as restricted in their scope as they are in Canada. See the remarks of J.E. Hodgetts, *Proceedings*, Institute of Public Administration of Canada, 1951, p. 353.

50. V.C. Fowke, "Royal Commissions and Canadian Agricultural Policy," *Canadian Journal of Economics and Political Science*, XIV, 1948, p. 168.

51. J.C. Courtney, "In Defence of Royal Commissions" *CPA*, Vol. XII, No. 2, Summer 1969, p. 198.

52. *Ibid.*

53. V.C. Fowke, "Royal Commissions and Canadian Agricultural Policy," p. 172.

54. G. Bruce Doern, "The Role of Royal Commissions in the General Policy Process and in Federal-Provincial Relations," *CPA*, Vol. X, No. 4, December 1967, p. 422.

55. I am oversimplifying Sir Geoffrey Vickers' thesis of the nature of policy-making, but this aspect of his theory can be simplified and used to give the reader a basic insight from a most stimulating book on the nature of policy-making. See Sir Geoffrey Vickers, *The Art of Judgement: A Study of Policy-Making* (London: Chapman and Hall, 1965) especially Chapter 18.

56. Donald V. Smiley, "The Rowell-Sirois Report, Provincial Autonomy, and Post-War Canadian Federalism," *Canadian Journal of Economics and Political Science*, Vol. XXV III, No. 1, February 1962, pp. 54-69.

57. When the Hall Commission's report was made public even writers in the left wing publication, *Canadian Dimension*, were astonished at the radical nature of the recommendations which came from a body appointed by the conservative administration of John Diefenbaker. A commission "well spiked with Bay Street influences" and "impeccable references" had done the impossible: "What hidden logic impelled these conservatively minded Canadians to make forceful recommendations that would stagger even the former CCF government of Saskatchewan?" Trevor Emrys, "Liberal Government Studies of the Hall Commission Report on Medicare," *Canadian Dimension*, (September-October 1964), p. 4.

58. Elsewhere we have described this complexity as one akin to "motionless equilibrium" where "each member of the cast desires to stab his neighbours, but is prevented by his neighbour's attempt to stab him, the while remaining in tableau, each unable to act because the balance of forces is precise." For an account of this complexity and the failure of the Gordon Royal Commission, see Chapter 10 of J.E. Hodgetts, W.E. McCloskey, Reginald Whitaker and V. Seymour Wilson, *The Biography of an Institution* (Montreal: McGill-Queen's Press, 1972), pp. 209-231. The above quote is from p. 217.

59. *Ibid.*, pp. 287-306.

60. Mr. Justice Thomas R. Berger, "Commissions of Inquiry and Public Policy" Public Administration Lecture Series, March 1, 1978. Public lecture delivered under the auspices of the School of Public Administration, Carleton University, Ottawa. See also V. Seymour Wilson, "The Role of Royal Commissions and Task Forces: in G. Bruce Doern and Peter Aucoin (eds.), *The Structures of Policy Making in Canada*, pp. 113-129 at p. 118.

61. *Ibid.*, p. 120.

62. A.M. Willms, "The Administration of Research on Administration in the Government of Canada," p. 412.

63. V. Seymour Wilson, "The Role of Royal Commissions and Task Forces," p. 120.

64. *Financial Post*, September 1, 1962, p. 3. Quoted by G. Bruce Doern, "The Role of Royal Commissions in the General Policy Process and in Federal-Provincial Relations," p. 417.

65. See C.W. Topping, "The Report of the Royal Commission on the Penal System," *CJEPS*, Vol. 4, No. 4, (November 1938), p. 559.

66. V.C. Fowke, "Royal Commissions and Canadian Agricultural Policy," p. 164. In our opinion this is one of the best articles written on royal commissions and the policy process in Canada. The following quote demonstrates the insights of Fowke:

> As for the use of royal commissions to enable governments to postpone action, this purpose is held to be reprehensible and is always concealed as carefully as possible from the taxpayer. Realism, however, should lead the taxpayer to admit that at times he forces governments to exactly this kind of procedure. With our modern cult of progress and of activism we apparently can never admit the possibility that under certain circumstances the best action may be no action at all. Governments consequently are driven to carry on all sorts of ostentatious and elaborate "busy work" of which the appointment of a royal commission may be as harmless and economical as any. (pp. 164-165).

For another article sympathetic to royal commissions see J.C. Courtney, "In Defence of Royal Commissions," *CPA*, Vol. XII, No. 2, Summer 1969, pp. 198-212.

67. G. Bruce Doern, "The Role of Royal Commissions in the General Policy Process and in Federal-Provincial Relations," p. 431.

68. J.E. Hodgetts, "Should Canada be de-commissioned? A Consumer's View of Royal Commissions," *Queen's Quarterly*, Vol. LXXX, No. 4, Winter 1964, pp. 475-490, at p. 489.

69. J. E. Hodgetts, "The Grand Inquest on the Canadian Public Service," *Public Administration* (Sydney), Vol. XXII, No. 3, September 1963, pp. 226-241.

70. T.H. McLeod, "Glassco Commission Report," *CPA*, Vol. 6 (1963), p. 390.

71. See J.E. Hodgetts et al., *The Biography of an Institution,* pp. 290-291, 328-329; for a further comment on the role of the bureaucracy when the Glassco recommendations of personnel administration finally got to the legislation stage, see J.R. Mallory and B.A. Smith, "The Legislative role of parliamentary committees in Canada: the case of the Joint Committee on the Public Service Bills," *CPA,* Vol. 15, No. 1, Spring 1972, pp. 1-23.

72. G.V. Tunnoch, "The Glassco Commission: Did it Cost More than it was worth?" *Canadian Public Administration* Vol. VII (September 1964), p. 389.

73. J.E. Hodgetts, "Public Power and Ivory Power," p. 277.

74. Norman C. Thomas and Harold L. Wolman, "The Presidency and Policy Formulation: The Task Force Device," *Public Administration Review* Vol. 29, No. 5, (September-October 1969), pp. 459-471.

75. Lloyd Axworthy, "The Housing Task Force: A Case Study" in G. Bruce Doern and Peter Aucoin (eds.) *The Structures of Policy-Making in Canada,* pp. 130-153.

76. Paul Hellyer, "How they killed public land banking: A political memoir," *City Magazine* Vol. 3, No. 2. December 1977, pp. 31-38 at p. 32.

77. John W. Langford, *Transport in Transition: The Reorganization of the Federal Transport Portfolio* (Montreal: McGill-Queen's University Press and the Institute of Public Administration of Canada, 1976) especially Chapters 3-8. For a concise view of the task force as an instrument of innovation see John W. Langford, "The Canadian DOT Reorganized: The Work of the Task Force on the Objectives and Structure for the Portfolio of the Minister of Transport," *The Transportation Law Journal,* 4, No. 1 (January 1972), pp. 91-111.

78. *Ibid.,* pp. 51-52.

79. Langford reports that before 1968 the use of the task force device as an investigatory tool was not uncommon within departments. However, it was only in the late 1960s that it was used as an instrument to bring in "outside" advice other than from a professional consulting firm, and as an "interdepartmental committee." For this latter aspect, see G. Bruce Doern, "The Role of Interdepartmental Committees in the Policy Process,: (unpublished M.A. thesis, Carleton University, 1966).

80. Fred Schindeler and C. Michael Lanphier, "Social Science Research and Participatory Democracy in Canada," *CPA,* Vol. XII, No. 4 (Winter 1969), p. 497.

81. Department of Communications, *Branching Out: Report of the Canadian Computer/Communications Task Force* (Ottawa: Information Canada, 1972). *Inter-alia* the task force dealt with the term of reference calling for it to examine the need for "adequate protection for privacy, right of access and freedom of speech in all elements of the national system." (Vol. 1, p. 211).

82. *The Community Health Centre in Canada—Report of the Community Health Centre Project to the Conference of Health Ministers,* July 21, 1972. For an assessment of the work

of this task force see R.L. Jones, "From health insurance to a health system—the Hastings Report," *The Canadian Forum*, Vol. LII, No. 623, December 1972, pp. 13-15.

83. For a statement by the task force's chairman indicating that its work will be public as much as possible see Jean-Luc Pepin, "The Task Force on Canadian Unity," *Optimum*, Vol. 8, No. 4, 1977, pp. 29-32.

84. A. Paul Pross, "Canadian pressure groups in the 1970s: their role and their relations with the public service," *Canadian Public Administration*, Vol. 18, No. 1, Spring, 1975, pp. 121-135.

85. For a good example of this point see D.A. Chant, "Pollution Probe: Fighting the Polluters with their own weapons," in A. Paul Pross (ed.), *Pressure Group Behaviour in Canadian Politics*, pp. 61-68.

86. Peter Aucoin, "Pressure Groups and Recent Changes in the Policy-Making Process," in A. Paul Pross, *ibid.*, pp. 174-192.

87. A. Paul Pross, "Canadian pressure groups in the 1970s," pp. 132-135.

88. *Ibid.*, pp. 133-134.

89. W. Wronski, "The public servant and protest groups," *CPA*, Vol. 14, No. 1, Spring 1971, pp. 65-71, at p. 68.

90. Helen Jones Dawson, "National Pressure Groups and the Federal Government," in A. Paul Pross (ed.) *Pressure Group Behaviour in Canadian Politics*, p. 42; Frederick Englemann and Mildred C. Schwartz, *Political Parties and the Canadian Social Structure* (Scarborough: Prentice-Hall, 1967), p. 105.

91. R. Presthus, *Elite Accommodation in Canadian Politics*, p. 153.

92. Helen Jones Dawson, "National Pressure Groups and the Federal Government." For a rebuttal of Dawson's claims see M.L. Friedland, "Pressure Groups and the Development of the Criminal Law," pp. 217-219.

93. Thomas A. Hockin, "The Advance of Standing Committees in Canada's House of Commons: 1965 to 1970," *CPA*, Vol. XIII, No. 2, Summer 1970, pp. 185-202; Robert Presthus, "Interest Groups and the Canadian Parliament: Activities, Interaction, Legitimacy and Influence," *CJPS*, IV, No. 4, pp. 444-460. For two pessimistic views as to whether this increase amounts to much see David Hoffman, "Liaison Officers and Ombudsmen: Canadian M.P.s and their Relations with the Federal Bureaucracy and Executive," in Thomas A. Hockin (ed.) *Apex of Power: The Prime Minister and Political Leadership in Canada* First edition (Scarborough: Prentice-Hall, 1971). Pp. 146-162. J.A.A. Lovink, "Prospects for Democratic Control" in John H. Hallowell (ed.) *Prospects for Constitutional Democracy: Essays in Honor of R. Taylor Cole* (Durham, N.C.: Duke University Press, 1976) pp. 36-52.

94. Presthus provides general empirical support for the assertion that most interest-group activity is aimed either directly or indirectly at the Cabinet and the bureau-

cracy. Parliament's role in the process is however not ignored: the majority in Presthus's sample "believe that lobbyists think, however wrongly, that if they can persuade a sufficient number of backbenchers to support a given policy, they may be able, in caucus, to change the mind of the relevant minister." Quoted in Fred Thompson and W.T. Stanbury, "The Political Economy of Interest Groups in the Legislative Process in Canada," R. Schultz et al., *The Canadian Political Process*, Third Edition (Toronto: Holt, Rinehart and Winston, 1979) ր 234.

95. There is still, of course, the traditional form of pressure *before* the legislation comes to the House, that is, at the pre-legislation stage while it is within the bowels of the politics-administration arch.

96. M.L. Friedland, "Pressure groups and the Development of the Criminal Law," pp. 220-221.

97. *Ibid.*, p. 236.

98. Quoted in Friedland, "Pressure Groups and the Development of the Criminal Law," p. 227.

99. *Ibid.*, p. 229. The device *amicus curiae* (literally meaning "friend of the court") has been an important vehicle for pressure groups to attempt to influence the development of judge-made law. Historically the *amicus curiae* was an individual who volunteered to assist the court. See Friedland, *ibid.*, pp. 225-227. See also the excellent study by James V. West. *Public Interest Groups and the Judicial Process in Canada: The Need for a More Realistic Jurisprudence.* Occasional Papers No. 5, April 1979. Department of Political Science, Carleton University.

100. *Attorney-General v. Lavell* (1973), 38 *Dominion Law Review* (3rd) p. 481.

101. *Morgentaler vs. the Queen* (1975) 53 *Dominion Law Review* (3rd), p. 161; (1975) Canadian Criminal Cases (3d), p. 449.

102. Reference re Anti-Inflation Act, (1978) 68 *D.L.R.* (3rd) 452; [1976] 2 *Supreme Court Review*, p. 373. See also the excellent article by Peter H. Russell, "The Anti-Inflation case: the anatomy of a constitutional decision," *CPA*, Vol. 20, No. 4, Winter 1977, pp. 632-665.

103. A. Alan Borovoy, "Civil Liberties in the Imminent Hereafter," *Canadian Bar Review*, 51, (1973), p. 94, also quoted in Friedland, *op. cit.*, p. 217.

104. Robert L. Heilbroner, *Between Capitalism and Socialism: Essays in Political Economics* (New York: Random House, 1970).

105. Robert L. Heilbroner, "National Economic Planning: The Need," *Economic Impact: A Quarterly Review of World Economics*, Number 15, 1976 (Washington, D.C.: U.S. Information Agency) pp. 20-25.

106. Government of Canada. *Agenda for Cooperation: A Discussion Paper on Decontrol and Post-Control Issues*, May 1977, p. 13.

107. Audrey Doerr, "The Role of White Papers," in G. Bruce Doern and Peter Aucoin (eds.) *The Structures of Policy-Making in Canada,* pp. 179-203.

108. *Ibid.,* p. 192.

109. *Ibid.,* p. 194. Doerr later adds that "It is doubtful that the actual participation in the policy-making process extended much beyond a circle of parliamentarians, organized interests and provincial premiers." (p. 197).

110. E.E. Schattschneider, *The Semi-Sovereign People.*

111. W. Wronski, "The public servant and protest groups," p. 71.

112. J.E. Hodgetts, *The Canadian Public Service, 1867-1970,* p. 4.

113. Leo Panitch (ed.) *The Canadian State: Political Economy and Political Power* (Toronto: University of Toronto Press, 1977), pp. 3-27.

114. U.S. President's Committee on Administrative Management, *Report with Special Studies* (Washington, 1939), p. 36.

Notes

The literature on pressure group interaction with the bureaucracy is not all that plentiful. We highly recommend one edited book, not only for its excellent and varied individual contributions, but for its very comprehensive bibliography on Canadian pressure group studies.
A. Paul Pross (ed.) *Group Behaviour in Canadian Politics* (Scarborough: McGraw-Hill Ryerson Ltd., 1975.

Two excellent articles which we highly recommend are:
1. M.L. Friedland, "Pressure Groups and the Development of the Criminal Law" in P.R. Glazebrook (ed.), *Reshaping the Criminal Law: Essays in Honour of Glanville Williams* (London: Stevens and Sons, 1978).
2. James V. West, *Public Interest Groups and the Judicial Process in Canada: The Need for a More Realistic Jurisprudence.* Occasional Paper No. 5, Department of Political Science, Carleton University, April 1979.

For other related material on this subject we recommend that the footnotes to Chapter 13 be checked for specific aspects.

Epilogue: Theory and Environment in Perspective

. . . bureaucracies not only implement the values of their community, they also embody them. As instruments of power, bureaucracies symbolize how power may be applied and to what ends. As instruments of rule, bureaucracies indicate how power is, in fact, exercised and by what right. . . . The structure of the state, then, affirms the society in a unique way, because its public administration establishes the general limits within which the life of a people can move.

Donna Robinson Divine

We have identified many characteristics of modern bureaucracy distinguishing it from traditional forms of administration. Using the work of Max Weber we have shown that these characteristics include division of labor, hierarchy of authority, written rules and regulations, and so on. We contend that the "ideal-typical" characteristics of modern bureaus embody a simple Weberian hypothesis that modern organizations based on rational-legal authority are more likely to have these attributes than earlier forms of administration. The ideal type allows us to place bureaucracy in a comparative historical setting. Following Albrow and others we also contended that the more an organization approximates the bureaucratic model, whatever the arrangements of characteristics within it, the more it will conform to rationalist criteria. Rationalism in this sense is defined as the organization of the individual's daily activities through *the division and coordination of legal authority*—the achievement of a methodical way of life.

However, these characteristics of bureaucracy tell us very little of its causes. In his comparison of traditional with bureaucratic means of administration, Weber was indicating that bureaucratization is but one aspect of the historical evolution toward rationalization of all institutional forms in modern societies. There are several preconditions leading to this evolution: the substitution of authority based on rules for authority derived basically from charisma or other personal attributes; a money economy that allows calculability of results and widespread literacy; mobility of resources; religious beliefs permitting trust amongst strangers; urbanization and so on. Rationalism in this sense embodies two other central meanings. First is *the scientific-technological rationalism*, which is a capacity to control the world through calculation or empirical knowledge and know-how (a condition for a money economy and superior mobility of resources). Second is a rationalism concerned with "the systematization of meaning patterns." As Wolfgang Schluchter puts it, this rationalism involves "the intellectual elaboration and deliberate sublimation of ultimate ends. In this sense rationalism is a consequence of cultured man's 'inner compulsion' not only to understand the world as a 'meaningful cosmos' but also to take a consistent and unified stance toward it."[1] This type of rationalism he calls a *metaphysical-ethical rationalism* (for example, religious beliefs). All of these forms of rationalism vary with social circumstances and are related to each other in changing ways.[2]

But the relative importance of these causes of bureaucratization lies in the fact that *they are environmental*, that is they are external to bureaucracy and arise largely as a result of certain historical processes. This is why we have emphasized environmental factors in the larger social and political environment as central to an understanding of modern Canadian public policy and administration. A study of environmental factors seems to suggest that formal procedures in bureaucracy are due in part to the historical era in which organizations are founded. This formalization in turn engenders hierarchical differentiation and differentiation gives rise to delegation of decision-making authority. Delegation of decision-making brings in its wake the central problem of administrative responsibility and control. Max Weber pointed to all of these paradoxes of rationality, and he remained ambivalent toward many of the aspects of rationalization. Bureaucratization had been a revolutionary process in sweeping away most aspects of traditionalism but in turn it has the full potential of becoming a Leviathan, an "iron cage" to entrap the rationalized individual: ". . . once fully established, bureaucracy is among those social structures which are hardest to destroy . . . Once administration has been completely bureaucratized, the resulting form of domination is practically indestructible."[3] The administrative state can be both a blessing and a curse to modern society. According to Weber, such a state embodied a rationalism of technological progress which had serious debilitating consequences for democracy. In recent decades we have seen how this faith in rationality has dominated our notions of public policy and administration, not only in the western European countries and North America, but in the socialist nations and in many areas of the "developing" world. This faith in rationality emerged unquestioned in the guise of a faith in technological development and economic growth. The age of technological progress was heralded as the answer for displacing the confusion of competing ideologies and the distaste for political conflict. Nearly one hundred years ago Weber saw this trend in Western society and his warning then is particularly appropriate for us in the 1980s: western civilization, he argued, must worry about what is in store for it when "the last ton of fossil fuel has been used up."[4]

To Max Weber, the liberal democrat, there was nothing deterministic about this trend. He believed that we control our own destinies, and the answer to our conundrums is to be sought in the structure and institutions we have devised to govern ourselves. Max Weber stood, along with many of us, as heirs to a long and distinguished tradition in political philosophy which maintains that politics is shaped to a great extent by its forms and structures. Structures extend, complete and even amend our values.[5]

Compared to the roles of the Canadian Senate and the House of Commons, two institutions which have engendered considerable skepticism as to their importance in public policy formation, consider for a moment Fritz Morstein Marx's catalogue of the functions of bureaucracy in western political systems:

It is a gatherer of facts that constantly accumulate as a byproduct of administrative activities. It is a surveyor of public needs as well as of governmental performance in meeting such needs. It is a recorder of interest pressures and public sentiments affecting the political course. It is an inaugurator of organizational devices and technical procedures suitable for attaining the government's ends. It is a fountain of ideas about what ought to be done to redress conditions that cry for remedy . . . it is a knowledgeable and skillful draftsman in converting broad understandings about desirable goals into the detailed language of regulatory measures.[6]

These are formidable political powers in any society attempting to achieve the day-to-day accomplishment of public purposes. Max Weber was well aware what the implications can be in this accumulation of power:

In view of the growing indispensability of the state bureaucracy and its corresponding increase in power, how can there be any guarantee that any powers will remain which can check and effectively control the tremendous influence of this stratum? How will democracy even in this limited sense *be at all possible?* [A further] question and the most important of all, is raised by a consideration of the inherent limitations of bureaucracy proper.[7]

Weber goes on to insinuate that bureaucrats will utilize their power simply because they are in possession of it, whether or not such power and know-how are competent to supply the solutions needed for the well-being of a society. He therefore insisted that the bureaucratic phenomenon, *including all its technical administrative means*, must be constantly subjected to scrutiny and attention by a vigilant social science and by all others in the polity who are moved by reason, legitimacy and responsibility.

Yet much social science pays only lip service to these insights. To much Canadian political science in the 1980s, for example, "structures" mean party and electoral systems and a legislature—and very little else. By ignoring the crucial role of administrative means in shaping political ends, much of social science has lost its relevance to a deeper understanding of policy analysis. Political theorist, C. B. Macpherson argues that "the serious difficulty about a democratic society is not how to *run* it but how to *reach* it."[8] (my italics), and Richard Simeon regards the study of public administration (as distinct from *his* conception of public policy) as no more than a "hole" from which public policy must be "rescued."[9] Alan Cairns, in his presidential address to the Canadian Political Science Association implicitly rejects these assumptions when he argues that "in the evolution of the division of labour between those who govern, and those who are governed, the energizing, proselytizing, and entrepreneurial role increasingly rests with *those civil servants and politicians with the capacity to influence policy and its administration.*"[10]

As we enter the decade of the 1980s Cairns' rebuke to Canadian political science that it has "failed to treat government with appropriate seriousness"[11] remains a lonely admonition in a discipline seeking the holy Grail of "real science." Too many Canadian political scientists in the 1980s are busily engaged in publishing empirical trivia to pay much attention to this call for relevance by Cairns. A few of them have stumbled upon the "study of public policy" but as yet they fail to realize that any investigation of the articulation, formulation and implementation of public policy cannot be seriously undertaken without a serious study and understanding of the administrative factor. Furthermore, this understanding must go beyond the presently fashionable empirical studies of bureaucratic career paths and elitist attitudes.

In the United States students of technological rationality fully recognize the central importance of the role of bureaucracy in public policy and administration. Many students of American public policy view with consternation the manner in which public policy has been reduced to the "ultimate criteria" of measurements and optimization. This has not occurred in Canada to the same extent, but increasingly Canadian students of technocracy are recognizing a vacuum in a field which traditionally was regarded as the province of political studies. Public policy and administration must continue to be components of a seamless web. Robert D. Miewald's views on the need for a rapprochement between American political science and public administration holds equal significance for us here in Canada.

Whether public administration, the child, was thrown out of the house of its parent or left of its own accord is of interest only to those anxious to carry on ancient feuds . . . neither has done much to advance our understanding of the administrative society. Political science, in its desire to be a "real science," has turned itself into the world's oldest floating trivia game. As an aggressively "practical" discipline, public administration has helped to reinforce the bureaucratic reality. Both are destined to become dead sciences, for without an appreciation of politics, administrative questions are, at best, technical problems. And without an appreciation of administration political questions are sterile exercises.[12]

Political Ends and Administrative Means

We have had, in the field of administration, too much synthetic philosophy disguised as a science and not enough examination of the relation of administrative devices and techniques to major political objectives. We need, far more than we have done in the past, to recognize the relativity of means to ends and to escape from the sterile conception that administration is an end in itself or that efficiency and economy are objectives superior to any others that may be sought. This can best be done by the acquisition of perspective and by the careful analysis of administrative devices and techniques in relation to the broad ends they are to serve.

J. Donald Kingsley

Footnotes to Epilogue

1. Wolfgang Schluchter, "The Paradox of Rationalization: On the Relation of Ethics and World," in Guenther Roth and Wolfgang Schluchter, *Max Weber's Vision of History, Ethics and Methods* (Berkeley: University of California Press, 1979), p. 15.

2. *Ibid.,* pp. 11-64.

3. Max Weber, *Economy and Society,* edited by Guenther Roth and Claus Wittich (Berkeley: University of California Press, 1978), p. 987.

4. Max Weber, *The Protestant Ethic and the Spirit of Capitalism.* Translated by Talcott Parsons (New York: Scribner, 1958), p. 181.

5. Donna Robinson Divine, "A Political Theory of Bureaucracy," *Public Administration* (London), Vol. 57, Summer 1979, pp. 229-231 at p. 229.

6. Fritz Morstein Marx, "The Higher Civil Service as an Action Group in Western Political Development" in Joseph La Palombara (ed.), *Bureaucracy and Political De-*

velopment (Princeton, New Jersey: Princeton University Press, 1963) pp. 62-95 at pp. 77-78.

7. Max Weber, "Parliament and Government in a Reconstructed Germany," Appendix II to *Economy and Society* (New York: Bedminster Press, 1968), p. 1401 ff (at p. 1403).

8. C.B. Macpherson, "Essay III: Problems of a Non-Market Theory of Democracy" in C.B. Macpherson, *Democratic Theory: Essays in Retrieval* (Oxford: Clarendon Press, 1973), pp. 38-76 at p. 74.

9. Richard Simeon, "Studying Public Policy," *Canadian Journal of Political Science*, IX, No. 4 (December 1976), pp. 548-580 at p. 549. Reading Simeon's article reminded us of that Jean Renoir film, "Rules of the Game," in which the house party sallies forth from La Colinière on a Sunday morning and shoots every bird and rabbit in sight for miles around. The carnage is incredible. Bang! Bang! Bang! go the pointed criticisms and down they crash. Before long the landscape is littered with the corpses of academic marksmanship.

10. Alan Cairns, "The Governments and Societies of Canadian Federalism," *Canadian Journal of Political Science*, X:4 (December 1977), pp. 695-725 at p. 703.

11. *Ibid.*, p. 698.

12. Robert D. Miewald, *Public Administration: A Critical Perspective* (New York: McGraw-Hill Book Co., 1978), p. 260.

Appendix

Present Scheduling of Corporation in the Financial Administration Act: (1980)

Subsection 66(3) of the Financial Administration Act suggests the following classification spectrum for Canadian Crown corporations.

Financial controls comparable to public departmental administration		Crown corporations treated as private sector organizations
Departmental Corporations	Agency Corporations	Proprietary Corporations

Schedule B (departmental corporations)

". . . a servant or agent of Her Majesty in right of Canada and is responsible for administrative, supervisory or regulatory services of a governmental nature."

Agricultural Stabilization Board
Atomic Energy Control Board
The Director of Soldier Settlement
The Director, Veterans' Land Act
Economic Council of Canada
Fisheries Prices Support Board
Medical Research Council
Municipal Development and Loan Board
National Museums of Canada
National Research Council
Science Council of Canada
Unemployment Insurance Commission

Schedule C (agency corporations)

''. . . an agent of Her Majesty in right of Canada and is responsible for the management of trading or service operations on a quasi-commercial basis, or for the management of procurement construction or disposal activities on behalf of Her Majesty in right of Canada.''

Atomic Energy of Canada Limited
Canadian Arsenals Limited
Canadian Commercial Corporation
Canadian Dairy Commission
Canadian Film Development Board
Canadian Livestock Feed Board
Canadian National (West Indies) Steamships Limited
Canadian Patents and Development Limited
Canadian Saltfish Corporation
Centennial Commission
Crown Assets Disposal Corporation
Defence Construction (1951) Limited
Loto Canada Inc.
National Battlefields Commission
National Capital Commission
National Harbours Board
Northern Canada Power Commission
Royal Canadian Mint
Uranium Canada Limited

Schedule D (proprietary corporations)

''i) is responsible for the management of lending or financial operations, or for the management of commerical and industrial operations involving the production of or dealing with goods and the supplying of services to the public
ii) is ordinarily required to conduct its operations without appropriations''

Air Canada
Canadian Deposit Insurance Corporation

Canadian Broadcasting Corporation
Cape Breton Development Corporation
Central Mortgage and Housing Corporation
Eldorado Aviation Limited
Eldorado Nuclear Limited
Export Development Corporation
Farm Credit Corporation
Federal Business Development Bank
Federal Mortgage Exchange Corporation
Freshwater Fish Marketing Association
National Railways
Northern Transportation Company Limited
Petro-Canada
Pilotage Authorities
  Atlantic Pilotage Authority
  Laurentian Pilotage Authority
  Great Lakes Pilotage Authority
  Pacific Pilotage Authority
Polysar Limited
St. Lawrence Seaway Authority
Seaway International Bridge Corporation Limited
Teleglobe Canada

NAME INDEX

SUBJECT INDEX